The Bible Speaks Today
Series editors: Alec Motyer (OT)
John Stott (NT)
Derek Tidball (Bible Themes)

The Message of
the Living God

D1169052

Titles in this series

The Message of the Living God

His glory, his people, his world

Peter Lewis

*Senior Pastor of the Cornerstone
Evangelical Church, Nottingham*

Inter-Varsity Press

To the people of Cornerstone Church, past and present, at home and abroad: 'How can we thank God enough for you, in return for all the joy we have in the presence of our God, because of you?' (1 Thess. 3:9).

InterVarsity Press
P.O. Box 1400, Downers Grove, IL 60515-1426
World Wide Web: www.ivpress.com
E-mail: mail@ivpress.com

Inter-Varsity Press
38 De Montfort Street, Leicester LE1 7GP, England

© *Peter Lewis 2000*

All rights reserved. No part of this book may be reproduced, stored in a retrieval system or transmitted in any form or by any means, electronic, mechanical, photocopying, recording or otherwise, without the prior permission of InterVarsity Press.

InterVarsity Press® is the book-publishing division of InterVarsity Christian Fellowship/USA®, a student movement active on campus at hundreds of universities, colleges and schools of nursing in the United States of America, and a member movement of the International Fellowship of Evangelical Students. For information about local and regional activities, write Public Relations Dept., InterVarsity Christian Fellowship/USA, 6400 Schroeder Rd., P.O. Box 7895, Madison, WI 53707-7895.

Inter-Varsity Press is the book-publishing division of the Universities and Colleges Christian Fellowship (formerly the Inter-Varsity Fellowship), a student movement linking Christian Unions in universities and colleges throughout the United Kingdom and the Republic of Ireland, and a member movement of the International Fellowship of Evangelical Students. For information about local and national activities write to UCCF, 38 De Montfort Street, Leicester LE1 7GP, England.

All Scripture quotations, unless otherwise indicated, are taken from the Holy Bible, New International Version®. NIV®. *Copyright* © *1973, 1978, 1984 by International Bible Society. Used by permission of Hodder and Stoughton Ltd. All rights reserved. "NIV" is a registered trademark of International Bible Society. UK trademark number 1448790. Distributed in North America by permission of Zondervan Publishing House.*

USA ISBN 0-8308-2402-2
UK ISBN 0-85111-509-8

Typeset in Great Britain by The Midlands Book Typesetting Company.

Printed in the United States of America ∞

British Library Cataloguing in Publication Data

A catalogue record for this book is available from the British Library.

Library of Congress Cataloging-in-Publication Data

Lewis, Peter.
  The message of the living God : his glory, his people, his world / Peter Lewis.
    p. cm.—(The Bible speaks today-Bible themes series)
    Includes bibliographical references.
    ISBN 0-8308-2402-2 (paper : alk. paper)
      1. God—Biblical teaching. 2. God—Knowableness—Biblical teaching. I. Title. II. Bible speaks today.
  BS544 .L49 2001
  231—dc21

00-047168

| 18 | 17 | 16 | 15 | 14 | 13 | 12 | 11 | 10 | 9 | 8 | 7 | 6 | 5 | 4 | 3 | 2 |
| 16 | 15 | 14 | 13 | 12 | 11 | 10 | 09 | 08 | 07 | 06 | | | | | | |

Contents

General preface

THE BIBLE SPEAKS TODAY describes three series of expositions, based on the books of the Old and New Testaments, and on Bible themes that run through the whole of Scripture. Each series is characterized by a threefold ideal:

- to expound the biblical text with accuracy
- to relate it to contemporary life, and
- to be readable.

These books are, therefore, not 'commentaries', for the commentary seeks rather to elucidate the text than to apply it, and tends to be a work rather of reference than of literature. Nor, on the other hand, do they contain the kind of 'sermons' which attempt to be contemporary and readable without taking Scripture seriously enough.

The contributors to *The Bible Speaks Today* series are all united in their convictions that God still speaks through what he has spoken, and that nothing is more necessary for the life, health and growth of Christians than that they should hear what the Spirit is saying to them through his ancient – yet ever modern – Word.

ALEC MOTYER
JOHN STOTT
DEREK TIDBALL
Series Editors

Author's preface

For me, God has always been 'the living God'. In my childhood I knew him as Father and Friend; in my early teens I gave my life over to him as Redeemer and Saviour; and in my years as a preacher of the gospel of our Lord Jesus Christ I have consistently felt and seen the witness of the Holy Spirit to the Word of God in the Scriptures. That is why the writing of this book has been for me a sustained act of worship. I hope others will be able to worship through it too. The ultimate purpose of theology is to lead us to the feet of the living God.

Having written a book on the person and work of Jesus Christ (*The Glory of Christ*, Hodder and Stoughton, London 1992, 2nd ed. 1997 [Moody Press, Chicago 1997]), I was eager to comply with the wishes of IVP to do one on the doctrine of God. The difference in method, however, was that this was to be more expository than systematic theology usually is, by following connected passages on a biblical theme rather than grouping texts and concepts under a prearranged scheme.

When I began to do that, two things struck me with fresh force. First, I was struck by the way God has 'incarnated' theological truth from the start. Instead of an abstract theology, we have the revelation of God in human lives. He is the God who speaks and acts at 'ground level'. This revelation has all the colour, pace and drama of human life, woven in with the speaking, caring, living and righteous God who will not be locked out of his world and whose self-revelation is closely intermeshed with the lives of his people. That is why expository preaching, if it is not submerged in our systematic theology, will always be gripping and relevant. The Bible is never dull, even though we preachers sometimes manage to make it seem so!

Secondly, I found myself concentrating on its first five books rather than trying to run through the entire Old Testament. It became clear that those are the massive foundational building-blocks of the Bible's doctrine of God, and that their teaching shaped the mind of the later prophets. It was all there from the start. Moses is the 'Paul' of the Old Testament! As a preacher, I am also aware of the need for evangelical congregatons to rediscover the Old Testament roots of their faith and for our preachers to capture in our pulpits the high drama and sacred relevance of Israel's Old Testament history.

I have felt, too, the need for the New Testament revelation of God, as the Father, the Son and the Holy Spirit, to be very explicitly and repeatedly enforced in the churches. This is the height of relevation, and it gives coherence to all distinctively Christian faith. Without its explicitly trinitarian roots the church would soon perish.

I have had to be selective in a number of ways, not only due to space but also due to the planning of other books in this Bible Themes series which will deal with a range of specific doctrines. The biblical commentaries and theological studies I have so freely quoted for their excellence will take the reader on where I have had to stop. Most of them are works by fellow-evangelicals, but not all. Walter Brueggeman, for instance, has written what has been called the first postmodern 'Theology of the Old Testament', a work massive in its erudition, controversial in its approach, and full of penetrating and challenging insights.

I must record my gratitude and sense of debt to three scholars who have scrutinized my manuscript and made many helpful suggestions: John Balchin, Alec Motyer and Derek Tidball. The faults that remain despite their good offices are down to me – and I wish I could rewrite the entire book! Particular thanks must go to Colin Duriez, my editor, for his unfailing encouragement and courtesy, and to Alison Linnell for her impeccable copy-editing. Special thanks to Eva Chambers for her well-thought-out study guide.

In this, the thirtieth year of my ministry among them, I have dedicated this book to the people I am privileged to serve at Cornerstone. We have grown together in the faith and love that are in Christ Jesus and are, by God's grace, growing still. 'May the grace of the Lord Jesus Christ, and the love of God, and the fellowship of the Holy Spirit be with you all' (2 Cor. 13:14).

Summer 2000   PETER LEWIS
Cornerstone Evangelical Church,
Nottingham
www.cornerstone-evangelical.org.uk

Chief abbreviations

AV	The Authorized (King James) version of the Bible (1611)
BST	The Bible Speaks Today
DLNTD	*Dictionary of the Later New Testament and its Developments*, ed. R. P. Martin and P. H. Davids (IVP, 1997)
ICC	International Critical Commentary
Int	*Interpretation*
ISBE	*International Standard Bible Encyclopedia*, ed. G. W. Bromiley, revised edition, 4 vols. (Eerdmans 1979–88)
NBC	*New Bible Commentary*, 21st Century edition, ed. D. A. Carson, R. T. France *et al.* (IVP, 1994)
NDT	*New Dictionary of Theology*, ed. S. B. Ferguson and D. F. Wright (IVP, 1988)
NIBC	New International Biblical Commentary
NICNT	New International Commentary on the New Testament
NICOT	New International Commentary on the Old Testament
NIDOTTE	*New International Dictionary of Old Testament Theology and Exegesis*, ed. W. A. VanGemeren, 5 vols. (Zondervan and Paternoster, 1997)
NIV	The New International Version of the Bible (1973, 1978, 1984)
RSV	The Revised Standard Version of the Bible (NT, 1946; second edition, 1971; OT, 1952)
TDNT	*Theological Dictionary of the New Testament*, ed. G. Kittel and G. Friedrich, translated by G. W. Bromiley, 10 vols. (Eerdmans, 1947–76)

TOTC	Tyndale Old Testament Commentary
TynB	*Tyndale Bulletin*
WBC	Word Biblical Commentary
WCF	Westminster Confession of Faith
WTJ	*Westminster Theological Journal*

Bibliography

Atkinson	David Atkinson, *The Message of Genesis: The dawn of creation*, BST (IVP, 1990).
Barclay	William Barclay, *The Revelation of John* (The Saint Andrew Press, 1974).
Barrett	C. K. Barrett, *The Gospel According to St. John: An introduction with commentary and notes on the Greek text* (SPCK, 1978).
Beasley-Murray	George R. Beasley-Murray, *John*, WBC, (Word, 1987).
Berkhof (1978)	L. Berkhof, *The History of Christian Doctrines* (Banner of Truth Trust, 1978).
Berkhof	——, *Systematic Theology* (Banner of Truth Trust, n.d.).
Berkouwer	G. C. Berkouwer, *The Providence of God*, Studies in Dogmatics (Eerdmans, 1972).
Blocher	Henri Blocher, *In the Beginning: The opening chapters of Genesis*, trans. David G. Preston (IVP, 1984).
Bray	Gerald Bray, *The Doctrine of God*, Contours of Christian Theology (IVP, 1993).
Bridge	Donald Bridge, *Signs and Wonders Today* (IVP, 1985).
C. Brown	Colin Brown, *Miracles and the Critical Mind* (Eerdmans/Paternoster, 1984).
R. E. Brown	Raymond E. Brown, *The Gospel According to St. John* (Geoffrey Chapman, 1971), vol. 1.
Brueggemann (1982)	Walter Brueggemann, *A Bible Commentary for Teaching and Preaching Genesis*, Int (John Knox Press, 1982).

BIBLIOGRAPHY

Brueggemann (1997)	——, *Theology of the Old Testament: Testimony, dispute, advocacy* (Fortress Press, 1997).
Caird	G. B. Caird, *The Revelation of St John the Divine* (A. & C. Black, 1966).
Calvin (*Genesis*)	John Calvin, *A Commentary on the First Book of Moses, called Genesis*, trans. John King (Baker, 1976).
Calvin (*Harmony*)	——, *A Harmony of the Gospels Matthew, Mark and Luke*, trans. Morrison (Eerdmans, 1980).
Calvin (*Institutes*)	——, *Institutes of the Christian Religion*, ed. John T. McNeill (Westminster Press, 1977).
Calvin (*Psalms*)	——, *A Commentary on the Book of Psalms*, trans. J. Anderson (Baker, 1979), vol. 1.
Carson (1978)	D. A. Carson, *The Sermon on the Mount* (Baker, 1978).
Carson (1991)	——, *The Gospel According to John* (IVP, 1991).
Cole	Alan Cole, *Exodus*, TOTC (Tyndale Press, 1973).
Craigie	Peter C. Craigie, *The Book of Deuteronomy*, NICOT (Eerdmans, 1976).
Davids	Peter H. Davids, *The First Epistle of Peter*, NICNT (Eerdmans, 1990).
Dumbrell	William J. Dumbrell, *Covenant and Creation: An Old Testament Covenantal Theology* (Paternoster, 1984).
Durham	John I. Durham, *Exodus*, WBC 3 (Word, 1987).
Fee	Gordon D. Fee, *The First Epistle to the Corinthians* (Eerdmans, 1987).
Gunton (1992)	Colin Gunton, *Christ and Creation* (Paternoster Press, 1992).
Gunton (1993)	——, *The One, the Three and the Many: God, creation and the culture of modernity*, The Bampton Lectures (Cambridge University Press, 1993).
Gunton (1997)	——, *The Promise of Trinitarian Theology* (T. & T. Clark, 1997).
Hamilton (1990)	Victor P. Hamilton, *The Book of Genesis, Chapters 1 – 17*, NICOT (Eerdmans, 1990).

12

Harris (1992)　　　　Murray J. Harris, *Jesus as God: The New Testament use of* theos *in reference to Jesus* (Baker, 1992).

Harris (1999)　　　　——, *Slave of Christ*, New Studies in Biblical Theology (IVP, 1999).

Harrison　　　　　　R. K. Harrison, *Leviticus*, TOTC (IVP, 1980).

Helm　　　　　　　Paul Helm, *The Providence of God*, Countours of Christian Theology (IVP, 1993).

Henry　　　　　　　Carl Henry, *God, Revelation and Authority*, 6 vols. (Word, 1976–83), vol. 6, *God Who Stands and Stays*.

Hoekema　　　　　　A. A. Hoekema, *Created in God's Image*, 2 vols. (Eerdmans/Paternoster, 1986).

Hubbard (*Hosea*)　　David Allan Hubbard, *Hosea*, TOTC (IVP, 1989).

Hubbard (*Joel and Amos*) ——, *Joel and Amos*, TOTC (IVP, 1989).

Hughes　　　　　　Philip Edgcumbe Hughes, *A Commentary on the Epistle to the Hebrews* (Eerdmans, 1977).

Kidner (1967)　　　　Derek Kidner, *Genesis*, TOTC (Tyndale Press, 1967).

Kidner (1973)　　　　——, *Psalms 1 – 72*, TOTC (Tyndale Press, 1973).

Kidner (1981)　　　　——, *The Message of Hosea: Love to the loveless*, BST (IVP, 1981).

Lane　　　　　　　William L. Lane, *Hebrews*, WBC 47B (Word, 1991).

Lewis　　　　　　　Peter Lewis, *The Glory of Christ* (Hodder & Stoughton, 1992).

Milne (1993)　　　　——, *The Message of John: Here is your King!*, BST (IVP, 1993).

Moo　　　　　　　Douglas Moo, *Romans 1 – 8*, The Wycliffe Exegetical Commentary (Moody Press, 1991; reprinted as *The Epistle to the Romans*, NICNT [Eerdmans, 1996]).

Morris (1965)　　　　Leon Morris, *The Apostolic Preaching of the Cross* (IVP, 1965).

Morris (1971)　　　　——, *The Gospel According to John*, NICNT (Eerdmans, 1971).

Morris (1973)　　　　——, *The Revelation of St John* (Tyndale Press, 1973).

Morris (1988)　　　　——, *The Epistle to the Romans* (Eerdmans/IVP, 1988).

BIBLIOGRAPHY

Motyer (1974)	J. A. Motyer, *The Message of Amos: The day of the Lion*, BST (IVP, 1974).
Motyer (1993)	——, *The Prophecy of Isaiah* (IVP, 1993).
Mounce	Robert H. Mounce, *The Book of Revelation*, NICNT (Eerdmans, 1977).
Newbigin (1986)	Lesslie Newbigin, *Foolishness to the Greeks: The gospel and western culture* (SPCK/Eerdmans, 1986).
Newbigin (1989)	——, *The Gospel in a Pluralist Society* (SPCK, 1989).
Newbigin (1998)	——, *Trinitarian Doctrine for Today's Mission* (Paternoster, 1998).
O'Brien	Peter T. O'Brien, *Colossians, Philemon*, WBC 44 (Word, 1982).
Oswalt	John Oswalt, *The Book of Isaiah, Chapters 1 – 39*, NICOT (Eerdmans, 1986).
Ramachandra (*Mission*)	Vinoth Ramachandra, *The Recovery of Mission: Beyond the pluralist paradigm* (Paternoster, 1996).
Ramachandra (*Gods*)	——, *Gods that Fail: Modern idolatry and Christian mission* (Paternoster, 1996).
Stott (1984)	John Stott, *Issues Facing Christians Today* (Marshalls, 1984).
Stott (1986)	——, *The Cross of Christ* (IVP, 1986).
Stott (1994)	——, *The Message of Romans: God's good news for the world*, BST (IVP, 1994).
Tate	Marvin E. Tate, *Psalms 51 – 100*, WBC 20 (Word, 1990).
Thielicke	Helmut Thielicke, *The Evangelical Faith*, 3 vols., trans. G. W. Bromiley (T. & T. Clark, 1974–82), vol. 2, *The Doctrine of Christ*.
Turner	Max Turner, *The Holy Spirit and Spiritual Gifts Then and Now* (Paternoster, 1996).
Warfield	B. B. Warfield, *Calvin and Augustine* (Presbyterian & Reformed Publishing Co., 1956).
Wenham (1979)	Gordon J. Wenham, *The Book of Leviticus*, NICOT (Eerdmans, 1979).
Wenham (1987)	——, *Genesis 1 – 15*, WBC (Word, 1987).
Wenham (1994)	——, *Genesis 16 – 50*, WBC (Word, 1994).
Witherington	Ben Witherington III, *Paul's Narrative Thought World* (Westminster/John Knox Press, 1994).
Wright	Christopher J. H. Wright, *Deuteronomy*, NIBC (Hendrickson/Paternoster, 1996).

Introduction:
How can we know God?

Woody Allen, in *Love and Death*, says at one point: 'If God would only speak to me – just once. If he would only cough. If I could just see a miracle. If I could see a burning bush or the seas part. Or my Uncle Sasha pick up the check.'

There, I think, you have the mixture of timeless longing and trendy cynicism which characterizes much of the Western mind-set and personality today. Allen wants God – but on his own terms. And God won't play. Allen wants God the conversationalist: 'If God would only speak to me – just once.' God has, in fact, given him a Bible recording 1,400 years of speech, but a cough for Woody outweighs a covenant with Abraham or even a Calvary for Christ.

He wants God the conjuror ('If I could just see a miracle') but gives no guarantees he'd do anything about it. He probably wants God the friend and God the therapist too, but all he has is human beings: commonplace, flawed, stubborn, exploitive. Like his Uncle Sasha, who always lets other people pick up the bill.

How then can we know God and how can we know that we know him, if not the Woody Allen way?

1. Points of contact

In his fine book on effective Christian apologetics, *Bridge-Building*, Alister McGrath writes:

> The first major insight encountered by the reader of Scripture is that God created the world. Is it therefore surprising that this creation should bear witness to him? Or that the height of his creation, human beings, should carry a recognisable imprint of his nature? And that this imprint might have considerable value as a starting point for apologetics? Paul believed passionately in the theological truth and apologetic importance of this insight (Romans 1 – 2).[1]

[1] Alister McGrath, *Bridge-Building* (IVP, 1992), p. 18.

Here is a God-given starting point within the created order itself which can act as a trigger, stimulating people to ask questions about the meaning of life or the reality of God. Through the generosity of God we have been left with a latent memory of him which can discern what Peter Berger famously called 'signals of transcendence' within human life.

However, McGrath continues:

> Points of contact are not in themselves adequate to bring people into the kingdom of God. They are starting points for that goal. Nor are they adequate in themselves to bring people to a specifically *Christian* faith ... The apologist must show that the Christian gospel is consistent with these points of contact. It is able to explain them – and more than that: it is able to deliver all that they promise, turning hints into reality.[2]

Because of universal sin, the falleness of our race from God and the corruption of the natural order, these things do not give us a sufficient knowledge of God or put us right with God. 'Fallen human nature is obliged to reflect upon a fallen creation ... Like a cracked mirror, or a misty window, it presents us with a distorted image.'[3] We find within ourselves and our history as a race all sorts of confused and conflicting knowledge and ideas about God. We have a deep dissatisfaction with life without God, and yet are runaways from him. As Augustine famously said, 'You have made us for yourself, and our hearts are restless until they rest in you.' McGrath comments:

> The doctrines of creation and redemption combine to interpret this sense of dissatisfaction and lack of fulfilment as a loss of fellowship with God which can be restored. Augustine captured this idea perfectly when he spoke of a 'loving memory' of God. It is a *memory* of God, in that it is grounded in the doctrines of creation and redemption, which affirm that we have partially *lost* something through sin – and are somehow made aware of that loss through God's grace. It is a *loving* memory, in that it is experienced as a sense of divine nostalgia, of spiritual wistfulness. There is a thirst to have more of that which we already have only in part.[4]

Yet there is not only desire for God but also an antipathy for God in fallen, rebellious, human nature.[5] Paul says, 'The sinful mind is hostile to God. It does not submit to God's law, nor can it do so.'[6]

---

[2] Ibid., p. 19. [3] Ibid., p. 23. [4] Ibid., p. 21. [5] Rom. 1:18. [6] Rom. 8:7.

There is an ignorance of God which is 'due to the hardening of their hearts'.[7] Sin has made us allergic to holiness and guilt has made us liable to punishment.[8] Therefore we are in flight from 'home' as well as nostalgic for it. Sin has broken the relationship which marked us out as such a special creation. Now, as a race, we stand in proud independence, and in profound ambivalence about the knowledge of God. We want this knowledge – up to a point, and we don't want it to control our lives. This ambivalence has to be faced and dealt with. God's grace helps us to do that. This is the grace that is alone sufficient to arrest us in our flight, to bring us to our knees, to begin the conversation *with* our Maker (and not just conversations with others about him), to make us seek to know God by his own light and not just by our own. Such a dependence on grace is the true starting point in any journey to God.

2. Knowing God

John Calvin does not begin his *Institutes* by speaking of the 'existence' of God, but of the 'knowledge' of him.[9] He doesn't begin by asking 'Does God exist?' but 'How can God be known?' Calvin insists that we know God only because he lets himself be known and, furthermore, that we know him properly only from within a relationship of humility, worship and love.[10]

Calvin's point is twofold. First, God must be known in his nature and character more than in terms of his essence. God's essence is largely beyond our knowing and it is enough for us to worship him in his immensity and his spirituality without presuming to go into matters infinitely beyond us. The question is not 'What is God?' but 'What am I meant to know of him which is proper to his glory?' Secondly, 'It is a favourite emphasis in Calvin that *pietas*, piety, in which reverence and love of God are joined, is prerequisite to any true knowledge of God.'[11] The knowledge of God must be personal, penitential and devout. In a word, it must be *responsive*. It cannot be merely acquisitive.

This attitude to knowing God takes us into the area of personal relationships at the start. God is not the static object of our enquiries but the One who takes the initiative in making himself known. When we apprehend his activity aright, we begin to seek him in the right way. We then want to see him by his own light and not just by our own. We begin to make the great discoveries which will revolutionize our thinking. We begin to see him as he really is in his goodness, purity and righteousness – and to see ourselves as we

[7] Eph. 4:18.   [8] Rom. 2:1–5.   [9] Calvin (*Institutes*), I. i.1.   [10] Ibid., I.i-ii.
[11] Ibid., I.ii.1.

really are in our sinfulness and need of him. We are brought to a position where God can lead us on to a true and saving knowledge of himself in the Son he gave for the salvation of our world.

Our knowledge of God will be responsive: the joyful discovery that he knows us and wants us to know him; that knowing him is the greatest thing in life, in this world and the next:

> This is what the LORD says:
> 'Let not the wise man boast of his wisdom
>   or the strong man boast of his strength
>   or the rich man boast of his riches,
> but let him who boasts boast about this:
>   that he understands and knows me,
> that I am the LORD, who exercises kindness,
>   justice and righteousness on earth,
>   for in these I delight,'
> declares the LORD.[12]

Apart from such joyful knowledge as this, knowing whether or not there is a God becomes a pointless exercise. Worse, it becomes the impudent affirmation of our priority over him, the priority of our curiosity about his existence over the character of the God who exists, and whose existence presses in on us on every side, challenging us at every level of our being: physical, personal, mental and moral.

3. The need for special revelation

While God has left his signature on creation, and while, to use a phrase of Jonathan Edwards, he communicates 'a sort of shadow . . . of his excellencies' in its beauty and intricacy, we can never by this arrive at the proper knowledge of God. There is a gulf between ourselves and God which can be bridged only from the divine side. The message of Scripture is that God *has* crossed that gulf and made himself known, not vaguely but specifically, not just informatively but savingly, in words of his choice to people of his choice.

Calvin likened God's use of human speech to the simplicities of baby-talk between a mother and her child – but it is baby-talk which stretches us to the utmost! Human language may not be adequate to say everything about God. It is adequate, however, for the purposes for which it was given, and it is adequate, if he chooses, to bring to us the personal self-revelation of the God who is Father, Son and

[12] Jer. 9:23–24.

Holy Spirit. If God chooses such talk, our philosophy of language and being must not despise it.

Part of our sinful arrogance is to think we can arrive at the knowledge of God without his word. But because of sin, natural theology ('human reasoning about God, under the conditions of sin, unaided by special revelation')[13] leaves us, still, with God as an unknown God.[14] We need the special revelation of the Scriptures, the revelation of himself which God gave to the patriarchs and prophets, which is confirmed by the witness of the Spirit in the hearts of God's people and which bears within itself its own authentication. Indeed, says Calvin, 'no-one can get even the slightest taste of right and sound doctrine unless he be a pupil of Scripture' without which we fall into error.[15]

> Just as old or bleary-eyed men and those with weak vision, if you thrust before them a most beautiful volume, even if they recognise it to be some sort of writing, yet can scarcely construe two words, but with the aid of spectacles will begin to read distinctly; so Scripture, gathering up the otherwise confused knowledge of God in our minds, having dispersed our dullness, clearly shows us the true God. This, therefore, is a special gift, where God, to instruct the church, not merely uses mute teachers, but also opens his most hallowed lips.[16]

If we turn aside from this, in favour of our own ideas of what God is or should be, we shall never reach the goal of knowing God. Even Paul called the splendour of the divine countenance 'unapproachable',[17] so that the knowledge of God 'is for us like an inexplicable labyrinth unless we are conducted into it by the thread of the Word; so that it is better to limp along this path than to dash with all speed outside it'.[18]

There is no rivalry here between the word of God as Scripture and the Word made flesh as Jesus Christ. The Word he is and the word he speaks are one Word: the unfolding self-revelation of God, beginning with the creation and reaching its climax in the person and work of Jesus Christ, his incarnation, atoning death and vindicating resurrection and exaltation. We meet the Word in his word – Old Testament and New. Alister McGrath pays due attention to Calvin's emphasis on Scripture and writes:

> Christianity is Christ-centred, not book-centred; if it appears to

---

[13] Calvin (*Institutes*), I.v.12, fn. 41.   [14] Acts 17:23.
[15] Calvin (*Institutes*), I.vi.2.   [16] Ibid., I.vi.1.   [17] 1 Tim. 6:16.
[18] Calvin (*Institutes*), I.vi.3.

be book-centred, it is because it is through the words of Scripture that the believer encounters and feeds upon Jesus Christ. Scripture is a means not an end; a channel, rather than what is channelled. Calvin's preoccupation with human language and supremely with the text of Scripture, reflects his fundamental conviction that it is here, through reading and meditating upon this text, that it is possible to encounter and experience the risen Christ. A concentration upon the means reflects the crucial importance which Calvin attaches to the end. To suggest that Calvin – or, indeed, anyone who pays high regard to God's self-revelation in and through Scripture – is a 'bibliolater', one who worships a book, is to betray a culpable lack of insight into Calvin's concerns and methods.[19]

4. The historic Christ

The Christian faith centres on a person who, on any account, remains one of the most powerful influences in world history. The historicity of Jesus of Nazareth is undoubted, except perhaps by a minority. There are near-contemporary references in the writings of the Roman historian, Tacitus, and the Jewish historian, Josephus. We have well over 5,000 ancient manuscripts of parts or the whole of books which now comprise our New Testament which go back to the fifth, fourth, third, and second centuries AD. It is one of the phenomena of history that the ancient world is littered with evidence of Jesus of Nazareth and the communities he founded. The earliest is a part of John's Gospel which palaeographers confidently date about AD 125, that is within 90 years of the events it records – astonishingly close in historical terms. Yet when this manuscript was copied, there were already Christian churches, communities of the resurrection, in existence. That existence we can trace back further still.

5. The risen Lord

The apostle Paul wrote his first letter to the Corinthians in about AD 52 or 53, about twenty years after Jesus' death. His claim in 1 Corinthians 15:1–11 that the various disciples and followers of Jesus had encountered him after his crucifixion as the risen Lord, could easily have been falsified by those who remembered the time and by the original followers of Jesus themselves. They could have said, 'It wasn't like that.' But they were preaching the same thing!

[19] McGrath, op. cit., pp. 28–29.

Moreover, Paul himself had been preaching this for eighteen years before he wrote to the Corinthians. It had been the central message of his long evangelistic and missionary career from the start. That takes us back to his Damascus road encounter with the exalted Christ and his immediate preaching in the local synagogue, that Jesus is the Son of God.[20] All that was just a year or two after the event and easily falsifiable at that stage.[21] So, by stages, the surprising facticity of the Christian message can be supported. By that I mean its nature as concrete fact in history; not mysticism, not philosophy, not even therapy!

The evidences for the resurrection of Christ are well known and they form a formidable body of proof, especially when the 'explanations' are examined and found to be inadequate: the empty tomb and the inability of the authorities to produce the body, the credible witnesses who were not expecting it but spent a lifetime preaching it, the resurrection 'appearances' themselves (not shimmering visions but concrete encounters and sustained seminars!), the impossibility of groups of people having the same hallucination, the improbability of a not-quite-dead and severely wounded Jesus convincing his disciples that he was Lord over death (not to mention walking the seven miles to Emmaus on recently crucified ankles and appearing behind locked doors). In such a scenario, if Jesus had not died, his integrity would have done.

6. The claims of Jesus

And that brings us to the most stubborn fact of all: a Jesus who says, 'I am meek and lowly of heart', and who yet says, 'Before Abraham was, I am.'[22] Jesus is a prophet who does not point away to God, but who preaches a gospel of 'I ams'; who claims to be the centre of history and the Judge at its end, 'that all may honour the Son just as they honour the Father';[23] and who sends his disciples out to 'make disciples of all nations, baptising them in the name of the Father and of the Son and of the Holy Spirit'.[24] Who is this who shares the honours with God, who speaks of a life and a glory with his Father 'before the world began', and who accepts the worship of the disciples and the confession of Thomas, 'My Lord and my God'?[25] Here in space-time history is a fellow human being, of undoubted

[20] Acts 9:20.
[21] Leon Morris writes: 'George Ogg dates the crucifixion as AD 33 and Paul's conversion as AD 34 or 35 (*The Chronology of the Life of Paul* [London, 1968], p. 200) and Martin Hengel likewise dates his conversion as AD 32–34 (*Between Jesus and Paul* [Philadelphia, 1983], p. 11), and N. A. Dahl puts it "only a couple of years after Christ's death" (*Studies in Paul* [Minneapolis, 1977], p. 2)' (Morris [1988], p. 534).
[22] John 8:58.   [23] John 5:23.   [24] Matt. 28:19.   [25] John 17:5; 20:28.

godliness and integrity, who says 'All things have been committed to me by my Father. No-one knows the Son except the Father, and no-one knows the Father except the Son and those to whom the Son chooses to reveal him.'[26]

It is not convincing to say that all this was put into the mouth of a harmless young rabbi by over-zealous disciples. To say that the Jesus of the New Testament is largely the creation of his admirers is to say that he was ordinary and they were extra-ordinary, he was pedestrian and they were sublime, he was parochial and they were magnificent. It is to have a boring Jesus and an exciting church (my experience has been otherwise!). It is to have the Sermon on the Mount, the parables of the kingdom, and the drama of Calvary and the resurrection created by fishermen turned lay-preachers and first-century schools of thought. Shakespeare by committee is nothing to it! But in fact it is Jesus who towers over them all, who has not been dwarfed by 2,000 years of on-going human history, who has changed the lives of millions, and who has sown the Western world with many of its (better) values.

The fact is that the Jesus the New Testament writers portray is not at all the kind of Jesus they would have invented. He was a different kind of messiah, preaching a different kind of kingdom to a different kind of people than anyone expected. It was he who shaped them, not they who shaped him. They wrote and lived in the impact of his uniqueness. What they would have invented would have been, at best, devoutly commonplace. Their fictional Jesus would never have spoken words which often seemed quite blasphemous to his critics. He would have been the model penitent not the sinless Son, the modest preacher of a message bigger than himself or the hero of messianic expectations who was tragically lost to Israel and the world.

But in fact he puzzled them, shocked them and far surpassed them with his claims. And when he died they did not understand or expect, or even, at first, believe in his resurrection from the dead. And when they did, they worshipped and served him with joy and great assurance all their lives.

That assurance we too can have – about God, about forgiveness, and about eternal life – if we listen to him and believe in him. No-one meets the deepest needs of our flawed and dying humanity like the Christ who said, 'Come to me, all you who are weary and burdened, and I will give you rest ... the Son of Man did not come to be served, but to serve, and to give his life as a ransom for many ... I am the good shepherd. The good shepherd lays down his life for the sheep ... My sheep listen to my voice; I know them, and they

[26] Matt. 11:27.

follow me. I give them eternal life, and they shall never perish; no-one can snatch them out of my hand . . . Do not be afraid. I am the First and the Last. I am the Living One; I was dead, and behold I am alive for ever and ever! And I hold the keys of death and Hades.'[27]

There have always been godly men and women who seem in particular ways to reflect God's character strongly and clearly. But Jesus is not simply one in that category of persons nor did his apostles present him as such. The New Testament does not say 'Jesus is like God', it says 'God is like Jesus'; it says that to see Jesus is to see God, to come to Jesus is to come to God, to be judged by Jesus will be to be judged by God. In a word, there will be nothing in God, no attribute or quality, no decision or purpose, that is not in Jesus Christ, the Son of God, the one in whom 'all the fulness of the Deity lives in bodily form'.[28] If we know and are right with the Son, we need not fear to stand before the Father. There will be no hidden menace, no terrible discovery, no final contradiction of our hopes, for, as A. M. Ramsay once put it, recalling 1 John 1:5, 'God is Christlike and in him is no unChristlikeness at all.'[29]

7. The inspired Scriptures

Yet, notwithstanding all this, Jesus did not come as the first and only witness to the Living God but pointed to a long unfolding revelation by God to Abraham, Moses and the prophets. He himself fulfilled much of that and in his own person and teaching took it to new heights. He never relegated, however, what we call the 'Old Testament' Scriptures to a lower level of inspiration or authority than his own words. On the contrary, he taught its divine authorship and abiding validity.[30] So did his apostles, the first and foremost teachers of the church, themselves writing inspired Scriptures for that ongoing church.[31]

The apostle Paul, having congratulated Timothy on his early education in the Old Testament, says 'All Scripture is God-breathed and is useful for teaching, rebuking, correcting and training in righteousness.'[32] Peter also expressly states that the prophets delivered a message that they were given, not a philosophy, or even a theology, that they had invented: 'Above all, you must understand that no prophecy of Scripture came about by the prophet's own interpretation. For prophecy never had its origin in the will of man, but men spoke from God as they were carried along by the Holy

---

[27] Matt. 11:28; Mark 10:45; John 10:11, 27–28; Rev. 1:17–18.   [28] Col. 2:9.
[29] Cited in John V. Taylor, *The Christ-like God* (SCM, 1992), flyleaf.
[30] Matt. 5:17–18; 22:41–45; Luke 22:25–28, 44; cf. John 14:26; 16:12–14.
[31] 2 Tim. 3:14–17; 2 Pet. 1:19–21; 3:1–2, 15–16.   [32] 2 Tim. 3:16.

Spirit.'[33] The prophets themselves continually made just this point and we read phrases like 'The word of the Lord came', 'Thus says the Lord' and 'The burden of the Lord' no fewer than 3,808 times!

It is this *objectivity* in the Christian faith, the objective revelation of God in Jesus Christ and also in the entire unfolding revelation of God in the Scriptures, both Old and New Testaments, that counters the extreme subjectivism of our age, whether we encounter it in existentialism, New Age mysticism, or the gentle but fatal cynicism of Woody Allen. However, that does not shut us up to a mere scholasticism, or to a purely intellectual recognition of the Scriptures. There has to be a work of God in us as well as beyond us if we are to know God, the God of the Scriptures, the God of the prophets and the apostles, the God and Father of our Lord Jesus Christ.

8. The need of God's Spirit

Corresponding to his work in the writers of scripture is the work of the Holy Spirit bearing testimony in the hearts of all God's people, sophisticated and simple, that this is the word of the Lord. The Scriptures do not derive their authority from the church, notwithstanding its work in recognizing the canon, but the church itself is 'built on the foundation of the apostles and prophets'.[34] Scripture exhibits evidence of its own truth and 'the highest proof of Scripture derives in general from the fact that God in person speaks in it.

This was an important point in Calvin's theology of the Word:

> If we desire to provide in the best way for our consciences – that they may not be perpetually beset by the instability of doubt or vacillation, and that they may not also boggle at the smallest quibbles – we ought to seek our conviction in a higher place than human reasons, judgements or conjectures, that is, in the secret testimony of the Spirit ... The testimony of the Spirit is more excellent than all reason. For as God alone is a fit witness of himself in his Word, so also the Word will not find acceptance in men's hearts before it is sealed by the inward testimony of the Spirit. The same Spirit, therefore, who has spoken through the mouths of the prophets must penetrate into our hearts to persuade us that they faithfully proclaimed what had been divinely commanded.[35]

Scripture, says Calvin, as the Word of God, is 'self-authenticated' but 'the certainty it deserves with us, it attains by the testimony of the Spirit':

---

[33] 2 Pet. 1:20–21. [34] Eph. 2:20. [35] Calvin (*Institutes*), I.vii.4.

For even if it wins reverence for itself by its own majesty, it seriously affects us only when it is sealed to our hearts through the Spirit. Therefore, illumined by his power, we believe neither by our own nor by anyone else's judgement that Scripture is from God; but above human judgement we affirm with utter certainty (just as if we were gazing upon the majesty of God himself) that it has flowed to us from the very mouth of God by the ministry of men ... Let us, then, know that the only true faith is that which the Spirit of God seals on our hearts ... Whenever, then, the fewness of believers disturbs us, let the converse come to mind, that only those to whom it is given can comprehend the mysteries of God (cf. Matt. 13:11).[36]

9. The people who listen

God is a speaking God – and a speaking God calls for a listening people. This book seeks to listen to God's voice in Scripture, to explore and apply the revelation of himself that God has made in Scripture to ourselves and our times. The listening posture is crucial for all knowledge of God from first to last; it is the natural posture of faith. Anselm of Canterbury described theological enquiry as 'Faith seeking understanding'. Anselm believed that faith was a necessary foundation and support for all further discovery. He wrote, in famous words: 'I do not seek to understand that I may believe, but I believe that I may understand: this I also believe, that unless I believe I will not understand.'[37]

This belief is not an eyes-shut leap in the dark, but a profound Spirit-wrought recognition of and response to the call of God which brings us to our knees in gratitude and adoration.[38] Jesus put it most simply and memorably: 'My sheep listen to my voice; I know them, and they follow me.'[39] Helmut Thielicke wrote, 'What we call our knowledge of Christ is imparted to us only as we achieve a relationship of trust in him.'[40] The human desire to understand God in a non-relational way is a profound expression of our fallenness. 'The first task of theology is to bring us to his feet.'[41] It is with such a conviction that this book is written, with the prayer that it may be used to keep us at the feet of God.

---

[36] Ibid., I.vii.5.   [37] Anselm, *Proslogion*, i.
[38] Matt. 11:25; 16:17; 1 Cor. 2:8–16.   [39] John 10:27.
[40] Quoted in Donald McCullough, *The Trivialisation of God: The dangerous illusion of a manageable deity* (NavPress, 1995), p. 71.
[41] Thomas Howard and J. I. Packer, *Christianity: The true humanism* (Word, 1985), p. 68.

PART 1: GOD AND HIS WORLD

Genesis 1:1 – 2:3
1. God the Creator

This is a book about God, but it cannot be about God alone. The Bible is not a book all about God, but rather it is all about God and people, God and us. It is not a tourist's guide to God, a walk around his perfections, a philosophical investigation. The Bible is God's saving revelation of himself in word and deed. It is history and prophecy, wisdom and worship; it is judgment and mercy, passion and redemption. It is redemptive event and world news, the greatest and best news the world could ever have: that God has come to save us from our sin and failure and to lift our fallen human lives into an eternal fellowship with his own divine life. The story of God is inextricably bound up with our story now – and there is a human being at the centre of the divine life to prove it!

1. God! (1:1)

In the beginning God created the heavens and the earth (1). Here is the revelation of a truth that touches every other truth. Here is the key to creation and the light that falls on every human life. Here we are told that *the secret of the universe is not a formula but a person.* From this one, first, given truth of the Bible all else will flow, giving new and profoundly important significance to all reality. All Christians have a theology of creation. They may disagree on processes and time-scales, but at the centre of their understanding of the origin of things and their ongoing existence is the personal Creator and Upholder of all things: the God of wisdom, power and goodness in infinite degree.

Today, we have cause to wonder at creation as much as any of our forebears and to seek to know the Creator. What kind of God is it who made the universe which we are only just beginning to measure and understand? What kind of God is it who made quasars and quarks, galaxies and gluons, pulse stars and peacocks, Betelgeuse and butterflies? The foundational revelation of Genesis 1 – 2 is that he is the infinite-personal God who is good and who does good. He has made a good creation, and, as the climax of his work on this planet, has made human beings in his image, for his glory and for personal fellowship with himself. Genesis 1 is at least as much about the Creator as it is about the creation: God is mentioned 34 times in 36 verses and the revelation we have of him there is foundational for the rest of Scripture.

2. The eternal God

In the beginning (1). In the first words of Scripture we are brought to the edge of all we can know and to the brink of all we can never know. We are brought to the beginning and edge of time to look into the abyss of eternity.

An old illustration of eternity in terms of time is still impressive even if it falls far short of the reality. Imagine a rock a hundred miles long, a hundred miles wide, and a hundred miles high. Once every thousand years a bird comes and sharpens its beak on the rock. Only when that rock has thus been worn away will one brief moment of eternity have passed! Even such a salutary analogy can be misleading, however, since eternity is, properly speaking, timelessness.

Yet, as we shiver on the brink of creation and look out on eternity, we find not emptiness but fullness: 'In the beginning *God*'! These opening words of Genesis tell us of the eternity of God; not of God 'in' eternity (as though somehow eternity was bigger than God) but of eternity *in God*. We learn that before there was anything else there was God. Before there was matter, time and space there was God: God who has no succession of moments in his own Being, God who alone is infinite and eternal, the uncreated Creator, unique in his eternity and all-sufficient in the infinite resources of his Being, the fullness of light, love, joy and meaning: 'From everlasting to everlasting you are God.'[1]

So the Bible puts us in our place at the start, and it is a very little place. In other respects it is a very special place too (as this same chapter in Genesis will show), but before we can overestimate ourselves it dwarfs us with infinities and immensities. It humbles our pride, it stills our chatter and it tells us to listen, like the children of the universe we are, to the self-revealing God. And as we stand on the brink of time and try to grasp the eternity of God we learn the first lesson even while we fail the first test: 'Where were you when I laid the earth's foundation . . . while the morning stars sang together and all the angels shouted for joy?'[2]

It is often and rightly said that the Bible nowhere tries to prove

---

[1] Ps. 90:2.   [2] Job 38:4, 7.

the existence of God. In Scripture God is not a deduction but a given. His existence is not 'proved' but presupposed. It is the first of truths. This does not mean that we cannot argue the case for God's existence and activity, that there are not confirmations and signposts in creation around us and in our own constitution as human beings. There are. But it does mean that we cannot, in fact, occupy 'neutral' ground which decides the issue irrespective of God's gracious self-disclosure, or which leaves God 'on one side' while we prove him – or not – and which necessarily denies him in order possibly to affirm him. He is not waiting at the end of our argumentation but is the One with whom the biblical revelation begins. In short, God is too all-encompassing to be at the end of anything, including an argument! So we find him at the beginning and at the end of the Bible, the beginning and the end of all wisdom – the alpha and the omega, the first and the last.

3. The creator God

... *God created the heavens and the earth* (1). Our minds stagger at the immensity of a finite universe, but beyond it all is the infinitude of God. Only now are we beginning to measure the universe, one part of which our forebears mapped and wondered at before us. Today we should wonder more than ever at the greatness of the God who 'created the heavens'.

Only the Maker and Sustainer of all this is greater than it all and he puts it into another perspective by his own infinite existence and by his Personhood and love. The universe is vast and dwarfs us. God is infinite and values us. The planets are old and human history becomes a blip on the screen. God is eternal and lifts human beings into an everlasting relationship with himself. The purpose of the writer of Genesis is to show that the God of the galaxies is the God of Abraham, Moses and Israel; that the people of God will never be lost among the gods of the peoples; that this God is the true God and his purposes will stand.

And so in one opening statement the author of Genesis 1 declares war on every contradictory or qualifying statement and challenges every other religious loyalty. God, this God, the one and only true God, created everything; he and no other, he, without help, created all things in heaven and on earth, stars and spirits, animals, plants and people. He created everything that is not God.

Today we know a great deal more about the physical world than our ancestors, but it should not make us less devout. We are only beginning to know mysteries and forces that have been there from the beginning of creation. No doubt there remains very much more to be known. But what we do discover will still be God's truth; it will not make God redundant because its whole existence testifies to him. He is not just the 'God of the gaps' in our knowledge but the God of the knower and the known, the God of every explicable process and unifying theory. At every point the universe is open to the God who created it but who also transcends it, and who can act as he pleases within it, to continue or suspend or redeem its natural laws. We may have 'come of age' in some respects but too often we are like cocky teenagers, enamoured with our own discoveries but still having a great deal to learn – and to re-learn.

Some argue strongly for a more or less literal understanding of these early chapters of Genesis;[3] others believe a conservative evangelical view of the Bible does not necessitate such an approach.[4] David Atkinson points out:

> The writer does not attempt, or want, to *explain* creation. With reverence, he wants to catch us up into its wonder. He is not concerned with the question 'How did God do it?' He would not, I think, have been terribly interested in our debates about the time-scale of evolution, or the physics of the First Three Minutes. These are not the questions he is asking. And when we bring such questions to the text, we are disappointed . . . The author does not say . . . He is concerned with something else. He is safeguarding and proclaiming something of the unsearchable mystery of God.[5]

Certainly the chapter is concerned with the theology rather than the science of creation, and its concern is to say who God is and what is his relation to the world we live in; but, as G. J. Wenham notes, it is 'more than a statement of theology, it is a hymn of praise to the Creator through whom and for whom all things exist'.[6]

4. The present God (1:2)

Now the earth was formless and empty, darkness was over the surface of the deep, and the Spirit of God was hovering over the waters.

Here we have a stage of creation where all seems dark, disordered and frightening. But *God* is there, all-powerful, purposeful and active: 'and the Spirit of God was hovering over the waters'. The Hebrew word here for 'spirit' is *rûah* and it can mean spirit or wind, and commentators differ on which of these is meant here. Victor Hamilton argues convincingly for the translation 'spirit', but even if

---

[3] See the survey of beliefs and arguments in Wayne Grudem, *Systematic Theology: An introduction to biblical doctrine* (Zondervan/IVP, 1994), ch. 15.
[4] Henry, vol. 6, chs. 5–9. [5] Atkinson, p. 17.
[6] Gordon Wenham, 'Genesis', *NBC*, p. 59.

we translate the Hebrew as 'the wind of God' it will be, as Gordon Wenham agrees, 'a concrete and vivid image of the Spirit of God'.[7] Everywhere else in the Old Testament the phrase used here indicates the Spirit of God (or a spirit from God).[8] Derek Kidner writes, 'In the Old Testament, the Spirit is a term for God's outgoing energy, creative and sustaining.'[9]

The rare Old Testament word for 'hover' occurs also in Deuteronomy 32:11 where a mother eagle hovers protectively over her young. There it illustrates Yahweh's protection, care and guidance of Israel in the nation's earliest days. Here it may suggest the Spirit 'waiting' to implement the creative word as soon as it is spoken.[10] Calvin sees the work of the Spirit as giving life to all creation: 'For it is the Spirit who, everywhere diffused, sustains all things, causes them to grow, and quickens them in heaven and in earth',[11] and says of this verse: 'the world . . . was an undigested mass; he now teaches that the power of the Spirit was necessary in order to sustain it . . . Therefore that scripture must be fulfilled, "Send forth thy Spirit, and they shall be created, and thou shalt renew the face of the earth," and so on the other hand, as soon as the Lord takes away his Spirit, all things return to their dust and vanish away (v. 29).'[12]

Here too the ideas of watchfulness and purpose may be present as the Spirit 'hovers' over the creative process. God does not create from a distance but as one intimately concerned and involved. Derek Kidner comments, 'An impression of Olympian detachment, which the rest of the chapter might have conveyed, is forestalled by the simile of the mother-bird hovering or fluttering over her brood.'[13] While the references to God speaking creation into existence and order in the rest of the chapter serve to preserve the proper *distance* that exists between God and his creation, this reference to the spirit of God serves to remind us of his close, personal involvement with all his work.

This closeness of God to his creation, his Presence over it and in it at every level, must surely inspire us with the right kind of creation-spirituality. It inspires neither the worship of nature, nor a forgetfulness of its woundedness due to the fall, but a respect for its value, a delight in its beauty and complexity, and a desire to recognize God in his works. The one eternal God, infinite in power and unchanging in goodness, still holds in being all that he called into existence and their processes: every blade of grass, each leaf on a tree, the gnat and the great whale, mountains and solar systems, and our own selves fearfully and wonderfully made. He is the God who is 'in touch' with his creation at every level: subatomic, macrocosmic, and every level

---

[7] Wenham (1987), p. 17.   [8] Blocher, p. 68   [9] Kidner (1967), p. 45.
[10] Alec Motyer in correspondence.   [11] Calvin (*Institutes*), I.xiii.14.
[12] Calvin (*Genesis*), vol. 1, pp. 73–74.   [13] Kidner (1967), p. 45.

between. When the insect lands on our hand, or the stars shine above our heads, we can worship the God of wisdom, power and unchanging faithfulness, in whom we also live and move and have our being, for 'he is not far from each one of us'.[14]

5. The God of order

What we have in the processes described in Genesis 1 is God ordering the earth. The phrase translated *formless and empty* (the attractive-sounding Hebrew terms are *tohû waḇohû*) refers not to a 'chaos' in the Greek sense (involving a spirit of disorder) but to the creation of a disordered state as the first stage in a process. God is the God of process as well as fiat. His 'days' can be hours or aeons. The thought of Genesis 1 moves not only between nothing and creation but also between disorder and order. Henri Blocher remarks: 'Now the emphasis on the order of creation is the one most loudly heard in the opening of Genesis. It is not for nothing that the throng of the creatures is there called literally an *army* (2:1), and that army . . . does not fight, it parades.'[15]

We can also see that a pattern of movement emerges in the rest of the chapter, after verse 2, from generalization to particularization.[16] Notice the ways in which days one, two and three parallel days four, five and six, moving in each case from form to fullness, from preparation to accomplishment. So, for instance, the light and dark of day one prepare for the lights of day and night in day four; the creation of sea and sky on day two prepare for the creatures of water and air in day five, and the fertile earth of day three prepares for the creatures of the land in day six. The first triad points to acts of *forming*, the second to acts of *filling*. God's personal involvement is specified at every point as the chapter moves through the creative process from disorder to order. In this a process of separation takes place between light and darkness, clouds and oceans, sea and land, and a process of population and classification begins among plants and trees, birds and fish, animals and human beings.

The most important thing we are told about this process is that it is *God's* way of proceeding. It is not automatic or self-enclosed, or the result of random chance, but the result at every point of his creative and directive Word. Eight times we read 'And God said' and each time the result of his commanding will is the fulfilment of what he purposed: 'And it was so.'

The author of Genesis 1 is concerned with order, pattern and categories which he sees in the creation around him. David Atkinson comments:

[14] Acts 17:27–28.   [15] Blocher, pp. 70–71.   [16] Hamilton (1990), p. 117.

Here is a mind that is not far from the interests of science. Indeed, the whole enterprise of science rests precisely on the assumption of an ordered world in which pattern can be discovered and categories established. The ordered rationality of the created world, deriving from the transcendent rationality of the creative Word, is a basic assumption – not usually expressed in those terms – of natural science. There would be no science at all without an ordered world.[17]

However, the natural order of the world is not a logically necessary order. It could have been otherwise. And this, the dependent, derived and contingent order of the world is a fact that provokes endless research and investigation. Stephen Hawking in one place asks the question: 'What is it that breathes fire into the equations and makes a universe for them to describe? The usual approach of science of constructing a mathematical model cannot answer the questions of why there should be a universe for the model to describe. Why does the universe go to the bother of existing?'[18] Genesis and the entire Bible answers the question not with a 'What' but a 'Who'!

6. The purposeful God (1:3–25)

In this chapter every stage of creation is attributed to the one and only Creator who proceeds systematically to order his world. In the familiar refrain 'And God said', the picture of God speaking is not meant to be taken literally but is a figure of speech for God's *personal* and *purposeful* creative activity and precludes random chance as being the key to creation or the cause of what exists. At each stage of the creation 'Let there be' precedes 'and there was'. In this way the writer rests all creation on the intelligence, will and purpose of its Creator.

Looking at the repeated wording of Genesis 1 and its message for its own day and ours, Derek Kidner observes that the simple phrase 'And God said' refutes a range of errors, ancient and modern, about God and our world: 'These eight specific commands, calling all things into being, leave no room for notions of a universe that is self-existent, or struggled for, or random, or a divine emanation.'[19] Here God's distance from, as well as his closeness to, creation is again preserved; creation is not God or any part of him but is called into

---

[17] Atkinson, p. 19.
[18] Stephen Hawking, *A Brief History of Time* (Bantam Press, 1988), p. 184, quoted in Ramachandra (*Gods*), p. 58.
[19] Kidner (1967), p. 46.

being by him, with full intent that it should reveal his wisdom in its design and his purpose in its complexity.

Roy Peacock, a professor in aerospace sciences and an authority on thermodynamics, writes of his own research and his growing awareness that 'What we are viewing is design, contrivance – not accident, chance.' He continues:

> The more I explore this subject, the greater is the conviction that, setting all else aside and from the scientific viewpoint alone, I see a designer who has contrived the most amazing cosmos whose characteristics are balanced on a knife-edge of improbability, ready to topple off should there not be the corrective 'hand on the windlass'. But it is a cosmos so fashioned that it would be the residence of man whom he would create. Stephen Hawking, examining the uniformity of the initial state of the universe, concluded that, so carefully were things chosen that 'it would be very difficult to explain why the Universe should have begun this way, except as the act of a God who intended to create beings like us'. That is a good, considered view, speaking of an intelligent creator. The *how* begins to direct us towards the *why*.[20]

David Wilkinson, formerly a theoretical astrophysicist, now a Christian minister and author, makes the same point:

> Why is the universe so ordered that science itself is possible? Science assumes that such an order underlies its laws, but it cannot explain why. And why can we understand the order? Einstein said, 'The most incomprehensible thing about the universe is that it is comprehensible.' The Christian says that the laws of physics are a reflection of the faithfulness of God the lawgiver, and we can understand them because that same God underlies the rationality of our minds. Why does the universe seem so well set up for life? Life in the universe is only possible because of a number of very sensitive balances in the laws of physics. Over the last 30 years, scientists have often been moved to ask the 'why' question, as we have discovered more. For example, if the energy levels in carbon and oxygen were only a fraction of a per cent different to what they are, there would be no carbon in the universe and therefore no you and me. Sir Fred Hoyle, who pioneered work in this area, stated that nothing had shaken his atheism as much as this discovery.[21]

---

[20] Roy Peacock, *A Brief History of Eternity: A Considered Response to Stephen Hawking's A Brief History of Time* (Monarch, 1989), p. 132.

[21] David Wilkinson, 'The Truth about Science', *Idea*, Sept.–Oct. 1996.

Notice, too, that the world, though contingent (dependent) in its existence, is also given a semi-autonomy, a kind of independence. It rests for its existence every moment on the goodness and power of God, but on that basis and within that divine gift it has within itself the means of self-propagation and self-determination. Thus we read of plants and trees: *Then God said, 'Let the land produce vegetation: seed-bearing plants and trees on the land that bear fruit with seed in it, according to their various kinds'* (v. 11) and of animals: *God blessed them and said, 'Be fruitful and increase in number and fill the water in the seas, and let the birds increase on the earth'* (v. 22). The laws of nature, the explanations of physics, the mechanisms of life, even 'a unified theory of everything' in the physical world should not suggest to us a denial of God but rather the perfection of a created order which is given semi-autonomy, the means under God to develop and perpetuate its own existence.

A point often missed is made by Walter Brueggemann, who observes that verses 3–25 stand as a protest against an exclusively human-centred view of the world: 'The creator God is not totally preoccupied with human creatures. God has his own relation with the rest of creation. The others are his faithful, valued and obedient creatures (cf. Mt. 6:26–29; 8:20; 10:29–31).' He points out that the first blessing of the Bible 'is not for humankind but for the other creatures who have their own relation to God'.[22] An awareness of this should make us kinder to animals, more concerned to preserve vanishing species, and even better gardeners! More widely, it should encourage us to continue the 'creation project' of developing the earth's good potential, especially in less favoured parts where human beings suffer under harsh conditions and which cry out for recognition, protection and development.

7. A good creation (1:31)

And God saw all that he had made, and it was very good (31). Seven times the refrain 'and it was good' acts as an approval-formula in Genesis 1 showing the pleasure and satisfaction of God at each stage of his creation and ordering of the world (vv. 4, 10, 12, 18, 21, 25, 31). To Walter Brueggemann the text proclaims that 'creation is a source of rejoicing and delight for creator and creature . . . All of creation is characterised by God's delight.'[23] He then goes on to quote from Proverbs 8:30–31 (RSV):

> I was daily his delight,
>   rejoicing before him always,

[22] Brueggemann (1982), p. 31.   [23] Ibid., p. 27.

> rejoicing in his inhabited world
> and delighting in the sons of men.

The Creator sees reflected in his creation something of his own goodness. It fits his purpose, but it also mirrors its Maker. In it both God and man can see something of the 'eternal power and divine nature' of God.[24]

We can see from this that the proper understanding of creation has a spiritual and moral dimension as well as a scientific and intellectual one. There is a quality as well as a quantity involved. God has made everything good in its time and place[25] because he is good and does good. Our own love of discovery, design and classification may be part of God's image in us, increasing the tragedy that we should lose sight of the Creator in the creation.

In some of the psalms which celebrate the goodness of creation in the light of the goodness of the Creator we have a two-way movement, as it were, of God saying 'It is good' and creation saying 'God is good'. Walter Brueggemann makes this point when he writes of psalms which celebrate God's generosity and the world's grateful response:

> Thus the morning and evening shout for joy (Ps. 65:8). God waters, enriches, blesses and crowns (vv. 9–11); and as a result the hills are wrapped in joy (v. 12) and sing and shout for joy (v. 13). God's movement toward creation is unceasing generosity. The response of creation is extended doxology (Job 38:7; Ps. 19:1).[26]

The place of human beings is to be the chief singers and conductors in the grand chorale of creation. In us it should find voice and expression in unique ways. We ourselves should never cease to marvel at ourselves and our world.[27] We should never lose the wonder, the 'Wow!' factor, the admiring echo of God's first judgment: 'God saw all that he had made, and it was very good.'

We see, then, that biblical religion is world-affirming in very important respects and not simply world-denying. It is simply not true that 'all is illusion'. Creation is real, matter matters, and if God rejoices in what is material as well as in what is spiritual, then so may we. There is a flight from the physical which is not a necessary part of true spirituality and which can wrongly refuse to enjoy the pleasures of the senses, the sights and sensations of embodied life, the joys of creativity, sexuality, athletics and hard work. Here too we find the mirror and justification of all our art, science and technology, our excitement at discovering and our satisfaction in

---

[24] Rom. 1:20.   [25] Eccles. 3:11.   [26] Brueggemann (1982), p. 28.   [27] Ps. 8.

achieving. Even in the world of the fall the validity of the good life as well as its limits can be recognized.[28]

8. Good – but not God! (1:14–16)

And God said, 'Let there be lights in the expanse of the sky to separate the day from the night, and let them serve as signs to mark seasons and days and years, [15]*and let them be lights in the expanse of the sky to give light to the earth.' And it was so.* [16]*God made two great lights – the greater light to govern the day and the lesser light to govern the night. He also made the stars.*

The goodness of creation, however, can never rival the goodness of the God of creation. All worship is due to him alone. His creation itself is brought into contempt when it is elevated above its place in the created order. At such times it has to be shown to be 'only' the creation. We can see an example of this in the way the writer of Genesis records the creation of the sun, moon and stars.

Vinoth Ramachandra asks: 'Why does the writer put the creation of the sun and the moon on the fourth day, after the creation of light, when it would have been obvious to everyone that they were the sources of light for the earth?' He replies to his own question:

> The reason becomes obvious when we recall that the worship of the sun and moon was very common in the writer's world (e.g. the great Chaldean city of Ur where Abraham came from was a famous centre of moon-worship). Also then, as now, many believed that human life was controlled by the motion of the planets ... The Genesis narrative 'de-bunks' this superstition. The heavenly bodies are simply creatures of God, lamps hung in the sky, with no divine power of their own. They are neither to be feared not worshipped. Nature is but a fellow-creature with human beings: both are dependent on and nourished by the Creator alone.[29]

Similarly, Victor Hamilton writes: 'Few commentators deny that this whole chapter has a strongly anti-mythical thrust. Perhaps in no other section – except the sixth day – does this polemic appear so bluntly as it does here.' Hamilton explains the terms used to denominate the sun and the moon, 'the greater light to govern the day' and 'the lesser light to govern the night':

---

[28] Eccles. 3:11–14; 5:18–20; 9:7–10.   [29] Ramachandra (*Gods*), p. 64.

37

The author's polemical concerns continue in these verses as indicated, first of all, by his choice of terminology. He uses the unusual expression 'the greater luminary' instead of the normal word for sun, *šemeš*, of which he was undoubtedly aware. In the same way he opts for the term *'the lesser luminary'* instead of the familiar word for moon, *yārēaḥ*. The choice of these terms may be due to the fact that these names for the sun and moon – which are very similar in other Semitic languages – are the names of divinities! Thus this text is a deliberate attempt to reject out of hand any apotheothising [making a god] of the luminaries, by ignoring the concrete terms and using a word that speaks of their function.[30]

So, to their superstitious devotees they are 'gods' but to the biblical writer they are no more than outsize lamps! Similarly all the stars together, in their countless masses, are but the 'also made' of God's work in a day!

Even today huge numbers of educated, sophisticated adults look for their 'star signs' and consult astrologers, believing that the positions of the stars have some power over human destiny. Others see them as but the debris of a 'big bang' which was somehow 'meant' to make this world – and us – possible (the weak-anthropic principle). Biblically minded believers, however, see that their lives and the destiny of the creation lie, not in the outworking of impersonal forces, real or imagined, but in the hand of a Personal Creator, Sustainer and Guide, the only true God. He alone must have the glory and honour of these things.

9. Human beings: the masterpiece of God (1:26–28)

Then God said, 'Let us make man in our image, in our likeness, and let them rule over the fish of the sea and the birds of the air, over the livestock, over all the earth, and over all the creatures that move along the ground.'

> [27]*So God created man*
> *in his own image,*
> *in the image of God*
> *he created him;*
> *male and female*
> *he created them.*

---

[30] Hamilton (1990), p. 128.

²⁸*God blessed them and said to them, 'Be fruitful and increase in number; fill the earth and subdue it. Rule over the fish of the sea and the birds of the air and over every living creature that moves on the ground.'*

With verse 26 the creation narrative reaches its climax. The first thing that we notice here is a change in the creation formula. It is no longer 'Let there be' but 'Let us make'. At once the reader is prepared for something particularly important and significant.

To suppose that the plural form of the verb ('Let us make') is an intentional reference to the Trinity is to read back a New Testament doctrine into the writing of an early Old Testament author. Some commentators see it as a human way of expressing God's deliberation, rather as we might say to ourselves 'Let's try this' or 'Let's do that'. Possibly it is God addressing his Spirit, mentioned in verse two, which would give us 'the first glimmering of a Trinitarian revelation'.³¹ Many writers old and new, including early Jewish commentators, have thought it most likely that God is addressing the heavenly court, the angels who are elsewhere mentioned as being present at the making of the world.³² Only God, of course, creates us, as the singular of the verb 'create' in verse 27 shows, but in this case we would have 'a divine announcement to the heavenly host, drawing the angelic host's attention to the masterstroke of creation, man'.³³

From Genesis 1 then, we learn not only what God is but who we are. Too often science leaves us dwarfed by huge time-scales that seem to say the whole history of humankind is just a blip on the screen. So we need this affirmation of our worth and place in the creation which is to be found neither in the measurement of time nor the investigations of science, but in the decision and purpose of God. It is from him in whose image we have been made that we get our true self-estimate and full value.

a. 'In his own image'

No term or phrase is more important in regard to the creation of humankind than the recurring phrase 'in our image'. Entire books have been written in answer to the question 'In what does the image of God consist?' The answers have included human reason, conscience, original righteousness, our relationship with God, our relationship with others, and our rule over the natural world. In the last analysis the image of God probably does not lie in any one thing

³¹ D. J. A. Clines, 'The Image of God in Man', *TynB* 19 (1968), pp. 66f., quoted in Blocher, p. 84.
³² Job 38:4, 7.   ³³ Wenham (1987), p. 28.

but in a uniquely human complex of qualities and relationships. It is our humanity in its fullness, not some detached part of it, which makes us 'like God'. As Wayne Grudem points out, there are moral, spiritual, mental, relational and even physical aspects of our humanity which show us to be more like God than the rest of creation. In fact, however, no list could do justice to the image of God in humankind, for as he says: 'a full understanding of man's likeness to God would require a full understanding of who God is in his being and actions and a full understanding of who man is and what he does'.[34] An Old Testament scholar remarks similarly: 'In the twentieth century a consensus has emerged concerning the image among O.T. scholars . . . The image is properly understood as referring to the entire human, not a part or property.'[35] Humankind is seen as God's representative on earth, given the task of dominion over the non-human creation and even, some would say, God's counterpart.[36]

The Dutch theologian Herman Bavinck has written: 'The entire world is a revelation of God, a mirror of his virtues and perfections; every creature is in its own way and according to his own measure an embodiment of a divine thought. But among all creatures only man is the image of God, the highest and richest revelation of God and therefore the head and crown of the entire creation.'[37]

Here, too, at the beginning of the Bible, we find the ground for a Christian ecology, a recognition of the value of creation and a response to the Creator of gratitude and responsibility. We are not only lords of creation but trusted stewards and managers of it, appointed to bring it to perfection, exploring its secrets, harnessing its powers and fulfilling its potential (1:26–30). As we recognize the power and wisdom of the Creator we shall be the more likely to value the creation and care for the environment. Here, doxology and ecology go together. Those who have heard God say of the earth 'It is good' should be the first to manage it well.

It is made clear later that it was not only the first, unfallen human beings who are in the image of God. The image is not lost through sin: 'Gen. 9:6 indicates that humans, as made in God's image, have an intrinsic worth that is related to God's own glory. Thus to harm or kill humans is to injure the majesty of God (cf. Prov. 14:31; James 2:9).'[38] It makes clear too, in an ancient world where only kings and their like were thought to be in the image of the gods, that all men and women were made in the image of their Creator and have a unique identity and value in the world.

However, while this 'natural' likeness remains, with its great

---

[34] Grudem, op. cit., p. 443.
[35] R. C. van Leeuwen, 'Form, Image', *NIDOTTE*, vol. 4, p. 644.   [36] Ibid.
[37] Quoted in Hoekema, p. 12.   [38] Van Leeuwen, op. cit., p. 645.

importance for our understanding of the unique nature and value of the human being, the biblical doctrine of sin and the New Testament theme of *re*-creation/redemption in Christ, show us that the 'moral' image of God 'in true holiness and righteousness' has been seriously defaced and largely lost. Only in Christ and in his final glory will the full image of God be restored in us.

b. Made to know God

In verse 28 we see human beings as uniquely *addressable* by God: God blesses and speaks to them as he does not speak to the animals. He addresses them as a person to persons. Because he is personal they can be persons too, interacting as such with him and others. Walter Brueggemann writes:

> It is important that of all the creatures of God's eight creative acts, God speaks directly only to human creatures. The others have no speech directed toward them at all. By contrast, in 1:28, God speaks to the human creatures, and in verse 29, he twice addresses them directly, 'you'. This creature has a different, intimate relation with the creator. This is the speech-creature *par excellence*. This is the one to whom God has made a particularly intense commitment (by speaking) and to whom marvellous freedom has been granted (in responding).[39]

c. Male and female in his image

In speaking of the creation of humanity, Genesis 2 adds the statement, 'And the LORD God formed the man from the dust of the ground and breathed into his nostrils the breath of life, and man became a living being' (2:7). Genesis 2 also tells us of the woman's creation out of Adam's side (2:21). He is *'is̆* (Man), she is *'is̆s̆â* (female Man); the exact and equal counterpart and fulfilment of *'is̆*. She is later given the name 'Eve'. We should notice that 'it is not Eve herself but simply the raw material that is taken from the man'.[40] Woman as such is made *a special creation* by God out of Adam as he made Adam *a special creation* out of the dust of the ground. The point, I believe, is to show that men and women are fundamentally equal; they are of one species. They are also distinct in their gender, with a distinction that is part of their identity and not a mere accident of their humanity. Gender distinctions are God-given and reflect him in equal and overlapping ways. It is not that either is less than the image of God but that both, and indeed the wider human society, in their complementarity and diversity, reflect more adequately the glories of that image and the glory of God who is in all and above

---

[39] Brueggemann (1982), p. 31.   [40] Hamilton (1990), p. 179.

all. Woman is not, as many of the ancients believed, an inferior form of man but an equal being, bearing the image of God as much as he. She is his counterpart and equal, his helper and his completion. Over this and all of his creation stands the verdict of the Creator: 'God saw all that he had made, and it was very good' (1:31).

11. The rest of God (2:2–3)

By the seventh day God had finished the work he had been doing; so on the seventh day he rested from all his work. ³And God blessed the seventh day and made it holy, because on it he rested from all the work of creating that he had done.

God's 'rest' is, of course, a relative not an absolute rest since God never ceases to work.[41] But it is a serious statement about a finished work and a settled, created order. We have now, in the creation, a reliable physics, a dependable system, a designed harmony in which, more and more, we can see how things work. The 'laws of nature', far from rendering God an unnecessary hypothesis, reflect his purpose and the perfection of his work. The built-in *order* of the universe makes all scientific knowledge and medical progress possible and the 'rest' of God in the first chapter of Genesis proclaims that finishedness which ensures the stability of natural law. God did not immediately set about making new, different or contrary laws in an unfinished creation, an alternative physics making a nonsense on Wednesdays of what was assured on Tuesdays. The integrity of the first creation was, and is still, preserved. We do well to remember this amidst the present hunger for the miraculous which threatens to lose the wonder of the everyday and the security of an established order. The life of the kingdom does not set aside the life of creation.

a. A faithful Creator

It is, of course, true that something has entered to disturb and disrupt the creation: it is both settled and unsettled. It no longer proceeds in all the ways God intended. Even the good laws and regularities of nature can now work against us and wreak havoc in the order of creation and in human life. The cancer grows as well as the child. It is no longer a case that 'God's in his heaven, all's well with the world.' It was because all was not well with the world that God left his heaven. The Babe of Bethlehem became the Man of Calvary.

Yet, in the grace of God, even this fallen creation retains much of its integrity, for he does not cease to work. God's act of creation was

---

[41] John 5:17.

no experiment; it was an act of commitment. The same divine Mind that rejoiced in the first creation rests also in full assurance about the restored creation and keeps faith with man and beast:

> The eyes of all look to you,
> and you give them their food at the proper time.
> You open your hand
> and satisfy the desires of every living thing.[42]

The 'rest' of God signified his contentment with what he had done. He had begun to share for ever his life with others, his existence with the existence of a marvellous creation and a race of beings 'in his image'. He would not go back on his intentions. From now on the eternal God would exist for ever in relation to time and space and a creation outside of himself. The day would come when he would take to himself a human body and a human nature. Nothing would ever be the same for God again – and he was well content.

b. The life of God shared with creation

The 'rest' of God on the seventh day leads to his blessing it as a sacred period for all time. It is not the later Jewish Sabbath as such that is for all time blessed. Rather, what is blessed is what it and this act of blessing betokens, that is, the life of God shared with creation which finds in him and his rest its true destiny.[43] Walter Brueggemann writes on the later institution of the Sabbath in Israel: 'The celebration of a day of rest was ... the announcement of a trust in this God who is confident enough to rest. It was then and is now an assertion that life does not depend upon our feverish activity of self-securing, but that there can be a pause in which life is given to us simply as a gift.'[44] Our part is to meet God's creation faithfulness with thanksgiving, a doxology renewed with every 'sabbath' and even in the little sabbaths of table-graces when we know that 'we live by gift' and are 'strangely sustained, nurtured and nourished'. These are the visible links in our lives between 'the overpowering miracle of creation and the daily reality of food'. So we are to respond to the revelation of blessing in the text of Genesis 1. 'We must listen to the text, but it does not stay in our ears. It leaps to our lips. The proclamation becomes a doxology.'[45]

12. A tract for the times?

The biblical account of creation was not written in a vacuum. It was

---

[42] Ps. 145:15–16. [43] Gen. 1:22, 28; 2:3; Rom. 8:18–25.
[44] Brueggemann (1982), pp. 35–36. [45] Ibid., pp. 35–36, 39.

43

written amidst the swirl of different and differing religions with their highly coloured myths, their many gods and their tribal and civilizational sense of identity and destiny. The early chapters of Genesis present an alternative world-view, indeed one hostile to those in wide circulation in the ancient Near East. Gordon Wenham describes Genesis 1 – 11 as 'a tract for the times', challenging ancient assumptions about the nature of God, the world and mankind.[46]

We realize just how different the biblical account of creation is when we read, for example, the Babylonian creation epic, *Enuma Elish*, the most important cosmological text of the ancient Mesopotamian world. It was compiled from earlier sources during the second half of the second millennium BC, that is around the time of Abraham. It was written as propaganda to demonstrate the supremacy of the Babylonian god Marduk over all the other gods. In payment for settling the long-standing conflict between the older, more static gods and the younger and more dynamic gods (is anything new?), Marduk was granted supreme authority. He made heaven and earth from the two halves, respectively, of the older god he had defeated (Tiamat, consort of the already slain Apsu). Then he made humankind (from the blood of another slain god, Kingu), 'for the service of the gods that they might be at ease' from having to irrigate and cultivate the land in order to grow food for themselves. Now human beings could do the work necessary and provide food for the gods by their sacrifices and devotions.[47]

Similarly, in the *Myth of Atra-hasis*, another ancient Mesopotamian account of the origins of mankind, the lesser gods complained of the work they had to do. They asked the mother-goddess Mami (or Nintu) to create mankind to bear their toil. The god Enki advised killing one of the gods 'that god and man may be thoroughly mixed in the clay'. Consequently, the mother goddess Nintu pinched off fourteen pieces of this clay mixture and fourteen birth-goddesses gestated them, producing seven male and seven female human beings.[48] So now you know!

From such examples we can appreciate Henri Blocher's comment that the first verse of Genesis dramatically and uncompromisingly 'breaks with all the mythologies of the ancient East'. He quotes the vivid sentence of another French scholar, Claude Tresmontant: 'Just as Abraham left his family and the land of his ancestors, so with its very first step, the metaphysics of the Bible leaves behind the metaphysics of the ancient world.'[49] In a classic work on the subject, Alexander Heidel, comparing the Babylonian myth of origins with

[46] Wenham (1987), p. xlv.
[47] See M. J. A. Horsnell, 'Religions: Assyria and Babylonia', *ISBE*, vol. 4, pp. 84–95.
[48] Ibid., p. 94; cf. Wenham (1987), p. 52.   [49] Blocher, p. 61.

the Genesis account, concluded that 'In the light of the differences, the resemblances fade away almost like the stars before the sun.'[50]

In these opening verses, and in the verses that follow, the uncompromising statement is made that this God and this God alone created all that is not God. This first clear note is sounded throughout the rest of the Scriptures without compromise.[51] He is the God who says, 'I am the LORD, and there is no other.'[52] All things exist by his will and for his glory.[53] Yet, as Wenham insists, 'Genesis 1 is more than a repudiation of contemporary oriental creation myths; it is a triumphant invocation of the God who has created all men and an invocation to all humanity to adore him who has made them in his own image.'[54]

Genesis 1 speaks today as it has spoken to men and women for millennia and we are made wiser and stronger for life as we listen to it. Its message is as relevant as ever, but we must be careful to understand what its message really is. Gordon Wenham writes:

The Bible-versus-science debate has, most regrettably, side-tracked readers of Gen. 1. Instead of reading the chapter as a triumphant affirmation of the power and wisdom of God and the wonder of his creation, we have been too often bogged down in attempting to squeeze Scripture into the mould of the latest scientific hypothesis or distorting scientific facts to fit a particular interpretation. When allowed to speak for itself, Gen. 1 looks far beyond such minutiae. Its proclamation of the God of grace and power who undergirds the world and gives it purpose, justifies the scientific approach to nature. Gen. 1, by further affirming the unique status of man, and his place in the divine program, and God's care for him, gives a hope to mankind that atheistic philosophies can never legitimately supply.[55]

---

[50] Quoted in ibid., pp. 33–34.
[51] E.g. Ps. 33:6, 9; Acts 4:24; 14:15; 17:24–25; Col. 1:16.   [52] Is. 45:18.
[53] Rev. 4:11.   [54] Wenham (1987), p. 10.   [55] Ibid., p. 40.

Genesis 1
2. Genesis for today

One night, after hours spent in observing the movements of the stars and planets, the great seventeenth-century astronomer Kepler said to his friends, 'I have been thinking over again the earliest thoughts of God.' Three hundred years later, Albert Einstein, though not of any orthodox faith, said he felt 'rapturous amazement at the harmony of natural law, which reveals an intelligence of such superiority that compared with it all the systematic thinking and acting of human beings is an utterly insignificant reflection'.[1]

The harmony, design and evidence of purpose that run through the entire creation, from the world of quantum physics to the worlds of distant galaxies and universes, from the intricacies of the human brain to the tantalizing ripples at the edge of the universe, cry out for recognition and explanation. The biblical testimony is that the primary explanation has already been given – by the God who made us and all things for his glory. Even apart from the special revelation of Scripture and even in their fallen state, human beings are made to see in the created world 'God's invisible qualities – his eternal power and divine nature'.[2] They are without excuse when they 'suppress the truth' they know.[3]

1. The God who continues to reveal himself

In the previous chapter we stayed fairly close to the text of Genesis 1. Here I want to broaden the same lessons out a little in terms of the Bible as a whole, applying some of them more closely to our own times. Martin Luther described the opening of Genesis as 'certainly the foundation of the whole of Scripture'.[4] We know God only because he makes himself known, in deed and word, by general

---

[1] Quoted in C. Colson, *Kingdoms in Conflict* (Hodder & Stoughton, 1989), pp. 66–67.
[2] Rom. 1:20. [3] Rom. 1:18–19.
[4] Quoted in Blocher, p. 16.

revelation in the creation and by special revelation in the Scriptures.[5] The God who meets us in the first chapters of Genesis is the God who continues to reveal himself to us in the rest of Scripture. There is a marvellous unity about the books that go to form our Bible, a collection of books written and edited by more than forty authors over a period of fourteen or sixteen hundred years. We do not find there is one God of the Old Testament and a very different God of the New. The elements of greatness and goodness, justice and mercy, love and wrath in the one true God are there from the early chapters of the first book to the final chapters of the last.

The opening of Genesis tells us something about *the goodness of God*. He did not have to make the world. He had evidently lived in the self-sufficient blessedness of his own eternal Triune Being. He did not make us because he was lonely; he made us because he is generous, good and loving. He did not need us, yet he ordained to bring us into existence, to give us the gift of sentient life and ultimately to take us into the perfect circle of his life and fellowship for ever. His goodness means that he is the standard of all that is good[6] and the giver of every good gift.[7] The self-giving nature of God's goodness should cause us to see God in all his works, and to praise him for them. At the same time it ought to cause us to seek him in and beyond them all.[8] The goodness of God is the presupposition of the fundamental goodness of creation.

This goodness is a matter that needs to be recognized and maintained by believers when so much evolutionary theory stresses a world built on suffering and therefore on evil. A thing is good if it fulfils the purpose for which it was created. God has made our interconnected world and its means of survival and growth. God and his creation do not cease to be good because the spider eats the fly or because larger animals eat smaller ones. It is true that our world is damaged and frustrated because of the fall of human beings from God.[9] But God does not cease to be good in creation, providence and grace. From God's goodness flow his love, mercy, patience and grace.

Genesis tells us something, too, about *the spirituality of God*, his *transcendence* and *immanence*. God is distinct from everything created. He is also at the centre of everything created; standing apart and standing within. He is so truly 'Spirit' that nothing in all creation can be worshipped as divine, and yet so involved that nothing in all creation is irrelevant or unknown. God's transcendence means that he is not to be 'located' spatially as created things are. He is not 'in' one place more than another, and there is not more of him in one

[5] Ps. 19:1–14.   [6] Ps. 119:68.   [7] Jas. 1:17.   [8] Ps. 73:25–26.
[9] Gen. 3:17; Rom. 8:22.

place than another. God is present in a way which transcends spatial terms. Millard Ericksen writes:

> All finite objects have a location. They are somewhere. This necessarily prevents them being somewhere else. The greatness of finite objects is measured by how much space they occupy. With God, however, the question of whereness or location is not applicable. God is the one who brought space (and time) into being. He was there before there was space. He cannot be localised at a particular point. There can be no plotting of his co-ordinates.[10]

However, God is immanent as well as transcendent. The immanence (not imminence) of God means his indwelling; it means that God is everywhere, present at every place in all of his creation at all times. As Ericksen puts it, 'The point here is that nowhere within creation is God inaccessible. Jeremiah quotes God as saying, "Am I a God at hand . . . and not a God far off as well?" (Jer. 9:23). The implication seems to be that being a God at hand does not preclude his being afar off as well.'[11] God is present in everything created yet he is infinitely removed from everything created because, in terms of his own essence, he transcends everything created: he is the God who is Spirit and who must be worshipped in spirit and in truth.[12]

It is this infinite difference – God's transcendence even where he is present – that underlies the biblical protest against idolatry,[13] including the well-nigh universal worship of the sun, moon and stars. Nothing can be worshipped, simply because nothing is God or any part of him. In the beginning God did not say 'Let *me* be light', but 'Let *there* be light.' This is in strong contradiction of much 'New Age' Western thought which sees everything as a part of 'God', including ourselves.

Genesis 1 tells us too about *the creativity, wisdom and power of God*. He is infinite and invisible. Yet his fingerprints are on every snowflake, and he writes his signature in the stars for us to read and recognize. What teems in the mind of God soon teems in the oceans of earth. The land becomes rich and abundant in plant and animal life. As the animals came out of Noah's ark two by two, so the wonders of creation and the creatures of planet earth come out of the great ark of the Divine Intelligence million by million. However he did it, he did it wonderfully, wisely and well. Genesis says it was with a word; John says it was by the Word; and Paul says that he who is the Word shall have the last word, when he reconciles to God

---

[10] Millard Ericksen, *Christian Theology* (Baker, 1985), p. 273.   [11] Ibid.
[12] John 4:24.   [13] E.g. Is. 44:9–11; 45:18–23; 46:8–10; 48:12–14.

'all things, whether things on earth or things in heaven' in a creation where God makes everything new.[14]

Throughout the chapter *the purpose of God* in creation is stressed. The progression from disorder to order – the movement which gives shape, beauty and life in all its forms – is not described as an automatic or self-enclosed process. Rather it is depicted as God's way of proceeding, the result at every point of his creative and directive word. God is the God of order. This is made clear by the repeated refrain 'And God said, "Let there be" . . . and there was.' The process is not specified, but the purpose is. Whether we think in terms of evolutionary processes or not, the one thing precluded here is random chance as the reason for life. It has been said that the probability of life originating from accident is comparable to the probability of a dictionary resulting from an explosion in a printing works. However, the opening chapter of the Bible does not speculate about a probability but proclaims a Person. Here is purpose, intention, guidance, direction, achievement. This purpose is said to reach its highest objective in the creation of humankind, male and female, which is created 'in the image and likeness of God'. From the start biblical truth sets man and woman in the context of both the creation and the Creator. Human beings have a unique relationship with both which defines them.[15]

The creation account ends in 2:2–3 with *the rest of God*. On the seventh day he 'rested', signifying a work completed, which would not be undone. This was no mere experiment, interesting but disposable; this is an act of commitment, even a covenantal act. The very existence of creation carries within it the promise of a future. For even in the world of the fall 'there remains, then, a Sabbath-rest for the people of God' for which the whole creation 'waits in eager expectation'.[16] And so the first chapters of the Bible link with the last. God made a world which has been spoiled, but God has a plan which cannot be spoiled. He has a sovereign purpose which mysteriously overarches human failure and cuts a path through fallen human history. The sovereign purpose of the all-good and all-powerful God is the first and final refutation of all fatalism and the antidote to all despair.

2. The infinite-personal God

Some systems, religions and philosophies have a god who is infinite but not personal. Fashionable 'New Age' ideas, for instance, often claim that what we call 'God' is everything in the universe including

[14] Gen. 1:3, 20; John 1:1–3; Col. 1:20; Rev. 21:5.
[15] Gen. 1:26–30; Pss. 8:1–9; 139:1–18; Acts 17:24–31; Rev. 21:3.
[16] Heb. 4:9; Rom. 8:19; Rev. 21:1–5.

ourselves. People have often held the view that 'nature' is God and 'God' only another word for nature. These ideas may superficially sound good but they are in fact devastating in their implications. They are new forms of an age-old philosophy called 'pantheism'. The word pantheism comes from two Greek words: *pan*, meaning all or everything, and *theos*, meaning God. It says that everything is God: the galaxies and the forces of nature, the seas and their teeming life, and the land with its animals, trees and vegetation. But were we to agree with this we would then, of course, have surrendered all idea of a truly personal God and even sacrificed the very idea of personality or personhood itself.

I can hug the yew tree but the yew tree cannot hug me back. The entire Milky Way cannot love and comfort me and dry my tears as can a person, or the God who is a person. Wayne Grudem writes:

Pantheism denies several essential aspects of God's character. If the whole universe is God, God has no distinct personality. God is no longer unchanging, because as the universe changes, God also changes. Moreover, God is no longer holy, because evil in the universe is also part of God. Another difficulty is that most pantheistic systems (such as Buddhism and many other eastern religions) end up denying the importance of individual human personalities: since everything is God, the goal of an individual should be to blend in with the universe and become more and more united with it, thus losing his or her individual distinctiveness.[17]

On the other hand, there are religions whose gods are personal but not infinite. Animism, for instance, sees spirits in rocks, trees and pools who can be benevolent or malevolent. Each is one among many other beings, far from being infinite in power or knowledge. Similarly, ancient paganism has its hierarchy of gods with particular areas of responsibility and degrees of power (like Mars, god of war, and Artemis, goddess of love), and who were capable of showing all-too-human lusts and cruelties. These were not infinite, and were also vulnerable to one another. The last opera in Richard Wagner's famous *Ring* cycle, The Twilight of the Gods, ends with Valhalla ablaze as the Norse gods fall prey to their own abuse of power. Hinduism also has millions of gods, again of very different character, who are supposed to have some form of personhood but who are not themselves infinite.

In contrast to all this the Bible presents us with a Creator who is

[17] Wayne Grudem, *Systematic Theology: An Introduction to Biblical Doctrine* (IVP/Zondervan, 1994), pp. 268–269.

both infinite and personal. Holding the two together is essential. God's being is so different from ours, his essence so unknowable to our creaturely minds, that there are times when we cannot say what he is: only, by contrast with what we know, what he is not. There are points at which we must proceed by negatives (the 'via negata' as the old divines called it). For instance, God is in-finite, not finite; im-mortal, not mortal; im-mense, not measurable. These things remind us how far beyond our best thoughts is his eternal glory. Yet God's infinitude must never be seen as emptiness but rather as full-ness; it is not only the absence of limitations but the fullness of perfections. He is infinitely holy, wise, just and good. It means, too, that he is not only unlimited but unlimitable, even by evil and the rebellion of the human race. His infinite goodness is the final truth and power. He is the sovereign God. This is an enormous comfort to us as it was to the author of Psalm 46:

> God is our refuge and strength,
> an ever present help in trouble.
> Therefore we will not fear, though the earth give way
> and the mountains fall into the heart of the sea . . .
> The LORD Almighty is with us;
> the God of Jacob is our fortress (46:1–7).

As we encounter God in his ongoing revelation of himself, we shall see that his real though divine personhood is expressed in striking human terms. So, for instance, we meet with his grief and anger in Exodus, his love and suffering in Hosea, his justice and judgment in Amos, his jealousy and joy in Isaiah, and his assumption of flesh-and-blood humanity in Jesus Christ. The Scriptures risk many of our misunderstandings to make the point, the supremely important point, that God is a personal being.

3. The God who creates out of nothing

The doctrine of the creation out of nothing (*ex nihilo*) is important because it preserves and affirms the aloneness of God as the Author and Sustainer of all creaturely existence, the Creator of everything that is not God. While *bārā'*, to create, is a term used with only God as its subject in the Hebrew Old Testament, modern scholarship warns us against reading too much into the particular Hebrew term used here. It is better to see the text of Genesis 1:1 as a whole 'as communicating an absolute beginning of the universe as well as the absolute sovereignty of God in bringing reality into being and ordering it according to his will'.[18] Others can only fashion out of existing materials but God created the original material that he and others order and use. This distinguishes the unique creativity of God.

The defence of creation *ex nihilo* is not merely a case of reading back into the account a later concern. All the early creation myths imagined the gods creating from pre-existing material. Victor Hamilton asks, 'Is it possible to believe that the author would leave, unchanged and unmolested, and thus endorse, one of the distinguishing concepts of the mythical world-view viz. the creation of the world from pre-existing matter which is outside the creator's divine activity?'[19] The author of Genesis 1 means his readers (or hearers) to learn that the true God called forth creation out of nothing and by nothing but his own unaided power. So the point is made at the outset that in the beginning there were not *two* (God plus eternal matter) but *One* (God only, God alone). Various texts elsewhere in Scripture similarly deny the eternal pre-existence of matter.[20]

The question is not merely speculative. It has far-reaching ramifications for both belief and behaviour. Firstly, Genesis teaches us that all matter owes its existence to nothing save God's will alone. He was not confronted with matter or energy as eternal as himself and which restricted his choices. Rather he chose in the freedom of his power and his love to bring into existence something other than himself – a universe of wonders and a world of beings made in his image. Colin Gunton writes:

> The doctrine of creation holds that the world and all it contains comes from the free, creative act of God. That divine freedom is the chief burden of the doctrine of creation out of nothing ... We come from nothing, in the sense that but for our calling into being by the love of God, we should not be. What might be called the existential point of the doctrine is, to cite Luther's famous words: 'that I should believe that I am God's creature, that he has given me a body, soul, good eyes, reason, a good wife, children, fields, meadows, pigs and cows ... Thus this article teaches that you do not have your life of yourself, not even a hair'.[21]

Secondly, this doctrine of creation out of nothing is important and is far-reaching in its implications, both for the biblical doctrine of

---

[18] R. C. van Leeuwen, '*br*''', *NIDOTTE*, vol. 1, p. 732, citing Eichrodt, Westermann and Wenham.

[19] Hamilton (1990), p. 105.

[20] E.g. Ps. 148:5; Prov. 8:22–27; John 1:3; Acts 4:24; Rom. 4:17; Col. 1:16; Heb. 11:3.

[21] Gunton (1992), p. 44.

God and for our understanding of personal responsibility. James Linsay notes: 'The eternity of matter, as something other than God, means its independence of God and its power to limit or condition him.'[22] And Helmut Thielicke writes:

When creation myths understand God as a kind of artist . . . who fashions the world out of existent material, man can be only partially and not totally responsible. The forces of guilt and the tragic entanglements which afflict him can be traced back to the cosmic material, which is often regarded as under a curse, and which determines the immobile situation of human existence, so that man cannot be held responsible for it. In this way much guilt is transformed into fate . . . When God creates out of nothing, then the man created by Him belongs to Him totally and must give himself back to Him as he has received himself from Him. If he has alienated and falsified himself, he can no longer refer by way of extenuation to realities which are taken from God's creative act and which thus exist apart from the guilt of man. For example he cannot refer to matter which drags him down and through no fault of his own poisons his existence. Nor can he refer to the blighting forces of fate which indwell the world from the very outset . . . instead man is totally guilty before God.[23]

If anyone is tempted to think that talk of 'creation myths' and 'fate' is irrelevant to our modern society, they would do well to reflect on the emergence of some contemporary excuses for human behaviour which transfer responsibility and blame on to pre-existing materials – from evolutionary forces to genetic pre-dispositions and 'promiscuous genes'! Human beings have always been experts at reducing their personal responsibility for their sinful behaviour.

4. The God who is not nature

The commanding word spoken throughout Genesis 1, '*Let there be . . .*', also shows *the distinction between God and his creation*. Biblical religion never confuses God and 'nature' as the rites and symbols of many ancient religions have done, from the fertility rites of ancient Baal worship to the *monism* (all is one) of much Hindu philosophy and Eastern thought. 'New Age' philosophy does this in the West in our own day. Here everything and everyone is seen as sharing in the universal 'deity' which is creation. The earth goddess 'Gaia' is again venerated as the planet is given an almost personal identity.

[22] James Linsay, 'Creation', *ISBE*, vol. 1, p. 802.   [23] Thielicke, vol. 2, pp. 54, 88.

The Bible retains this distinction between God and his creation throughout. God is not 'everything', though he holds everything in being. He is distinct in his own being and essence from his creation even though he is present in power and wisdom at every point of its molecular and subatomic life. It is this that underlies the biblical protest against every kind of idolatry. We must not make a god of anything which has been made *because it is not God*. It has a dependent (contingent) existence, depending on him for its creation and its continuance. Only God the Creator is *self-existent*, owing his existence to nothing outside of himself.

This is a basic reason why we cannot 'prove' the existence of God scientifically in the ways we are often challenged to do. If God were discoverable at the level of physics he would simply be another piece of phenomena with which physics has to do. As Paul Helm puts it:

> If God's relation to the physical universe is capable of being understood scientifically, then God would be a part of the physical universe. Investigating God and the universe would be like investigating the relationship of one planet to another, or of one galaxy to another ... But according to Scripture God is not part of the physical universe ... In the language of theology, God *transcends* the universe.[24]

That is why we need the self-revelation of the infinite-personal God in and above all observations and arguments. This is the God who revealed himself to patriarchs and prophets; the God who says 'Here I am' as well as 'Let there be'; the God who revealed himself in word and deed, and supremely in the Word made flesh; the God whose ongoing revelation of himself by the Holy Spirit in the hearts and minds of his people enabled the apostle Paul to say: 'For God, who said, "Let light shine out of darkness", made his light shine in our hearts to give us the light of the knowledge of the glory of God in the face of Christ.'[25]

5. God and the recovery of purpose

If the world was created by a person, it was created for a purpose. Conversely, the loss of the one must eventually lead to the denial of the other.

In his book *Foolishness to the Greeks*, Bishop Lesslie Newbigin frequently protests against the denial of purpose which has characterized modern scientific theory, and which has devastating results on human self-consciousness and society. With the rise of

---

[24] Helm, p. 70.   [25] 2 Cor. 4:6.

Newtonian science it was held that the real world was governed not by purpose but by natural laws of cause and effect: 'To have discovered the cause of something is to have explained it. There is no need to invoke purpose or design as an explanation.'[26] From this came the modern divisions between facts and values: 'The public world is a world of facts that are the same for everyone, whatever his values may be, the private world is a world of values where all are free to choose their own values and therefore to pursue such a course of action as will correspond with them.'[27] 'There is in this view a world of facts that is the real world, an austere world in which human hopes, desires, and purposes have no place. The facts are facts, and they are value-free.'[28]

From this emerged the denial that human values can flow from the (scientific) facts, that we can get to what 'ought to be' from what 'is'. Justice and morality are not regarded as objective realities or standards in the universe outside of ourselves and our own choice. Yet the irony is, as Newbigin points out, that the very mind which denies purpose presupposes it in the decisions and methods of its own enquiry. This is a dichotomy that runs through our culture: 'We all engage in purposeful activity, and we judge ourselves and others in terms of success in achieving the purposes that we set before ourselves. Yet we accept as the final product of this purposeful activity a picture of the world from which purpose has been eliminated.'[29]

This has crucial implications for human life and for our own self-understanding. If creation was without purpose, then human life is without any purpose other than that which we ourselves manufacture for our comfort. We may whistle in the dark to keep our spirits up. But if we are the accidental throw-up of evolutionary forces or an original 'big bang' then we came from nothing meaningful and are going to nothing meaningful. In the last analysis human life becomes futile. To the contrary, however, we see everywhere around us evidence of design and progress. Meaning and purpose are built into the deepest fabric of the universe. Even the 'big bang' is seen, by many of those scientists who champion it as a theory, as having been exquisitely orchestrated so as to have made possible our own world and its atmosphere, given our speed through expanding space.

The recovery of purpose is one of the greatest and most urgent needs of Western society. Values in any culture are based on some vision of the ultimate purpose of things. The modern scientific view does not provide such a basis. The education of entire generations of children and young people is seriously incomplete and inadequate

[26] Newbigin (1986), p. 25.　　[27] Ibid., p. 36.　　[28] Ibid., p. 77.　　[29] Ibid., p. 78.

when education is based on such a purely scientific world-view. As Newbigin puts it:

> That the development of the individual person is governed by the program encoded in the DNA molecule is a fact every educated person is expected to know and accept. It will be part of the curriculum in the public school system. That every human being is made to glorify God and enjoy him for ever is an opinion held by some people but not part of public truth. Yet if it is true, it is at least as important as anything else in the preparation of young people for their journey through life.[30]

The Bible is full of purpose from its first chapter to its last. That purpose is defined by God, in his power and goodness. The purpose of God does not stop with the world and creation at large as it was then or as it now is, or with human beings as they have been or are. It includes what our world, animate and inanimate, human and animal, will be, in the destiny marked out for it. This is a destiny forfeited by the fall of humanity but recovered by Christ in his victory at the cross. Colin Gunton writes:

> Creation was not simply the making of the world out of nothing, not even that world continually upheld by the providence of God, but the making of a world destined for perfection, completedness. To be a creature means to be a being called and directed to a future perfection. Those who first proclaimed that the chief end of man is to glorify God and enjoy him for ever enunciated a profound truth ... Not only are we called to give our souls and bodies as living sacrifices of praise to our creator, but along with them the whole creation, represented as it is in the sacramental elements of water, bread and wine.[31]

The purposes of the Creator, however, are not only denied but openly challenged in our time. We saw in the previous chapter the emphasis on order at the creation. This is an essential part of the biblical world-view: that there is an order to things, that there are boundaries, distinctions, limits, places where things, animals and people belong in the God-given order of creation. We are living in a time when people are impatient of the order of God and determined to cross the boundaries of morality and even nature. Good and evil are synthesized in a modern dialectic, and sexual boundaries are crossed in various ways. Even the distinction between humans and animals is blurred, with talk of animal rights (rather than human

---

[30] Ibid., p. 38.   [31] Gunton (1992), pp. 45–46.

responsibilities) and even human rights for certain endangered species of ape. Part of us longs for the order and unity, the place and purpose, that are in God. Yet we are in revolt against it because we are in revolt against him, his holiness and his rule. So we lament the confusion we provoke and curse the darkness we create. As Henri Blocher notes:

> Once the knowledge of God is lost, the sense of God wanders among created things and not finding him, seeks for his substitute in their dissolution. Once the knowledge of God is lost, mankind accuses finitude of causing his disorder, whereas that disorder is the fruit of disobedience. Once the communion is lost, mankind wants to replace it with confusion.[32]

a. We matter because God matters

In their book *Stephen Hawking: a life in science*, Michael White and John Gribben quote Hawking's conclusion from modern science's observation of the size of the physical universe around us: 'We are such insignificant creatures on a minor planet of a very average star in the outer suburbs of one of a hundred thousand million galaxies ... that it is difficult to believe in a God that would care about us or even notice our existence.[33] But the experience of our littleness and creation's vastness is not new. Three thousand years ago the psalmist wrote of it – but with a very different conclusion. For the psalmist might have known much less about creation than modern scientists, but he knew far more about God!

> O LORD, our Lord,
> how majestic is your name in all the earth!
> You have set your glory above the heavens ...
> When I consider your heavens,
>   the work of your fingers,
> the moon and stars,
>   which you have set in place,
> what is man that your are mindful of him,
>   the son of man that you care for him?
> You made him a little lower than the heavenly beings
>   and crowned him with glory and honour.[34]

The psalmist knew that creation was big even if he did not know just how big. He also knew that God was bigger, so much so that size was irrelevant to him. The God who was great in big things was even

[32] Blocher, pp. 72–73.
[33] M. White and J. Gribben, *Stephen Hawking: A life in science* (Penguin, 1992), p. 166.
[34] Ps. 8:1, 3–6.

greater in small things – including his tender regard for us. And the psalmist has something to teach us here. For he knew that we are not simply bits of nature, but 'crowned with glory and honour', the glory and honour of being human, made in the image of our Creator, and as such only 'a little lower than the heavenly beings'. He knew his God and therefore knew himself and his fellow human beings in a crucial respect; some modern scientists have yet to catch him up!

Without this knowledge we live in restlessness and anxiety, always on the edge of despair. The attempt of secular humanism to understand, affirm and fulfil people without God misses both his glory and the true glory of being human. R. C. Sproul writes:

> The humanist rejects God while affirming loudly the value of people. He joins hands with Christians and Jews to march for human rights, to eliminate slavery, to halt the oppression of the poor, to build hospitals, to care for men and women in misery. He exalts the virtues of honesty, justice and compassion but he must crucify his mind to do it. The humanist is caught in the vicious contradiction of ascribing dignity to the creatures who live all their lives between the poles of meaninglessness. He lives on borrowed capital, deriving his values from the Judaeo-Christian faith, while at the same time repudiating the very foundation on which those values are set ... We stare in wonder at his ability to get being from nothingness, dignity from insignificance, personality from impersonality and marvel at his ability to stand firmly with both feet planted in mid-air.[35]

In contrast to all this the Bible roots human origins in the creativity of God, locates human identity in the image of God, and rests human destiny in the purposes of God.

b. God and the knowledge of ourselves

We were created for a unique, personal and eternal relationship with God. It is this destiny which sets us apart from the rest of creation. Earlier we saw that an exclusive centredness on humankind failed to recognize God's blessing on the rest of creation. However, there is a right kind of 'anthropocentrism', a proper and balanced people-centredness to be drawn from the biblical doctrine of creation and the divine purpose for our world. Men and women are neither merely bits of nature, nor simply well-evolved animals. There is no equivalence of value between humans and animals, or between us and anything else. The recognition of the supreme value of human

[35] R. C. Sproul, *In Search of Dignity* (Regal Books, 1983; Pickering & Inglis, 1984), pp. 93–94.

life and dignity lies at the heart of biblical values and ongoing human rights.

Vinoth Ramachandra notes how the Genesis account relates us both to the rest of creation and, uniquely, to the Creator:

> Thus men and women, according to the Genesis narrative, possess a dual nature. They are *creatures*, belonging to the rest of the animal kingdom: created on the sixth day, along with all the other creatures of the earth, and (in the following chapter) said to be formed 'from the dust of the earth' ... pointing to our human creatureliness (as if to say, 'they didn't drop from heaven like some immortal gods') and our relatedness to the earth. We share most of our DNA with other living organisms, we live on the exhalation of plants, and our well-being depends on the maintenance of sensitive balances in the biosphere.
>
> But the other side of the truth about us is equally clear and vitally important: humans alone are stamped with the image of the Creator, called into a *personal* relationship with him which defines human life as more than merely biological. Human beings alone are addressed by God. To the Creator, we exist not only as objects but as subjects. Human uniqueness consists not in the fact that we talk with each other, rather that God talks to us and invites us to reply. In other words, we are invited to become part of the conversation that is the divine life ... It is this fact of personhood, established by creation, that confers dignity and value to every human life. We alone are treated as moral agents, commanded by the Creator and held morally responsible to him for our actions.[36]

Genesis 1 fittingly reaches a climax not only with our creation as lords of creation but with our unique *addressibility* by God. This is the hallmark of humanity. Even in the world of the fall human beings have what Calvin calls 'a sense of divinity' that is not to be confined to a certain type of person. Francis Crick, with James Watson, discovered the structure of DNA. He has suggested, perhaps half seriously, that there might be a religious gene, one that determines whether an individual becomes a believer: 'There's probably something in people's brains that makes them more susceptible to religion than others.'[37] Now it may well be that some people are genetically predisposed to a mystical or philosophical 'bent'. But Christianity is far more than that. Jesus did not say 'Come to me, all you who are genetically inclined', but 'Come to me, all you who are weary and burdened'.[38] Every human being has the capacity and

---

[36] Ramachandra (*Gods*), p. 66. [37] *The Times*, 22 May 1994. [38] Matt. 11:28.

potential for a relationship with God. His grace is not for one 'type' of person but for all 'types' everywhere and always.

Moreover, biblical religion as a whole is not a mystical religion or a philosophy of ideas only, but a faith centring on God's self-revelation and involvement in human history. It is about his speech, his covenants, and his mighty acts in human history, in the story of Israel and, supremely, in the incarnation and atonement of the Son of God. The death and resurrection of Jesus Christ are concrete events in history, rooted in time and place. The influence of biblical religion and its demands challenge and affect our everyday practical living as much as our thought-life and our feelings. Such religion is as accessible to the 'practical' as to the 'mystical' type. The apostle Paul clearly teaches the universal capacity among human beings to recognize God in his creation, as well as the universal tendency to suppress or otherwise avoid the true implications of that knowledge.[39]

6. The God who entrusts us with his world

The psalmist says to God, of humanity:

> You made him a little lower than the heavenly beings
> and crowned him with glory and honour.
> You made him ruler over the works of your hands;
> you put everything under his feet.[40]

That is our glory but it has also been our shame. The fall of the race has affected our world in all sorts of ways. Throughout our history we have abused our environment and misused our trust:

> Overgrazing, deforestation and similar errors of sufficient magnitude to destroy civilisations, have been committed by Egyptians, Assyrians, Romans, North Africans, Persians, Indians, Aztecs and Buddhists [as well as Christians]. Centuries before the Christian era, Plato commented, in his *Critias*, on the deforestation of Attica. Since primitive times man has been altering his environment dramatically in ways that upset the ecological balances. Early hunters used fire to drive out their game. Agricultural people everywhere clear fields and dam streams and wipe out stock predators and kill plants that get in the way of their chosen crops.[41]

[39] Rom. 1:18–21.   [40] Ps. 8:5–6.
[41] Thomas Sieger Derr, 'Ecology and Liberation: a theological critique of the use and abuse of our birthright', *WSCF* (1973), p. 19.

The indiscriminate felling of trees in North Africa and Arabia since 5,000 BC has resulted in rapidly expanding deserts. While some famines are natural (e.g. Ethiopia 1984), others are entirely man-made (e.g. Somalia 1992) through war and the looting of relief supplies. Modern crises of pollution are getting worse. In 1976, in Seveso, Italy, large amounts of dioxin – a highly poisonous and durable chemical – were released into the atmosphere leaving the immediate area uninhabitable. In 1984, in Bhopal, Northern India, 30 tons of another poisonous gas escaped, killing 3,500 people and leaving 300,000 with long-term health problems. In 1986, in Chernobyl, Ukraine, a nuclear reactor overheated. Thousands faced cancers as a result and pollution spread across Europe. Even now sheep which have been grazed on land in North Wales cannot be sold for human consumption.

With its command to 'subdue' the earth, the text of Genesis 1 has, in recent years, been held up as doing great harm with its supposed mandate of pillage and exploitation.[42] But in fact it speaks of responsible management, it is 'a mandate of power and responsibility', 'power exercised as God exercises power'. Thus the task of 'dominion does not have to do with exploitation and abuse. It has to do with securing the well-being of every other creature and bringing the promise of each to full fruition'.[43]

Throughout much of human history human beings have abused the environment and mistreated animals, both domestic and wild. The way forward, however, is not in levelling down human kind by claiming equal rights for animals, or in losing human uniqueness in the diversity of life on our planet. Rather it is in recognizing that our responsibility to the environment and to animals is unique because of our unique identity, status and answerability to the Creator. Such a way ahead will include seeing all our sciences, arts, work and leisure as our continuation of 'the creation project'. The world then comes to be what it was meant to be, had God's regents (man and woman) peopled its territories, 'subdued' its forces, and realized its potential, offering it all up to God in devotion and praise. Professor T. F. Torrance, speaking of just one of the great disciplines of modern society, writes:

Science is a religious duty, while man as scientist can be spoken of as the priest of creation, whose task it is to interpret the books of nature, to understand the universe in its wonderful structures and harmonies, and to bring it all into orderly articulation, so that it fulfils its proper end as the vast theatre of glory in which the

[42] Cf. Lynn White, 'The historical roots of our ecologic crisis', *Science* (1967), 155:1203–1207.

[43] Brueggemann (1982), p. 32.

Creator is worshipped and praised. Nature itself is dumb, but it is man's part to bring it to word, to be its mouth through which the whole universe gives voice to the glory and majesty of the living God.[44]

Human beings are crucial to the world's future and even to its meaning. In us alone the spiritual and the material worlds meet, for we have a spiritual and a material side to our nature. In our perception and appreciation the diverse but related parts of creation meet and form an offering to the God who created them. Moreover, at the centre of the story of redemption and fulfilment is the work of one human being who has taken his human nature to heaven – the risen Christ. At the centre of the universe there is a human being who thus gives unique and everlasting significance to the race he made and joined, reversing for ever the corrupting effects of our fall. It is he, too, who is the Redeemer of the entire creation, which finds in him its true and proper centre. In speaking of the salvation of the creation as a whole by the work of Christ, Colin Gunton warns:

> Today, with all our ecological guilt and anxiety, we are perhaps over-concerned to play down the anthropological dimensions of the gospel ... Thus today there is much talk of creation-centred spirituality, sometimes as if it were the creation and not the creator that we worship. In many places there is to be found a tendency to pantheism, the pagan and the dehumanising effects of which will reveal themselves all too soon. If they are to be avoided, it must be remembered that it is not creation that was made in the image of God, but men and women ... it is the personal that is central, the non-personal peripheral.[45]

Gunton adds, 'That does not rule out an ecological concern, but it cannot be of independent interest. The creation is represented before God first by Christ and then, in dependence upon him, by us.'[46]

7. God's Sabbath rest

The 'rest' of God in Genesis 2:2 has a further significance for us, as the New Testament book of Hebrews makes clear: 'There remains, then, a Sabbath-rest for the people of God; for anyone who enters God's rest also rests from his own work, just as God did from his.'[47] The Jewish weekly Sabbath pointed forward to this final state of

---

[44] T. F. Torrance, *Transformation and Convergence in the Frame of Knowledge: Explorations in the interrelations of scientific and theological enterprise* (Christian Journals, 1984), pp. 163–164, quoted in Gunton (1992), pp. 119–120.
[45] Gunton (1992), pp. 32–34.   [46] Ibid., p. 34.   [47] Heb. 4:9–10.

renewal, the renewal of the whole of creation and of God's new humanity. The same is true of the Christian weekly commemoration of the resurrection of Jesus Christ, which for ever underwrites the integrity of creation, establishing its redemption and renewal in the form of a 'new heavens and a new earth'.[48]

For it is not in Genesis 1 – 2 that we find the final confirmation of the divine purposes, but in the New Testament witness to the bodily resurrection of Jesus Christ. It is confirmed in the incarnation and atonement of the Son of God: his assumption of a human body, his entering into creaturely relations with the world around him (his Father's world, our world), and in the atoning and reconciling work of the cross. This confirmation is evident in the tested materialness of Jesus' ongoing, risen life,[49] and in the form of his glorified humanity, imperishably human even in heaven. Here we see the validation of the created order and the guarantee of its perfection. We find the promise of a new heaven and a new earth, in which nothing vile and corrupt shall have a place, in the Christ of the resurrection, the first-fruits of a future order of being; in the God–Man who ate, walked and talked with the wondering and joyful disciples, and whose resurrection is the promise and power of our own.

This resting of God, its earthly commemorations, and our own longing for our heavenly rest, must not lead to a contempt for everything in between. The new creation does not invalidate the old, rather God's rest after the creation of the old has within it the promise of the new. God's satisfaction and rest at the completion of creation is the presupposition of history and the promise of its fulfilment in him. There we too shall be taken into the rest God enjoys, a rest, not of inactivity, but of 'joyful service and unclouded worship'.[50] It marks an end to the frustrating and painful toil of life in a fallen creation[51] and an endless joy in an unending kingdom where the living God will dwell in the midst of his redeemed people.[52] Carl Henry writes:

> The Bible correlates the Creator God not only with primal creation but also with a coming new creation (Isa. 65:17f.; Acts 3:21; 2 Pet. 3:13; Rev. 21:1–8) and with the regenerative recreation of penitent mankind (2 Cor. 5:17ff.). The eternal Christ, the mediator of divine creation, is openly manifested in the incarnation as the one through and for whom God made the universe and through whom God redeems rebellious mankind and the disordered

---

[48] Rom. 8:19–21; Col. 1:20; Rev. 21:1–6.

[49] 'Look at my hands and my feet. It is I myself! Touch me and see; a ghost does not have flesh and bones, as you see I have' (Luke 24:39).

[50] Hughes, p. 162.   [51] Rev. 14:3.   [52] Rev. 21:3.

cosmos (John 1:1–3; 1 Cor. 8:6; Col. 1:16; Heb. 1:2, 10 ... The 'whence' and the 'whither' of the universe cannot be divorced; in Christ the whole creation has its basis (Rev. 3:14) as well as its final goal (Heb. 1:11f.).[53]

In a restless world and an uncertain life, where many are looking for meaning and for security, we need to point men and women to the Creator God who *is* the meaning of life. He is the Saviour God who has found a way to bring exiles into his presence, sinners into his rest, by Jesus Christ, the incarnate Son of God, who himself was the agent of creation, and who himself is its redeemer.

8. The creation call to worship

The revelation of Genesis 1 is not given to leave us informed but unchanged; God's purpose is not to satisfy our curiosity, but to direct our activity. It is also given as a call to worship the Creator in the midst of his creation:

> 'You are worthy, our Lord and God,
>   to receive glory and honour and power,
> for you created all things,
>   and by your will they were created
>   and have their being.'[54]

We live in a fallen, damaged world where men and women are rebellious, self-centred and cruel. Yet it is a world still full of the mercy and goodness of God; still full of a wonder and beauty which proclaims the Creator who dwells in the beauty of holiness. Gerad Manley Hopkins writes of this in his poem 'God's Grandeur':

The world is charged with the grandeur of God.
    It will flame out, like shining from shook foil;
    It gathers to a greatness, like the ooze of oil
Crushed. Why do men then now not reck his rod?
Generations have trod, have trod, have trod;
    And all is seared with trade; bleared, smeared with toil;
    And wears man's smudge and shares man's smell: the soil
Is bare now, nor can foot feel, being shod.

And, for all this, nature is never spent;
    There lives the dearest freshness deep down things;
    And though the last lights off the black West went

[53] Henry, vol. 6, p. 112.   [54] Rev. 4:11.

Oh, morning, at the brown brink eastward, springs –
Because the Holy Ghost over the bent
World broods with warm breast and with ah! bright wings.

A right understanding of redemption will never leave behind a right understanding of creation. By the cross, creation is not effaced but established.[55] At the end of the Bible the God of creation and redemption, in the tri-unity of his being and operations, is adored.[56]

[55] Col. 1:20.   [56] Rev. 4:11; 5:9; 21:17.

Genesis 2 – 3
3. God the betrayed

Why is the world, as we now see it, a mixture of beauty and brokeness? Why are human beings as they are, a mixture of dignity and degradation? Why is God as he is toward us as a race, so near and yet so distant, to be loved yet also to be feared, merciful and wrathful, loving and judging? In the third chapter of Genesis we have the biblical explanation of all this, with its account of the fall of the human race in Adam from its first honour and safety to its present disgrace and insecurity.

We shall never know fully the cost to God of his decision to bring into being a creation, a universe, and orders of moral beings outside of himself. Within their own Trinitarian life Father, Son and Holy Spirit lived in eternal blessedness, a life complete and unmixed with sorrow. But with the decision to create there was the decision to open up that life to suffering and rejection as the cost of sharing their eternal blessedness with others. Where we look back, God looked forward: to the defection of angels, to the rebellion and fall of humans, and to the corruption of his bright and beautiful creation. We cannot imagine the depth of pain in the Godhead as he contemplated our human history of cruelty and selfishness, of exploitation and greed, of godlessness and inhumanity. The wonder is that he went through with it!

Yet these things are not all that he knew. He knew too, from the foundation of the world, the truth of its fall and the cost of its redemption.[1] The contemplation of these things was surely only outweighed by his contemplation of creation redeemed, renewed and restored in Christ. Today, millions walk in darkness; then, millions will rejoice in the light. Now, sickness, disappointment, pain and tears are inevitable accompaniments of life in a fallen world; then, 'He will wipe every tear from their eyes. There will be no more death or mourning or crying or pain, for the old order of things' will

[1] 1 Pet. 1:20.

have passed away.[2] Then, the new heavens and the new earth will reflect their Creator's original plan and full intention.

1. God the final authority (2:16–17)

And the LORD God commanded the man, 'You are free to eat from any tree in the garden; [17]but you must not eat from the tree of the knowledge of good and evil, for when you eat of it you will surely die.'

Notice it is *God* who sets forth the prohibition; it is God who says what is good and what is evil. Human beings are given a wide area of freedom. We are free to explore our world, to develop its potential, and to make decisions for ourselves and for the world over which we have been given so much power. But we are not given the choice of what will be good and what will be evil. That is a decision made for us by our Creator. He is good and does good. He defines good and evil by what he is. He sets the limits of our moral life by the laws of his own. God is the standard of all moral good and the source of moral absolutes. His character and his will are the final authority.

We live in an age when people increasingly want to choose their own morality, write their own commandments, make their own rules of right and wrong. Personal choice is the great good, tolerance the only absolute. We are busy relabelling the trees of the Garden, with disastrous results. The prophet Isaiah once cried out in the name of God:

> 'Woe to those who call evil good
>   and good evil,
> who put darkness for light
>   and light for darkness,
> who put bitter for sweet
>   and sweet for bitter.'[3]

The ultimate impudence is committed when sin is justified and virtue despised. It is the final confusion, opening a chasm into anarchy and despair at the feet of the society that chooses it.

The decision of Adam to be self-legislating brought with it diverse consequences. Although thereafter he was the possessor, by use, of tremendous determinative power, and thus 'like God', yet he was 'unlike God' in that he would constantly be uncertain of the

[2] Rev. 21:4.   [3] Is. 5:20.

nature of the issues before which he was placed. He would never be able to foresee the consequences of the choices he would make. Having power to choose, he would continue throughout life and history to be the captive of his choices. Putting himself in a position of moral defiance to his Creator, he plunged himself into a life of tension and absolute moral uncertainty ... unable to control himself or his world.[4]

It is also ironic that the explanation of our present condition is not simply our own choice, but includes our folly in allowing ourselves to be manipulated by outside forces. Even when we first declared independence from God we did so because someone else persuaded us. Forces outside us have been pulling our strings ever since.

Without explanation or introduction an anti-God power appears in the form of a serpent in Genesis 3:1. Several New Testament passages take up this symbolism in connection with Satan, 'that ancient serpent', as he is called in the book of Revelation.[5] Jesus spoke of this event when he said the devil was 'a murderer from the beginning ... a liar and the father of lies'.[6] It is justifiable to see the Genesis serpent, therefore, not merely as a creature, but as a figure for a personal being later called Satan, the accuser.[7]

This is the Bible's way of making it clear that evil is the product of created beings. It is not a dark force within God or a dark deity in the universe who is equal and opposite to the good God, as certain dualistic philosophies taught. Later Scriptures will speak clearly of the rebellion and fall of angelic beings who were created good.[8] But here we have no explicit reference to Satan, only this veiled reference to a non-human agency which misrepresents God and seduces the woman.

2. The slandered God (3:1)

Now the serpent was more crafty than any of the wild animals the LORD God had made. He said to the woman, 'Did God really say, "You must not eat from any tree in the garden"?'

The first thing the serpent does is to slander God, representing him as ungenerous and unreasonable. He said to the woman, 'Did God really say, "You must not eat from any tree in the garden"?' In fact, God had said, 'You are free to eat from any tree in the garden' (2:16). The generosity and abundant goodness of God are sidelined. All his kindness in making them lords of the world he had created is set

---

[4] Dumbrell, pp. 38–39.   [5] Rev. 20:2; cf. Luke 10:18f.; 2 Cor. 11:3–4.
[6] John 8:44.   [7] Job 1:6; Zech. 3:1.   [8] 2 Pet. 2:4; Jude 6.

aside in favour of the one restriction placed upon them. In a travesty of the truth God is represented as denying them the means of happiness and the possibility of fulfilling their potential. Victor Hamilton describes it as 'an attempt to create in the woman's mind the impression that God is spiteful, mean, obsessively jealous and self-protective'.[9]

We see the repetition and success of this temptation every day of our lives. Men and women who refuse to acknowledge God's daily goodness to them are ready at all times to blame him for life's frustrations and ills. God is for many only an opponent, a threat and a restrictor of freedoms: sexual, social and scientific. All religion is resented and despised as a chain to hold the human race back from its true potential ('You shall be as gods!'). His kindness is forgotten, his limits resented, his laws transgressed. This is commonly followed by the self-justification that blames God, not ourselves, for the bitter harvest we reap. Since Eve listened to Satan, no being in the universe has been so much or so wickedly misrepresented and ill-used as the Supreme Being, the God who is holy, wise, just and good. He has been ignored, despised and defied in our world.

3. The distanced God (3:2–5)

The woman said to the serpent, 'We may eat fruit from the trees in the garden, ³but God did say, "You must not eat fruit from the tree that is in the middle of the garden, and you must not touch it, or you will die." '

⁴'You will not surely die,' the serpent said to the woman. ⁵'For God knows that when you eat of it your eyes will be opened, and you will be like God, knowing good and evil.'

At first the woman corrects the serpent's account, but with two features which might be meant by the author to betray a wavering trust. The serpent has significantly used a name for God (*Elohim*) which, while valid and important (it is used frequently throughout the Pentateuch, and often stresses his supremacy as the Sovereign Lord), is different from the name for God which is used in the rest of chapters 2 – 3 (*Yahweh Elohim*). The ancient name 'Yahweh' was given new significance in Moses' time[10] as the covenant name of God for his people Israel, the name which denoted a unique relationship and obligation. We cannot be sure of its use as an address of worship before the time of Genesis 4:26. However, in verse 3, the woman takes up the name that Satan has used, 'God' (the distant Creator) instead of 'the LORD God' (the covenant Partner). No doubt the writer means us to notice this!

⁹ Hamilton (1990), p. 189.   ¹⁰ Exod. 3:15.

The woman then corrects the serpent, but not quite accurately. The LORD God had said, 'You are free to eat from any tree in the garden' except the tree of the knowledge of good and evil. Eve leaves out the 'any' and adds to the ban on *eating* from the tree of the knowledge of good and evil her own words: 'and you must not touch it, or you will die'. Gordon Wenham says:

> These slight alterations to God's remarks suggest that the woman has already moved slightly away from God toward the serpent's attitude. The Creator's generosity is not being given its full due, and he is being painted as a little harsh and repressive, forbidding the tree even be touched. Indeed the way 'lest you die' follows 'touch' suggests that not just eating it but touching it may be lethal.[11]

The serpent is 'crafty' in the art of seduction as in everything else. Without ever telling her directly to eat of the forbidden fruit, he continues his onslaught on God, this time more obviously. He replies, 'You will not surely die ... For God knows that when you eat of it your eyes will be opened, and you will be like God, knowing good and evil' (vv. 4 and 5).

Notice at this point how the discussion has already side-lined God. The debate about him takes place not in the presence of God, but in his absence. He himself is not consulted! That is the beginning of every false philosophy and of all false religion. It is also the beginning of every morally wrong decision and the foundation of every ungodly lifestyle. God's word is not heard, or sought, but stifled. Instead, human autonomy, human reason, human self-will decides the issue: 'Shall I or shall I not?', 'Is it like this or is it like that?', 'Has God said or has he not?', 'Is it true or is it false?' Even God's self-revelation is judged as though we were a higher power: 'Is the religion of the Bible, is Christianity, keeping me down, holding me back, stopping me from fulfilling myself?'

4. The first lie (3:4–5)

'You will not surely die,' the serpent said to the woman. [5]'For God knows that when you eat of it your eyes will be opened, and you will be like God, knowing good and evil.'

The snake cannot decide for her but he can motivate her in wrong directions. He begins with an outright lie: 'You will not surely die.' Looking back to this event, Jesus says of the devil, 'He was a

[11] Wenham (1987), p. 73.

murderer from the beginning, not holding to the truth, for there is no truth in him. When he lies, he speaks his native language, for he is a liar and the father of lies.'[12]

The first lie was that they would not actually die. Some see a half truth here as they did not physically die. However, Satan could not have known in advance of the decision by God to postpone physical death. Others, from the parallel in 1 Kings 2:30–46, take the Hebrew expression to mean, 'on that day you will fall under the power of a death sentence', which might not be carried out immediately. Others point out that death itself is a bigger concept and reality than physical death. It is to be defined in terms of God as well as earthly life, and is in essence separation from God as well as from life in this world. Eventually it involves what the last book of the Bible calls 'the second death',[13] which is not non-existence but a final and eternal separation from the Creator and from the bountiful gift of life as it was meant to be. Whatever the explanation, the serpent sought to diminish the force of God's warning and so the original liar accused God of lying. The God of all truth is not to be trusted! To this day men and women live in the denial of judgment to come, even though Jesus Christ spoke of it in terrible terms.[14] The suggestion is still 'Did God really say . . . ?'

What follows is the final slander of God, and the fullest enticement to rebellion on the part of the people God had made. The snake purports to know what is in the mind of God, and what is his real motive in prohibiting the one tree: 'For God knows that when you eat of it your eyes will be opened, and you will be like God, knowing good and evil.'

The possibility, indeed the assurance, held out is that they will be 'like God'. But they are *already* like God, made 'in his image'. That image could only have increased in beauty and glory if they had developed with God. Human beings would have been led to higher and higher stages of honour, happiness and glory if they had trusted him. Our entire history as a race would have been different, involving the lives and eternal futures of millions. But human beings fell for the lie that they could be more free only if God was less in control. The lust was kindled to be 'like God' in ways they were never meant to be, to grasp a new power as well as to taste a new experience. Satan, writes Henri Blocher, 'projects the false perspective of a rivalry between God and man; he suggests that man will be less free as God will be the more sovereign, and vice versa'. He adds, 'How many generations since that very first one have swallowed the

---

[12] John 8:44.   [13] Rev. 20:14.
[14] E.g. Matt. 7:21–23; 25:41–46; Mark 9:42–50; Luke 16:19–31.

same bait?'[15] Walter Brueggemann writes: 'The prohibition which had seemed a *given* is now scrutinised as though it were not a given but an *option* ... The givenness of God's rule is no longer the boundary of a safe place. God is now a barrier to be circumvented.'[16]

And so we read of the fateful act of considered rebellion against God in which there lies, quite literally, a whole world and history of woes: *When the woman saw that the fruit of the tree was good for food and pleasing to the eye, and also desirable for gaining wisdom, she took some and ate it. She also gave some to her husband who was with her, and he ate it* (3:6).

The woman moves from commitment to doing God's will to commitment to doing her own will and becomes, with her husband 'who was with her', the first of millions to do so. For sin is in essence autonomy over-against God, the determination that I will live by my own preferred rules. It is the decision to make my will central and God's will peripheral.

Sin is not properly understood until it is seen in terms of our relationship with God our Creator and his acknowledged and welcomed Lordship in our lives. A life in sin is not necessarily a scandalous life; it might be a very respected, useful and admired life. But if it is God-less it is profoundly sinful. Sin is a flight from, a rebellion against, and an antipathy to God, where self is central and supreme. Sin is not simply a broken code but a broken relationship; not only a relationship lost but a relationship renounced.

5. The fatal results (3:7–15)

Some years ago, my wife Valerie and I were reading the Valentine messages in *The Times* – with a good deal of amusement, I must say. There was one, however, which has lived with us. It was not from a lover to a lover but from children to their parents, and it read simply but unforgettably: 'The rebels failed; for our Utopia was the home we fought to leave.'

That is the truth about our human race, which fought to leave God for freedom and progress only to find its freedom frustrated and its progress hampered by its own sinfulness. Our 'utopia' was our destiny in God. Our determination to seek or to build other utopias – ideological or material – have all ended, and must all end, in failure and unfulfilled longing. Only our home in God, reconciled and obedient for ever, is a real and sufficient utopia for us, for we were made for him.

The results of Satan's temptation and Adam and Eve's joint fall were a complete reversal of expectations. They didn't find utopia;

---

[15] Blocher, p. 139.   [16] Brueggemann (1982), pp. 47–48.

instead they found that the effects of sin ruined their till now perfect existence.

a. Sin diminishes us

No sooner were their eyes *opened* than *they realised that they were naked* (3:7). They could not even cope with the knowledge of each other, let alone other mysteries of 'good and evil'. Instead of being empowered they were diminished, for they knew as they were never meant to know, and not even then as God knows (I read verse 22 as irony).

They came to know evil only by becoming evil. The evil they came to know was the evil which corrupted them so that they could no longer bear to see or be seen in full frontal openness and honesty. The knowledge they gained was the wrong knowledge and the price of knowing 'good and evil' in this way was terrible. It left them shocked, fearful and self-absorbed.

In the 1960s the fashionable 'new morality' of the *Honest to God* debate claimed that the fall was really 'a fall upwards' towards moral maturity, a necessary stage in human development. There is indeed a way of knowing evil as God knows evil, and that comes from listening to God and doing good. But there is also a way of knowing evil which comes of doing evil. The second of these diminishes, distorts and desensitizes our true understanding of evil. In C. S. Lewis's novel *Perelandra* (our Venus), the Genesis temptation is replayed on another planet with another Adam and Eve. This time the logic of Satan's temptation is exposed as a false logic and he is successfully resisted. The new race can enter its future unspoiled. At the end, the Venusian Adam, the King of Perelandra, says:

> 'We have learned of evil; though not as the evil one wished us to learn. We have learned better than that, and know it more; for it is waking that understands sleep and not sleep that understands waking. There is an ignorance of evil that comes from being young: there is a darker ignorance that comes from doing it, as men by sleeping lose the knowledge of sleep.'[17]

We would do well to remember the point made here when someone tells us we cannot know that something is wrong until we have tried it, or that we will find our true self, or sexuality, or freedom, only by experimenting with things that are now forbidden us by others. It is not sleep that understands waking but waking that understands sleeping. The more you are awake to God, the more you will be aware of moral and spiritual realities; the more you will find your

---

[17] C. S. Lewis, *Perelandra* (Pan Books, 1983).

true and God-given identity. Sin does not develop and mature us; it wounds and weakens us. It leaves us naked and ashamed. It does not make us more, it makes us less – in every way.

Adam and Eve's entire situation is now changed; nothing remains the same. As Brueggemann perceives: 'The *prohibition* of 2:17 is violated. The *permission* of verse 16 is perverted. The *vocation* of verse 15 is neglected. There is no more mention of tending and feeding. They have no energy for that. Their interest has focused completely on self, on their new freedom and the terror that comes with it.'[18]

b. Sin alienates us from God

The focus away from God and towards self shows itself most dramatically in Adam and Eve's negative reaction to the sound of the Lord God as he was walking in the garden 'in the cool of the day': *they hid from the LORD God among the trees of the garden* (3:8).

The impression given is of a regular occurrence, their Creator and friend spending 'quality time' with these two people at the end (or perhaps the beginning) of each working day. Their privilege was immense. At other times they might have run to meet him but now they hid from him.

The first and worse thing sin does is to produce an antipathy to God in the sinner, an allergic reaction to his purity, an inability to tolerate his insistent demand for righteousness, a hostility to his Lordship. We find his approach threatening. So, in guilt and fear, 'they hid from the LORD God among the trees of the garden'. And mankind has been hiding behind the trees ever since: behind the trees of false religions, false philosophies, self-righteousness and worldly preoccupations. Even religion, even the true religion, can be used as a screen, a cover, a last-ditch defence against the unbearable approach of the Holy God who exposes our nakedness and our need, our mixed motives and our moral failure.[19]

6. God seeking (3:9-13)

The call of God to Adam in verse 9 is essentially rhetorical: '*Where are you?*' Wenham thinks it suggests that 'the Judge of the whole earth is calling man in order to demand an account of his conduct'.[20] As he notes, however, another side of the action is indicated by Franz Delitzsch, who remarks, 'It was God their creator, who now as God the redeemer was seeking the lost. In this way God seeks to

---

[18] Brueggemann (1982), p. 48. [19] Rom. 1:18–25, 28–32; 8:6–8.
[20] Wenham (1987), p. 76.

draw rather than drive them out of hiding. What follows will show a mixture of judgement and mercy.'[21]

The pair emerge shame-faced from among the trees and God begins his interrogation. Even now he allows the man opportunity to confess his crime rather than charge him with transgression (3:10–11). However, all that he meets with are evasions (3:10) and excuses (3:12–13). The man blames the woman and the woman blames the serpent. Worse, Adam says in his own defence, *'The woman you put here with me – she gave me some fruit from the tree and I ate it'* (3:12). Here he puts himself last in a series of 'reasons' which include God himself, with God as the main cause of his predicament: 'The woman *you put here with me*.' As Hamilton notes, 'Through rationalisation the criminal becomes the victim and it is God and the woman who emerge as the real instigators in this scenario.'[22] Doesn't that sound familiar? It is all too characteristic of human beings that for their own sin they blame others, or circumstances, or fate, or their genes, and ultimately God for 'making me that way'. It has been said that the epitaph for our times will be 'It wasn't my fault.'

God's silence, then as now, is a mixture of mercy and dignity. God isn't in the dock – we are! Adam isn't struck down for such a blasphemy and God disdains to defend himself in such a 'court'. He takes sin and human decisions seriously, weighs us all in perfect balances, and finds us wanting. In the words of Ecclesiastes,

> This only I have found:
> God made mankind upright,
> but men have gone in search of many schemes.[23]

'What is this you have done?' (3:13) is said rhetorically to the woman and for her sake rather than God's. The enormity of her act has only begun to strike her. She blames the snake, forgetting that she and her husband were meant to rule over such 'creatures', not to be directed in moral decisions by them. Here is a fatal role-reversal. In this way she minimizes her freedom, which the external forces of evil could not penetrate and destroy without her permission. To this day, the excuses 'I didn't know', 'I didn't realize', 'I was deceived' are favourites among those whose defences were foolishly lowered by themselves and who entered into dialogue with temptation.

7. God promising (3:15)

God's response to the original sin of the original pair comes in the form of a curse placed upon the snake, the earth and the human

---

[21] F. Delitzsch, *A New Commentary on Genesis*, 2 vols. (1888; Klock, 1978), vol. 1, p. 157.

[22] Hamilton (1990), p. 194.   [23] Eccles. 7:29.

beings – who must suffer deprivation and loss, conflict and pain, and above all, death, as a result of their rebellion against God and abandonment of his ways.

Yet, even when the curse is being pronounced, the promise is included: *'And I will put enmity between you and the woman, and between your offspring and hers; he will crush your head and you will strike his heel'* (3:15).

Here is a statement that evil will not entirely conquer human affairs; that the demonic will not be allowed to absorb the human; that, because of a 'divinely implanted hostility' ('I will put en- mity'),[24] conflict will continue between 'the offspring' of the serpent and that of the woman. The statement comes with, perhaps, the hint of a fatal wounding and a final victory over the dark powers represented by the snake. The serpent, as we have seen, represents Satan and symbolizes sin, death and the power of evil. It is primarily anti-God. It is also anti-human, because human beings are made in the image of God. The struggle between the offspring of Eve and the serpent-race indicates the long struggle between good and evil in the world, between pro- and anti-God forces, between humanity's fulfilment in God and Satan's attempt to poison and destroy the race God made in his image and for himself. Each would 'batter' the other in a centuries-long struggle. Eventually the fight would be won decisively, not by us alone, but by God sending his Son to fight for us. As Hermann Ridderbos writes:

> All the Old Testament prophecies that have reference to the war waged ever since Paradise between God and Satan have come to stand in an entirely new light through the advent of Jesus Christ, and have acquired the highest possible relevance.[25]

Church tradition has seen in verse 15 the *protoevangelium*, the first announcement of the gospel, the first messianic prophecy in the Old Testament. If that is so, then these words find their supreme fulfil- ment in the Son of God: 'Since the children have flesh and blood, he too shared in their humanity so that by his death he might destroy him who holds the power of death – that is, the devil – and free those who all their lives were held in slavery by their fear of death.'[26] By his cross he 'disarmed the powers',[27] triumphing over them in the

[24] Walter Kaiser Jr, *Toward an Old Testament Theology* (Zondervan, 1991), p. 36; Kaiser argues strongly from the Septuagint version for a 'collective notion which included a personal unity in a single person who was to obtain victory for the whole group he represented'.
[25] Herman Ridderbos, *Paul: An Outline of his Theology*, trans. J. R. De Witt (SPCK, 1977), p. 514.
[26] Heb. 2:14–15.   [27] Col. 2:15.

very hour and by the very event which they thought signalled their complete victory. That definitive and crucial triumph is one which will be shared by all the people of God in all their trials and setbacks. As the apostle Paul assured the Christians at Rome, 'The God of peace will soon crush Satan under your feet.'[28] The book of Revelation depicts in vivid and terrifying imagery the final conflict and overthrow of evil and its demonic agent(s).[29]

8. God judging (3:16–19)

To the woman he said,

> *'I will greatly increase your pains in childbearing;*
> *with pain you will give birth to children.*
> *Your desire will be for your husband,*
> *and he will rule over you.'*

[17]*To Adam he said, 'Because you listened to your wife and ate from the tree about which I commanded you, "You must not eat of it,"*

> *'Cursed is the ground because of you;*
> *through painful toil you will eat of it*
> *all the days of your life.*

> [18]*It will produce thorns and thistles for you,*
> *and you will eat the plants of the field.*
> [19]*By the sweat of your brow*
> *you will eat your food*
> *until you return to the ground,*
> *since from it you were taken;*
> *for dust you are*
> *and to dust you will return.'*

The final overthrow of evil is still in the future, however, and we must now face squarely the reality of the curse which sin has brought upon the earth and which in various ways manifests itself in human life and even in aspects of our redeemed and reconciled Christian lives. The curse is given in the form of a prophecy of what will happen, but its outworking is not an automatic process. The Bible reminds us of the personal nature of God's love of righteousness and wrath for sin too often for us to do that.[30]

---

[28] Rom. 16:20.   [29] Rev. 2:9; 20:10.
[30] See e.g. Exod. 20:5; 32:11–12, 14; Pss. 78:38; 85:2–7; Ezek. 7:8–9; Mic. 6:8; Nah. 1:1–8.

a. The curse and human relationships

The consequences of sin in the world are spelt out in dire predictions. Sin will continue to make inroads into human life and history even on a more-than human scale, 'striking the heel' of all human progress and achievement, culture and civilizations, fostering wars and conflict, and often driving its human tools to furious and even self-sacrificing evil. To this day we see it issuing in blind hatreds, suicidal destructiveness and holocausts of destructive evil that are bigger than any mere human agency.

Human relationships will be disturbed and disrupted, even that most intimate relationship of man and wife (3:16). The blessing of procreation will be marred by pain and danger, and the self-giving of one-flesh marriage will be abused and lessened by the desire to rule and manipulate. As Kidner puts it, 'To love and to cherish' becomes 'To desire and to dominate.'[31] We may see here the beginning of centuries and millennia of male domination and female subjugation, an abuse which no view of biblical headship can defend.

b. The curse and the created order

There will also be conflict between human beings and their environment: a world they fail to 'subdue' and develop as they would like; a world where men and women fall prey to natural disasters and the result of their own mismanagement; a world which Ecclesiastes describes with all its glory and futility. The earth itself will be cursed because of humanity and human sin, not only the soil which is explicitly mentioned (3:17) but the animal kingdom too[32] – in fact 'the whole creation.'[33] Human beings will work in a hostile environment and their own lives will be at many points a painful journey, ending in death: 'for dust you are and to dust you will return' (3:19).

So, as Kidner strikingly remarks, sorrow, sweat and dust answer the fantasy 'you will be like God'.[34] Death itself will bring to dust the person who was made from dust but who was not made to die. Death in these chapters is shown to be penal, not natural, where human beings are concerned. Those who were finally made 'in the image of God' were made to share the immortality of their Creator. If Adam and Eve had not rebelled and fallen so far beneath their privilege, God would have led us on to other, higher levels of life, without the tragedy and the obscenity of death. Ben Witherington III sees further consequences of the fall when he writes:

> The charter of human existence was to be inferior to God but superior to the rest of creation ... By listening to the serpent

[31] Kidner (1967), p. 71.   [32] Rom. 8:19–22.   [33] Rom. 8:22.
[34] Kidner (1967), p. 71.

[Adam and Eve] broke the chain of the created order, submitting to those they were supposed to rule over . . . Seeking to be as gods, Adam and Eve became more like the lesser creatures in several ways: (1) the human story, like that of other sentient beings, becomes red in tooth and claw, an endless struggle for survival, an endless competition for superiority; (2) the human story, like that of other creatures, becomes the story of a sort of moral promiscuity common among the lesser animals; (3) the human story even degenerated into the worship of parts of creation (animals, natural forces, even human beings) as if they were the Creator.[35]

We shall never begin to understand why our world is as it is if we do not take seriously the third chapter of Genesis. How else can we understand the evil that is in the world and in our own hearts; our pride, self-centredness and rebelliousness against the holy rule of God. The importance of recognizing the real historicity of this event has been well expressed by Witherington:

> . . . not only does Paul believe the story of Adam and Eve to be theologically profound, but it seems clear from texts like Romans 5 and 1 Corinthians 15 that he also believes it to be historically true. He does not think that he is dealing with 'cleverly devised myths,' for he consistently bases his statements about the eschatological Adam, Christ, on the assumption that the first Adam really was the first created human being, who along with Eve really did commit the first sin (cf. 1 Cor. 15:45–49; 2 Cor. 11:3), causing the mess humanity has found itself in ever since. This is also evident from the way Paul treats death – not as a natural closure to human life, but as the enemy (1 Cor. 15:21). The story of Christ in Paul's thought presupposes this larger Story, and the former cannot be understood fully without the latter.[36]

No book of the Bible faces such facts more memorably than Ecclesiastes. It speaks of the streaks of meaninglessness, futility and vanity that run through all of life and spoil the brightest and the best in a bright and beautiful world. It squarely faces the riddle of life 'under the sun', but it also holds fast to God who is over all, to be trusted, worshipped and adored.[37] It reminds us too that things were not always like this and that we, not God or blind fate, are at the heart of our predicament.[38]

---

[35] Witherington, p. 13.　　[36] Ibid., p. 30.　　[37] Eccles. 12:1, 13–14.
[38] Eccles. 7:29.

9. God staying (3:20–24)

The last act in the drama of Genesis 3 is the expulsion of Adam and Eve from the garden God had prepared for them. Again we have mingled elements of judgment and mercy. In kindness God makes them 'garments of skin' to protect them in the world outside: 'Whereas the human couple could only produce inadequate loincloths (3:7), God provided them with a proper outfit.'[39] However, in justice and in judgment, God shows how decisive and irreversible Adam and Eve's sin has been. They are forbidden the tree of life and driven quickly out of the protected region by God himself (3:23), and the way back is unmistakably barred by an angelic being with a sword of fire (3:24).

It is only as we read on in Genesis that we make the most surprising discovery of all. We see it in the worship of Abel and the warning to Cain, in the godly line of Seth, and in the life of Noah. Their stories show, as the rest of the book and all the books that follow will show, that though he exiled Adam and Eve from the garden, *God went out from the garden with them!* The God whom we betrayed has not left us. The Creator, Lawgiver and Judge has become the Shepherd, Healer and Saviour.

10. God's second Adam

The world into which Adam and Eve passed was a very different world from the one they had known previously. It is powerfully exposed by Paul, in his letter to the Romans and elsewhere, as a world where sin and death reign because of their rebellion. It was and would be a world where all had sinned and fallen short of the glory of God,[40] where none would be righteous, where no-one would seek God, where all would turn aside and become unprofitable.[41] It is a world where sin, having entered, remains dominant, universal, reigning as a power.[42]

In Romans 5 Paul tells us how this state of affairs came about and what God has done about it. He tells us that human history has been shaped decisively by two 'heads': Adam, the head of the old humanity, and Christ, the head of a new humanity. Every human being is crucially related to, or 'in', one or the other. We are in one by natural birth and in solidarity with him we share his sin and downfall.[43] We are in the other by faith and receive as a gift the grace and righteousness of God.[44] Notice how in that entire passage Paul keeps repeating phrases that point to the two decisive acts of these

---

[39] Wenham (1987), p. 84. [40] Rom. 3:23. [41] Rom. 3:10–20.
[42] Rom. 3:9; cf. Gal. 3:22. [43] Rom. 5:12. [44] Rom. 5:17.

men: the one act of the one man Adam in a rebellion which cursed his world and corrupted his race, and the one act of the one man Jesus Christ who 'was delivered over to death for our sins and was raised to life for our justification'.[45] The great theme of the paragraph is 'the power of Christ's act of obedience to overcome Adam's act of disobedience'.[46]

Every human being now is born outside the garden. What was done there involved us all, for 'in this way death came to all men, because all sinned'.[47] As Hermann Ridderbos convincingly shows, Paul does not mean that death comes to all because of the personal choices of each individual. Rather, each and every person shares in a collective identity, and in solidarity with Adam suffers because of Adam's sin.[48] Hence Paul's words 'and in this way death came to all men' and the explicit statements of verses 13 and 14. Adam's sin is the one fixed, first transgression that was the sin of all by virtue of their relation to the first Adam which resulted in death for all.[49] Adam's sin was the sin of all on account of their connection with 'the one man' and by it many were made (literally, 'constituted') sinners. Paul does not, of course, mean this to be taken in abstraction from the present situation of personal sinfulness. He means it only as an explanation of sin's first and decisive entrance into the world and our subjection to its calamitous regime. Paul's aim in doing this is to show that God has provided for us a new Head instead of Adam – Jesus Christ. In solidarity with him we receive, not the condemnation of God for Adam's self-assertion, but the justification of God by Christ's obedience.[50]

Even the Redeemer from God was born far from the garden, in a stable and 'in the likeness of sinful flesh'. Even for him the way back to Paradise was by another route – the cross – in order that he might take us with him. For, 'just as the result of one trespass was condemnation for all men, so also the result of one act of righteousness was justification that brings life for all men'.[51]

Derek Kidner writes, 'It took the work of the last Adam to bring home to us our full downfall in the first Adam',[52] and it is only in the death of Jesus Christ that we see sin's full seriousness. If it took the full resources of the Son of God to atone for sin we can see how great an evil sin is in God's sight. Yet the victory of Christ at the cross is such that it far exceeds Adam's act. One man's act of self-assertion brought sin and death, but in God's grace another man's self-sacrifice brought the gift of justification and life into a guilty, dying world:

---

[45] Rom. 4:25.   [46] Moo, p. 326.   [47] Rom. 5:12.
[48] Ridderbos, op. cit., pp. 96–99.   [49] Rom. 5:15–18.   [50] Rom. 5:15, 19.
[51] Rom. 5:18.   [52] Kidner (1967), p. 67.

> O loving wisdom of our God!
> When all was sin and shame,
> A second Adam to the fight,
> And to the rescue came.[53]

Now there is a way out of the old humanity and into a new humanity in Christ Jesus. It is the way of faith in him as the Son of God who loved us and gave himself for us. We have a choice! We had no choice about being in the first Adam. Belonging to a fallen humanity we were born into human failure and folly. But now we have a choice, an open door into a new state. We can be rescued, taken up into the Last Adam, born again into a new humanity, saved for eternity because Jesus is Lord. We who had become slaves of death can 'reign in life through the one man, Jesus Christ':

> But the gift is not like the trespass. For if the many died by the trespass of the one man, how much more did God's grace and the gift that came by the grace of the one man, Jesus Christ, overflow to the many! Again, the gift of God is not like the result of the one man's sin: The judgment followed one sin and brought condemnation, but the gift followed many trespasses and brought justification. For if, by the trespass of the one man, death reigned through that one man, how much more will those who receive God's abundant provision of grace and of the gift of righteousness reign in life through the one man, Jesus Christ.[54]

If God took the one first sin of Adam so seriously, how seriously he must have taken 'the accumulated sins and guilt of all the ages'[55] and how astonishing that he should be willing, and at such cost, to justify sinners in Christ his Son. But that is the character of God's 'abundant grace' which has 'overflowed' to millions. Now the reign of sin and death is broken in every life which is taken up into the life of the Son of God. These things may remain to trouble us but they are no longer decisive for us. The reign of sin and death has been definitively replaced by the reign of grace, overruling death and enabling us to 'reign in life' in and through the last Adam. He bore the judgment we deserved that we might receive the justification we did not deserve[56] and that the whole people of God might 'reign in life' through the one act of the one Man of Calvary.

---

[53] Hymn, 'Praise to the Holiest in the height', John Henry Newman (1801–1890).
[54] Rom. 5:15–17.
[55] C. E. B. Cranfield, *The Epistle to the Romans* (T. & T. Clark, 1977), vol. 1, p. 286.
[56] Gal. 3:13.

Genesis 6 – 9
4. God the committed

1. The God who shelters

Everyone has heard of Noah's ark. Thousands of children are quite sure they know what it looked like; after all, they have its picture, in a book or on their bedroom wall, with all sorts of animals in it or going into it or coming out of it. Why do children love the story? Possibly because it has become a symbol of safety in a world of danger, the sign of a Great Parent and his care, the reassurance we all need that in a world of sin, calamity and even judgment, there is a divine purpose, a thread of meaning, a door of hope. And because children like animals!

It is easy for the cynic to fasten on the dark side of this near-universal judgment, but it is interesting that the biblical focus, in Old Testament and New, is not on the many that were lost but on the few that were saved. The cynic might say, 'What is that compared to cities, tribes and populations lost?' The answer of the story is that from the eight who were saved new cities, tribes and populations were formed, repopulating the earth, giving violent, godless humanity a new start, setting the scene for a new work of God which continues the salvation-history of the world to this day, from Noah to us.

It is poor arithmetic that says only eight were saved. The message is that humanity was saved. In a sense there were uncounted millions in that ark, millions of men and women, boys and girls, of all nations – a world begun again that continues to this day. The judgment indeed was terrible but the mercy was even greater than the judgment. We, every one of us, are beneficiaries of it: spared for new possibilities and a new future. That is why the story of Noah's ark has never been forgotten. With its elements of judgment and mercy, warning and hope, stern morality and abiding love it sets us in a moral universe where order is the last word and God's purposes will prevail.

2. The God who grieves over sin (6:1–8)

Human civilization had developed but so had human sin. The line of
Cain had grown in power and in arrogance, the arts had flourished
but there was a sickness at their heart, cities were built but they
became centres of intrigue and violence where corruption lived in
concentrated form. Above all, godlessness reigned. Eden was
forgotten; the human race was 'going it alone'.

Alongside this, however, God was at work in the godly line of
Seth, with its famous representative, Enoch, who, in the words of
Genesis 5:24, 'walked with God; then he was no more because God
took him away'. Noah was of that line, but the line had so
diminished in true godliness that by the time of the flood only he is
mentioned as walking with God (6:9) among the people of his time.
Human civilization was given up to pride and violence. By the time
of Noah it was so far from being what it was meant to be that God
determined to show his intense opposition to sin in a way which
would never be entirely forgotten.

It is of first importance that we see the flood as God's judgment
upon sin, as the expression of his holy wrath on account of sin, and
as the demonstration of his grief and indignation in the face of
universal human sin. Human terms are used in verses 5–6 to describe
the divine reaction, but notice that it is the *sin* and not just the judgment that follows that grieves God: *The LORD saw how great man's
wickedness on the earth had become, and that every inclination of
the thoughts of his heart was only evil all the time. The LORD was
grieved ... and his heart was filled with pain.*

Even the reference to Noah in verse 8 is a statement of grace not
of due: the wonder is that he found favour with God. It is, in some
ways, not so clear from the NIV translation that the Hebrew text
repeatedly emphasizes an unrelieved universality in verses 5–7 of
which Noah could not but be a part. The sequence in these verses is
of the human race universally sinful (6:5), universally a grief to God
(6:6) and universally consigned to death (6:7). Within this unrelieved
universality, Noah, equally fallen, equally under sentence with all
the others, was made a recipient of grace. Noah did not find favour
because he was a righteous man; he was a righteous man because he
was favoured, because God had chosen him in grace. The word for
'favour' here is *ḥēn* (it equals the Greek *charis*) and is never in
response to merit.

It is at this precise point that the biblical picture of God is
revolutionary in its ancient Near Eastern setting. It is important that
we understand human depravity, widespread corruption, and human
accountability as the background to the judgment that follows. It is

the distinguishing feature of the biblical account and flows from an understanding of the character of God as holy, righteous and sin-hating, who has created a universe backed by ethical principles that imply a moral response. W. G. Dumbrell remarks: 'A notion of such an accountability of man for moral faults introduces into the biblical flood narrative ideas which would have been generally revolutionary in the ancient world and lends to them … a theological distinctiveness.'[1]

3. The gods who are helpless

There are other stories of a great flood, some of them very ancient indeed. Those originating in Mesopotamia contain some striking similarities to the biblical account.[2] However, the differences are even more striking than the similarities and show the uniqueness of the biblical revelation. For instance, in the Atrahasis epic human beings had become so populous that their noise keeps the god Enlil awake. After several failed attempts to eradicate the race by means of plague, drought and famine he eventually unleashes a great flood (which Atrahasis survives by building a boat). And in the Babylonian Gilgamesh epic we read:

> The gods were frightened by the deluge
> And, shrinking back, they ascended to the heaven of Anu.
> The gods cowered like dogs
> Crouched against the outer wall.[3]

Gordon Wenham brings out the many contrasts between the biblical understanding and that of the myths:

> The plurality of divinities creates uncertainty about the future as far as mortals are concerned, and the pettiness of the gods' motives in destroying mankind contrasts starkly with the stern moral tone of the biblical account. Man is damned in the latter not for making a noise but because of his incorrigible evil for ruining the earth and committing violence … If the sending of the flood shows the capricious nature of mesopotamian deities, its effects demonstrate their weakness. When the storm arrived they were unable to control it; they were frightened and 'cowered like dogs' … Yet as soon as 'God remembered Noah' and caused a wind to pass over the earth (compare God's breath in creation), the waters receded. The omnipotence and control of Yahweh is again demonstrated.

[1] Dumbrell, p. 13.
[2] See, in particular, Wenham (1987) and Hamilton (1990).
[3] Wenham (1987), p. 161.

The closing scenes of the epic, after the flood, serve to point up the differences between biblical and Babylonian attitudes to the divine. Here too, the flood hero offers a sacrifice when he comes out of the ship. Here too, the sacrifice is acceptable. But the responses are very different:

> Gilgamesh continues by describing the gods 'crowding like flies around the sacrifice', greedily jostling for places at the open-air barbecue. Since mankind had been created to feed the gods, obviously the latter had gone hungry while there were no men around to present offerings. Then Enlil, chief executive among the gods arrives and is surprised to discover survivors of the flood. Clearly he is neither omnipotent nor omniscient. The recriminations that follow underline the fact that the gods do not agree or act in concert, whereas in Genesis the divine speeches that follow the sacrifice reassert the creator's lordship over his creatures and his determination to uphold the cosmic order and his mercy toward mankind. Throughout the flood story, then, Genesis paints a completely different portrait of God from the standard ancient theology.[4]

Wenham also observes that, 'While Genesis builds up the character of God, it very much reduces the dimensions of the flood hero.'[5] Noah is not a king as his counterpart in the other stories seems to be. He does not, as in the myths, dominate the scene with his activity nor is he made into a god, together with his wife, as in the Gilgamesh epic. In fact our last sight of him is the unflattering story of his drunkenness and shame. Thus the biblical narrator cuts even the heroes of the Old Testament down to size!

4. The moral seriousness of God (6:9–17)

The first thing we learn in these verses is *the moral seriousness of God*. The God of the Genesis flood story is ethical in his holiness and righteous in his anger. The great and central requirements of this God are moral and spiritual. If these convictions do not keep pace with the advancement of a civilization or society, theirs or ours, then or now, that civilization or society is ultimately doomed to fall under the judgment of God. The growing lack of moral seriousness in modern society is a sickness that has grown with startling rapidity in our times. American theologian David Wells quotes the research published in 1991 in the book *The Day America Told the Truth: What People Really Believe about Everything that Matters*, by

---

[4] Ibid., p. 165.   [5] Ibid., p. 166.

James Patterson and Peter Kim. It might have been written about Britain or elsewhere in the Western world. He writes:

> Americans today, say researchers James Patterson and Peter Kim, 'stand alone in a way unknown to any previous generation'. They are alone, not least because they are without any objective moral compass. 'The religious figures and Scriptures that gave us rules for so many centuries, the political system which gave us laws, all have lost their meaning in our moral imagination.' While the great majority of Americans believe that they actually keep the Ten Commandments, only 13% think that each of these commandments has moral validity. It is no surprise to learn that 74% said they will steal without compunction; 64% say they will lie if there is an advantage to be had in doing so; 53% say that given a chance they will commit adultery ... What may be the clearest indicator of the disappearance of a moral texture to society is the loss of guilt and embarrassment over moral lapses ... While 74% will steal without compassion, only 9% register any moral disquiet. While pornography has blossomed into a four billion dollar industry ... only 2% experience guilt about watching. And, not surprisingly, at the center of this slide into license and moral relativism is the disappearance of God. Only 17% define sin as a violation of God's will.[6]

And this in a society with a far greater church-going population than Britain (40% compared with under 10%) and where a third of the population claim to be born again!

Hebrews 11:7 says, 'By faith Noah, when warned about things not yet seen, in holy fear built an ark to save his family. By his faith he condemned the world and became heir of the righteousness that comes by faith.' Noah's 'holy fear' was not fear of the flood so much as fear of God. We do not hear of someone being 'God-fearing' today do we? It is a term that has fallen out of use, not because we have a better understanding of God but because the sense and implications of his holiness have been lost. But the God of the Bible is awesomely powerful, utterly just and unbearably holy: his purity is a white-hot flame and sin cannot live in it.[7] Only those whose folly is as great as their ignorance will find nothing in God to fear. Only toy lions are cuddly; the real thing can be fearful! It is God in his holiness, confronting us in our sinfulness, that has the most terrible possibilities for us – for any of us: 'The lion has roared – who will not fear?' cried an Old Testament prophet.[8]

[6] David Wells, *Losing our Virtue: Why the church must recover its moral vision* (IVP, 1998), pp. 58–59.
[7] Gen. 18:25; Deut. 32:4; Hab. 1:13; Rom. 1:18.   [8] Amos 3:8.

In C. S. Lewis's children's book, *The Lion, the Witch and the Wardrobe*, the human children have met the beavers, some of the talking animals of Narnia, and are hearing for the first time about Aslan, the Great Lion, the true King of Narnia, the Christ-figure of the book. Narnia is a land held in perpetual winter by the Witch. The animals know that only the coming of Aslan can save their world. Mrs Beaver says: 'If there's anyone who can appear before Aslan without their knees knocking, they're either braver than most or else just silly.' 'Then he isn't safe?' said Lucy. 'Safe?' replied Mr Beaver. 'Don't you hear what Mrs Beaver tells you? Who said anything about safe? Course he isn't safe. But He's good. He's the King, I tell you.'[9]

The choice, whether in the imaginary Narnia or the real world of today, is between the real God and the fancied God, between the God of the prophets and the cardboard cut-outs of postmodern pastiche, between the historic Christ and the contemporary gurus. But we must face the words and warnings of Jesus that a greater judgment than the flood awaits the world 'at the coming of the Son of Man' when 'all the nations' will be gathered before him and he will say to many, 'Depart from me, you who are cursed, into the eternal fire prepared for the devil and his angels.'[10] Aslan is not a tame lion!

5. The covenant of God (6:18)

At the start of the biblical account the key statement on Noah's significance in his godless generation is given in Genesis 6:9: 'Noah was a righteous man, blameless among the people of his time, and he walked with God.' It is important to note that the righteousness spoken of here is, as is usually the case in the Old Testament use of the term, *righteousness within a relationship*. It indicates a lifestyle and a conduct arising from a relationship with God and loyal to that relationship. Noah's was not merely a legal or simply an ethical righteousness. The relationship with God was the source and sustaining power of it. Noah did not walk with God because he was righteous; he was righteous because he walked with God. Walking with God was not the reward of his righteousness but the ground of it. His righteousness arose out of a pre-established relationship.

This relationship is called a *covenant* relationship in verse 18: '*But I will establish my covenant with you, and you will enter the ark — you and your sons and your wife and your sons' wives with you.*' We shall see in a later chapter the importance of this term in biblical

---

[9] C. S. Lewis, *The Lion, the Witch and the Wardrobe* (Collins, 1988).
[10] Matt. 24:39; 25:32, 41.

revelation, but here it denotes a very special relationship in which God was committed to his servant Noah. A covenant was the most solemn and binding undertaking known in the ancient world. God's covenant here is that he is committed to this world he has made; he is committed to the future of the race of unique beings he made 'in his image'; he will uphold his world in all its wonder and variety.

The term 'establish' might lead us to think that the covenant was being newly set up. But in fact it is spoken about as something already in existence, to which God is continually faithful, and in which Noah is said to have his place. 'Establish' is a misleading translation. The verb used here (*qûm*) is not used of covenant inauguration (*kārat*); rather it implies the implementation of an existing covenant. William G. Dumbrell argues that it would be best to think of our terms 'obligation' or 'commitment' when we read 'covenant' here, and that 'I will establish my covenant' should be understood as 'I will maintain my (already-existing) covenant'.[11]

6. The covenant-keeping God (8:1, 20–22; 9:1–17)

On the day Noah entered the ark the deluge came. God shut him in and the world out. For forty days the waters rose, and for a hundred and fifty days the ark floated above universal death. Then we read that *God remembered Noah . . . and he sent a wind over the earth and the waters receded* (8:1).

The day came when one surviving family and a whole menagerie of animals came out of the ark to repopulate the devastated earth. Noah's first act was to build an altar to the Lord. I like the words of David Atkinson here: 'The boat builder now builds an altar. He steps out of the tomb of his ark into the fresh air and daylight of his Easter morning, kneels down in the mud and says his prayers.'[12]

But God has something to say too, for he is the God of mercy as well as judgment in a fallen world. God meets Noah's act of worship with a revelation: '*Never again will I curse the ground because of man, even though every inclination of his heart is evil from childhood. And never again will I destroy all living creatures, as I have done. As long as the earth endures . . . day and night will never cease*' (8:21–22).

a. The covenant confirmed

At the beginning of Genesis 9 we have echoes of the first chapter of Genesis in the speech of God, as though God were starting a new world with a new Adam and Eve: 'Be fruitful and increase in number and fill the earth.' Earlier we had read, 'The LORD was grieved that

---

[11] Dumbrell, pp. 16, 20–26, 31.   [12] Atkinson, p. 148.

he had made man on the earth' (6:6), and the resulting destruction appeared to indicate that God had discarded his covenant because of human sin. Now, however, God makes plain what the preservation of Noah and his extended family had already suggested, namely, that he did not consider his covenant to be annulled, or his original creation intent to have lapsed since he had established it before Noah, before the generations of the fall after Adam, and even before the creation of Adam himself. God's covenant was established on his foreordained grace, not on human response or human merit. The New Testament will make even clearer God's plan to deal with human sin and failure.[13]

Once again human beings are to rule the earth and subdue it, but now, as an explicit counter-force to the proud and violent nature of fallen man so evident before the flood, the bottom line for civilizations and communities in the new world is to be the sanctity of human life as the nearest thing to God in the created world:

> 'Whoever sheds the blood of man,
> by man shall his blood be shed;
> for in the image of God
> has God made man' (9:6).

Finally, we have the solemn covenant made with Noah and his sons and also with every living creature in Genesis 9:11: *'I establish my covenant with you: Never again will all life be cut off by the waters of a flood; never again will there be a flood to destroy the earth.'*

b. The rainbow in the cloud

God therefore confirms his creation covenant with Noah and his descendants and includes in it 'every living creature on earth'. When he says, 'Never again will all life be cut off by the waters of a flood; never again will there be a flood to destroy the earth', he does not mean simply that there will never again be such a flood in particular but that he will never destroy the earth he has made or mankind for whom he has an ultimate purpose. The entire creation-order will be upheld and preserved in the goodness of God until he fulfils his original intention for it. The strong language of 2 Peter 3:5–7, 11, where he speaks of the present world being reserved for fire and destruction, should not be taken literally, in my view, since Peter also speaks of the world of the flood being destroyed without meaning its annihilation and replacement. So the 'new heaven and earth' will be a renewed not a replaced creation.[14]

God says he is bound to creation by a commitment freely entered

---

[13] Eph. 1:3–10.　　[14] Rom. 8:21

into, a commitment that still stands. The sign of that commitment will thenceforth be the rainbow in the cloud – the most appropriate symbol in a world of threatening storms and abiding providence. William Dumbrell comments: 'The divine commitment, given at this time, never again to send a flood ushers in presumably the time of forbearance to which Paul refers in Rom. 3:25.'[15] God announces that throughout the course of human history and in the face of many provocations: '*Whenever the rainbow appears in the clouds, I will see it and remember the everlasting covenant between God and all living creatures of every kind on the earth*' (9:16). Dumbrell explains this divine 'remembering':

Of course, we must not think that something additional to and outside of the divine nature is necessary to stimulate God to provide for the obligation to which he has committed himself, for we would hesitate to ascribe memory lapses to the Creator of the universe! For the use of 'remember' in the Old Testament is hardly ever, as it invariably is with us, simply a reference to the power of the psychological recall of the past. Biblically, when the past is 'remembered', what is most often meant is that what is done in present experience is logically dependent upon some past event. This is what is meant in Genesis.[16]

God also clearly has a point in saying all this to Noah. The rainbow is a covenant sign for him and his descendents also. 'Covenant signs express covenant promises to covenant people.'[17] What the rainbow in the clouds means to God it can now mean to Noah. 'When he sees the bow he will be drawn yet again into faith in the promise.'[18]

God was fully aware of our human bias toward sin. He knew that the flood that had washed the world clean had not washed the heart of humanity clean, even in Noah's family, and in Noah himself. God knew in advance our continuing history of idolatry, violence and immorality. Yet he knew too what he would do from within history – curbing its corruptions, fostering its civilizations, calling its generations to life-changing faith in the true God. When the time had fully come, he knew he would send his own Son to be what Adam and Noah could never be, and to do for a lost world what patriarchs and prophets could never do. So Christ Jesus came: the centre of history, the last Adam, the Second Man, the Lord from heaven, the new Beginning of a world without end.

Jesus Christ is our Ark now: big enough for the whole world,

---

[15] Dumbrell, p. 26.   [16] Ibid., p. 31.   [17] Alec Motyer in correspondence.
[18] Ibid.

strong enough to withstand the shocks of life, the rising waters of death, and the upheavals of the last judgment. There is safety here in the Son of God, sent to be for us all the shelter, the salvation we so desperately needed. He is our Ark and safe passage into the new world that God has planned. From that Ark, at the general resurrection, we will emerge to inherit a new heaven and a new earth.[19] For the end of God's plan is not the destruction but the renewal of the earth. The rainbow hangs in the air as a sign and a promise of a new day coming, clear shining after rain, the home of righteousness.[20]

c. Freely but firmly committed

The covenant with Noah shows that God will continue to be committed to and involved in human history. The depth of that commitment and the degree of his involvement will be shown most fully in the incarnation and redemptive suffering of Jesus Christ, 'God with us'.[21] The biblical message stands in stark contrast with some other religious and philosophical approaches to the world in its disorder. In Buddhism, for instance, the life of the arhat, or saint, is one that transcends the needs, sufferings and fears of the ordinary life in a balanced *detachment*. The Japanese writer and former missionary Kosuke Koyama engages with some of the major doctrines of Theravada Buddhism and writes in this regard:

> The arhat-ideal is radically different from the spirituality expressed in the lives of the people of Israel (the Old Testament) and of the church (New Testament). There God is portrayed strongly as an anti-arhat God in that he is deeply engaged in history. He rules history. His direction is not away from history (detachment – 'eyes lowered'), but towards history (attachment – 'I have seen the affliction of my people who are in Egypt'). Perhaps this is the basic contrast between Theravada Buddhism and the Judeo-Christian faith: the two histories, the two eyes.[22]

d. Covenant and creation

The beginning of the covenant relationship and the naming of its beneficiaries are indicated in Genesis 9:8–17:

> Then God said to Noah and to his sons with him: [9]'I now establish (maintain, perpetuate) my covenant with you and with your descendants after you and with every living creature that was with you ... [16]Whenever the rainbow appears in the clouds, I will see it and

---

[19] Rev. 21:1.   [20] 2 Pet. 3:11–13.   [21] Matt. 1:23; cf. Heb. 2:14.
[22] Kosuke Koyama, *Water Buffalo Theology* (SCM Press, 1974), p. 153; quoted in David Burnett, *The Spirit of Buddhism: A Christian Perspective on Buddhist Thought* (Monarch, 1996), pp. 247–248.

remember the everlasting covenant between God and all living creatures of every kind on the earth.'

[17]*So God said to Noah, 'This is the sign of the covenant I have established between me and all life on the earth.'*

As there is no earlier use of the word 'covenant', even in the Garden of Eden narrative, and as the reference to the wider creation is so clear here, Dumbrell is convinced that the only logical place to look for the establishment of anything like a covenant, with its God-initiated commitment, is Genesis 1:1. He writes, 'The very fact of creation involved God's entering into relationships with the world' and 'The covenant which was confirmed with Noah had been brought into existence by the act of creation itself.'[23] The act of creation itself, he says, involved God in a commitment to what he had brought into existence, a commitment in which he freely obliged himself to fulfil his first intentions for the human race and indeed the whole created order. Hence the repeated references in Genesis 9:8–16 to all other life on earth as well as human life. Dumbrell argues from his analysis of Genesis 1 – 9 that there can be only one divine covenant, and that any theology of covenant must begin with Genesis 1:1: 'All else in covenant theology which progressively occurs in the Old Testament will be deducible from this basic relationship.' And so he proceeds to trace and examine 'the chain of connection which having moved from creation to Noah, leads us from Noah to Abraham, from Abraham to Sinai, to David, to the Jeremianic new covenant and thence to Jesus its fulfiller'.[24]

This does not mean that God's commitment is not free because it is present in creation from the start. God brought creation into being knowing in advance of the defection of the rebellious angels and of mankind yet determined not to let sin and corruption have the last word. God was therefore committed to his creation before the fall and he has not abandoned that commitment since, despite the defection of the human race. He has freely determined that his first intentions would eventually be brought to fruition, that there would be 'a sabbath rest' for the people of God and the whole creation.[25] Dumbrell writes on this:

> By the divine rest on the seventh day the goal of creation is indicated, a goal which will be maintained notwithstanding sustained human attempts to vitiate it. Not only does the seventh day rest note the goal to which creation points, but it is the call to man to begin history holding firmly in view that 'the goal of creation, and at the same time the beginning of all that follows, is the

---

[23] Dumbrell, pp. 41, 43.   [24] Ibid., p. 42.   [25] Heb. 4:3–4, 9.

event of God's Sabbath freedom, Sabbath rest and Sabbath joy, in which man, too, has been summoned to participate'.[26]

This notion of divine rest which humanity is thereafter invited to share becomes a dominant one later in the Old and New Testaments, and the institution of the Sabbath[27] becomes the particular covenantal sign of the concept: 'On the Sabbath, therefore, Israel is to reflect upon the question of ultimate purposes for herself as a nation, and for the world over which she is set.'[28]

7. The God who enters into relationships

A covenant is often defined briefly as 'a promise ratified by an oath'. Dumbrell, however, makes the point that 'the covenant is not to be identified with the promises or demands bound up with it. Covenant refers to the relationship from which promises and demands will flow.' The God who speaks in covenant language throughout the Old Testament and into the New ('This cup is the new covenant in my blood'[29]) is the God who enters into *relationships*. It is the form of his self-giving and his openness to receiving. David Atkinson quotes an old scholar to the effect that the rainbow, in originating from the effect of the sun upon clouds and water, 'typifies the readiness of the heavenly to pervade the earthly', adding, 'Heaven and earth can come together.'[30] That is precisely what God wants to do with his creation and with humankind in particular. He is the God whose holiness sets him apart from all that is not God. But he is also the God whose goodness and love bridges the gap between himself and his creation. In the story of redemption we find the awesome and holy God whom the heavens cannot contain is also the down-to-earth God. He is the one who came down to earth, even when it had no room for him in its fallenness, that he might redeem us and reconcile us to himself. And at the end of the Bible we have God declaring in 'a loud voice from the throne . . . "Now the dwelling of God is with men, and he will live with them." '[31]

[26] Dumbrell, pp. 34–35.   [27] Exod. 31:13–17.   [28] Dumbrell, pp. 34–35.
[29] Luke 22:20.   [30] Atkinson, p. 166.   [31] Rev. 21:3.

Genesis 8 – 9
5. Providence: God who sustains

Linus and Lucy were watching the rain through their living room window. 'Boy, look at it rain,' Lucy exclaimed with a frown. 'What if it floods the whole world?' To this, the ever-confident Linus replied, 'It will never do that. In the ninth chapter of Genesis, God promised Noah that would never happen again, and the sign of the promise is the rainbow.' Upon hearing these reassuring words, Lucy broke out in a big grin. Looking again at the torrential downpour outside, she noted, 'You've taken a great load off my mind.' Linus seized this teachable moment. 'Sound theology has a way of doing that!' he announced to his young companion.[1]

1. The reliability of God (8:22; 9:12–16)

The theology of Israel was not a theology of fear but of confidence. The religion of the Old Testament was not a religion of anxiety, but a faith firmly founded on a covenant-making and covenant-keeping God; a God who made promises for all to hear, and placed his rainbow in the sky for all to see. He is a God who committed himself in Israel's history, that future generations might see *that* story as *their* story. The promises are made to the children as much as to the father, that they might walk in trust and obedience.

> '*As long as the earth endures,*
> *seedtime and harvest,*
> *cold and heat,*
> *summer and winter,*
> *day and night*
> *will never cease*' (8:22).

---

[1] Stanley J. Grenz, *Created for Community: Connecting Christian belief with Christian living* (Victor Books/S P Publications, 1996), p. 41.

'Whenever I bring clouds over the earth and the rainbow appears in the clouds, I will remember my covenant between me and you and all living creatures of every kind' (9:14–15).

What we have in Genesis 8:22 and 9:12–16 is God's promise to Noah to sustain his world, to order the course of nature, and to preserve and guide the world and the human race throughout its history. What we have in Psalm 119 is the celebration of stability due to the faithfulness of God, Creator, Redeemer and Saviour:

> Your word, O LORD, is eternal;
>   it stands firm in the heavens.
> Your faithfulness continues through all generations;
>   you established the earth, and it endures.
> Your laws endure to this day,
>   for all things serve you.[2]

There is an unhealthy preoccupation with the supernatural and the miraculous that has no theology of the normal, and misses the glory of God in the regular and the predictable. Today, between an unbelieving secularism and a credulous supernaturalism, we hear less and less about the doctrine of the divine providence.

The two main aspects of God's providence in theological thinking are God's *sustenance* of all things (holding all creation in being, with all its laws of growth and development) and God's *government* over all things (overruling all events in the world and in the history of mankind in order to lead them to his final purposes of judgment and salvation). It is largely the first we shall consider here, reserving the second for a separate chapter.[3] We must not forget, however, that it is both aspects of God's providence which make up the whole doctrine.

When God brought the creation into being, with all its marvellous complexity and order, and pronounced it 'good', he signified an approval of it and a commitment to it; a commitment grounded in himself as 'the only wise God' whose decisions and work are uniquely serious. Henceforth creation would reflect and communicate to human beings the truth of 'his eternal power and divine nature'. It was an expression, not of his being but of his mind, his wisdom and his goodness. As such, God has always been committed to his creation, including its non-human and inanimate parts and components, and supremely he is committed to human kind.

When Adam and Eve rebelled God could have scrapped 'the human experiment', if an 'experiment' was all it had been. But we

---

[2] Ps. 119:89–91.   [3] See chapter 20, 'The sovereignty of God'.

learn from the living God that none of these things took him by surprise and that, instead of eliminating the divine intentions for our world and its race, he revealed a plan that nothing could annul.[4] God was still committed to the world, even to the world of the fall and the flood, and to the ongoing world, with its long history of painful progress and drastic setbacks.

2. Providence as sustenance (8:22)

The Old Testament is full of the recognition that God is constantly at work sustaining his creation[5] and this helps to explain its frequent attitude toward second causes. They are not denied, rather the sense of God at work in the world is paramount. Nothing in all creation has an independent existence. Secularist and materialist philosophies have leant far the other way in more recent times. The sense of God at work in nature or human history has been largely lost in Western society. God's marvellous creation around us has become simply 'the environment', and in the story of human affairs 'progress' has replaced 'providence'. Biblical faith, however, rescues us from such blindness and we are able to recognize the Creator in his works, and to trust his power to lead history towards his destined end.

In the New Testament we read that in response to Satan's temptation to satisfy his hunger by making stones into loaves of bread, Jesus said, 'Man does not live on bread alone, but on every word that comes from the mouth of God.'[6] This was a quotation from the Old Testament book of Deuteronomy, where Moses reminds the people of Israel of the long years they survived in the scrub-land between Egypt and the Promised Land because God gave them 'manna' enough to feed the entire nation. The point Jesus is making, as Calvin noted,[7] is not that people need doctrine as well as food, but that it is the word of God that makes food nourishing, his will and energy that makes things 'work', his kindness that keeps us in existence. It is not 'bread' or anything else necessary for life that does its work in independence of God. These things do not work 'alone'. Nothing and no-one has more than a semi-autonomous existence. All things are contingent, depending on him who created them and who keeps them in being with all their characteristics and powers.

3. The everywhere-active God

God's work of providence is no less mighty than his original work of creation and brings equal glory to him. The 'rest' of God in

---

[4] Gen. 3:15; cf. Eph. 1:3–10. [5] See e.g. Job 37 – 38; Pss. 19; 104. [6] Matt. 4:4.
[7] Calvin (*Harmony*), vol. 1, p. 138.

Genesis 1 does not mark the end of God's involvement with creation, only a transition of his working into a new phase of activity. Providence now takes over from creation. Creation called all things into being; providence keeps all things in being.

In an essay entitled 'A scientist in God's world', the late Professor Donald MacKay vividly illustrates this from the understanding of modern physics:

> Ask a physicist to describe what he finds as he probes deeper and deeper into the fine structure of our solid world, and he will tell you a story of an increasing *dynamic* character. Instead of a frozen stillness, he discovers a buzz of activity that seems to intensify as the magnification increases. The molecules he pictures as the stuff of the chair you are sitting on and of the body sitting in it – are all believed to be in violent motion, vibrating millions of times in a second, or even careering about in apparent disarray, with an energy depending on the temperature ... According to modern physics, it is to such elementary *events* – myriads of them, continually recurring – that we owe all our experience of the solid world of objects.[8]

Such images, says Professor MacKay, illustrate a key concept: 'We can call it *dynamic stability*.'[9] The stability of things in our world is real enough. There is no hint in Scripture of unreality or illusion about the solid contents of our world.

> They are as real as we ourselves, as real as their Creator has conceived them to be. But their stability is nevertheless declared to be a dynamic, contingent [dependent], stability. It is only in and through the continuing say-so of their and our Creator that they cohere or 'hold together' (Col. 1:17) ... the Bible has no room for the idea of matter as something eternally self-sufficient or indestructible ... In the end, for biblical theism, the only solid reality is God and what God holds in being.[10]

4. God's two books

This is the teaching of the Bible throughout its varied periods of composition, the teaching of Old and New Testaments. To this day, it is also the foundation, recognized or not, of the entire scientific and medical enterprise: an ordered creation, coherent, comprehensible and reliable because it is called into being and kept in being

---

[8] Donald MacKay, *The Open Mind and Other Essays* (IVP, 1988), pp. 21–22.
[9] Ibid., p. 22.   [10] Ibid., pp. 23–24.

by its Creator who regards his creation with intense and sustained seriousness.

The old writers often spoke of 'God's two books': the book of nature and the book of salvation. The Bible was incomparable and alone was sufficient in showing the way of salvation, but God was no less the author of the book of nature, which showed his power, wisdom and goodness to his own glory. They saw no conflict between these two books, which had but one Author! They also recognized the different (though overlapping) ways in which we discover and respond to the truths revealed in both: hearing, believing and obeying the one in the context of a personal relationship and discovering, experimenting with and utilizing the other as lords of creation given a mandate to rule it wisely, search it thoroughly, and develop its potential in proper humility.[11]

5. God and the scientist (9:12–16)

All truth is God's truth, and scientific discovery today invites faith and challenges unbelief, rather than the reverse. Alister McGrath writes:

> One of the most significant achievements of modern science has been its demonstration of the ordering of the world. It has disclosed an intelligible and delicately balanced structure, raising questions which transcend the scientific, and provoke an intellectual restlessness which seeks adequate explanation. The fundamental human instinct to discern order within the world seen at work so clearly in the Old Testament wisdom literature is in its element when confronted with the findings of physical science, which seek to present an amazingly ordered cosmos. And it prompts questions. Perhaps the most fundamental could be summarized in a single word: Why?[12]

Such a sense of order running throughout the physical world is an important common link between Christian faith and science, two things which should not be seen as irreconcilable enemies or even strangers to one another. What the scientist and the Christian have in common is that they both expect the world to make ultimate sense – even when they are puzzled by an immediate problem which does not. They both proceed on a basis of faith, and in each case it is one that precedes and underlies their investigations. They can both say, in their different ways, as Anselm, 'I believe in order to understand.'

[11] Gen. 1:26–30; 2:19–20; Job 38:12–33.
[12] Alister McGrath, *Bridge-Building* (IVP, 1992), p. 63.

The scientist presupposes a world which is regular, constant and uniform in its physical laws, that is 'the central – indeed we might say the foundational – assumption of modern natural science, which comes remarkably close to being an article of religious faith.'[13] It may be said, 'But that is because the scientist finds this in his or her scientific investigations.' However, even when the investigator turns up an observation which indicates that nature is not uniform, the main presupposition is not challenged. As Alister McGrath observes:

> The doctrine of the uniformity of nature is actually treated as lying beyond falsification. If the experimental results appear to contradict it, these results are, in practice, not interpreted as implying that nature lacks uniformity; the more probable explanations urged are either that the experiment is flawed, or that subsequent experiments or developments in theoretical analysis will explain the result without the need to reject the notion of the uniformity of the natural world.[14]

It is, however, a sign, not of human cleverness, but of human sin when men and women recognize and rely on the order and stability of nature but refuse to recognize and rely on the Creator whose wisdom, power and patience keeps them and their world in being. The scientific method has been made the only way of knowing anything that can be known. But God is not to be known as other things are known; he is not part of the universe he made. He is to be known in other ways: by his own self-revelation and by our personal encounter with him. As Calvin said at the outset of the modern experiment: 'To be so occupied in the investigation of the secrets of nature as never to turn the eyes to its Author, is a most perverted study; and to enjoy everything in nature without acknowledging the author of the benefit is basest ingratitude.'[15] He warns against making second causes substitutes for the First Cause, God: 'Philosophers think not that they have reasoned skillfully enough about inferior causes, unless they separate God very far from his works. It is a diabolical science, however, which fixes our contemplations on the works of nature, and turns them away from God.'[16]

It is in utter contrast to this fixation that the psalmist could write,

> Your faithfulness continues
>   through all generations;
>   you established the earth, and it endures.

[13] Ibid., p. 212.   [14] Ibid., p. 211.   [15] Calvin (*Genesis*), vol. 1, p. 60.
[16] Calvin (*Psalms*), vol. 1, p. 479.

Your laws endure to this day,
for all things serve you'.[17]

The existence of what used to be called the 'laws of nature' is a revelation of God's commitment to and purpose for his creation. In particular it is the constant sign of his kindness, forbearance and mercy toward all of humankind. The ordered, dependable, even predictable universe is no indication of his absence, as the cynical mockers of Peter's day suggested in their taunt: 'Where is this "coming" he promised? Ever since our fathers died, everything goes on as it has since the beginning of creation.'[18] Looking back to the destruction of the flood and the covenant with Noah, Peter replies that the world is not abandoned but 'reserved' and 'kept' in being for a final judgment. Meanwhile the present time is full of significance and hope, for 'The Lord is not slow in keeping his promise, as some understand slowness. He is patient with you, not wanting anyone to perish, but everyone to come to repentance.'[19]

Thus the rainbow in the cloud holds out both promise and warning, assurance and admonition. The message is as ever, 'Seek the LORD while he may be found; call on him while he is near.'[20] The God of the covenant is a God of salvation and judgment; the covenant itself makes demands and threats; from it proceed both promises to those who rely on it and warnings to those who reject it and place themselves outside its provisions and beyond its help.

6. The question of miracles

We live in a God-created, God-sustained world where the natural order is his active, ongoing work of wisdom, power and faithfulness. Into that world sin has come, bringing with it disorder, wrath and the curse.[21] Yet, even in the world of the fall, God made a covenant with Noah that he would continue to uphold the fundamental order of creation, including what we call 'natural laws'. These observable, reliable, predictable mechanisms of physical life form the basis of much of our lives: of daily work, of national economics, of medical and scientific progress. Without them life would be a nightmare of insecurity.

We do not live in the 'open world' of the animist where natural laws are nothing and spiritual forces (divine and demonic) are everything – maturing or blighting harvests, healing or destroying people, capriciously sending success or failure. Rather we live in a world of natural order, of cause and effect, of in-built laws of crea-

[17] Ps. 119:90–91.   [18] 2 Pet. 3:4.   [19] 2 Pet. 3:9.   [20] Is. 55:6.
[21] Gen. 3:17–20.

tion. Yet we do not live in the 'closed world' of scientism either, where God is locked out or irrelevant or has become the prisoner of his own laws. It is by his personal action that they are kept in existence and it is by his personal action that their existence is ordered. They do not operate of themselves but by his power and at his will. We live in the 'controlled world' of biblical providence where God upholds what he has created but shows, too, his sovereignty over all created forces and things.[22]

a. A world of order and disorder

In the world of the fall, however, the reliable progressions of the natural order now work against us as well as for us. God's created order has been disturbed. Fallen humanity now falls victim to its crushing regularity; the cancer grows as well as the baby; disease progresses by natural laws which are not easily controlled; we find ourselves trapped in a world of danger, illness and death. In such a world God has acted in ways that give security in good times[23] and hope in bad times.[24] That hope includes the eventual reordering of nature in a new heavens and a new earth, a world where sin, death and disease among his people will be no more. It anticipates the world of the resurrection, whose powers have already entered our world with the coming of Christ but have not yet filled up our world or replaced the present order (and disorder) of things. Colin Brown writes:

> The same Creator may act within the world and he may act on the world. In both cases there is a resultant order. Thus in the last resort, all miracles may turn out to be expressions of contingency [one thing depending on another], though the contingency may include that of the 'new creation' as well as that of the 'old'. The kind of miracles that the Christians believe in are not pure random manifestations. They are manifestations of a divine ordering of the nature with which we are familiar, and of the eschatological order of the Christian hope. In neither case could they have come about if nature had been left to itself. For this reason miracles cannot be the object of scientific investigation, for science can only deal with nature as it is left to itself.[25]

b. Jesus and the kingdom of God

The fact of miracles is not disputed in Scripture, although it would be wrong to think that the Bible is full of them. In the Old Testament most of the recorded miracles cluster in two periods which were critical for Israel's life as the people of God: the times of Moses

[22] Carson (1978), pp. 87–90.   [23] Ps. 91.   [24] Ps. 42.   [25] C. Brown, p. 292.

and Elijah. Miracles otherwise are not commonplace and, of course, signs and wonders that were everyday events would hardly be especially significant or wonderful! There is, however, a larger reason for the economy of miracles that we have in the Old Testament and even, to a lesser extent, in the New.

Jesus came preaching and practising the presence of the kingdom of God with all its ramifications – spiritual, social and physical.[26] Here, in and through Jesus, God's final destiny for humankind and for the whole creation begins. This is marked by a reconciliation and a renewal which will reverse the effects of the fall and take the human race and their world, on to what it was meant to be from the beginning.[27]

Jesus and his mighty works belong together.[28] They are signs of the kingdom. They announce and inaugurate a new age[29] which is both here and yet to come, which is already and not yet. If there is a sign-hunger in the Gospels which is condemned,[30] at there is a sign-presence in Acts which is celebrated.[31] Indeed, the church herself becomes a sign in her existence and character and gifts,[32] pointing forward to God's future.

Even in the Acts of the Apostles, however, we see evidence that miracles were never 'on tap' and that miraculous powers were not 'possessed' by anyone, even the apostles. They inspire awe even among the believers.[33] The church cannot perform them at will but must pray[34] and wait the Lord's will. Miraculous activity occurs in generous bursts at some times[35] and selectively at others.[36] Sometimes the most greatly used servants of Christ have to wait[37] and sometimes they wait in vain.[38] The faith-formula of Jesus[39] is not a reference simply to a human decision but to a special, divinely given faith, a divine moment in which believers are taken up in cooperation with God. Such special faith in first *given* and only then *exercised* with insight and entire confidence.[40]

It is important in all this to recognize that the old order of creation and the new order of the kingdom of God are both of God. The extremes of living as though the kingdom has not come or as though its fullness were here for us now (in theological terms, the extremes

[26] E.g. Luke 4:17–21; 11:20; cf. Matt. 10:2–7; 13:1–52.
[27] Gen. 1:31; Rom. 8:19–23; Col. 1:19–20; Rev. 21:1, 5; 22:1–5.
[28] Matt. 11:4–6; John 14:9–11.   [29] John 14:12–14.
[30] Matt. 12:39; 16:4; John 6:14–15, 26, 30; 1 Cor. 1:22.
[31] Acts 2:19, 22, 43; 4:30; 5:12; 6:8; 7:36; 14:3; 15:12.
[32] Rom. 12:3–8; 1 Cor. 12:7–11; 1 Pet. 4:10–11.   [33] Acts 2:43.
[34] Acts 4:30–31.   [35] Acts 5:12–16; 19:11–12.   [36] Acts 9:32–42.
[37] Acts 16:18.   [38] 2 Cor. 12:7–10; 2 Tim. 4:20.
[39] 'If you have faith ... Nothing will be impossible', Matt. 17:20; cf. 9:29; John 14:12–13.
[40] E.g. Acts 3:16; 9:34, 40; 14:8–10.

of an under-realized eschatology and an over-realized eschatology) are true neither to Scripture nor to day-by-day reality, as Paul had to tell the Corinthians.[41]

c. Real but rare

Miracles are always *possible* because God is always sovereign in the universe he sustains and never a prisoner of his own laws. Miracles are always *serious* because they are breaches of a general and covenanted order which maintains stability in creation and on which all our lives depend, as well as all medical and scientific progress. Miracles are always *significant* because they are signs of the kingdom of God which is here to stay.[42] They are real, but they are *rare* because they belong to a world that is as yet future. They are never ordinary because we are not yet in the new earth,[43] and such powers most properly belong to the resurrection state,[44] that glorious future when we shall bear the likeness of the man from heaven.[45]

Meanwhile, in health and in sickness, in our expectations of an ordered world and in our sufferings when our own private world is disordered, we can trust the God of the ordinary and the extraordinary that our times are in his hand. Nothing is impossible for him – except to go back on his promise of the day when the dwelling of God will be with humankind, when 'There will be no more death or mourning or crying or pain, for the old order of things has passed away.'[46]

---

[41] 1 Cor. 4. [42] Mark 16:17–20. [43] 2 Pet. 3:13; Rev. 21:1. [44] John 20:19.
[45] 1 Cor. 15:49. [46] Rev. 21:4.

PART 2: GOD AND HIS PEOPLE

Genesis 11 – 18
6. God of the promise

G. Campbell Morgan, a popular Bible teacher of the first half of the twentieth century, used to divide Genesis into three parts: chapters 1 – 2: *generation*; chapters 3 – 11: *degeneration*; chapters 12 – 50: *regeneration*. These divisions can, of course, be oversimplified since we see God at work in the history of salvation from chapter 3 onwards. We see it in the promise of Genesis 3:15, in the story of Abel and the godly line of Seth, and in the life of Enoch and the deliverance of Noah. Indeed it has been noted that each of the narratives involving illustrations of the fall 'moves beyond a divine punishment which the act of sin provokes, to a divine act of forgiveness or a mitigation of punishment which follows'.[1] It would be rather more accurate to say, therefore, as recent scholars, that the theme of Genesis 1 – 11 as a unit is 'creation – uncreation – recreation'.[2] Yet Genesis 12 does mark a new beginning and one to which chapters 1 – 11 form a prologue.

1. From the city of mankind to the city of God (11:31–32)

The degenerative effects of sin on human life and civilization are a main part of the message of Genesis 3 – 11. From Cain and Lamech to the builders of Babel, pride and violence, greed and fear, lust and envy are seen to be endemic in a world that has rebelled against God and sought its own good apart from him.[3] These chapters form the prelude to Genesis 12 and all that follows. In them it has been made clear that the resources of human history are not enough to meet and deal with the fact of human sinfulness. The answer must come from *beyond* human history *into* human history. Whatever processes of technological, social or religious evolution may have been going on

---

[1] Dumbrell, p. 62.
[2] D. J. A. Clines, quoted in R. C. Van Leeuwen, *'br'' NIDOTTE*, vol. 1, p. 732.
[3] Cf. Rom. 1:28–32.

in the world, here God breaks into history from beyond history to do a new and decisive thing.

Vinoth Ramachandra notes the contrast between the arrogant city Babel, with its great human resources, and God's choice of one man to do what he alone can do:

> The Hebrew Bible sets the call of Abraham and the emergence of the people of Israel against the dramatic background of the story of creation and the alienation of all the 'families of the earth' from their Creator ... It is on the heels of the depressing narrative about collective human rebellion (Gen. 11) that we read of God's call to Abraham: to distance himself from Babylon, the archetypal city of human arrogance and wickedness, and to begin an adventure in the wilderness alone with God. The covenant that God makes with him in Genesis 12 is ultimately for the blessing of 'all the families of the earth'. God works with the one man and his family while his gaze, so to speak, is on all the families of the earth. God's final word on even Babylon itself is not one of judgement but of hope – but a hope that will be mediated through the heirs of Abraham.[4]

'The God of the biblical revelation, then', he continues, 'is the God of universal history. But he brings that history to its goal ("salvation") through the particular history of a particular people. This interplay between the universal and the unique runs right through the Old Testament narrative.'[5] The end of God's salvation-history will not be Babel (or Ur, or London, New York, Brussels or Beijing) but the city of Revelation 21 – 22, human civilization filled with the glory of the nations and the presence of God. It was the vision of such a future which sustained Abraham, 'For he was looking forward to the city with foundations, whose architect and builder is God.'[6]

a. Ur of the Chaldees

The story begins in one of the great cities of the ancient world, 'Ur of the Chaldees' as it later became called. The great city of Ur (if, as most commentators think, it is Ur in southern and not northern Mesopotamia which is meant) lay in what we would call southern Iraq, about 220 miles south-east of modern Baghdad. From the dawn of recorded history it had been an important centre of conquest, administration and culture at various times. In the 1920s archaeologists discovered under the desert sands at Ur some of the richest finds in the history of archaeology including over 1,800

---

[4] Ramachandra (*Mission*), p. 230.   [5] Ibid.   [6] Heb. 11:10.

private graves and tombs, 16 royal tombs and six 'death pits' that contained the mass burials of servants who were put to death when the monarch died so that he would have his proper status and entourage in the next world.

During the time of Abraham, in its third dynasty, about 1800 BC, some 300,000 people lived in Ur, a huge population for those times. Among other things it was an important centre of moon-worship and boasted a mighty 'ziggurat', a tower like the tower of Babel, with its temple to Nanna, the Sumerian moon-god at the top. Rather like a wedding cake, a ziggurat rose in square sections each of which was smaller than the one it rested on; each level was reached by means of a staircase which wound around the outside of the structure. The ziggurat of the later city of Babylon was 280 feet high. The huge base of the tower of Ur, with its great outside staircase, can still be seen and it is very impressive even by today's standards. Now, the whole area is desert, barren and lifeless, but 4,000 years ago it was humming with life and activity, a centre of culture and commerce that reached out over many hundreds of miles.

b. Let there be light!

It was there that God did a new thing, something that would affect the history of the world. God chose one man in the crowds; a man whose name was *Abram*, which meant 'exalted Father'. Later, God would change his name slightly to *Abraham*, which meant 'father of a multitude'. From the Genesis text we might think that the call of God came to Abraham in Haran, but Acts 7:2–3 makes it clear that there was an initial call in Ur. It may well have been that Abraham had to wait until the death of his father Terah, the leader of the clan, before he could leave.[7] By this time the semi-nomadic family of Terah was in Haran, an important trading centre in what we would call northern Syria and also a centre of moon-worship to which the clan of Terah was presumably attached.

In Haran the call of Abraham was renewed. In the obscurity of one man's private life God does a new thing and marks one of the most far-reaching turning points in history. Walter Brueggemann comments:

> The one who called the worlds into being now makes a second call. This call is specific. Its object is identifiable in history. The call is addressed to Abraham and to barren Sarah. The purpose of the call is to fashion an alternative community in creation gone awry, to embody in human history the power of the blessing . . . The call to Sarah and Abraham has to do not simply with the

[7] Acts 7:4.

forming of Israel but with the re-forming of creation, the transforming of the nations. The stories of this family are not ends in themselves but point to God's larger purposes.[8]

It is this that makes Genesis 12:1–3 one of the most important passages in the entire Old Testament, even, we may say, in the entire Bible. 'What is being offered in these few verses', says William Dumbrell, 'is a theological blueprint for the redemptive history of the world now set in train by the call of Abram . . . The kingdom of God established in global terms is the goal of the Abrahamic covenant.'[9]

2. God's elective call (12:1)

The call of God summoned Abram to a series of separations: from country (semi-nomadic groups could also own land and 'belong' to a specific place), and from clan and kindred and the ancestral deities they worshipped. As William Dumbrell notes: 'The call was to abandon all natural connections, to surrender all social customs and traditions, to leave land, clan and family. These were the very areas of strong attachment which in the ancient world would have been thought to provide ultimate personal security. Whatever binds him to the past is to be broken in this call which now comes to him to be the father of a nation.'[10] He adds: 'We may rightly term the call of God to Abram an elective call, and remind ourselves that such a sovereign act of God conferred greatness rather than rewarding it.'[11]

It was not Abraham who found God; it was God who found Abraham. In later times Israel will know that its founding father was once a Mesopotamian whose family worshipped other gods, that the pit out of which they were dug was no more than common clay, that the nation was hewn from the rock of fallen humanity and that only grace, free and unmerited favour, made the difference.[12] The biblical doctrine of election begins here and is rehearsed in unapologetic ways from Abraham to Israel[13] and to all believers.[14] Here are grounds for everlasting gratitude but none at all for self-congratulation or for apathy and smugness. Abraham is called, but 'all peoples on earth' will be blessed through him (3:3). Israel is chosen – but she is chosen to be a light to the nations.[15] Similarly, the New Testament believers, 'God's elect' are a people chosen to 'declare the praises of him who called you out of darkness into his wonderful light'.[16]

---

[8] Brueggemann (1982), p. 105.   [9] Dumbrell, pp. 66, 78.   [10] Ibid., p. 57.
[11] Ibid.   [12] Josh. 24:2; Is. 51:1.   [13] Deut. 7:6–8.   [14] Eph. 1:4–6.
[15] Is. 49:6; Acts 13:46–48.   [16] 1 Pet. 1:1; 2:9.

a. The logic of election

In his book, *The Gospel in a Pluralist Society*, Lesslie Newbigin has written:

> There is surely no part of Christian teaching which has been the subject of so much ridicule and indignant rejection as the doctrine of election. How absurd for intelligent, educated people to believe that almighty God should have his favourites, that he should pick out one small tribe among all the families of mankind to be the special subjects of his attention. Is it not a piece of ignorant egotism? There can be few places where this is felt more keenly than in India, with its immensely ancient and venerable traditions of religious experience and sophisticated theological reflection. How can one believe that almighty God has hidden the secret of truth for all these centuries from the great saints and scholars of India, the men and women of India, the men and women who were composing some of the greatest religious literature in the world at a time when the tribes of western Europe were wild barbarians, and that India should have to wait three thousand years to learn the secret of eternal salvation from the descendants of these barbarians? But the scandal is certainly not peculiar to India. It was Rousseau who said that he could not understand why, if God had something to say to Jean-Jacques Rousseau, he could not say it directly but had to go through Moses to say it.[17]

b. No private salvation

The first step toward an answer to such questions, Newbigin replies, is to ask what assumptions lie behind them.

> What is implied in the complaint that I ought not to have to depend on another for that which is necessary for my salvation? One has only to pose this question to uncover a whole set of assumptions which have to be questioned, assumptions which go to the heart of what it is to be human. Some of these assumptions have a very long and venerable history, and here I am thinking of the Indian traditions which have taken it as self-evident that the knowledge of God and the path to salvation must be in the last analysis a matter for the individual soul. Of course the seeker may need the help of a spiritual guide, but in the end the journey must be made alone. Salvation, if we want to use that word for that which is understood as the goal of human being, is in the end a matter of the relation between the individual soul and the Eternal.

[17] Newbigin (1989), p. 80.

It is in accordance with this way of understanding matters that the initiative lies with the seeker: he must search for and find a spiritual guide, and he may well go from one to another until he finds the guru who can lead him. The guru is not sent out to lost souls. It is for others to seek him.[18]

He continues, 'Modern Western culture has worked with analogous assumptions. Kant's famous slogan "Dare to Know", in which he summed up what was meant by enlightenment, was a summons to the autonomous human reason to trust its own powers and to dare to question the accepted traditions.'[19] Newbigin's response to such attempts to bypass relationships, to strip away the accidents of history, and to see the human relation with God as 'the relation of the alone to the alone' is to say:

> There is, there can be, no private salvation, no salvation which does not involve us with one another . . . God's saving revelation of himself does not come to us straight down from above – through the skylight, as we might say. In order to receive God's saving revelation we have to open the door to the neighbour whom he sends as his appointed messenger . . . There is no salvation except one in which we are saved together through the one whom God sends to be the bearer of his salvation.[20]

c. God's way of communicating truth

In our fashionable and often conceited individualism, we want a private revelation of reality that renders others unnecessary to us. But God shows us that others are necessary to us, that both life and thought are dependent upon what others have found and experienced. So too, God invests the knowledge of himself in one man, one family, one nation, that it may be communicated to all men and women, families and nations through the meeting of mind with mind, heart with heart, and life with life. God has no other way of world missions than that which is mediated by human beings.

The point is similarly made by Vinoth Ramachandra, who writes:

> Why does God not reveal himself directly to every individual human soul? The biblical answer, never explicit but presupposed from beginning to end, is simply that human beings are not autonomous spiritual/rational 'essences', abstracted from their location within social and material relationships that develop through space and time. Biblical teaching about election can be grasped only when seen as part of the characteristically biblical

[18] Ibid., p. 81.   [19] Ibid.   [20] Ibid., pp. 82–83.

way of understanding human reality. Human life consists in mutual relationships: a mutual interdependence that is not simply a temporary phase in the journey towards salvation but one that is intrinsic to salvation itself. If God's way of blessing 'all the families of the earth' . . . is to be addressed to those families in their concrete situations, and not to unreal abstractions such as 'immortal souls' or 'autonomous selves', then it must be accomplished through election – calling and sending *some* as vehicles of that blessing for *all* – so that human community may be freed from fragmentation and recreated in communion with God.[21]

This is what Lesslie Newbigin calls 'the logic of election' which underlies and precedes 'the logic of mission'.[22]

3. God's disruptive call

Abraham is not called simply to adopt a new set of ideas, insights or spiritual perceptions which leave his outward life untouched. He is not called to a new but privatized religion. The call of God, as so often, is disruptive.

a. A new devotion

First of all, for Abraham it is a call to a decisive turning away from the past, to a public rejection of his ancestral religion. This God is a jealous God, like a faithful husband he will brook no rivals, not even a mixture of old and new.

As Christian believers we are often rebuked for supporting Christian missions. We are told in the fashionable thinking of the day that each nation, tribe or people-group should be left undisturbed to worship their own gods in their own way and that we must be content to worship our God in our own way. What is really being said in such cases is that we must treat God as our own 'tribal deity', a personal, and by implication, local god. This is the very antithesis of the biblical revelation and understanding of God as the infinite-personal God who wants all the families of the earth to know him in the light of his self-revelation which challenges every inadequate and unworthy concept of our Creator who wants to be our Saviour.

It has never been easy to respond to the call of such a God. The pull of the world, the expectations of those around us, the pressures of life, all combine at times to keep us from doing so.

As pastor of a very international church I have seen how painful it

[21] Ramachandra (*Mission*), p. 233.   [22] Newbigin (1989), p. 80.

has been for affectionate and loyal children from south-east Asia to reject the ancestor worship that bound their family together, that was believed to take on in bliss generations of ancestors, and that gave their own parents hope of being blessed in the afterlife because of the worship, in turn, of their own children. Yet many have recognized every good thing and every high ideal in their Buddhist background but have said 'It is not enough'. This is because they have heard great good news for a sick and dying world, a world where men and women have not lived up to their ideals, where 'all have sinned and fall short of the glory of God', including the sages of the nations. The news is of the One who sent his only Son to die for the sins of the world, that men and women might receive as a gift the forgiveness of sins and the life eternal.

Others came out of Islam because they realized that Jesus was more than a prophet, that his death was a necessary atonement for sin, and that men and women are saved for eternal life, not by their own prayers and good deeds, but by the righteousness of God made available for failed sinners, by faith in the Son of God who loved us and gave himself for us.

These disruptions, which took Abraham from Ur and Haran, and which still take many from what have hitherto been familiar and trusted dependencies, are part of the cost of following God's call in a fallen world. Jesus, standing yet again in the place that only God could occupy in human hearts and priorities, made it clear that no-one who followed him could expect to escape the disruptive decisions and transferred loyalties that true discipleship involved: 'Do not suppose that I have come to bring peace ... a man's enemies will be the members of his own household. Anyone who loves his father or mother more than me is not worthy of me ... and anyone who does not take his cross and follow me is not worthy of me. Whoever finds his life will lose it, and whoever loses his life for my sake will find it.'[23]

b. A new context

The call of Abraham was not only to a new devotion but to a new context also. It was a call to a promised land: '*Go to the land I will show you*' (12:1). In the years to come 'the land' would be an essential part of Israel's conscious inheritance in God, uniting outer and inner, life and thought, work and worship, even this world and the world to come. For Israel 'the Land' had sacramental significance. Every tribe, clan and family's share in the land was important because it signified their place in the covenant God had made with Abraham for him and all his descendants after him.

[23] Matt. 10:34–39.

Hence, for example, the importance of the detailed records of Joshua 15 – 22 for the descendants of the tribes and clans mentioned there. The land itself had a significance far beyond its present state and condition. While it was considerably more productive then than now, the designation of it as 'a land flowing with milk and honey' was not without hyperbole since it was a land of stones and steep mountains also. Isaiah extends the concept into the final phase of salvation, when God creates new heavens and a new earth, and rejoices over a restored and complete people enjoying the heritage God had planned for them.[24] In this way, the Promised Land pointed forward to the restitution of all things, for God's salvation has, from the beginning, involved the whole creation, which he pronounced good and to which he has always been wholly committed.

What is of greatest importance in the New Testament revelation at this point is that it is by Jesus Christ, and his atoning work on the cross, that God was pleased to reconcile to himself a creation as well as a human race which was fallen and spoiled.[25] It will be at the second coming of this same Jesus that creation will be restored.[26] The writer of Hebrews says that Abraham looked forward 'to the city with foundations, whose architect and builder is God',[27] but the writer of Revelation makes the point clear that the place where that 'city' (really the people of God) will be built will be the earth which God made for humankind.[28]

4. Great nation . . . great name . . . great blessing (12:2–3)

> *'I will make you into a great nation*
> *and I will bless you;*
> *I will make your name great,*
> *and you will be a blessing.*
> [3]*I will bless those who bless you,*
> *and whoever curses you I will curse;*
> *and all peoples on earth*
> *will be blessed through you.'*

It is quite clear that the writer of Genesis means us to remember what he has written of the city and tower of Babel in the previous chapter while we are reading these verses in Genesis 12. At every point there are contrasts drawn here with that account. In Genesis 11:1–9 the men of Shinar, as Jacques Ellul points out, built their city and its tower not only to consolidate their power and increase their

---

[24] Is. 65:17–25.   [25] Col. 1:20.   [26] Rom. 8:19–22.   [27] Heb. 11:10.
[28] Rev. 21:1–4; cf. Ps. 115:16; Is. 11:9; 25:6–9; 65:17–18.

prestige but 'to exclude God from his creation', to establish their 'unity in separation from God'.[29] The cities of mankind have always done that. They 'mark the advance against God', as Ellul vividly puts it. The city, any city, not only Babel, 'is a tower in order to seize for herself what belonged to God, she is a wall to protect herself against God's interventions'.[30]

God alone, however, can define greatness and has it in his gift to bless. So he says here, not to a thrusting civilization, but to a man of his own choice, 'I will make you into a great nation' (12:2). Where the Babel-builders say 'Come let us build', God says to Abraham 'I will bless you.' Where the motivation of the builders is 'Come, let us build ourselves a city . . . so that we may make a name for ourselves', God says to a man who lives in tents 'I will make your name great.' This greatness however will not be turned inward ('a name for ourselves') but outward ('all peoples on earth'). The Babel project failed because God confused their language: 'By the confusion of tongues, by non communication, God keeps man from forming a truth valid for all men. Henceforth, man's truth will only be partial and contested.'[31]

The Abraham project, however, will not fail because God has kept alive the truth that sets men and women free from bondage and superstition, that sanctifies them for God, and brings them to the only point of unity that God has established in history – himself. In all the millennia of conquest and coexistence, of live-and-let-live, of interaction and estrangement, the world has never found the unity it needs and fears. Only in God will all peoples on earth find their universal centre and common life. And the place where that unity can be discovered and enjoyed is now in Christ Jesus: 'Remember that at that time you were separate from Christ, excluded from citizenship in Israel and foreigners to the covenants of the promise, without hope and without God in the world. But now in Christ Jesus you who once were far away have been brought near through the blood of Christ.'[32] The Pentecost of Acts 2 will give that new illustration and force, signalling the reversal of Babel: 'Now there were staying in Jerusalem God-fearing Jews from every nation under heaven. When they heard this sound, a crowd came together in bewilderment, because each one heard them speaking in his own language.'[33]

Thus early in redemptive-history are we led to the truth that God is a missionary God and that he has plans, not for one nation to know him, but for all nations to know him, not in their own image, not as their ancestral gods, but as the God who revealed himself

[29] Jacques Ellul, *The Meaning of the City* (Paternoster, 1997), p. 16.   [30] Ibid.
[31] Ibid., p. 19.   [32] Eph. 2:12–13.   [33] Acts 2:5–6.

definitively to Abraham, Moses and the prophets and who himself came into our world and for its peoples in Jesus Christ.[34]

5. Human pain and God's promise (15:1–5)

When God called Abraham from Haran he was already 75 years old and Sarah 65. Throughout their years of marriage they had carried within them a great pain. They were childless. Gordon Wenham writes: 'Childlessness was viewed as an unmitigated disaster in the ancient world. Without children there was no-one to carry on your family line or preserve the family inheritance, no-one to look after you in old age, no-one to carry out the funerary rites and secure your soul's rest in the world to come.'[35] Children, especially male children, were regarded at that time as adding considerable prestige to a man's life in a man's world. The absence of children, on the other hand, was considered more than a misfortune; it was regarded as a curse, a sign of disfavour by the gods or, as in later Israel, by the One true God. For Sarah especially there would have been the hurtful experience of cruel contempt in a society that had little place for a woman who could not bear children.

Personal grief and social stigma made childlessness a terrible thing then, and it is a hard thing now, in a very different society. Writers on childlessness today all speak of the levels of shock, denial, grief and anger which have to be worked through by childless couples.

> For many infertile couples, the question comes in the context of their religious beliefs: 'Is God angry with us? Is he punishing us by not letting us have children?' Infertility generates feelings of guilt and worthlessness. You may find yourself bargaining with God, promising anything in exchange for a child. This goes back at least as far as Biblical times. Hannah, longing for a child, prayed, 'O LORD Almighty, if you will only look upon your servant's misery and remember me, and not forget your servant but give her a son, then I will give him to the LORD for all the days of his life' (1 Sam. 1:11).[36]

We can feel Abraham's pain in Genesis 15, several years after his call and the first giving of the promise. Nothing had happened in those years, though Abraham had increased greatly in wealth, prestige and power. When God says to him in a vision: *'Do not be afraid, Abram. I am your shield, your very great reward'*, Abraham replies, 'O Sovereign LORD, what can you give me since I remain childless and

---

[34] Heb. 1:1; cf. John 8:12.   [35] Wenham (1987), p. 334.
[36] Beth Spring, *Childless* (Lion, 1989), p. 28.

the one who will inherit my estate is Eliezer of Damascus?' The suggestion is that this man, a member of his household, will become his heir by adoption. 'Clearly', writes Walter Brueggemann, 'the faith to which Abraham is called is not a peaceful, pious acceptance. It is a hard-fought and deeply-argued conviction'.[37]

So far the promise of offspring had been made and renewed three times (12:2, 7; 13:15–16) and one can imagine the excitement and expectations each of those occasions must have generated. But those times had come and gone without any change in Sarah. How much disappointment there must have been and how faith must have been tested. Even strong faith needs encouragement for it is capable of doubting itself even if not God. Here, God gave Abraham the renewed promise of a son, and more, in such a way that every time Abraham looked up at the stars he would remember this event and be reminded of the divine plan for him.

We have a God who is willing, not only to give us promises, but to repeat and renew them in different ways when they are made. How easy it is for any of us to forget, for impressions to fade, for an experience, even of God, to lose its force! We all need our reminders, our 'night sky'. Yet we have something more, something Abraham did not have. We have the Scriptures which are better than the stars. Abraham had a silent witness, we have a talking Book. We have a Bible studded with the promises of God: psalms that reflect our turmoil and radiate God's peace; histories that show us that the Lord reigns above the chaos of life and history; prophets who offer us not their own theories and ideas but 'the word of the Lord'; and above all a Son who says, 'You believe in God, believe also in me.'

6. The righteousness of faith (15:6)

Abraham's story, early in the Old Testament, highlights the Bible's consistent emphasis on faith in God as the key factor in any relationship with him. It is so because in faith a person goes out of themselves and relies on God: faith is a believing dependence on God; it is a trust that gives him the credit of his truthfulness, his reliability and his goodness; it is a person's commitment to God as his or her God and to his promises as the sure foundation of his or her life. Notice that here and everywhere it is a reasoned response to a recognized revelation. It is not a vague hope or a blind trust. As ever, 'faith comes from hearing the message'.[38] It is the response of the person to God's call based on God's known character. It is the opposite of that dependence on self that characterizes fallen, rebellious human nature. It is itself the gift of God and the sign of grace,

---

[37] Brueggemann (1982), p. 141.   [38] Rom. 10:17.

the undeserved favour of God in active and powerful operation on the heart.[39]

In Genesis 15:6 we have a statement that would be, for the apostle Paul, the central statement of Abraham's life of faith and the key truth that distinguishes a religion of faith from a religion of works: *Abram believed the* LORD, *and he credited* (reckoned) *it to him as righteousness.* Paul, in Romans 4 and Galatians 3, uses this passage and this verse against Jewish legalists who wanted Gentile believers to be circumcised as a means to enter into a right relationship with God and who wanted them to keep the law of Moses as a condition of maintaining a right relationship with God. For Paul this was a denial of the sufficiency and even the character of the work of Christ and of the way of faith. He points out that Abraham was credited with righteousness simply on account of his faith, before his circumcision spoken of in Genesis 17 and no less than 400 years before the giving of the law to Moses on which Paul's Judaizing opponents based so much. God's way of salvation has always been by faith, not by works, even by works once commanded under the law. It has been pointed out more than once that Paul's argument here hinges on the fact that the first Jew was a Gentile! Paul, however, also looks *beneath* the relationship with God that Abraham's faith received, to the foundation on which that relationship rested. It rested on the very righteousness of God, given as a gift, to be received by faith 'from first to last',[40] 'a righteousness from God, not from ourselves, and which comes, not from law-keeping, but through faith in Jesus Christ to all who believe'.[41] 'The words "it was credited to him" were written not for him alone, but also for us, to whom God will credit righteousness – for us who believe in him who raised Jesus our Lord from the dead. He was delivered over to death for our sins and was raised to life for our justification.'[42] The relationship between God and the sinner cannot rest on anything meritorious in the sinner. It is undeserved favour.

The Genesis text therefore cannot mean that God simply lowered the standard and accepted Abraham's faith *in lieu* of righteousness as either its equivalent or its acceptable substitute. Abraham believed God and God credited to him a righteousness which was not his or his faith's but God's: God's provision, God's imputation, God's gift, God's own righteousness. God credited to Abraham a righteousness that was not his and he could do so only because of the future work of Christ. Paul knew that the foundation of every relationship with God was the righteousness of Christ who became for us all 'wisdom from God – that is, our righteousness, holiness and

---

[39] Cf. Is. 28:16; 30:15; Hab. 2:4. [40] Rom. 1:17. [41] Rom. 3:21–22.
[42] Rom. 4:23–25.

redemption'.[43] His concern therefore was to gain Christ and to be found in him, 'not having a righteousness of my own that comes from the law, but that which is through faith in Christ – the righteousness that comes from God and is by faith'.[44] On this basis Jewish and Gentile believers enter the kingdom of God on the same footing, as equals; and Abraham, the once-idolator from Ur of the Chaldees, is seen as the father of all who believe, Gentile as well as Jew.[45]

7. The God who covenants (15:7–18)

In chapter 15 we have what is surely one of the strangest and most dramatic experiences in Abraham's long life. God responds to Abraham's cry, 'O Sovereign LORD, how can I know that I shall gain possession of it?' by directing him to take a heifer, a goat and a ram, cut them in two, and, in accordance with the customs of the time, to arrange the halves opposite each other on the ground. A dove and a young pigeon are also added but kept whole. As the sun was setting, Abram fell into a deep sleep, and a thick and dreadful darkness came over him (15:12). Gordon Wenham writes, 'The "deep sleep", "fear", and "darkness" all suggest awe-inspiring divine activity (cf. Gen. 2:21; Isa. 29:10; Ex. 10:21, 22; 14:20; 15:16; 23:27; Deut. 4:11; Josh. 2:9) and are closely associated with the exodus and conquest, appropriately introducing the prophecy in the next verses.'[46]

God first speaks and then manifests his presence visibly. This is called a 'theophany', a manifestation or appearance of God in some form. In 15:17 God assumes the form of 'a smoking brazier and a blazing torch'. The brazier would have been a large earthenware pot filled with smoking charcoal. Smoke and fire are often symbolic of the presence of God.[47] God, in this form, walks between the severed bodies of the sacrificial animals in a recognized covenant ritual. It may be shocking that God should symbolically take upon himself the threat, the curse even, suggested by walking between the severed corpses of the animals (as a man might say with a gesture across the throat, 'The gods/The Lord do so to me if I betray this agreement'),[48] and some discount this element. But in this way God accommodates himself to the customs of the time in order to show Abraham his complete seriousness in fulfilling his promises.[49] Here again, as with Noah, God involves himself unilaterally in an obligation: no undertaking to make it valid is exacted from Abram, and God binds himself with an oath.[50] All this is not to suggest that no response of acceptance and obedience is expected, only that they are not conditions in the usual sense found in covenantal arrangements

---

[43] 1 Cor. 1:30. [44] Phil. 3:9. [45] Rom. 4:16–17; Gal. 3:8–9, 29.
[46] Wenham (1987), pp. 331–332. [47] E.g. Exod. 13:21; 19:18; 20:18.
[48] Cf. Jer. 34:18. [49] Cf. Gen. 22:6; 26:3. [50] Cf. Heb. 6:13.

in the ancient Near East. 'Acceptance and obedience are responses within the divine covenant, not elements in a *quid pro quo* bargain.'[51]

In spite of the unforgettable nature and high drama of this incident, several years pass and Sarah, discouraged to the point of unbelief, persuades her husband to take her personal slave, the Egyptian Hagar, as a second wife to act as a surrogate parent. This was a widely known and accepted way forward for childless couples, but it was not God's way for Abraham and Sarah, and as a result of this piece of manipulation everyone involved suffered – including the child, Ishmael, whose desert descendants were the centuries-long enemies of Israel.

8. The demands of the covenant (17:1–9)

When Abram was ninety-nine years old, the LORD appeared to him and said, 'I am God Almighty; walk before me and be blameless. ²I will confirm my covenant between me and you and will greatly increase your numbers.'

³Abram fell face down, and God said to him, ⁴'As for me, this is my covenant with you: You will be the father of many nations. ⁵No longer will you be called Abram; your name will be Abraham, for I have made you a father of many nations. ⁶I will make you very fruitful; I will make nations of you, and kings will come from you. ⁷I will establish my covenant as an everlasting covenant between me and you and your descendants after you for the generations to come, to be your God and the God of your descendants after you.

⁸The whole land of Canaan, where you are now an alien, I will give as an everlasting possession to you and your descendants after you; and I will be their God.'

⁹Then God said to Abraham, 'As for you, you must keep my covenant, you and your descendants after you for the generations to come.'

Here God reminds Abraham of his accountability and the necessity of walking in a manner suitable to the relationship which has been established between God and him and which has been confirmed in covenantal form. The personal tone, 'Walk before me and be blameless', is important for, as William Dumbrell notes: 'The covenant is not to be identified with the promises or demands bound up with it. Covenant refers to the relationship from which promises and demands will flow.'[52] These demands are not strictly the condition of the covenant. God does not say to Abraham 'I will if you will', but 'I will, therefore you must.' Obedience to the covenant is the

---

[51] Alec Motyer in correspondence.　　[52] Dumbrell, p. 77.

condition of enjoying its blessings; disobedience brings chastisement. But through all, the covenant holds because it rests on God's purposes and faithfulness, not on man's deservedness.

The primary demand of the covenant is for loyalty to the gracious relationship with God which it confirms. This loyalty is called 'faithfulness'. As God is faithful to his covenant undertakings, so he calls for exclusive worship and that righteousness which is consistent with the character of God, which walks in his ways, which 'does justly, loves mercy and walks humbly' with God the covenant Partner.[53]

Notice how the covenant made with Abraham is considered to have been made with his descendants also:

> [7]'*I will establish my covenant as an everlasting covenant between me and you and your descendants after you for the generations to come, to be your God and the God of your descendants after you ...* [9]*As for you, you must keep my covenant, you and your descendants after you for the generations to come.*'

Israel is 'a people formed by God's word to hear his promises and do his purposes'.[54]

9. The sign of the covenant (17:10–14)

In Genesis 17 we also have the sign of the covenant between God and Abraham and his descendants. That sign was to be the circumcision of all males born into or bought into Abraham's household. Circumcision was an ancient rite among many peoples, probably marking the entrance into manhood. Here, however, it is invested with new religious meaning. It is taken up and used as an outward sign in the flesh of the Abrahamic covenant, marking one as a member of the covenant community. It is, as Leslie Allen notes, 'A God-given reminder and confession of the distinctive status of recipients of the covenant.'[55] 'The permanent marking of the body', writes Wenham, 'reflects the eternity of the covenant between God and Israel (Gen. 17:7, 13, 19)'[56] and was a constant reminder of the obligations of the covenantal relationship. It was, says Dumbrell, 'a sign of covenant separation and thus consecration'.[57] Circumcision signifies the donation of the promises first and foremost, hence Genesis 17:1–8 precedes verses 9–14 which imply the appropriation of the covenant. Grace is always prior to obedience; obedience is the grateful response to grace. However, the objective importance of

---

[53] Mic. 6:8.   [54] Brueggemann (1982), p. 117.
[55] Leslie Allen, 'Circumcision', *NIDOTTE*, vol. 4, p. 474.
[56] Wenham (1994), p. 24.   [57] Dumbrell, p. 74.

circumcision was not allowed to obscure the fact that the physical mark was, in and of itself, not enough. Eugene Carpenter writes:

> Circumcision appealed to Israel to walk before the Lord. It did not create a change in persons; therein lay its weakness. Hence, God's appeal to Israel was to 'circumcise (*mwl*) [the foreskin of] your hearts,' i.e. change your inner heart and attitude and serve me (Deut. 10:16). This appeal was ineffective; hence God would circumcise their hearts (Deut. 30:6). Jeremiah picks up the deuteronomic concern for circumcision of the heart ... He instructs Israel to be circumcised to the Lord, removing the foreskin of their heart (Jer. 4:4). God will punish everyone circumcised in his foreskin (flesh) only.[58]

10. El Shaddai

In Genesis 17 God reveals himself by means of a new name, *El Shaddai*: 'I am God Almighty' (17:1). Whatever the etymology of this may be, it is the way the term is used that is most important for us. William Dumbrell notes helpfully:

> The use of this name in the patriarchal narratives from this point on is associated with *the resolution of extreme difficulties* between the content of covenantal promises and the reality of the situation in which the patriarchs found themselves at the time. This note of *powerful intervention* which the name seems to imply is well brought out by the customary Greek Old Testament translation of 'God Almighty'.[59]

It will be illustrated unforgettably in the 'impossible' birth of Isaac (18:14). We read in 18:1–2, *The LORD appeared to Abraham near the great trees of Mamre while he was sitting at the entrance to his tent in the heat of the day. Abraham looked up and saw three men standing nearby.* Commentators are divided on whether this is another theophany, in which God assumes human form and comes with two angelic beings similarly disguised, or whether all three are angels representing God. (It should certainly not be seen as a manifestation of the Trinity!) The visitors tell Abraham plainly that the appointed time has come. Sarah, now 89, has heard it all before (several times!) and laughs incredulously at first, but when they show an uncanny knowledge of her (hidden) presence, her thoughts and her new name (no longer Sarai but Sarah), she too, according to the writer of Hebrews, believes. *Then the LORD said to Abraham,*

---

[58] Eugene Carpenter, '*mwl*', *NIDOTTE*, vol. 2, p. 869.   [59] Dumbrell, p. 73.

'Why did Sarah laugh and say, "Will I really have a child, now that I am old?" Is anything too hard for the LORD? I will return to you at the appointed time next year and Sarah will have a son' " (18:13–14).

One year later, when Abraham was 100 and Sarah 90, the impossible happens. We read in 21:2, 'Sarah became pregnant and bore a son to Abraham in his old age, at the very time God had promised him. Abraham gave the name Isaac to the son Sarah bore him.' They named the son 'Isaac', which means 'he laughs', perhaps because in chapter 17 Abraham had laughed when God had yet again promised him a son (at 99!) and in chapter 18 Sarah had laughed when the three visitors confirmed the time. Now Sarah says, 'God has brought me laughter, and everyone who hears about this will laugh with me' (21:6). No-one would have laughed 'at her' because quite apart from natural feelings they would have been awed by the miracle and convinced of her and Abraham's great favour with God.

11. Trusting the promise-maker

The message that runs through the Abraham narrative is that God's promises can be trusted because God himself can be trusted. He is the God of faithfulness and truth. 'Abraham', says the writer of Hebrews, 'considered God faithful who had made the promise',[60] and so must we. Abraham trusted God through long years of delay; and then after years of rejoicing in the fulfilment of those promises in Isaac, he was again tested; this time to sacrifice the child of the promise and with him all visible assurance about the future (22:2–3). The victory of faith which Abraham won on that day is reflected in God's response which carries with it a note of strong excitement:

> The angel of the LORD called to Abraham from heaven a second time and said, 'I swear by myself, declares the LORD, that because you have done this and have not withheld your son, your only son, I will surely bless you and make your descendants as numerous as the stars in the sky and as the sand on the seashore. Your descendants will take possession of the cities of their enemies, and through your offspring all nations on earth will be blessed, because you have obeyed me' (22:15–18).

The fact that God had sworn on oath to do this for Abraham and his descendants was determinative for Israel's future faith and sense of destiny. Walter Brueggemann writes:

---

[60] Heb. 11:11.

Israel's testimony to Yahweh as a promise-maker presents Yahweh as both powerful and reliable enough to turn life in the world, for Israel and for all peoples, beyond the present circumstance to new life-giving possibility. Yahweh's promises keep the world open toward well-being, even in the face of deathly circumstance . . . The Book of Genesis understands the urgency of transmitting the solemn oath of Yahweh to the next generation of Israel, for it is this oath that gives Israel power to survive and prosper in demanding and debilitating circumstances.[61]

Brueggemann points out that on a few occasions[62] the fulfilment of the promises is recorded but that, more characteristically, 'Israel waits and hopes – in joy, in perplexity, in eager longing, but also in wonderment and near-despair, because most often the promises are not yet kept, and Yahweh's oath is held in abeyance. This abeyance marks Israel as a people of hope, waiting in expectation.'[63]

It is a lesson that has to be learned in the life of faith, that many of God's cheques are post-dated. The promise is given but we cannot read the time of their fulfilment. Many of the Old Testament saints had to wait long years before they received what was promised. Joseph waited twenty years for his prophetic dream to be fulfilled; Moses waited forty years before he could even begin the work he had set his heart on; David was king-in-waiting, anointed by Samuel, years before he succeeded Saul. And Abraham, promised a child when he was no longer young, had to wait twenty-five years from the time he was first promised a son with Sarah.

We so often want promise and fulfilment to come with very little space between. We live in a society where credit cards 'take the waiting out of wanting'. We pray – and expect the answer by next week; we claim a promise – but everything continues the same and we get discouraged. At such times we are to keep our eyes upon the Promise-Maker. It has always been the condition of victory – however long it takes.

a. Living in the promises of God

Abraham is the supreme example of faith in the entire Old Testament history. He is called 'the friend of God' by both Isaiah in the Old Testament and James in the New.[64] The apostle Paul calls him 'the father of us all', that is, all who believe.[65] If Abraham is the father of all who believe, including us, then as believers we too have begun the life of faith which he demonstrated. Consequently, his experience is our instruction, his example is our inspiration, and his

---

[61] Brueggemann (1997), pp. 164, 168.   [62] E.g. Josh. 21:42–45.
[63] Brueggemann (1997), p. 169.   [64] Is. 41:8; Jas. 2:23.   [65] Rom. 4:16–17.

goal – the city of God[66] – is our goal. To an extent we ourselves are an ongoing part of his story: the story that began in Genesis 12:1–3.

The writer to the Hebrews, looking back over Israel's history and the heroes of faith, concludes: 'These were all commended for their faith, yet none of them received what had been promised. God had planned something better for us so that only together with us would they be made perfect.'[67] Yet we too await the final fulfilment of all that has been promised. We have the revelation of Christ and the beginning of his kingdom but we do not yet have all that he will bring with him at his Coming. For the patriarchs and their descendants, 'Living in terms of the promises of God without experiencing the eschatological reward became characteristic of faith itself.'[68] They lived between promise and fulfilment in one dispensation and so do we in another. Walter Brueggemann captures the victory of faith in laying hold of the promises of God:

> *Promise* is God's mode of presence in these narratives. The promise is God's power and will to create a new future sharply discontinuous with the past and the present. The promise is God's resolve to form a new community wrought only by miracle and reliant only on God's faithfulness. *Faith* as response is the capacity to embrace that announced future with such passion that the present can be relinquished for the sake of the future.[69]

That is still the position and the victory of faith. If it has the promises of God, it has the certainty of their fulfilment.

b. Avoiding unnecessary anxiety

The nineteenth-century Baptist preacher and evangelist C. H. Spurgeon used to say, 'If God had meant to run back from any promise, he would surely have run back from the promise to give his only begotten Son; but having fulfilled that, what promise is there that he will ever break?'[70] It is precisely on the fact of that supreme giving that every other giving is predicted and guaranteed.[71] Calvary – its cost and its triumph – is the measure of the divine reliability, the strength of the promises and the depth of the love on which we build our lives and journey to God's promised future.

I once read the story of a man who crossed the Mississippi on foot when it was frozen over. Half way across he lost his nerve and began to panic. He finished the crossing crawling on his stomach, soaked and chilled. Imagine his feelings when, having got to his feet on the

---

[66] Heb. 11:10. [67] Heb. 11:39–40. [68] Lane, vol. 2, p. 392.
[69] Brueggemann (1982), p. 106.
[70] C. H. Spurgeon, *The Metropolitan Tabernacle Pulpit* (1990), vol. 46, p. 19.
[71] Rom. 8:31–32.

other side, he saw another man, sitting on a large sled loaded with pig-iron, wave cheerily to him as he crossed right over the river in complete safety!

It will be like that for some Christians travelling through life with 'only' the word of the Lord Jesus Christ to rely on: some anxious, fearful and hardly daring to think that God can cope with their failures, doubts and inadequacies; others driving on with confidence and joy, trusting the weight of their whole lives on the God who cannot lie. Like the man crawling on ice feet thick, so many believers are inching towards survival when they could be striding towards victory; creeping along on our own pilgrim's progress when we could be moving in confidence and power through our society and generation, telling others what God has done and what God can do for them. When we come to stand before God surely the thing we will most regret is that we didn't take him at his word more fully. His promises are not thin ice.

Trust him in good times and bad; when you have all you could wish for *and* when you are forced to say, 'You have given me no children ... no job ... no partner in life ... no relief from weakness or pain ... no converts in my family, among my children.' He will love you and help you. He may not give you all you want, not even what you want most in the world next to God. But there is one thing he will give you: he will give you himself, now, in the tears and also one day in glory, where every tear will be wiped away, where there will be 'no more death or mourning or crying or pain',[72] only life with God in unimaginable glory and everlasting joy.

[72] Rev. 21:4.

Exodus 3; 7 – 12; 15
7. The God who rescues a people

1. Our decisions and God's delays (3:1–3)

When God met Moses it was at an altogether unexpected time and in an altogether unexpected way. First of all God was forty years late. A British prime minister, Harold Wilson, once said that a week was a long time in politics. Certainly when a cabinet minister leaves office after an election or a scandal, the journey from being powerful and popular to being powerless and forgotten is often very short and swift. I doubt if politics in ancient Egypt was any more sentimental.

There had been a time when Moses was 'somebody'. He was raised by one of the daughters of the reigning pharaoh. He was educated in the most sophisticated civilization of the day. He was a 'friend in high places' for the Hebrews, to whom he belonged by birth, and, it would appear, by sympathy too. No doubt he had connections, talents and a political future: all the opportunities to do good on a wide scale and in particular to ameliorate the conditions under which the Hebrews suffered, to argue their case, to relieve their distress. However, God does nothing of what Moses expects, in order that he might do something far beyond expectations; but he does so in his own way and according to his own timetable.

Moses had all the advantages and he determined to use them to champion the cause of his people. However, he ended up a murderer on the run. When God's work is not done in God's way it is likely to end in confusion and failure. For Moses the price of doing it his way was high.

Forty years later Moses was nothing and nobody; at least not where it mattered. Egypt had forgotten him, even the Israelites had forgotten him. He was yesterday's news, yesterday's hope, a long-forgotten fugitive, living in the scrub land of the wilderness, keeping sheep; all advantages gone, all connections dead. But although he did not know it, Moses was now on the verge of his life's work.

We should apply this early lesson to ourselves. Perhaps we wanted this and we worked for that and we had plans for other people, and they were good goals and plans. Perhaps they were even plans for special and much-needed Christian service in one field or other. Then illness came, or a bad decision, or a set of events beyond our control. Life has many disappointments. But God is not one of them! Our greatest work and our greatest victory in life is to place our hearts and lives into the hands of God with each aspiration and achievement, and with each failure and disappointment also. We may yet find that he does with us and through us more than we can ever ask or imagine, even if they are different from what we ask or imagine.

Moses not only had the cargo of worldly connections which had to be left behind in Egypt, he also carried around with him the fat of pride and self-reliance which had to be sweated off in the deserts and disappointments of the Midian years. We too may be most useful to God when we feel our usefulness to him and to anyone is at an end. When we come to the end of ourselves we step on to the endless and limitless plan of God – God the infinite, eternal, all-sufficient 'I am'.

2. When God meets a man (3:4–6)

The story of the liberation from Egypt really begins at the lowest point for both Moses and Egypt. Then, on a day like any other, and while shepherding his father-in-law's sheep, Moses leads the flock on to the mountain of Horeb, also called Sinai. There God spoke to him out of the bush that burned with strange fire and a new chapter of history was begun.

'Do not come any closer,' God said. 'Take off your sandals, for the place where you are standing is holy ground.' ⁶Then he said, 'I am the God of your father, the God of Abraham, the God of Isaac and the God of Jacob.' At this, Moses hid his face, because he was afraid to look at God.

Confronted by the God of Abraham, Isaac and Jacob, he is reminded that in the presence of the Holy One there is danger as well as glory. When God tells Moses that the ground is holy he means that it is so because he himself is there: it is really he who is holy and his presence makes that part of the desert a holy place. Later we shall find that many things in the tabernacle will become holy by association with God.

The Hebrew word 'holy' (*qāḏôš*) probably comes from a root which means 'cut', and it literally means 'cut off', 'separated', 'set apart', 'different'. God is 'holy' because he is 'set apart' from everything else in his infinite and eternal being. Thus the first use of the term was simply to describe the Godness of God, his distance from all that is created and dependent. But the term soon acquired moral dimensions since God is infinitely removed from corruption as well as creatureliness. Thus holiness came to stress the purity and uncompromising righteousness of God. His holiness, then, has an ontological and essential character (God is holy in his being and essence) and the infinitude of his being awes the angels nearest to his throne.[1] His holiness also has a moral character that brings sinners to their knees.[2]

Love called Moses by his name but holiness told him to be careful: 'Do not come any closer,' God said. 'Take off your sandals, for the place where you are standing is holy ground' (3:5). This is a lesson that holds good throughout Scripture.[3] We must never lose our sense of awe before the holy majesty of God. We can be intimate with him but never casual. Even his love must not be taken for granted: it led to Calvary where in our place Another cried out in the awful darkness of judgment.

3. The God who answers prayer (3:7–10)

[7]*The LORD said, 'I have indeed seen the misery of my people in Egypt. I have heard them crying out because of their slave drivers, and I am concerned about their suffering.* [8]*So I have come down to rescue them from the hand of the Egyptians and to bring them up out of that land into a good and spacious land, a land flowing with milk and honey . . .* [10]*So now, go. I am sending you to Pharaoh to bring my people the Israelites out of Egypt.*

It must have seemed to many Israelites amid their ever-increasing hardships as slaves in Egypt that God had abandoned them, that he was deaf to their prayers. Gradually, true religion declined among them[4] and the God of Abraham no longer seemed the sovereign God that their illustrious forebear had worshipped and trusted. But God is still the same, undiminished and unchanged by the centuries. And this is still his people. He has heard their crying out and he is 'coming down to rescue them' at last. George Knight observes:

> This naive anthropomorphic language is put into the mouth of God. Yet it reveals what the modern Jewish scholar Abraham Heschel has called 'the pathos of God'. 'I have heard their cry', virtually 'their scream'. The vast gap between man and God is crossable by God, though not in the reverse direction, cf. Gen.

---

[1] Is. 6:2–3.   [2] Is. 6:5.   [3] Cf. Rev. 1:17.   [4] Josh. 24:14; cf. Ezek. 20:7; 23:8.

3:24 . . . God had then come down into the chaos of Egypt, out of the realm of the holy, in order to rescue his people from suffering and to bring them up into a wholly new situation. The descent of other gods in the Near East was for their own glory. This descent and then ascent, however, of which Moses now learns, is being made in order to rescue a bunch of slaves![5]

This national memory of God as the One who heard the cries of his people in Egypt and delivered them becomes the paradigm for the prayers of the oppressed in later times[6] and Yahweh becomes known as the one who hears the cry even of the individual.[7] This God is the God who hears prayers: 'O you who hear prayer, / to you all men will come',[8] and this is movingly expressed by Solomon in his prayer at the dedication of the temple in Jerusalem.[9]

4. The God who names himself (3:11–15)

Moses is told that the time has come for his people's liberation from Egypt and that he is to lead them out of Egypt to Canaan, the land God gave to Abraham: *'So now, go. I am sending you to Pharaoh to bring my people the Israelites out of Egypt'* (3:10). Moses knows that the leaders of the tribes will demand his credentials as a spiritual leader: *Moses said to God, 'Suppose. . . they ask me, "What is his name?" Then what shall I tell them?'* (3:13). This would be their way of asking Moses the identity of the divine being who had sent him. 'The name of the Lord' stands for the nature of the Lord. The question 'What is his name?' is intended to identify the character and essence and self-revelation of the One who had spoken to Moses. Allen Ross explains that 'name'

> . . . can also signify the nature or attributes of the person named. This is especially true with regard to God. In Exod. 34:5–7 the Lord's proclamation of 'the name of the Lord' is followed by a listing of divine attributes . . . Likewise, the 'naming' of the Wonder King, the Messiah, in Isa. 9:6 is more of a description of his nature, than throne names or titles to be used: 'And his name shall be called [NIV: And he will be called] Wonderful Counsellor, Mighty God, Everlasting Father, Prince of Peace.' Thus to pray 'in the name of the Lord' could mean to pray with confidence in the nature and ability of God.

[5] Knight, p. 20.   [6] 1 Kgs. 8:33–34, 44–53; cf. Pss. 80; 107; 136.
[7] E.g. Pss. 5:2; 18:6; 34:15; 40:1; 106:44–45; 116:1–2.   [8] Ps. 65:2.
[9] 1 Kgs. 8:27–30, 32, 34, 36, 39, 41–43, 45, 49.

Ross concludes, 'If the power of a name is directly related to the power of the one named, then the name of the Lord is understandably the predominant force in the Old Testament. The name of the Lord is Yahweh, in all that fullness of divine power, holiness, wrath, and grace that he revealed in his nature.'[10]

In what follows, Moses is given a further revelation of God in words and a demonstration of his power in supernatural signs.

a. 'I am who I am'

To mark this new stage of Israel's history, God gives new significance to an old name: *Yahweh*. This consists of a new and awesome disclosure of his eternal being and commitment to his people. Out of the strange fire of the burning bush God identified himself in the mysterious and yet profoundly impressive announcement, '*I AM WHO I AM*', adding, '*This is what you are to say to the Israelites: "I AM has sent me to you"* ' (3:14).

Biblical scholars have long debated the precise meaning and even translation of this. In the Hebrew language the various forms of the verb are more flexible than their English counterparts. In Exodus 3:14 the form is imperfect and the possibilities range from 'I used to be' to 'I continuously (or characteristically) am' to 'I will be'. In the case of the Hebrew verb 'to be', the simple form and the causative form are identical, so that here it could equally well mean 'I cause to be', so that we could translate it, 'I bring to pass what I bring to pass.' Furthermore, the Hebrew verb 'to be' expresses active presence rather than mere existence, so that we have here not a mere philosophical statement about the being of God but an announcement that he is the *active* God. It is significant that in Exodus 3:14–17, and even more in 6:6–7, the divine Name ('I am Yahweh') is linked with the exodus actions of God.

Brevard Childs makes the point that what is being said to Moses in 3:14–15 is that Yahweh's nature will be known from his future acts, particularly from the now imminent liberation from slavery in Egypt,[11] but we must note that the word is before the act and that this is essential if the act is to be understood. As Alec Motyer has remarked: 'Without verbal revelation of meaning the Exodus is a national migration arising fortuitously out of a coincidence of natural disasters.'[12] In a similar way the Christ-event of the Gospels will need the apostolic teaching to reveal its true and full meaning or the story of Christ will be reduced to the tragically commonplace in a world where babies are born in harsh conditions and the innocent die with the guilty.

[10] Allen Ross, '*šēm*', *NIDOTTE*, vol. 4, pp. 148–150.

[11] B. S. Childs, *Exodus* (SCM Press, 1974), p. 76; quoted in Dumbrell, p. 84.

[12] Alec Motyer in correspondence.

The form of the verb 'to be' in 'I AM WHO I AM' (3:14) could well be future, giving us 'I will be who I will be' or, as we could render it, 'I will be who I am' or 'I am who I will be'. Terence Fretheim thinks this last suggestion 'may well be the best option'. He adds:

> The force of the name is not simply that God is or that God is present, but that God will be faithfully God for them in the history that is to follow (see verses 16–17). The use of the same verbal form in 3:12 and 4:12, 15 (cf. 6:7; 29:45) also suggests this. God will be God with and for this people at all times and places; the formula suggests a divine faithfulness to self. Israel need not be concerned about divine arbitrariness or capriciousness. God can be counted on to be who God is.[13]

We may compare the grammatical form of 'I am what I am' with Exodus 33:19: 'I will be gracious to whom I will be gracious.' The latter plainly states Yahweh's unfettered freedom, his sovereignty, in bestowing grace and choosing the objects of his favour, and the former reveals his unfettered freedom, his sovereignty, in determining how he will reveal himself. The statement 'I AM WHO I AM' suggests that the speaker is conditioned by nothing outside himself. He is the self-conditioned God; eternal in his being and unbounded in his freedom and resources. Yahweh is the self-conditioned Deity who can be to his people all that he chooses to be and all that they need him to be. In this covenant context his 'I AM WHO I AM' implies 'All that I am I will be for you.'

However puzzling and mysterious the statement may be, the two really important things it reveals about God to the Israelites are that his resources are limitless and his action is continuous. He is the 'God of all grace'; the same God who blessed Abraham, Isaac and Jacob (3:6) will be with Moses (3:12) and the people of Israel (3:15–17). He is the self-existent, self-sufficient, infinite-personal, covenant-keeping God. In his unfathomable and unlimited being, God was putting himself at the disposal of his beloved people: he who was all things in himself would be all things to them.

Here is the 'surpassing joy' of knowing this God as our God and of knowing that our salvation is decided, determined and conditioned not by what we are but by what he is. How terrible it would be if God said to us not 'I will be to you all that I am' but 'I will be to you all that you are to me. I will match your faith, your piety, your resources out of my own, level for level, quality for quality, hour for hour!' If he does not surpass us then he does not save us. If we are not saved by a love as great as himself we cannot be saved by a love as great as our own selves. But grace calls me to leave the little island of my own piety and to trek inland on the great continent of God's faithfulness and to answer his 'I AM' with my own joyful and worshipful 'Yes, Lord, you are.'

b. ' "Yahweh" – this is my name'

The actual name *Yahweh*, given in verse 15 and translated here and throughout the Old Testament as 'the LORD', gathers up and runs together some of the sounds of the Hebrew phrase 'I AM WHO I AM'. 'Yahweh' was a kind of shorthand for 'I AM WHO I AM.' It is a verbal component of the verb 'to be', probably a form of the third person singular. Hereafter, every time an Israelite said, heard or read this name of God, he or she would remember both the greatness and the grace of God and the covenant relationship which it enshrined.

So 'Yahweh' becomes the personal name of Israel's God and is found about 6,800 times in the Hebrew Old Testament books. The form in which 'Yahweh' appears there, however, is as four Hebrew consonants, transliterated as YHWH, and the pronunciation 'Yahweh' is 'only an educated guess, constructed largely from early Christian references'.[14] It is by this name that Israel is to link past, present and future in the God who will be faithful to his promises: *The LORD [Yahweh], the God of your fathers – the God of Abraham, the God of Isaac and the God of Jacob . . . This is my name for ever, the name by which I am to be remembered from generation to generation'* (3:15).

The use of 'The LORD' – often capitalized – as a translation of 'Yahweh' in most of our English Bibles is in some ways unfortunate. It obscures the fact that Yahweh is a name, not a title. It seems to originate from the Septuagint translators, Jewish scholars who translated their Hebrew Scriptures into Greek, and who wrote the Greek word *kyrios* (Lord) rather than transliterate the Hebrew, YHWH. In the intertestamental period in synagogues it became the practice to read the Hebrew word *ᵃdōnāy* (my Lord) for 'Yahweh' out of reverence for the sacred name itself, and in copies of the Hebrew Scriptures the vowels of *ᵃdōnāy* were added to the consonants of Yahweh to ensure this. The old translation, *Jehovah*, is entirely artificial, being the consonants YHWH plus the vocalization of *ᵃdōnāy*.

5. God's 'strong hand' and 'outstretched arm' (7 – 12)

The 'redemption' of Israel from slavery in Egypt and their (eventual) settlement in the Promised Land is the great and central event of Old

[14] Ibid.

Testament history, the paradigm of God's salvation and the demonstration of his being, power, justice and faithfulness. It has its own place in the national memory and is rehearsed by psalmist and prophet both in praise of God and in rebuke of an unfaithful people. Indeed, the story of the plagues of Egypt, the 'Red Sea' deliverance and the wilderness journey to Canaan has become widely known wherever the biblical faith has taken root.

However, even among conservative biblical theologians and commentators there have been differences in the precise understanding of what was involved at various times in the historical event. Some, for instance, see all the plagues as wholly supernatural and so inexplicable on a natural level,[15] while others think that they are in most cases natural phenomena and that the miracles lie in their timing and intensity without the need for a wholly supernatural work.[16]

The Bible does not tend to draw the sharp distinction we often make between the natural and the supernatural precisely because God is the God of both. There is an important lesson here. The division of reality into the 'natural' and the 'supernatural' can easily end up with 'God' being placed in the realm of the 'supernatural' with spirits, demons and gods and divorced from the natural world in which we live our everyday lives. There is, of course, a supernatural realm, no less real than this one, but God is not less here than there and not more sovereign there than here, even if his glory is uniquely manifested in heaven.

a. The mockery of Pharaoh and the gods

The plagues of Egypt, described in Exodus 7 – 12, the 'blows' of God which rained down on the back of a proud and cruel regime, appear to be a mixture of the natural and the supernatural and we can see that mixture right through the narrative from the turning of the Nile to blood to the final destruction of Pharaoh's army in the sea of reeds. Three words occur in these chapters and beyond: 'miracles', 'signs' and 'wonders'. The word 'signs' occurs 79 times in the Old Testament, 25 of those occurrences referring to the plagues of Egypt. The point about something being a sign is that it points beyond itself to something greater. In Exodus, as in John's gospel which speaks regularly of Jesus' miracles as 'signs', we must not stop at the sign any more than we should stumble at it. 'The question', as one writer puts it, 'is not "How on earth did he do that?" Rather it is "What can I see of the power and grace of God in this? How must I react? What does he want of me?" '[17]

---

[15] E.g. Durham, pp. 97, 128.   [16] E.g. Cole, pp. 90–91, 93, 98.   [17] Bridge, p. 61.

In this whole series of events Yahweh made a mockery of the 'gods' and religion of Egypt[18] and showed a proud nation that he alone was God: *'And the Egyptians will know that I am the* LORD *when I stretch out my hand against Egypt and bring the Israelites out of it.'*[19] Egyptian religion acknowledged some 80 gods at this time, many of which had their reputation affected in some way by the plagues, though 'the argument for an Egyptian deity or sacred institution lurking behind each plague is not compelling'.[20] In the midst of 'their' territory he paralysed their supposed efficacy and protected his own people. More particularly the plagues showed Yahweh's power over Pharaoh who was regarded as the god of the Egyptian state and was responsible for maintaining cosmic order on earth.[21] James Hoffmeier writes further:

> The Hebrew expressions 'strong hand' and 'outstretched arm' in the Exodus narratives, it has been suggested, were deliberately employed for polemical purposes against the Egyptian concept of Pharaoh's powerful all-conquering arm, a concept that was ubiquitous in Egyptian art and literature ... This proposal is supported by language in the Pentateuch that describes Yahweh's arm defeating that of Pharaoh, thus demonstrating the superiority of the God of the Hebrews over Pharaoh (cf. Ex. 15:6, 12, 16; Deut. 9:29; 26:8).[22]

This is not the place to analyse the plagues themselves, but in them Yahweh overrules the gods of Egypt, who are shown to be helpless, even in the areas of their supposed 'specialities'. The Israelites, in Goshen, meanwhile, are unaffected by the plagues which devastate the land of their captors.

Terence Fretheim has pointed out that beyond the vindication of Yahweh's power over the cosmic, physical order, we also have here his judgment in the realm of moral order. He considers this to be a central theological concern in Exodus and writes that 'the theological grounding for the plagues is an understanding of the moral order, created by God for the sake of justice and well-being in the world. Pharoah's moral order is bankrupt, severely disrupting this divine intent, and hence he becomes the object of the judgment inherent in God's order'.[23]

Ultimately, however, as Hoffmeier notes, 'God's purpose was to convince Israel that he was their God and that he alone could redeem Israel for himself.'[24] This purpose is seen in 6:6–7:

[18] Exod. 12:12; 18:10–11; Num. 33:4.
[19] Exod. 7:5; cf. 8:19; 9:14, 17–18, 20; 10:7.
[20] James K. Hoffmeier, 'Plagues of Egypt', *NIDOTTE*, vol. 4, p. 1056.
[21] Ibid., p. 1057.   [22] Ibid., p. 1056.   [23] Quoted in ibid., p. 1058.   [24] Ibid.

Therefore, say to the Israelites: 'I am the LORD and I will bring you out from under the yoke of the Egyptians. I will free you from being slaves to them and will redeem you with an outstretched arm and with mighty acts of judgment. I will take you as my own people, and I will be your God. Then you will know that I am the LORD your God, who brought you out from under the yoke of the Egyptians.'

b. The danger to Israel

Even the Israelites are in danger from the wrath of God in the last plague, however, and only the blood of the Passover lamb keeps the angel of death from slaying their firstborn. For these people too are sinners: their faith is weak and faulty, as subsequent history will show, and God's holiness is a danger to them also. They must learn that they are only saved by the mercy of God and by the blood of the lamb. On the Passover, J. Barton Payne writes:

> God... did not limit paschal observance to that original passover ... He proceeded to establish a perpetual, annual passover feast (12:14) ... designed, first of all, to serve as a memorial of Israel's deliverance from Egypt (vv.14, 17, 24–27) ... But its purpose exceeded that of a mere memorial. The reason that the passover feast and sacrifice had to be perpetual was due to the fact that Israel's firstborn children continued perpetually to be God's and stood, therefore, in constant need of divine redemption (Ex. 13:2; Num. 3:13). The explanation, in turn, for this continuing obligation in respect to the children's lives is found in the fact of sin, specifically, of Pharaoh's rebellion against God (Ex. 13:15).[25]

In the New Testament, the apostle Paul will make good use of this when he tells the Corinthians: 'Get rid of the old yeast that you may be a new batch without yeast – as you really are. For Christ, our Passover lamb, has been sacrificed. Therefore let us keep the Festival, not with the old yeast, the yeast of malice and wickedness, but with bread without yeast, the bread of sincerity and truth.'[26]

We must never take God for Granted. We must never forget his just judgment. We must remember that even as his redeemed people we must all appear before the judgment seat of God,[27] though it is now revealed to be also the judgment seat of Christ.[28] We must stand in awe of his purity and justice even as we shelter under the blood of a sufficient atonement. Perfect love casts out one type of fear but it establishes another kind – a godly reverence and awe: 'Therefore,

[25] J. Barton Payne, *The Theology of the Older Testament* (Zondervan, 1962), p. 403.
[26] 1 Cor. 5:7–8.   [27] Rev. 20:12.   [28] 2 Cor. 5:10.

since we are receiving a kingdom that cannot be shaken, let us be thankful, and so worship God acceptably with reverence and awe, for our "God is a consuming fire".'[29]

6. God, sovereign in judgment and salvation

A constantly recurring theme in these chapters is the hardening of Pharaoh's heart. Sometimes it is said that Pharaoh hardened his heart.[30] Sometimes it is said that the Lord hardened his heart.[31] The double hardening (God's and Pharaoh's) is an indication that God's action is not arbitrary. Always, Pharaoh is seen to be responsible for his actions and wilful in his intent, and always Yahweh is seen to be in sovereign control and acting in righteous judgment. It is Yahweh of Israel, not the gods of Egypt, who has brought Pharaoh to this point of power on the stage of history (9:16).

The apostle Paul quotes from these chapters in his letter to the Romans to show God's unfailing purposes of salvation for those who are his true people and also to show his judgment upon and sovereign control over fallen men and women in a fallen world. In a humbling and uncompromising series of statements he affirms God's sovereignty in salvation and judgment.[32] Men and women, however defiant, however unbelieving, like to think they have God 'on a string'; that they alone are in control of their destiny, not God; that they can change at any time and that God will always come to terms. But Paul knows that they belong to the world of Pharaoh, a fallen world, where the entire race rebelled and fell in Adam.[33] He then pictures God as a potter making things out of clay: out of the same 'lump' making different vessels, some for special and some for common use.[34] So, Paul argues from various scriptures, in a world which has rejected him, God has sovereignly ordained to choose some and to leave others, to have mercy on some and to harden others, to raise up a Pharaoh on the stage of history and to humiliate his pride and punish his wickedness in spectacular ways so that his name [God's] might be proclaimed in all the earth.[35]

Paul is not telling us that God creates or ordains some men and women to salvation and others to damnation irrespective of human sin and fallenness (in Paul's picture God is seen as working upon an already fallen race, the 'clay' is fallen, sinful human nature). Nor is he telling us that men and women have no free will; only that they use that freedom to rebel against God.[36] His concern is to assert the sovereignty of God even over those who, like Pharaoh, defy him. So he does insist that God is sovereign even over the fallenness of the

[29] Heb. 12:28.   [30] E.g. Exod. 7:13; 8:15, 19, 32; 9:34.
[31] E.g. Exod. 4:21; 9:12; 10:1, 20, 27; 11:10; 14:8.   [32] Rom. 9:14–24.
[33] Rom. 5:12–14.   [34] Rom. 9:21.   [35] Rom. 9:17.   [36] John 6:43–44, 63–65.

world he had made so well and the race he had made in his image and likeness. In his sovereignty he changes some by the power of his grace and mercy while, as Paul puts it in Romans 1, 'giving others over'[37] to their lust, pride, envy, greed, folly and sin – and to their own choice to live in defiance of him: 'For he says to Moses, "I will have mercy on whom I will have mercy, and I will have compassion on whom I will have compassion." '[38]

As we apply that to Pharaoh we see a powerful tyrant punished with his own sin, his stubborn heart hardened further, his confident sovereignty shattered by the supreme Sovereign, 'the blessed and only Ruler, the King of kings and Lord of lords',[39] a warning in history to all leaders of nations who despise God. And as we apply it to ourselves, we see that in our own small world we too might have said, as Pharaoh, *'Who is the LORD that I should obey him? . . . I do not know the LORD.'*[40] But the God of Moses and Paul, who says, 'I will have mercy on whom I will have mercy, and I will have compassion on whom I will have compassion', had mercy on us – and we can only worship, love and serve him as our God for ever and ever.

The subsequent account of the wilderness wandering of Israel will show that there were Israelites, too, who hardened their hearts and who stand as a warning to the church that nominal religion is just another form of unbelief.[41]

We see in all this the reality of God's wrath and sin's hardening power. When God is kept out of a life he can allow sin and forces beyond a man or woman's power to take them further than they ever meant to go: a flirtation can become a ruinous affair, an experiment can become an addiction, a small dishonesty can grow into a criminal activity, a holiday from God can become an eternal exile.

7. God as kinsman-redeemer

When Moses was given his commission by Yahweh, he was told to say to Pharaoh, *'Israel is my firstborn son . . . Let my son go, so that he may worship me'* (4:22–23). In Exodus 6:6, Yahweh tells Moses to speak to the Israelites on his behalf saying, *'I am the LORD and I will bring you out from under the yoke of the Egyptians. I will free you from being slaves to them and will redeem you with an outstretched arm and with mighty acts of judgment.'* The particular word for 'redeem', chosen out of several other possible words, is *gāʾal*, which involves 'redemption by one obligated through relational ties'.[42] John Durham translates 'I will redeem you', therefore, as 'I will act as your rescuing kinsman'.[43] Similarly in Exodus 15:13, in the song

---

[37] Rom. 1:24, 26, 28.　　[38] Rom. 9:15.　　[39] 1 Tim. 6:15.　　[40] Exod. 5:2.
[41] Ps. 95:8–11; cf. Heb. 3:7–19.　　[42] Durham, p. 72.　　[43] Ibid.

of Moses and Miriam, Durham translates 'the people you have redeemed' as 'this people you have redeemed as kinsmen'.[44]

The *gō'ēl* or 'kinsman-redeemer' in ancient Israel was a relative whose right it was to buy back land alienated from the family[45] or a relation who had sold himself into slavery to pay off a debt or to survive poverty.[46] Boaz and Jeremiah provide Old Testament examples of this law in action.[47] The prophet Isaiah, in particular, frequently uses this term (24 times in all!) to describe Yahweh's redemption of his elect people.[48] However, here is Exodus, in the Egyptian situation, the stress falls on their liberation from slavery.

In such cases a ransom price was necessary. Here the deliverance of Israel from bondage in Egypt was effected by the One who had bound himself to them and regarded them as his people, his family, his 'son'. As next of kin he has the right to purchase the freedom of enslaved Israel.

Later biblical teaching will show that the symbolic price of blood in the Old Testament, whether sprinkled on the doorposts or poured out at the foot of the altar, will become the blood of God's own Son,[49] the sign of his death as an atoning sacrifice.[50] The divine Kinsman-Redeemer would, in time, buy out of a greater bondage the whole Israel of God.[51]

The kinsman-redeemer could similarly buy land that had been alienated from the original owner. Once bought back into the family, the particular parcel of land which had been 'redeemed' became the possession of the kinsman who had purchased it. So also Israel had, by redemption, passed into the service of Yahweh, the Father of the nation, who was also their King. They were his by creation and adoption, by covenant and purchase, doubly bought and dearly loved: 'For your Maker is your husband – the LORD Almighty is his name – the Holy One of Israel is your Redeemer (*gō'ēl*); he is called the God of all the earth.'[52]

8. God as cosmic ruler

The song of Moses and Miriam, sung with cymbals and dancing on the far side of the Red Sea from Egypt, is, says John Durham, 'far more than merely a hymn of Yahweh's victory over Pharaoh and his Egyptians in the sea'. It is 'more a celebration of Yahweh and the kind of God he is'. As such, Durham concludes, 'it is a kind of summary of the theological base of the whole book of the Exodus.'[53]

---

[44] Ibid., p. 200.   [45] Lev. 25:28.   [46] Lev. 25:48.
[47] Ruth 2:20; 3:9; 4:3–4; Jer. 32:7.   [48] E.g. Is. 49:7; 54:5–8.
[49] Acts 20:28; 1 Cor. 5:7.   [50] Rom. 3:25; Heb. 9:12, 14; 10:4, 10, 14.
[51] Gal. 3:26 – 4:7; 6:16.   [52] Is. 54:5; cf. 43:14–15.   [53] Durham, p. 210.

> *'I will sing to the LORD,*
> *for he is highly exalted.*
> *The horse and its rider*
> *he has hurled into the sea.*
> *The LORD is my strength and my song;*
> *he has become my salvation'* (15:1–2).

Moreover, the event it remembers is of far-reaching significance. The 'redemption' from Egypt has the place in the Old Testament mind and memory that the ultimate redemption in the cross of Christ has in the New. In the song of Moses an image is developed which will reappear many times in the Old Testament: the image of Yahweh as a mighty warrior who fights Israel's battles and defeats her enemies (15:3).

The boast of the enemy in verse 9 echoes the contempt which the world powers have always had for the people of God.

> *'The enemy boasted,*
> *"I will pursue, I will overtake them,*
> *I will divide the spoils;*
> *I will gorge myself on them.*
> *I will draw my sword*
> *and my hand will destroy them."* '

One is reminded of Joseph Stalin's cynical question: 'And how many battalions does the Pope have?' G. K. Chesterton remarked that Christianity had been thrown to the dogs at least three times in history, but in each case it was the dog that died!

The central part of the song (15:11–13) celebrates the incomparableness of Yahweh and his unfailing love for his people:

> *'Who among the gods is like you, O LORD?*
> *. . . Majestic in holiness, awesome in glory, working wonders?*
> *You stretched out your right hand*
> *and the earth swallowed them.*

> *'In your unfailing love you will lead*
> *the people you have redeemed.*
> *In your strength you will guide them to your holy dwelling.'*

The song ends with the confident awareness that the present experience is 'simply an historical demonstration of the realities of divine cosmic rule through redemption'.[54] God who is God here is

[54] Dumbrell, p. 103.

God everywhere. He who governs history in this event has future history under his sovereignty. He will lead his people into their inheritance, for '*The* LORD *will reign for ever and ever*' (15:18). Yahweh as cosmic ruler will be a theme carried on in the Old Testament[55] and carried over into the New Testament in the exaltation and rule of Jesus Christ as the Son of God, Lord over fallen history, Judge and Saviour.[56]

There will come a time when we shall all be 'on the other side' of the divide between this fallen world of Pharaohs, Caesars and Führers, where power, money and fashion rule, and the world of God's future, Christ's glory and 'a new heavens and a new earth, the home of righteousness'.[57] On that great day the church of God, gathered from all times and all peoples, will know the joy of a full salvation, a final deliverance and an endless glory.

[55] E.g. Pss. 96 – 99; 106; 135; Is. 40; 49; 60; 63; 66.
[56] Matt. 28:18; John 5:22–30; 2 Cor. 2:14–16; 2 Thess. 1:5–10; Rev. 5:1–14.
[57] 2 Pet. 3:13.

Exodus 19:1–25
8. The unapproachable God

When God confronted Moses and spoke to him from within the strange fire of the burning bush, he called him to lead the people of Israel out of slavery in Egypt and on to Canaan, the land God had promised Abraham generations before. In Exodus 3:12 we read God's words to Moses, given as a sign that this destiny would be fulfilled: 'I will be with you. And this will be the sign to you that it is I who have sent you: When you have brought the people out of Egypt, you will worship God on this mountain.'

1. Israel at the mountain of God (19:1–6)

In Exodus 19:1–2 we see Moses with a nation at his back; the tribes of Israel with their families, flocks and herds, their hopes and fears, camped around the foot of Sinai, also called Horeb, the mountain of God. Behind him are the 'impossible' realities of the exodus from Egypt – the confrontation with Pharaoh, the ten plagues of Egypt and the deliverance of the Red Sea – and before them are all the possibilities of a new national life in their own land.

And here, at Sinai, it is as if Moses has brought a bride to her husband, for Yahweh, the great 'I am', is to make this nation, out of all the nations on earth, his nation, his holy people, elect and precious. Israel will be the bride of God and the wedding ceremony will be at the foot of the mountain of God. There God will say, 'I do', and Israel will say, 'I do', and something quite unique in the history of a fallen world will have begun.

The coming of God to his people at Sinai has been described as 'the most important event of Exodus and even of the Old Testament itself'; it is 'the formative event of Old Testament faith'.[1]

³*Then Moses went up to God, and the LORD called to him from the mountain and said, 'This is what you are to say to the house of Jacob*

[1] Durham, pp. 259, 265.

and what you are to tell the people of Israel: [4]*"You yourselves have seen what I did to Egypt, and how I carried you on eagles' wings and brought you to myself.* [5]*Now if you obey me fully and keep my covenant, then out of all nations you will be my treasured possession. Although the whole earth is mine,* [6]*you will be for me a kingdom of priests and a holy nation."* [1]

God's words in 19:3–6 form an important preamble to 'the Sinaitic covenant' and state his special relation to Israel. The picture is evoked of an eagle teaching its young to fly; the great bird stirring up the nest built on high places, pushing the flustered, fluttering young who are ready to fly and don't know it, out into space and then, as they fall, catching them on her strong wings, soaring up and letting them fall and then repeating the process until they can fly on their own.

So Israel was a fledgling and an untutored people, young and vulnerable, journeying into an unknown future through an unfamiliar desert. But the presence of God was the strong, protective force which had brought them thus far and which would lead them to their Promised Land.

Sometimes we feel very vulnerable on our journey to God's future: unprotected, inexperienced and wondering how we will cope. God himself leads us on to new stages of faith and new challenges in life. We flap and flutter and sometimes spiral down toward disaster, but the wings of God are there, strong and secure. They are never a substitute for action and effort; we too must learn to fly, to grow in wisdom, love and power, but they are our safety, security and encouragement. In the words of a more human metaphor: 'The eternal God is your refuge, and underneath are the everlasting arms.'[2]

In Exodus 19:5–6 we find three significant terms by which God describes his people, Israel: a treasured possession, a kingdom of priests and a holy nation.

a. God's treasured possession

This first description is a reference to a monarch's private fortune as distinguished from his royal domain.[3] This people are to be Yahweh's private property. The image is then expanded: God is God over the whole earth, the cattle on a thousand hills are his, and the pride of the nations, but Israel is to be 'the crown jewel of a large collection, the masterwork, the one-of-a-kind piece'.[4]

In the preamble to his covenant at Sinai, God states clearly the uniqueness of Israel's privilege and calling. The conditional form of

---

[2] Deut. 33:27.   [3] Cf. 1 Chr. 29:3.   [4] Durham, p. 262.

the covenant pertains to the nation's enjoyment of covenant privileges such as prosperity and protection, but it must not obscure the unconditionality of Abraham's (and Israel's) election or of God's commitment to the covenant itself. As Gordon McConville notes, 'The distinctive characteristic of the Mosaic covenant is its setting of God's laws relating to Israel's life in the framework of a theology of election of Israel by grace.'[5]

b. God's kingdom of priests

In the ancient world it was not unusual for the king to have his own group of priests.[6] Israel is also called to be 'a kingdom of priests' (19:6). Christopher Wright comments:

> Common political terms are used here: 'kingdom' and 'nation', but they are placed, almost with a touch of irony, alongside words that were the opposite of 'common' – 'priestly' and 'holy' ... But what is meant by calling the whole nation 'priestly'? A priest, in Old Testament thought and practice, stood between God and the people, a mediator in both directions. He represented God to the people, both in his person and example (cf. Lev. 21 – 22), and especially in his role as teacher (Deut. 33:10; Hos. 4:6; Mal.2:4–7). Through the priests, the word and will of God were to be made known to the rest of the people. Now if Israel as a nation were to be a priesthood, the implication is that they would represent God to the peoples of mankind in an analogous way. God's way would be made manifest in their life as a nation.[7]

As John Durham puts it, this was to be 'a kingdom run, not by politicians depending upon strength and connivance but by priests depending on faith in Yahweh, a servant nation instead of a ruling nation'.[8] Its greatest service to the world of nations would be to bring them the knowledge of the true God so that 'all peoples on earth' would be blessed by the children of Abraham just as God had promised Abraham himself.

c. God's holy nation

The third term here is 'a holy nation'. As we have seen earlier, the word 'holy' means 'cut off' or 'set apart'. God is 'set apart' from everything finite and created and from everything sinful and corrupt. It is his glory to be 'holy', 'set apart' and 'different'. The wonder is that he should take a people and set them apart for himself – take them, moreover, in all their humanness and sin, and lift them

---

[5] Gordon McConville, '*bᵉrît*', *NIDOTTE*, vol. 1, p. 749.   [6] Davids, p. 92.
[7] Wright, pp. 40–41.   [8] Durham, p. 263.

to the God-side of creation to be dedicated to him. But that is what God does to Israel, and what he does to us. Notice that Israel is made holy by an act of God in undeserved love and grace before she herself is fit for it or becomes holy in her national life. The second follows the first. Grace is always first. We love because he first loved us.

Yet the second does follow (at least in true Israel) and must follow. As Alan Cole puts it, 'Ultimately, God's holiness becomes a compelling moral demand on his people (Lev. 7:20).'[9] The precise nature of that demand will be filled out in the rest of the book and in the books that follow it. Christopher Wright, in his study of the laws of Deuteronomy and their implications for us today and our knowledge of God and his will, writes:

> The social shape of Israel was not an incidental freak of ancient history, nor was it just a temporary, material by-product of their spiritual message. It was an integral part of what God had called them into existence for. God's message of redemption through Israel was not just verbal; it was visible and tangible. They, the medium, were themselves part of the message ... the holiness of Israel was not a merely spiritual matter but had very practical implications. Now we can see it was not an exclusive or inward-looking distinctiveness. Rather it was God-centred precisely in order that it should be directed to the benefit of the rest of mankind, for 'the whole earth is mine'. And in order for it to have that 'outward' orientation in an effective way, their holiness needed to be given social, community, 'flesh'. That is why the purpose of God for Israel, expressed in Exodus 19:6, is so closely dependent on their obedience to the covenant law laid down in the preceding verse. It would be as they lived out the quality of national and social life demanded by the law they were about to receive, with its great chords of freedom, justice, love and compassion, that they would function as God's holy priesthood; as a nation, among the nations, for the nations (cf. Ps. 99:1–4).[10]

God is different and he makes his people different, holy as he is holy, called to live different lives, to be his display people, 'a showcase to the world of how being in covenant with Yahweh changes a people'.[11]

d. And that means us too

The result of all this would be that in a distant century, in another millennium, an apostle of the new covenant would be able to write

---

[9] Cole, p. 145. [10] Wright, pp. 40–41. [11] Durham, p. 263.

to mixed churches of Jews and Gentiles who believed in Jesus Christ as the Son of God, the Saviour of the world,

> But you are a chosen people, a royal priesthood, a holy nation, a people belonging to God, that you may declare the praises of him who called you out of darkness into his wonderful light. Once you were not a people, but now you are the people of God; once you had not received mercy, but now you have received mercy.[12]

As Israel was meant to be, so our New Testament church communities are meant to be in their life together: working models of the kingdom of God, touches and foretastes of a final reconciliation when Christ will reign over a redeemed people in perfect faith and love. That is why our churches must be communities of faith and love reaching out into a world which is so often a world of suffering and alienation – a kingdom of priests, aware of their priestly identity and calling.

2. Unapproachable holiness (19:7-25)

One feature of Exodus 19 is the number of times Moses goes up to and comes down from Mount Sinai. It is clearly one of the ways in which the message of unapproachable holiness is brought home to the Israelites and ourselves as readers:

[3]Then Moses went up to God ... [7]So Moses went back ... [8]So Moses brought their answer to the LORD ... [14]After Moses had gone down the mountain ... [24]The LORD descended to the top of Mount Sinai and called Moses to the top of the mountain. So Moses went up and the LORD said to him, 'Go down and warn the people so that they do not force their way through to see the LORD and many of them perish' ... [25]So Moses went down ...

Moses brings this life-changing declaration of God's intent to the elders of Israel (19:7) and the whole people with them vow to do all God required of them (19:18). This is Israel's 'I do' in the marriage ceremony. After Moses has returned to Yahweh with the reply of the people and Yahweh has informed the people through Moses that he will give Moses special access to himself (19:9), God announces that he is going to come down to Mount Sinai in the sight of all the people, not just to Moses, but to the entire nation who are to make themselves ready to meet their God.

At Sinai one of the first lessons the people of Israel are taught is that sin has made God dangerous: 'With the advent of Yahweh,

---

[12] 1 Pet. 2:9-10.

Mount Sinai would become holy by virtue of his special Presence there, and that holiness would constitute a danger to all persons and everything forbidden contact with it.'[13] Even when they are ritually prepared they are still in danger:

[10]*And the* LORD *said to Moses, 'Go to the people and consecrate them today and tomorrow. Make them wash their clothes* [11]*and be ready by the third day, because on that day the* LORD *will come down on Mount Sinai in the sight of all the people.* [12]*Put limits for the people around the mountain and tell them, "Be careful that you do not go up to the mountain or touch the foot of it. Whoever touches the mountain shall surely be put to death* ... [22]*Even the priests, who approach the* LORD, *must consecrate themselves, or the* LORD *will break out against them."'*

There are to be boundaries around the mountain itself, manned presumably by archers or slingers. Anyone breaking through, as the vast number of people gather at the sound of the ram's horn, would be shot. The boundaries are there, in fact, for the protection of the people. They could not live surrounded, unprotected, by the Holy Presence of God. Only those ignorant, foolish or contemptuous enough to cross the boundary are in danger. This is not a tourist's God!

Superficially it seems a strange contradiction: called to belong yet kept at a distance. But Israel who is 'holy' by God's choice and act is herself deeply unworthy, fickle and untutored in the things of God. It will be a main teaching of Leviticus and the sacrificial system that God is dangerous because he is holy and the people are unclean, and when the holy comes into contact with the unclean there is a reaction which spells death for the sinner. Even Moses, in a later chapter, will be told, 'You cannot see my face, for no-one may see me and live.'[14] Only the grace of God in the gift and acceptance of an atoning sacrifice can enable sinners to live in his presence.[15] We need God to protect us from God!

The coming down of Yahweh is told in a few unforgettable sentences:

[16]*On the morning of the third day there was thunder and lightning, with a thick cloud over the mountain, and a very loud trumpet blast. Everyone in the camp trembled.* [17]*Then Moses led the people out of the camp to meet with God, and they stood at the foot of the mountain.* [18]*Mount Sinai was covered with smoke, because the* LORD

[13] Durham, p. 265; cf. 2 Sam. 6:6–8; 1 Chr. 13:9–10.   [14] Exod. 33:20.
[15] Lev. 17:11.

*descended on it in fire. The smoke billowed up from it like smoke
from a furnace, the whole mountain trembled violently,* [19]*and the
sound of the trumpet grew louder and louder. Then Moses spoke and
the voice of God answered him.*

Here is a vision of God and some basic lessons about God which we
must all learn, even today. The God we worship is awesome and our
worship of him must never lose the element of appropriate awe:

> My God, how wonderful Thou art,
>   Thy majesty how bright!
> How beautiful Thy mercy-seat,
>   In depths of burning light!
>
> How wonderful, how beautiful,
>   The sight of Thee must be,
> Thine endless wisdom, boundless power,
>   And aweful purity![16]

He is our Father, but he is our holy and heavenly Father, a father like
no other, the Lord, the King. We may not stroll up to him with our
hands in our pockets, whistling!

At this point we should consider the Ten Commandments, the
great decalogue of fundamental principles for the covenant community which God gave to Israel. However, they are so important that
they will be dealt with separately in the next chapter, not because
they should be detached from the narrative and context in which we
find them, but only because they occupy a large space in this narrative and tell us crucial things about the God of Abraham, Isaac and
Jacob, the God and Father of our Lord Jesus Christ.

---

[16] Hymn, 'My God, how wonderful Thou art', by Frederick William Faber (1814–
1863).

Exodus 20:1–21
9. God in ten words

1. The God who speaks (20:1–2)

It has been said that when God wanted to tell people what he was like he gave them the Ten Commandments. In other words, God describes himself ethically rather than physically (although elsewhere there are plenty of familiar pictures, such as shepherd, king, husband, and various anthropomorphisms, too). However, there is far more here than mere 'ethics' as people commonly think of them – split off somehow from religion. It is true that there are some very ethical people who have no religious beliefs. It is equally true that they owe their possession of those moral standards to their unacknowledged Creator. However, in the Ten Commandments we have not a universal ethic but a covenant code, not the ethic of humanism but the face of God.

The Ten Commandments are not a set of rules for a secular society but a summary of what is owed by the people of God to their Saviour and their Lord. Even in transposing their significance to our own lives and societies we have to remember that the Ten Commandments are primarily about a relationship with God. The life they outline is a life lived in grateful and loving response to his election, salvation and authority: '*I am the* LORD *your God*' (20:1). It must be clear to us therefore that the Ten Commandments do not represent salvation by works but the life expected of a people already redeemed by the blood of the lamb – of the Passover and the cross!

After re-enforcing the prohibitions given earlier, God speaks. He speaks not only to Moses and Aaron who are permitted to come close, but also to the entire nation assembled at the foot of the mountain. He gives them in person the Ten Commandments with their crucial introduction: '*I am the* LORD *your God, who brought you out of Egypt, out of the land of slavery.*' Thus he sets his law firmly in the context of his preceding and all-determining grace.

Again and again, in Exodus, Deuteronomy and elsewhere, the point is made that *all Israel* heard the voice of God and his commandments. This was not an occult spirit, a deity who hid in dark corners, who stayed in mystery, but One who acted in history, decisively and unforgettably, for the redemption of his people and who did and spoke as no other 'god' had done to any nation.[1]

2. The Ten Commandments

The Ten Commandments are sometimes called 'The Ten Words'.[2] Looking back to their promulgation forty years later, Moses reminded the people of the 'appearance' of God at Sinai: 'Then the LORD spoke to you out of the fire. You heard the sound of words but saw no form; there was only a voice.'[3] Christopher Wright makes the perceptive comment:

> What really mattered at Sinai, then, was not that there had been a *theophanic manifestation* of God, but that there had been a *verbal revelation* of God's mind and will. Sinai was a cosmic audiovisual experience, but it was the audio that mattered. It has been observed that Hebrew society never developed a visual religious culture, unlike Greek society. Part of the reason lies in the aniconic [imageless] nature of Israel's worship, linked to the point made in verse 15 about seeing no 'form' of God. But a more significant and more positive reason lies in the emphasis Israel placed on its 'auditory' culture. God was to be heard, and through hearing, obeyed. The ear, as the organ of understanding and obedience in relation to the spoken word of God, was more religiously and ethically significant than the eye.[4]

The Ten Commandments themselves are 'the centre and focus of the whole Pentateuch' and 'the very heart of the whole Old Testament'.[5] They summarize the uniqueness of God, his moral character and his will for the life of his people. It has been said that 'the commandments are God's nature expressed in terms of moral imperatives'. Alan Cole adds: 'and it is significant that God chose to reveal Himself so, rather than in terms of philosophical propositions. So, to the Israelite, He is the God of history (verse 2) and of daily life (verses 13ff.) rather than the God of speculation.'[6]

---

[1] See e.g. Exod. 20:8–20; Deut. 4:9–14, 32–40; 9:10; Neh. 9:13.
[2] Exod. 34:27; Deut. 4:13; 10:4.   [3] Deut. 4:12.   [4] Wright, p. 50.
[5] Muilenburg, quoted in Durham, p. 284.   [6] Cole, p. 152.

3. New Lord, new lifestyle (20:3–11)

Walter Brueggemann writes that Yahweh's right to command is perhaps 'his defining and characteristic marking' in the Sinai tradition of Exodus, Numbers and Deuteronomy 12 – 25. He contrasts the command of Pharaoh with that of Yahweh:

> The Exodus narrative, which creates the contexts for the encounter at Sinai is the tale of Yahweh wresting Israel from enslavement to the commands of Pharaoh and bringing Israel under the command of Yahweh. Thus it is the exchange of one command for another. When Israel came under this alternative command of Yahweh at the outset, Israel willingly obeyed (Exod. 19:8). The Exodus was not a contextless emancipation. Rather it was an exchange of overlords ... As Exodus is not a contextless emancipation, so the commands of Yahweh at Sinai do not replicate absolute Egyptian power; Yahweh, moreover, is not a sovereign like Pharaoh. That is, the new 'command society' of Sinai is one of dignity, freedom and well-being.

He concludes, 'It is important not to stress the command structure of Sinai without appreciating the emancipatory impulse of Yahweh. Conversely, it is impossible to appreciate the emancipatory impulse of Yahweh, operative in the Exodus narrative, without paying close attention to the command structure of Sinai.'[7]

The New Testament too, in its way, will make the point that we have been saved to be holy, redeemed to belong to God; that, having been bought with a price, we are not our own; that we have been predestined to be conformed to the image of his Son.[8]

a. No other gods!

The first commandment, '*You shall have no other gods before me*' (literally 'before my face'), prohibits Israel adding the worship of any other deity to that of Yahweh. Yahweh was to have no rivals in Israel; they were his covenant people and he was their exclusive Lord. Christopher Wright says, 'A possible translation would be, "You shall have no other gods *as rivals to me*." For what is at stake is not a matter of philosophical orthodoxy ("You shall believe that only one God exists"), but a matter of practical loyalty.'[9] The point is that it is possible to defend a theoretical monotheism while engaging in a real polytheism. He applies this sharply to some fashionable thinking of our own times:

---

[7] Brueggemann (1997), pp. 182–183.   [8] Rom. 8:29; 1 Cor. 5:7–8; 6:19–20.
[9] Wright, p. 68.

It is sometimes alleged that, if there is only one God in reality, then what people worship must be (or must represent) that God. This is the kind of twisted logic that underlies the ideology of pluralism in the debate over world religions. Such a view requires a concept of 'God' that is so abstract that, even though it is grammatically singular, it can accommodate any number of 'faces'. Thus phrases like Ultimate Divine Reality, or The Real, or Transcendent Being, are used, and we are asked to accept that all religions, all concepts of God (or denials of personal deities as well) are equally valid in their partial portrayal of this mysterious, ineffable reality at the centre. Against this, one must, first of all, point out that the first commandment is inseparably linked to the prologue. That is, it does not say, 'You must acknowledge that there is only one ultimate divine reality, however you choose to define or worship "it" '; but rather, it says quite explicitly, 'I am Yahweh . . . no other gods before *my* face.' And secondly, one has to point to the NT development of this issue precisely in a highly pluralistic religious context. The difference then is that God is portrayed as defined in Jesus Christ.[10]

In his classic treatment and application to us of the Ten Commandments, John Calvin tells us that in forbidding us to have strange gods, 'God means we are not to transfer to another what belongs to him'. What this is he sums up under four headings: 1. *Adoration*, including veneration, worship and 'the submission of our consciences to his law'. (This releases us from the compulsions of superstition.) 2. *Trust*, which he defines as 'the assurance of reposing in him that arises from the recognition of his attributes, when – attributing to him all wisdom, righteousness, might, truth and goodness – we judge that we are blessed only by communion with him'. (This releases us from primitive fears of 'fate' and provides the ground of our peace of mind.) 3. *Invocation*, which is 'that habit of our mind, whenever necessity presses us, of resorting to his faithfulness and help as our only support' (which offers us a way out of fear and false reliance). 4. *Thanksgiving*, which is 'that gratitude with which we ascribe praise to him for all good things'. (Where many people speak of 'good luck' the Bible speaks of 'blessing'.)[11]

b. The God who is alive

Walter Brueggemann thinks that 'we may see in the prohibition of images an assertion of the unfettered character of Yahweh, who will not be captured, contained, assigned, or managed by anyone or

---

[10] Ibid., p. 69.   [11] Calvin (*Institutes*), I.viii.16.

anything, for any purpose'.[12] The second commandment, 'You shall not make for yourself an idol' (20:4) (literally a shaped image) is usually understood to relate to Yahweh's invisibility or his incomparability. Christopher Wright, however, makes the further point that

> Although the Israelites repudiated actual physical images of Yahweh, they were not lacking in creativity when it came to rhetorical imagery for Yahweh, drawn vigorously from the created and human order. Israel's language imagery for Yahweh made him very 'visible' to the mental eye through a rich and often daring anthropomorphic and metaphorical style. The affirmation that Yahweh is *personal* seemed more urgent than fear about his invisible spirituality'.[13]

He continues:

> Yahweh is the *living* God, and any carved statue is necessarily lifeless. Something that can *do nothing* is no image of the God who can *do all things*. The only legitimate image of God, therefore, is the image of God created in his own likeness – the living, thinking, working, speaking, breathing, relating human being (not even a statue will do, but only the human person) ... As the speaking God, Yahweh reveals, addresses, promises, challenges, confronts, demands. Any attempt to turn Yahweh into a voiceless statue effectively gags God. Idolatry therefore is fundamentally an escape from the living voice and commands of the living God.[14]

The motivation for this prohibition is given in the words in verse 5, 'for I the LORD your God am a jealous God'. In Old Testament language God's 'jealousy' is his strong devotion. It is his passionate commitment to his own glory, honour and Name, and, as his 'jealous love' for Israel, it is his passionate commitment to his people. Here 'jealous' means something like 'protective'; God is protecting a very special relationship. God's 'jealousy' is not an evil thing but is what Christopher Wright describes as 'a function of his covenant commitment to his people.' As such it is as much reassuring as threatening. He continues:

> The covenant relationship between God and God's people really means something only if God is totally committed to it. A God who was not jealous for the reciprocal commitment of God's people would be as contemptible as a husband who didn't care

[12] Brueggemann (1997), pp. 184–185.   [13] Wright, p. 70.   [14] Ibid., p. 71.

whether or not his wife was faithful to him. Part of our problem with this profound covenantal reality is that we have come to regard religion, like everything else, as a matter of 'consumer choice', which we have virtually deified for its own sake. We resent monopolies. But the unique and incomparable, only living God makes necessarily exclusive claims and has the right to a monopoly on our love ... Jealousy is God's love protecting itself.[15]

c. The God who will not be used

'*You shall not misuse the name of the* LORD *your God*' (v. 7). Misusing God's name can be done even in acts of worship; empty, insincere or presumptuous acts of worship misuse God's name.[16] It can also be done in perjury in the law courts or at the city gate where blasphemy against God and injustice against neighbour meet, a situation denounced with particular vigour by the prophets.[17] It can be done in any attempt to manipulate God's existence for one's own ends, as for example in the rhetoric of trade which called God to witness to the superior quality of the goods offered or in various superstitious practices where to know the secret name of the 'god' was thought to tap into its power and use it for one's own ends.

Jesus echoes this commandment when he warns his disciples not to use unnecessary oaths, including the Jewish circumlocution 'by heaven' for Yahweh (under any of his names). In a world of half-truths and lies, Jesus warns us: 'Simply let your "Yes" be "Yes", and your "No" be "No"; anything beyond this comes from the evil one.'[18]

John Durham notes that the name 'Yahweh' occurs some 6,828 times in the Old Testament and 'Elohim' 2,600 times. These 'together with other names, titles and epithets' of God add up to an impressive total and 'suggest how important the use of the divine names in the confession and worship of ancient Israel actually was'.[19] Today, wherever 'God' is no more than a convenient swear-word there is no sense of the significance or incomparability of God. But with us it must be different and we must take care that we do not take God for granted or misuse his name and its significance, even when we mean well, by lightly using phrases such as 'The Lord told me' or 'The Lord did this or that' or 'The Lord has promised me this or that' outside of Scripture. We must not mortgage his reputation on our good intentions.

---

[15] Ibid., pp. 71–72.   [16] E.g. Is. 1:13; Amos 4:4; Jer. 7:1–4; 23:17, 21.
[17] E.g. Is. 5:20–23; Amos 5:12–13.   [18] Matt. 5:34–37.   [19] Durham, p. 287.

d. The God who shares his rest

'*Remember the Sabbath day by keeping it holy*' (v. 8). Walter Brueggemann pays particular attention to the fourth commandment, 'where we find at the core of creation the invitation to rest'.[20] The sabbatical principle, he writes, 'holds that on a regular basis, the rhythms of a life of faith require a cessation of all activity as an act of acknowledging the rule of Yahweh and handing one's life back to Yahweh in gratitude'.[21] The Deuteronomic version also roots the Sabbath in the exodus memory and concerns rest for slaves.[22]

Walter Brueggemann writes: 'The command on Sabbath also looks forward: to a human community, an Israelite community peaceably engaged in neighbour-respecting life that is not madly engaged in production and consumption, but one that knows a limit to such activity and so has, at the centre of its life, an enactment of peaceableness that bespeaks the settled rule of Yahweh.'[23]

The fourth commandment also restated Israel's core identity and uniqueness as the people of God. John Durham writes: 'Keeping the Sabbath for them is a testimony of Israel's election and deliverance; in Egypt there was no day of interruption of the unending round of forced labour', so God 'commands them to celebrate the Sabbath as a "stopping day" proclaiming not only their dependence upon Yahweh but also their independence of all other peoples and powers'.[24]

Significantly, as Christopher Wright notes, 'Even the aliens, the non-Israelite residents, were included in this surprisingly egalitarian law.' He quotes the observation of N. Lohfink: 'While many human societies divided work and leisure along class lines (slaves, women, and the lower classes did the work; leisure was for the more privileged), the biblical Sabbath principle by contrast divides work and leisure horizontally in time, not vertically in society. All should work and all should have rest.' Wright concludes: 'The Sabbath was thus one part (arguably the most important part) of OT law's concern for workers, and especially for those most at risk in the world of work'. Then, with an eye to modern times, he adds, 'Harold Macmillan is reported to have described the Sabbath as the first and greatest worker-protection act in history.'[25]

All this has something to say to our own society where an individual's value is so often economically determined (as was the case of the Israelites in Egypt). It rebukes both bad management practices which abuse the human person (and their families) and the 'workaholic' culture which makes false gods of status and material

---

[20] Brueggemann (1997), p. 185.   [21] Ibid., pp. 187–188.   [22] Deut. 5:12–15.
[23] Brueggemann (1997), p. 185.   [24] Durham, p. 290.   [25] Wright, p. 76.

things. 'Alienated from God as the source of our fulfilment and rest, we endow work and the whole economic enterprise with a significance beyond its God-given role.'[26]

4. God's laws and our lives (20:12–17)

The relationship between the first four commandments and the last six is expressed well by John Durham: 'The first four commandments set forth the principles guiding Israel's relationship to Yahweh; the last six commandments set forth the principles guiding Israel's relationship with the covenant community, and more broadly with the human family. As the second, third and fourth are in many ways extensions of the first commandment, the first four commandments are the foundation for the final six commandments.'[27] They relate to the sanctity of family, human life, marriage and truth in Israelite society and to the rights of ownership and the importance of right attitudes. They set forth in broad principles those laws and attitudes which ensure and preserve a just and fair society.

John Calvin, whose words remind us that human nature has not changed radically since the sixteenth century, points out that without the first four commandments the remaining six will not flourish: 'God has so divided his law into two parts, which contain the whole of righteousness, as to assign the first part to those duties of religion which particularly concern the worship of his majesty; the second, to the duties of love that have to do with men.'

He continues:

Surely the first foundation of righteousness is the worship of God. When this is overthrown, all the remaining parts of righteousness, like the pieces of a shattered and fallen building, are mangled and scattered ... It is vain to cry up righteousness without religion. This is as unreasonable as to display a mutilated, decapitated body as something beautiful. Not only is religion the chief part but the very soul, whereby the whole breathes and thrives. And apart from the fear of God men do not preserve equity and love among themselves. Therefore we call the worship of God the beginning and foundation of righteousness.[28]

a. The God who puts us in families

John Durham also shows the connection between the specific commandment in verse 12 to 'Honour your father and mother' and what has gone before it:

[26] Ibid., p. 74.   [27] Durham, p. 290.   [28] Calvin (Institutes), II.viii.11.

Just as the relationship with Yahweh is the beginning of the covenant, so this relationship is the beginning of society, the inevitable point of departure for every human relationship. The first relationship beyond the relationship with Yahweh, who according to the OT is the giver of life, is the relationship to father and to mother, who together are channels of Yahweh's gift of life. No other human relationship is so fundamental, and none is more important. The fifth commandment is thus both as foundational to commandments six through ten as the first commandment is to commandments two through four, and is also the logical link from the relationship of Israel with Yahweh to the relationship of Israel to humankind.[29]

The relevance of this commandment to our own society has been pointed out by Alan Cole:

> Those who build a society in which old age has an honoured place may with confidence expect to enjoy that place themselves one day. This is not a popular doctrine in our modern world, where youth is worshipped, and old age dreaded or despised. The result is the folly by which men or women strive to remain eternally youthful, only to find it an impossible task. This commandment is part of the general attitude of Israel to old age (as symbolising and ideally embodying the practical wisdom of life) commended throughout the Old Testament (Lev. 19:32), and found in many other ancient peoples, notably the Chinese.[30]

b. The God who values life

'*You shall not murder*' (20:18). From earliest times the sanctity of human life was predicated on man as being 'in the image of God'.[31] This commandment is not a denouncement of capital punishment or participation in a just war. Rather, its focus is intentional homicide, including blood feuds in the covenant community. The 'shedding of innocent blood' is condemned in the strongest terms in the Old Testament, as are the illicit passions that lead up to it: jealousy, lust, greed and rage.[32] Whatever the complexities of the modern debate about abortion, euthanasia and genetic engineering, the value of human life, reflected in the sixth commandment and affirmed in its many Old Testament and New Testament echoes, should be our starting point.

Jesus reminds us that God is the One who searches the heart and indicates the extent of this prohibition when he warns against unjust

[29] Durham, p. 290.   [30] Cole, p. 158.   [31] Gen. 9:6; cf. Jas. 3:9; 1 John 4:20.
[32] Gen. 4:5; 1 Sam. 25:33–34; 2 Sam. 11:2–3; Prov. 1:11–16; cf. Lev. 19:17; Matt. 5:21–22.

anger and contempt which in any degree endangers or devalues unique human life.[33] John Calvin characteristically articulates its positive counterpart when he says: 'The purpose of this commandment is: the Lord has bound mankind together by a certain unity; hence each man ought to concern himself with the safety of all.'[34]

c. The God who protects marriage

The seventh commandment, '*You shall not commit adultery*' (v. 14), like the fifth, is concerned to protect Israel's life as the covenant people of God at both family and societal levels. The religious and social dimensions of the commandment cannot be separated. Durham observes, 'Everywhere in the ancient near east adultery was a crime against persons; but in Israel it was first of all and even more a crime against Yahweh.'[35] Wright states that it 'protected the sexual integrity of the marriage bond at the heart of the family' and says:

> We should remember that for the Israelite, family was not just one couple and their own children but the cluster of such families in three generations that constituted the extended household. Within that kinship 'molecule', the marital integrity of each 'nuclear' couple was carefully defined, both by this primary prohibition of adultery and by the range of limitations on sexual intercourse in Leviticus 18:6–18, which has been shown to be primarily designed to protect the inner sexual relationships of the extended family.[36]

Then, as now, adultery was far from being the concern only of the two people involved, it had both horizontal and vertical dimensions.

Jesus indicated God's concern for inner integrity and heart-purity in this prohibition.[37] as well as the inclination of fallen human nature to transgress it in thought, word or deed.[38] The apostle Paul locates it in a list of sins which indicate how one sin can lead to, or provoke, others, as lust and adultery can lead, and often have led, to discord and violence in the community.[39] God gives sex its high and proper place in human life and correspondingly warns of the seriousness of behaviour and attitudes which devalue, exploit or pervert human sexuality. In a society which trivializes and commonly degrades sex, the people of God need to be on their guard and to show a better and wiser way.

d. The God who respects property

'*You shall not steal*' (20:15). Walter Brueggemann, commenting on the last six commandments, makes this point:

[33] Matt. 5:21–22.   [34] Calvin (*Institutes*), II.viii.39.   [35] Durham, p. 294.
[36] Wright, p. 80.   [37] Matt. 5:27–30.   [38] Mark 7:20–23; cf. Eph. 5:1–7.
[39] Gal. 5:19–21.

The commandments concerning human social relationships (Ex. 20:12–17) seek to make human community possible by setting limits to the acquisitive capacity of members of the community – the capacity to seize and confiscate by power or by cunning what is necessary to the life of the neighbour . . . This set of limitations has in purview both the protection of persons and the protection of property. We may imagine that the protection of property is to be understood in the first place not as a rule of property, but as a defence of the weak against the rapacious capacity of the strong.[40]

No-one has better captured the sense and spirit of this commandment in its Old Testament context than John Calvin, who observes: 'It follows, therefore, that not only are those thieves who secretly steal the property of others, but those also who seek gain from the loss of others, accumulate wealth by unlawful practises and are more devoted to their private advantage than to equity.'[41] Christopher Wright describes how Calvin goes on to include in his discussion

> . . . a whole variety of socio-economic pentateuchal legislation including exploitation of hired workers, just treatment of aliens, accurate weights and measures, security of landmarks, laws relating to debt, interest and pledges, bribery, trespass, injury, and damage to property. He also argues that the prohibition implies a corresponding affirmative – to seek the good of the neighbour by generosity and kindness. Accordingly he also includes in his 'supplements' laws concerning rights of gleaning, sabbatical release of slaves and debt pledges, jubilee and redemption laws, and levirate marriage![42]

e. The God who loves truth

'*You shall not give false testimony*' (v. 16). Modern scholars tend to agree that the ninth commandment is connected to the judicial process in Israel where the testimony of at least two witnesses was required to sustain a charge and the penalty for false accusation was severe. An accusation proven false brought upon the accuser the penalty that would have fallen on the innocent man.[43] The prophets pointed to corruption in the law-courts as evidence of Israel's terminal state of spiritual decline and proximity to final judgment.[44] Moreover, the reputation of Yahweh was involved with that of Israel. Israel was to be a community which demonstrated to the world the character of Yahweh in righteousness, truth and justice.

---

[40] Brueggemann (1997), p. 185.
[41] Calvin (*Harmony*), vol. 3, p. 11, quoted in Wright, pp. 82–83.
[42] Wright, p. 83.   [43] Deut. 19:15–21.   [44] Is. 10:1–4; Jer. 7:9; Amos 5:7–13.

Calvin insists on a wider application of this commandment, however, believing that 'perjuries, in so far as they profane and violate God's name, are sufficiently dealt with in the Third Commandment'. He writes:

> The purpose of this commandment is: since God (who is truth) abhors a lie, we must practise truth without deceit toward one another. To sum up, then: let us not malign anyone with slanders or false charges, not harm his substance by falsehood, in short, injure him by unbridled evil speaking and impudence. To this prohibition the command is linked that we should faithfully help everyone as much as we can in affirming the truth, in order to protect the integrity of his name and possessions.[45]

With a shrewd understanding of human nature Calvin observes, 'We delight in a certain poisoned sweetness experienced in ferreting out and in disclosing the evils of others', but also adds, 'Indeed, this precept even extends to forbidding us to effect a fawning politeness, barbed with bitter taunts under the guise of joking.'

In ancient Israel or sixteenth-century Geneva or our modern world, the politics of life remain much the same!

f. The God who appoints limits

The importance of the Ten Commandments is that they internalize the law of God. That is clear from the tenth and last commandment, '*You shall not covet*' (v. 17), since covetousness is a hidden, internal thing. Jesus interpreted the seventh commandment in the light of the tenth when he forbade heart-adultery,[46] and Paul came under conviction when he faced up to its implications.[47] In a way the tenth commandment tells us how we are to regard the other nine, not merely with outward conformity or in a legalistic performance, but with the heart.

The Ten Commandments are not given as laws in the legislative sense but as fundamental principles of life for those living in relationship with Yahweh as the people of God. Here love and law meet in a willing obedience which gives to God and neighbour their due, for, 'If anyone says, "I love God", yet hates his brother, he is a liar'.[48] 'In terms of the dynamic of the covenant, covetous desires toward the wife, household or possessions of a brother-neighbour constitute hatred.'[49]

The serious nature of this sin is given considerable emphasis in the New Testament. Jesus warned his hearers about covetous greed and

---

[45] See Exod. 23:1, 7; Lev. 19:11, 16 (Calvin's references). [46] Matt. 5:27–28.
[47] Rom. 7:7–12.   [48] 1 John 4:20.   [49] Wright, p. 85.

illustrated his warning with one of his most dramatic parables.[50] It kept the rich young ruler from eternal life.[51] James saw it as the cause of other serious sins[52] and Paul exposed it as idolatry in one of its most common manifestations.[53] Covetousness puts things in the central and controlling place which belongs to God only. Hence its link with idolatry. If things become idols it is covetousness which sets them up. Peter O'Brien observes, 'In the catalogues of vices covetousness is the mark of a life which lacks the knowledge of God.'

Christopher Wright stringently applies this to our own time and society and writes:

> Thus the commandments come full circle. To break the tenth is to break the first. For covetousness means setting our hearts and affections on things that then take the place of God. It is not surprising then, conversely, that a whole culture that systematically denies the transcendent by excluding the reality of the living God from the public domain, as Western societies have been doing for generations, also ends up turning covetous self-interest into a socio-economic ideology, rationalised, euphemised, and idolised. Knowing full well that you cannot serve God and mammon, we have deliberately chosen mammon and declared that a person's life *does* consist in the abundance of things possessed. And when a society has so profoundly and deliberately abandoned the first and tenth commandments, the moral vacuum that results from the loss of all those commandments in between soon follows.[54]

While we cannot simply overlay a modern, secular society with these unique covenantal Old Testament laws, they show that fundamental human rights and duties are based on the absolutes which flow from God's character. They show that we can never separate the rights of men and women and children from the right of God to human love, faithfulness and obedience. They show too, that he is more than Lawgiver and Judge and that his will and plan for human beings is that they know him as the God who saves and who calls all men and women to enter a relationship with himself. Thus they still speak strongly and with great authority to every society in every place and generation.

---

[50] Luke 12:13–21.   [51] Matt. 19:16–22.   [52] Jas. 4:1–3.   [53] Col. 3:5; Eph. 5:5.
[54] Wright, p. 86.

5. Wanted – a mediator (20:18–21)

The sound of the voice of God going out among the hundreds of thousands of Israelites, on top of the awesomeness of the divine presence, was too much. The people, utterly overcome by the proximity of such holiness, cry out to Moses, *'Speak to us yourself and we will listen. But do not have God speak to us or we will die'* (20:19). *There* is the cry for a mediator, the sense of need for one who can stand between holy God and sinful man. The entire priesthood of Israel will reinforce that, and the New Testament will reveal that 'There is one God and one mediator between God and men, the man Christ Jesus.'[55] So, *the people remained at a distance, while Moses approached the thick darkness where God was* (20:21).

The New Testament writer of Hebrews uses this incident and passage to draw a contrast between the privileges of God's people then and now, but only because the blood of Jesus, the mediator of the new covenant, has achieved the great and final reconciliation:

> You have not come to a mountain that can be touched and that is burning with fire ... If even an animal touches the mountain, it must be stoned ... But you have come to Mount Zion, to the heavenly Jerusalem ... to Jesus the mediator of a new covenant, and to the sprinkled blood that speaks a better word than the blood of Abel.[56]

Even so, God is of such a nature that it remains to be said to every generation of his people: 'Therefore, since we are receiving a kingdom that cannot be shaken, let us be thankful, and so worship God acceptably with reverence and awe, for our God is a consuming fire.'[57]

It is surely fair to say that awe is in danger of becoming the forgotten emotion among Christians today. This is not because we know better but because we know less! We have lost sight somewhat of the awesome holiness of God. We have become desensitized to sin. We do not realize how extraordinary it is that we can survive in God's presence. The fact that it took a Calvary for us to 'have confidence to enter the Most Holy Place'[58] should make us think again: 'Christ redeemed us from the curse of the law, by becoming a curse for us'.[59]

There is only one place on earth more awesome than Sinai and that is Calvary. There God the One and Only did not come down to a mountain but was lifted up on a cross. There the Son of God, who

---

[55] 1 Tim. 2:5.   [56] Heb. 12:18–24.   [57] Heb. 12:28.   [58] Heb. 10:19.
[59] Gal. 3:13.

had come in our human nature, bore the penalty for our human sin, our great rebellion against God. There the Judge was judged in our place and the One who had given the commandments died for those who had broken them.

Deuteronomy
10. God the lawgiver

James Moffatt once made the point that 'To be justified by faith is God's gift. But it is more than a gift; it is a vocation, a career.'[1] Israel as a nation is to face that compelling fact as she receives the law at the foot of Sinai and is called to live out her unique privilege in covenant loyalty, in responsible living, in national life and personal lifestyle as a 'different' people. Israel as a nation has been made 'holy' by an act of God at Sinai.[2] Now she must live out that holiness in conformity to the God who has separated the nation from all others and made them his own people, chosen and loved.

Following on from the Ten Commandments we find in Exodus 21 – 23 what is often called 'The Book of the Covenant'. This is a miscellaneous collection of laws for Israel in its life in the Promised Land, governing everything from the treatment of livestock to the protection of slaves. This collection of laws is repeated and filled out forty years later in Deuteronomy, a name which means 'second [giving of the] law'. Its purpose is to bring all of Israel's life, 'every detail of it – public and personal, cultic and economic – under the aegis of the God of the Exodus'.[3] Here we enter the whole area of command more deeply as we examine the law, the Torah, of the Sinaitic covenant.

1. Guidance and gratitude

The characteristic feature of the Sinai covenant is the law which was given to Moses. It is important to understand, however, that it is not law as a means of salvation but law as the sequel to salvation. They

---

[1] James Moffat, 'Righteousness', in James Hastings (ed.), *Dictionary of the Apostolic Church*, vol. 2, quoted approvingly by B. B. Warfield in *Critical Reviews* (Baker, 1981), *Works*, vol. 10, p. 459.
[2] 'I am the LORD who makes you holy'; 'I am the LORD who sanctifies you'; 'I am the LORD who sets you apart' (Exod. 31:13; Lev. 20:8; 21:8).
[3] Brueggemann (1997), p. 186.

were already a redeemed people, and it was Yahweh, as their kinsman-redeemer, who had redeemed them out of Egypt and made them his nation.

William Dumbrell makes the point that our English word 'law' is to an extent an unfortunate translation of *tôrâ*. The Hebrew word includes the notion of *guidance* and *instruction* as well as categorical imposition: 'What is primarily involved in this Hebrew term is direction for life within the framework of the presupposed relationship.'[4] Covenant itself is a relationship from which promises and demands flow: 'In the Old Testament, adherence to law is thus not so much a matter of fulfilling a legal demand as demonstrating by way of national or personal life that a share of divine blessing has been entered.'[5]

That is why, in the Psalms and elsewhere, the law is celebrated in a non-legalistic sense as a source of strength, comfort and guidance.[6] Peter Enns notes the consistently positive attitude to the law in the Old Testament:

> The law is the psalmist's delight (Ps. 1:2; 119:70, 77, 92, 174). It is an object of devotion (2 Chron. 31:4) and of careful study and observance (Deut. 6:25; 31:11–13; Josh. 1:8; Neh. 8:3, 13). It is a source of wonder (Ps. 119:18) and grace (119:29). It is precious (119:72) and true (119:142). It is not only to be obeyed but loved (119:97, 113, 163, 165). The prophet looks forward to the day when the law of God will become part of the very inner fabric of God's people: 'I will put my law in their minds and write it on their hearts' (Jer. 31:33). It is to be taught to their children (Deut. 31:33; cf. 11:19–21).

Enns then adds the comment, 'This positive view of the law may be best understood in the context of covenant. The law is an expression of God's love for and commitment to his people. While enjoying a special relationship with Yahweh, the Israelites received the privilege of conducting their entire lives in accordance with his standards of conduct, which are themselves reflections of his character.'[7]

2. Law and grace, then and now

Under the new covenant, the Mosaic law and the Mosaic dispensation of law are superseded by Christ who is 'the end of the law . . . for everyone who believes',[8] summing it up and surpassing it in his own perfect righteousness which becomes ours by faith. He himself

---

[4] Dumbrell, p. 91. [5] Ibid. [6] E.g. Ps. 119:129–136.
[7] Peter Enns, 'Law of God', *NIDOTTE*, vol. 4, pp. 896–897. [8] Rom. 10:4.

replaces the law, yet does not leave us lawless, but conforms us to his image by the Holy Spirit who 'writes the will of God in our hearts', turning the written law into a living principle, internalizing the law of God and working in us a love for goodness and a power of obedience which we did not have before.[9]

It is important to recognize, however, that the background to the law is grace and that the context of the law is covenant. This is essential for an understanding of the law of Moses in its original setting and proper use. Walter Brueggemann, in his *Theology of the Old Testament*, gives considerable space to 'Yahweh, the God who commands' and writes: 'In its most pervasive testimony, the witness of the Old Testament asserts: "Observe what I command (*ṣwh*) you today" (Ex. 34:11). Commandment dominates Israel's witness about Yahweh. Yahweh is a sovereign ruler whose will for the world is known and insisted upon. Israel, as the addressee of the command, exists and prospers as it responds in obedience to these commands.'[10] After a closer examination of the laws of Exodus, Leviticus and Deuteronomy he observes: 'A student of Old Testament theology must think seriously about how this affirmative tradition of obligation, rooted in the God who commands, is now to be appropriated in a Christian tradition tempted to antinomianism, and in a modern tradition tempted by an illusion of autonomous freedom.' He offers two perspectives that are intended to avoid legalism on the one hand and antinomianism on the other:

First, the obedience to which Israel is summoned in this testimony is 'Exodus obedience'. The God of Israel intends that the emancipatory power of the exodus tradition should be a constant practice of Israel, permeating its public and institutional life. Thus the commands, rightly understood, are not restraints as much as they are empowerments. Those who obey are able to participate in the ongoing revolution of turning the world to its true shape as God's creation.

Second, in its Torah piety, Israel understood Yahweh as the true subject of its desire (cf. Pss. 27:4; 73:25), so that Israel wanted nothing so much as communion with Yahweh. This communion, which may have a mystic dimension, is however rooted in obedience that is inescapably the first element of communion.

He concludes by applying this to our modern society:

It is not excessively alarmist to say that our present acquisitive society, in its crisis of greed and brutality, is a society that tries to

---

[9] 1 Cor. 9:21; Jer. 31:33; Gal. 5:13–25.   [10] Brueggemann (1997), p. 181.

live outside of command. Such a way of life recognises no limit, until finally such brutality arrives at the nihilism of Auschwitz. The truth of the testimony, 'Yahweh who commands', is that unfettered autonomous freedom is in fact not available. Life is fundamentally relational, and the One who instigates and stands as the source of life's relatedness is the God who commands ... The commands of Yahweh are not social conveniences or conventional rules. They are, according to this testimony, the insistences whereby life in the world is made possible. Sinai articulates what Yahweh has intended for the well-being of the earth.[11]

An example of the ideological and self-serving use of the law might be seen in the actions of the Judaizers of the apostle Paul's day. Paul knew that the coming of Jesus Christ had radically changed the place of the law and that a new covenant had come into force. Yet, like the writer of Psalm 119, Paul also knew that the law is 'holy, righteous and good'.[12] But when it was misused, as the Judaizers were doing in making it, and circumcision in particular, a condition of salvation, it became something else. Indeed it became yet another of the superstitious God-substitutes, 'the basic principles of this world' by which fallen men and women hope to ward off judgment.[13] It changed the proclamation of the gospel from 'Christ alone' to 'Christ plus circumcision', 'Christ plus the law'.

3. God's law and likeness

I once heard it said that Deuteronomy was Jesus' favourite book. This may or may not be the case, but it is a fact that he quotes it more than any other.[14] The casual reader flicking through its pages might see it as a dusty collection of ancient laws with no relevance for us today. Jesus saw it in another light, and so should we. It was his Father's law and likeness, his wisdom and his will. In fact Deuteronomy has been described as the heartbeat of the Old Testament.

The people of Israel are at the borders of the Promised Land, at last ready to take up their inheritance. For forty years a fickle and failed generation has lived and died in the desert. With all the wonders of their deliverance from Egypt behind them, and every sign of God's presence among them, they still did not have the faith and courage to enter the Promised Land and displace the Canaanites. Now their children's generation is ready to be God's people in God's land.

---

[11] Ibid., pp. 200–201.   [12] Rom. 7:12.   [13] Col. 2:20.
[14] E.g. Matt. 4:4, 6, 10; 5:31, 38; 15:4; 18:16; 22:37.

But what sort of people are they going to be in that land and what kind of society are they going to create? Here God confronts a new generation with his demands on them as a nation. Nearly forty years before, at the foot of Mount Sinai, God had presented the nation with his Ten Commandments and filled out some of their implications for future and settled Israelite society in Exodus 20 – 23, 'The Book of the Covenant'. The book of Deuteronomy repeats and supplements that earlier code; it is 'preached law' and lays down God's directives for the national life of this people he had made his own possession, his holy nation. It may be said to have two great determining factors: God as the basis of Israel's life and Israel as a model for the nations. Justice and mercy should characterize human life and society wherever God's will is done.

4. God, the foundation of life (6:4–7; 7:6–11)

Deuteronomy begins with a theology of recent history as Moses recounts the wilderness wanderings after the failure at Kadesh Barnea, its lost opportunities, God-given victories and new possibilities. The Ten Commandments are repeated and the call is made to begin a new stage of Israel's ongoing story. Notice again that Israel's law is rooted in a relationship with God, a unique, undeserved and challenging relationship.

This was to be the secret of Israel's unique and revolutionary society: their law was rooted in grace, their obedience was to be a willing response to God's love, their present grew out of a past redemption, the deliverance from Egypt. Now they were to create a just and equal society under God which would be a light to the nations.

Here is an important New Testament perspective on the life of obedience too. Christianity is, first and foremost, about what God has done for us in Jesus Christ, not about what we must do for God. Then, what we must do for God is in *response* to this in love and gratitude. Our good works and cleaned-up lives are not a way of earning salvation but flow from a salvation which is unearned and free; God's gift at the start not his wages at the end. The Christian is someone who is motivated by gratitude, not by fear or uncertainty: 'Love so amazing, so divine, / Demands my soul, my life my all.'[15] This is not an excuse for sin but the foundation of all righteousness; so it was in Israel and so it is for us.

We all want a better world, don't we? We see and hear of so much crime, poverty, cruelty and suffering. Moreover, we have just emerged from a century marked by slaughter unparalleled in all

---

[15] Hymn, 'When I survey the wondrous cross', by Isaac Watts (1674–1748).

human history. Why are we still in this state after thousands of years of progress?

I believe the answer to that is well illustrated on the walls of the United Nations Building in New York. In one place there is a text from Isaiah 2:4: 'They shall beat their swords into ploughshares and their spears into pruning hooks. Nation shall not lift up sword against nation, neither shall they learn war any more.' Significantly, the first part of that verse has been left out: '*He* will judge between the nations and settle disputes for many peoples.' Why was the reference to God left out? Because the text was a gift of the Soviet Union to the United Nations, and the Soviet Union was militantly atheistic in its Communist ideology!

There are many others who want peace without the God of peace; the inconveniences of sin removed, but not sin's essential principle – independence from God. But we will never fulfil our human potential and destiny without God, because a relationship with him *is* our supreme and highest destiny, because we were made to love and serve him in a divine-human partnership, and because without him our human greed and folly will continue to be the ball and chain we drag with us through the centuries of human progress. All our laws and high-mindedness cannot eradicate these things; we cannot legislate for the heart, which only God can can change.

David Wells, in his book *Losing Our Virtue*, writes:

> We are seeing on an unprecedented scale the birth of a world civilisation ... [but] ours is the first major civilisation to be building itself deliberately and self-consciously without religious foundations. Beneath other civilisations there have always been religious foundations, whether these came from Islam, Hinduism, or Christianity itself. Beneath ours there are none and it is no surprise to learn that 67% of Americans do not believe in the existence of moral absolutes and that 70% do not believe in absolute truth – truths that should be believed by all people in all places and at all times. We are building a world of the most marvellous ingenuity and intricacy but it is arising over a spiritual vacuum ... we are now having to depend upon litigation to do what self-restraint, moral principle, religious belief, the family and the church once accomplished.[16]

The late Lord Denning, formerly Master of the Rolls in England and Wales, makes much the same point as Wells:

---

[16] David Wells, *Losing Our Virtue: Why the church must recover its moral vision* (IVP, 1998), pp. 23–24.

And what does it all come to? Surely this, that if we seek truth and justice, we cannot find it by argument and debate, not by reading and thinking, but only (as our forefathers said) by the maintenance of true religion and virtue. Religion concerns the spirit in man whereby he is able to recognise what is truth and what is justice: whereas law is only the application, however imperfectly, of truth and justice in our everyday affairs. If religion perishes in the land, truth and justice will also. We have already strayed too far from the faith of our fathers. Let us return to it, for it is the only thing that can save us.[17]

5. God's model community

The nation of Israel is to settle in the Promised Land, but what sort of people are they going to be in that land? Notice that it is not simply a matter of what kind of individuals but what kind of community. That is the question the book of Deuteronomy addresses.

There is an important lesson for us in that. God is concerned about human beings in their community life. God himself has lived from eternity in the community life of Father, Son and Holy Spirit, Three in One: knowing each other, loving each other, rejoicing in each other. Israel was to be a community which in some ways was to be like God in its community life, love and order. Christopher Wright, in his study of the laws of Deuteronomy and their implications for us today, writes: 'The primary ethical thrust of the Old Testament is, in fact, social . . . the Old Testament is absorbed with what it means to be the living people of the living God'.[18]

We tend to think of 'holiness' as a matter of personal and even private piety. But the book of Deuteronomy shows us that the holiness God requires of us is very practical and involves to a high degree the way we treat other people and live together. In the Old Testament laws, as Dr Wright points out, this holiness includes 'generosity to the poor at harvest time, justice for workers, integrity in judicial processes, considerate behaviour to other people, equality before the law for immigrants, honest trading and other very "earthy" social matters'.[19] Without this dimension of holiness, Israel's worship will never be acceptable: 'Failure to honour God in the material realm cannot be compensated for by religiosity in the spiritual realm.'[20]

All of the laws, of course, belong specifically to Israel as a

---

[17] Rt. Hon. Lord Denning, 'The Influence of Religion on Law', *Lawyers Christian Fellowship*, 1 May 1989.
[18] Wright, p. 10.   [19] Ibid., pp. 26–27.   [20] Ibid., p. 60.

particular culture at a particular stage in history. Some of them merely illustrate the 'difference' of Israel, her singularity as the Lord's people, a kind of badge or a marker of identity. Some of them belong to the Old Testament dispensation pointing forward to the once-for-all work of Jesus Christ, the Son of God and Redeemer of his world-wide people. A few may seem strange and even harsh to us, so distant are we from these times more than three thousand years ago.

But if we are wise we shall find here information and illustration touching the character of God and his will for all people and all times. Christopher Wright tells us: 'We need to see how any particular law functioned in its own Israelite context and what moral principles underlie it. It is those principles which then feed our ethical thought and action in our own environment.'[21] He tells us, 'A basic moral principle pervades biblical ethics', namely, 'the service of God and mutual human care are inseparably bound together'.[22] He shows us the compassionate drift of Old Testament laws:

> The breadth of situations covered by this category of law is very impressive. It includes protection for the weak, especially those who lacked the natural protection of family and land, namely the widows, orphans, Levites, immigrants and resident aliens; justice for the poor; impartiality; generosity at harvest time and in general economic life; respect for persons and property, even of an enemy; special care for strangers ... even care for animals, domestic and wild and for fruit trees.

Christopher Wright speaks of 'the warm heart of these Old Testament laws',[23] with their concern for freedom, rest and protection.

a. The God of fresh starts (15:1–18)

In Deuteronomy 15, for example, we see how the cycle of debt is broken for every Israelite every seven years when debts are cancelled in the Sabbath year. Any Israelite who had sold himself into slavery (in Israel this was not harsh but a kind of indentured labour, a period of domestic service) to work off his debts was to be set free with the means to start again in livestock and crops. For God is the God of fresh starts.

We can easily see the implication of this in churches to help, to give, to forgive as we have been forgiven by God. Even in society at large there must be escape routes from poverty for individuals and nations; not always hand-outs but always footholds, opportunities

[21] Ibid., p. 158.   [22] Ibid., p. 156.   [23] Ibid., pp. 156–157.

to climb out, with help, even from the holes our mistakes, folly or sin can get us into. Third World debt is so huge in some cases that half the national income is swallowed up paying interest to wealthy Western countries and banks, so that the principle is never reduced and in many cases new loans have to be taken out to pay more of the interest already owed. Such nations cry out for a fresh start. However, where corruption is endemic there are no easy answers.

b. The God who gives stopping places (16:1–17)

Deuteromomy 16, with its instructions about the annual feasts, reminds us that there were, by law, regular times of refreshment and festival in Israel and every family and individual was to be involved. They were truly 'holy' days but they were also 'holidays'. Besides the weekly Sabbath and the monthly new moon feast there were five great annual festivals in Israel. Three of them were pilgrimage feasts (Passover, Weeks/Pentecost and Tabernacles) lasting a week each and involving travel to Jerusalem in later years, in caravans of families, neighbours and friends. We can imagine the pleasure and excitement among Israelite children when their families were able to make the journey with its travel, its brief encampments, and reunions – a few days at the seaside today is nothing to it! Psalm 84 celebrates the journey as well as the destination and the Psalms of Ascent[24] may well have been sung at different stages on the journey.

One of the most engaging and insightful moments in C. S. Lewis's Narnia series is when Aslan plays with the children, rolling in the grass with them and carrying them on his strong back. The idea of God at play with us is, perhaps, both daring and delightful, but there are more daring pictures and metaphors than that in the Old Testament, and with the Jesus of the Gospels before us it does not seem so unlikely.

While worship was essential and central to these festivals, the 'rest' from labour of the weekly Sabbath day is always emphasized. This is a reminder to governments and businesses, large and small, that people are not machines or mere economic components to be driven constantly or moved about thoughtlessly. In recent decades great harm has been done by management practices and worker-abuse which have ignored or defied this principle. At last these practices are being recognized as 'counterproductive' – a poor enough motive in itself – as marriages founder and employees break down.

c. The God who protects

Various principles of justice and mercy are built in to Israelite life in Deuteronomy 17 – 25. In chapter 17 the law courts are established

---

[24] Pss. 120 – 134.

and respect for law is enforced. Even kings are not above it, and in the future each new king is to make his own copy of the law of God so that he does not act like the absolute monarchs of the surrounding nations (vv. 14–20). The king is only ever *primus inter pares* (first among equals) in covenant with God and the people to rule wisely and is responsible to God for his rule over the covenant community. This reminds us that governments, presidents, prime ministers and monarchs one day must all give account to God, the Judge of all the earth.

In Deuteronomy 19 there are safeguards for difficult cases, such as the three 'cities of refuge' set up in the heart of the land. A man who had committed accidental homicide could flee to one of these cities to be safe from the passion and reprisal of the murdered person's family. The proud and unforgiving blood feuds which marked many societies were not to be tolerated in Israel.

6. Church and state

These are only a few of the diverse laws of Deuteronomy and, earlier, Exodus. They serve to remind us that God is a God of justice, mercy and truth, who commands righteousness and gives peace in a society where his ways are respected and his will is done.

As Christians we must surely be champions of such principles in our own societies: fostering their growth, protesting their abuse and illustrating their beauty in our own working and domestic lives. This is why we need to have a biblical theology of work for everyone and it is why we need Christians to take an active part in the political and social structures which shape their nation's life.

We do not now live in a *theocracy* – a nation governed directly by God – but in a *democracy* – government by the whole population, usually through elected representatives. In modern history, as well as ancient, there have been two extremes in the matter of God and government: 'those who want to eliminate religion from political life' and 'those who want religion to dominate politics'.[25]

God, according to Scripture, has instituted the state, its government and authority to restrain sin and to promote a just social order.[26] One of the most common errors in these democratic times is to imagine that the role of government is determined solely by the will of the people. That is not true. As well as being answerable to their people, the leaders of the state are answerable to God. If the state kow-tows to populist (or group-pressure) demands for institutionalized racism, abortion on demand, or any other thing

---

[25] Charles Colson, *Kingdoms in Conflict* (Hodder & Stoughton, 1989), p. 46.
[26] E.g. Rom. 13:1–7; 1 Pet. 2:13–17.

inherently wrong, then the state cannot wash its hands of responsibility. It will suffer the built-in judgments of national evils and will share in the final judgment of God upon both leaders and people.[27]

At times the church has drawn unwarranted conclusions from the Old Testament laws and tried to mix church and state, religion and politics, persuasion and legislation in ways that were disastrous. The church must neither ignore the state nor seek to dominate it for her own ends – not even to promote the kingdom of God: ' "Not by might nor by power, but by my Spirit," says the LORD.'[28] But while the church is not a *ruling power*, she must nonetheless be a *prophetic voice* wherever tyrants deny human rights, wherever ruthless and greedy business practices crush and cheat the defenceless, and wherever old evils in new forms grow in a society.

God's people are to be salt and light in those societies, living out their message. Christian people should be responsible citizens, good bosses, reliable employees, caring fellow-workers, loyal and loving family members and faithful church members. As communities, our churches should be 'working models' of the world God wants and prototypes of the world that shall be when 'the dwelling of God is with men and he will live with them'.[29]

[27] See Charles Colson, op. cit., p. 91.   [28] Zech. 4:6.   [29] Rev. 21:3.

Exodus 32 – 34
11. God of glory and grace

1. A great apostasy (32:1–8)

After the confirmation of the covenant with the people and the elders of Israel in Exodus 24, Moses was called into the presence of God on the top of Sinai. He entered the cloud of glory and stayed there forty days and forty nights. There the arrangements for Israel's worship were set down: directions concerning the making of the Ark of the Covenant, the table and the lamp stand, the tabernacle frame and hangings, the altar, priestly garments and priestly equipment and the shape of worship for centuries to come. Much more would follow in God's further directions to Moses in the Tent of Meeting, recorded in Leviticus.

Exodus 32, however, records the terrible contrast between what was happening at the top of Sinai and what was taking place at its foot. Over the forty days, the mood among the people passed from awe and fear to impatience (32:1) and they decided to shape their own ritual and direct their own worship. Aaron, cowed by the widespread feeling and perhaps wanting to prevent something worse, succumbed to popular wishes. He utilized what was probably a familiar ancient near-Eastern symbol of deity, a golden calf, and declared a festival to Yahweh (32:5). The result was a mixture of debased Yahweh-worship and immorality (32:6). Here, as John Durham writes, everything Israel has gained

> ... is thrown into terrifying jeopardy by a shattering act of disobedience that threatens to plunge Israel into a situation far deadlier and more ignominious than Egyptian bondage at its worst. The special treasure people ... are suddenly in danger of becoming a people with no identity at all ... fragmented by the centrifugal forces of their own selfish rebellion and left without hope in a land the more empty because it has been so full of Yahweh's own Presence ... An Israel from whom Yahweh's Pres-

ence has departed is far worse than an Israel that had not known that Presence.[1]

a. Yahweh on their own terms

Durham carefully locates the exact nature of the offence of Israel in this act of apostasy. The account in Exodus 32:1–6: is not, he says,

> ... an account of the abandonment of Yahweh for other gods; it is an account of the transfer of the centre of authority of faith in Yahweh from Moses and the laws and symbols he has announced to a golden calf without laws and without any symbols beyond itself. Moses is the representative of a God invisible in mystery. The calf is to be the representative of that same God, whose invisibility and mystery is compromised by an image he has forbidden ... The calf represented Yahweh on *their* terms. Yahweh had made clear repeatedly that he would be received and worshipped only on *his* terms.[2]

It was like a bride having an affair on her honeymoon, playing fast and loose with her husband of days. A later psalm, ringing with indignation, contempt and sorrow would recall: 'They exchanged their Glory for an image of a bull, which eats grass.'[3]

b. 'I can worship my God in my own way'

Here is an early warning about natural religion and the attitude that says, 'I worship my God in my own way', without any care for his self-revelation in Scripture, his church, or his revealed will for our lives and our worship.[4] It is true that the law was 'only a shadow' of the good things that were coming,[5] that Christ has done what the law could not do in saving us,[6] that Christ has replaced the law, abolishing its sacrifice and priests and embodying in his own life and death the whole will of God,[7] and that in sending his Spirit in the new dispensation he has internalized the law of God as a ruling power in the lives of God's people.[8] Yet all that does not mean we can worship God in ignorance,[9] pride[10] or in a manner detached from daily life.[11]

2. The God who rages (32:9–35)

The full implication of Israel's act of apostasy becomes apparent in the rest of the chapter. Yahweh says to Moses, '*Now leave me alone*

[1] Durham, p. 418.   [2] Ibid., p. 422.   [3] Ps. 106:20.
[4] Heb. 10:25; 12:28; 13:17.   [5] Heb. 10:1.   [6] Heb. 10:1–7.   [7] Heb. 10:8–14.
[8] Heb. 10:16; cf. Jer. 31:33.   [9] Eph. 4:11–13.   [10] Rom. 12:3–8.
[11] Rom. 12:1–3.

*so that my anger may burn against them and that I may destroy
them. Then I will make you into a great nation'* (32:10). Israel's act
of covenant-betrayal leaves her facing annihilation: God can fulfil
his promise to Abraham through Moses without them. But Moses
pleads with God for Israel's life (vv. 11–14) and God agrees to spare
the nation.

The divine wrath, however, is forcefully expressed when Moses
comes down to the camp. The stone tablets containing the
commandments engraved by God are shattered at the foot of the
mountain, symbolizing the shattered relationship between Yahweh
and Israel (v. 19). The people are made to drink the detritus of their
own idol, which was probably made of wood overlaid with gold,
rather than of pure gold (v. 20). The Levites are sent to slay the guilty
without allowing any social or familial factors to intervene, *and that
day about three thousand of the people died* (vv. 27–28). Even this,
however, does not atone for Israel's great sin nor can Moses himself,
even in the sacrifice of himself, hope to do this (vv. 32–33), nor does
the plague that follows (v. 35).

3. The God who withdraws his presence (33:1–6)

At first God tells Moses he will no longer be the presence in Israel's
midst. Instead, he will send 'an angel' to drive out the tribes so that
Israel can take possession of Canaan, but he himself will not go with
them *'because you are a stiff-necked people and I might destroy you
on the way'* (v. 3). Indeed, because of Israel's persistent tendency to
rebel, God's presence in their midst will be dangerous and perhaps
even fatal (33:1–3).

The command in verse 1 to leave Sinai, the mountain of God,
seems to echo the expulsion from Eden. 'In the place of his Presence,
there will be only Absence. It is a punishment, announced at this
point in the sequence of the Book of Exodus, that negates every
announcement, every expectation, every instruction except those
now being given. There will be no special treasure, no kingdom of
priests, no holy nation, no cloud of Glory.'[12]

The result in the camp is immediate dismay and a fearful
uncertainty about the future. Without God, Israel is nothing, just
one nation among many. She has lost her identity. She no longer has
a world destiny. In the absence of God she ceases to exist as the
people of God. Memory is not enough; birth is not enough;
Abraham is not enough. 'No people, no matter how religious they
are and for whatever reasons, can be a people of God without the
Presence of God.'[13]

---

[12] Durham, p. 437.   [13] Ibid., p. 448.

There is a lesson here for us all. The Israelites who took part in the great apostasy did so at the foot of Sinai and after every experience of the majesty and the goodness of God. They stand (or fall!) as a terrible warning of what great temptation can do, of what ambushes await the people of God, even in the most favourable places, even at the most sacred times. It is possible to move from sacrament to sin in an hour. It is possible to go from the best ministry in the world to the worst sins of the city in an evening. It is possible to know the best doctrine but live the worst life. We are called to a godly fear that draws on God every hour, not in superstitious or unhealthy anxiety but in humble reliance and peaceful confidence, never dictating to him, willing to wait for him, true in worshipping him.

This holds true for every divine–human relationship in any age. Where would we be without the gracious presence of the Lord in our lives? God knows, but you and I may have an inkling! So, when Satan offers you the golden calf of an alternative loyalty, when you are tempted to turn your back on all the kindness and grace of the One God, when you are tempted by the world to 'chuck' Christianity, remember it is a thousand times better to 'chuck' the golden calf.

4. The God who relents (33:7–23)

In 33:12 Moses pleads with God his own inability to lead the people in God's absence. He presses God for a final decision as to himself and the people, for earlier God had left a glimmer of hope, telling the people, '*I will decide what to do with you*' (v. 5). He recalls the times (unrecorded) when God had said to Moses, 'I know you by name and you have found favour with me' (v. 12). He expresses his conviction that without the presence of God he could not continue to find such favour and pleads for the nation, '*Remember that this nation is your people*' (v. 13).

a. 'My Presence will go with you'
The reply of Yahweh in verse 14 is exactly what Moses has pleaded for: '*My Presence will go with you and I will give you rest.*' Literally it is 'My Face will go with you', and the remainder of the statement may be rendered either 'Thus will I give you rest [in the Promised Land]' or 'Thus will I quiet you.' Durham renders it, 'Thus will I dispel your anxiety.'[14] In relief and response Moses replies, '*If your Presence does not go with us do not send us up from here*' (v. 15). It is a confession that neither he nor Israel is anything without the presence of Yahweh and his blessing. What is the Promised Land

[14] Ibid., p. 444.

without that? So also for us, without the blessing of God's presence what are any of the glittering prizes of life: the fulfilment of all our ambitions, the successes of our lives, the possessions, the popularity, the applause?

Yahweh's reply is decisive: '*I will do the very thing you have asked, because I am pleased with you and I know you by name*' (v. 17).

b. 'Show me your glory'

At this point, as God comforts Moses with the reassurance of his love, his choice and his approval (we might see it as a statement saying, 'Well done, good and faithful servant'),[15] Moses utters his momentous request. He asks God what no-one had asked him before. Earlier, in Exodus 4:1–2, he had asked for signs for others; now he asks for a reassurance for himself: *Then Moses said, 'Now show me your glory'* (v. 18).

It seems clear that Moses is asking here for something beyond all previous revelations of the glory of Yahweh, such as the glory of the Lord in the cloud which he not only saw (16:7, 10) but entered (24:16–17). He had known times with the Lord which are described as 'face to face' (33:11). Durham thinks that the phrase 'face to face' there is to be understood as an idiom of intimacy, not as a reference to theophany.[16] However, even if there was more to it than that,[17] it remains the case that previously Moses had seen no more than 'the form of the Lord' and not the very being, the essential glory of Yahweh.[18] In his closest proximity the face of God had been hidden in darkness (20:21) or obscured by the bright cloud (33:9). Now, Moses wants more as love wants more of its beloved. He wants the privilege of seeing God in his unveiled glory, in his full beauty, in his innermost being. It is, of course, impossible but love often wants the impossible, such as to be with the human beloved 'always and for ever'.

c. 'No-one may see me and live'

God responds to this request with a statement of his sovereignty: *And the LORD said, 'I will cause all my goodness to pass in front of you, and I will proclaim my name, the LORD, in your presence. I will have mercy on whom I will have mercy, and I will have compassion on whom I will have compassion*' (v. 19). 'His favour and his compassion are given only on his terms.'[19] Then God explains why Moses cannot see his presence: he tells his beloved servant, '*You cannot see my face, for no-one may see me and live*' (v. 20). 'The gap

---

[15] Cf. Matt. 25:21, 23.   [16] Durham, p. 443.   [17] See Num. 12:8.
[18] Cf. Exod. 24:9–11.   [19] Durham, p. 452.

between the finite and the infinite is too great; it is an experience of which man is incapable.'[20] Indeed, sin has made such unmediated proximity fatal. We still need the cloud, the screen, the distance: too near the sun and we burn up; we can only take so much of God. Above all, we need a mediator. The people of Israel chose Moses (20:19) but the New Testament family learn that there is a better mediator as well as a better testament and dispensation.[21]

The verses which follow build up the tension involved in the approach of God in his glory. Moses is told that though he cannot see the face of God, yet the glory of his presence will 'pass by' and Moses will be sheltered in a cleft of the rock and covered with the protecting hand of God until the danger has receded. Only God can protect him from God! The receding glory will be as much as he can bear: *'You will see my back, but my face must not be seen'* (v. 23).

When God does eventually pass in front of Moses, what is revealed is neither light nor fire but the personal character of God as loving and gracious, holy and just. Durham writes:

> But though Yahweh does indeed come to Moses in theophany [an appearing of God], what he gives to Moses is quite specifically *not* the *sight* of his beauty, his glory, his Presence – that, indeed, he pointedly denies. What he gives rather, is a *description*, and at that, a description not of how he *looks* but of how he *is*.
>
> The calling out of the name 'Yahweh' as an accompaniment or perhaps even a conclusion to the passing of Yahweh's [goodness] is an important clue to what Yahweh promised Moses. [Goodness] refers, not to an appearance of beauty but to a recital of character . . . to Moses' request for a look at his Presence, Yahweh replied 'I will reveal to you what I am, not how I look.'[22]

5. What is God like? (34:5–8)

Then the LORD came down in the cloud and stood there with him and proclaimed his name, the LORD [Yahweh]. [6]And he passed in front of Moses, proclaiming, 'The LORD [Yahweh], the LORD [Yahweh], the compassionate and gracious God, slow to anger, abounding in love and faithfulness, [7]maintaining love to thousands, and forgiving wickedness, rebellion and sin. Yet he does not leave the guilty unpunished: he punishes the children and their children for the sin of the fathers to the third and fourth generation.' Moses bowed to the ground at once and worshipped.

---

[20] Ibid.   [21] 1 Tim. 2:5; Heb. 3:3–6; 8:6; 9:15.   [22] Durham, p. 452.

There is a remarkable omission in chapter 34. When God does pass by there is no mention of Moses seeing his receding glory, though he presumably did. Even that privilege is displaced by something greater: the definitive statement of God about his innermost character – his compassion, his mercy, his patience and his love. These are so much the central glories of God's being that visions of his outward brightness are secondary to them and he first and foremost wants us to know him by these things.

The lesson is clear: God wants us to know him as he truly is, not just to have vague feelings or even bright visions, but to know him, the infinite-personal God, in his true character. And to do that we are first summoned to listen to God's word about himself. That is why teaching is so important in the church: the teaching and preaching of the Scriptures, God's inspired Word and self-revelation.[23] If we are only interested in lovely feelings and occasional visions or mystical experiences or signs and wonders, we are in danger of falling into a mere mysticism at one extreme or an outright scepticism at the other.

It is true that we must move from knowing about God to knowing him. But the revelation is also the route. This is the God we seek: the one who seeks us first. This is the God who speaks: that we might find him to be this in our own experience. This is the God who puts first things first – not spiritual experience, but himself as the God who is experienced, not the wonders of God but the God of wonders, not the mercies of God but the God of all mercy and grace, not even the glories of God but the God whose greatest glory is his inmost character, his moral perfection, his holiness, his goodness, his uprightness, his love. When Moses asked of God, 'Now, show me your glory', God gave it to him in this form.

R. Moberly has called Exodus 34:5–7 'the most extensive statement about the name, i.e. the character, of God in the Bible', pointing out that it is 'a statement found, moreover, on the lips of God himself – and thus representing the very heart of God's self-revelation within Israel'.[24] We shall therefore examine it in some detail.

a. 'The compassionate and gracious God'

These two words, compassionate and gracious, are found together 13 times in the Old Testament, eleven of them as part of a long liturgical formula that spells out God's divine attributes.[25] The Hebrew word here translated 'compassionate' is *raḥûm*. The

---

[23] 2 Tim. 3:16–17; 2 Pet. 1:19–20.
[24] R. Moberly, *"mn"*, *NIDOTTE*, vol. 1, p. 428.
[25] Mike Butterworth, *'rḥm'*, *NIDOTTE*, vol. 3, p. 1094.

singular, *reḥem/raḥam*, is the word for 'womb', and carries with it 'a picture of the tender care bestowed on an infant when it is most vulnerable'.[26] The link with 'womb' makes it essentially maternal love, the love which surges and overflows, as in 1 Kings 3:26. The basic meaning of the root 'signifies a warm compassion, a compassion which is ready to go the second mile, which is ready to forgive sin, to replace judgement with grace'. It 'goes beyond the realm of legal rights into the realm of grace and hope'.[27]

Our English word 'compassionate' implies drawing alongside someone who is suffering, understanding their suffering ('standing under' their situation with them) and even suffering with them. But when we suffer, isn't there the tendency to think that God is punishing us for our sins and even that God has deserted us? From such words as this, and what they signify of God's heart, we may have the assurance that God is never closer to us than when we feel he is far from us.

The verb *ḥānan* (*ḥnn*), 'to be gracious' or 'to show favour', is one of the most important terms used to describe God's love for men and women. It occurs 41 times in the Old Testament with God as the subject, and a further 24 times we read of his *ḥen*, his 'grace'. Grace is 'undeserved favour at the hands of a superior',[28] it is 'love, but for the undeserving'.[29] The New Testament uses the Greek word *charis* for this. Its variety of contexts shows, as Terence Fretheim demonstrates, that 'God's grace is finally rooted, not in what people do, but in his disposition to be gracious in ways beyond any human formula or calculation . . . all in the service of God's will that as many as possible experience that grace (Jon. 4:2)'.[30]

God's grace issues in his gracious actions; grace is not only an attitude but an activity also. It means God 'going out' to relieve, encourage and save us. It means too that he does so because of something in him, not because of something in us. Grace is always unmerited favour, undeserved salvation, free and unforced love. He is the God of all grace.

b. 'Slow to anger'

We may all thank God he is! We don't like working beside or living with someone who has a short fuse, do we? It's not so much like walking on eggshells as between land-mines. If God were quick to anger we would have been history before we were news! Many Christians still think of God as an unsparing boss ready to come down on us like a ton of bricks at the first let-down. But we are

[26] Ibid., p. 1093.   [27] Ibid., pp. 1094–1095.
[28] Norman H. Snaith in J. Barton Payne, *The Theology of the Older Testament* (Zondervan, 1962), p. 164.
[29] Ibid.   [30] T. Fretheim, writing in *NIDOTTE*, vol. 2, p. 205.

reminded repeatedly in the Old Testament that Yahweh is 'slow to anger'. Gale Struthers notes:

> The phrase, 'slow to anger' ('*erek 'appayîm*) is included in a listing of the Lord's attributes seven times, together with his other attributes: love (*ḥeseḏ*), fidelity (*ʾemeṯ*), compassion (*raḥûm*) and graciousness (*ḥanûm*); see Ex. 34:6; Neh. 9:17; Ps. 86:15; 103:8; Joel 2:13; Jon. 4:2. Num. 14:18 simply links the Lord's slowness to anger with his love (*ḥeseḏ*).[31]

The Hebrew term translated 'slow to anger', *'erek 'appayîm*, is literally being 'long-tempered' as contrasted with 'short-tempered'.

Of course we play fast and loose with him at our peril, but while we can never persuade him to compromise his righteousness, we can count on him to help us in our struggle with our sins and failures. Why? Because he is 'slow to anger, abounding in love and faithfulness, maintaining love to thousands, and forgiving wickedness, rebellion and sin'.

c. 'Abounding in love and faithfulness'

The particular word for the divine love here is *ḥeseḏ*, often translated 'steadfast love' or 'unfailing love'. Marvin Tate translates *ḥeseḏ* by the term 'loyal love' because of its associations with loyalty and faithfulness to an established relationship. Loyalty is not merely an attitude nor is it something static. It is faithfulness in action.[32] 'In general,' says Tate, '*ḥeseḏ* refers to the obligation assumed by one person to act on behalf of another, who is usually dependent on the aid of the first and helpless to function adequately without it'.

It is the word David uses in his great psalm of repentance, Psalm 51: 'Have mercy on me, O God, according to your unfailing [*ḥeseḏ*] love.' Just as Israel's existence was threatened by the great apostasy, so David stood before the passionate wrath of God because of his sin with Bathsheba and his murder of her husband. Only God's *ḥeseḏ* stands between him and utter exclusion from the presence of the Lord. 'Thus in Psalm 51 the suppliant appeals for mercy on the basis of God's willingly-assumed and continued obligation (his "loyal love") to act for the removal of anything, including guilt, which threatens the welfare of an individual (or people) for whom he is responsible.'[33]

The term *ḥeseḏ* occurs 246 times in the Old Testament, just over half of them in Psalms. 'It is commonly used of the attitudes and

---

[31] Gale Struthers, "*np*', *NIDOTTE*, vol. 1, p. 464.
[32] See K. D. Sakenfield, *Faithfulness in Action: Loyalty in Biblical Perspective* (Fortress Press, 1985), quoted in Tate, p. 13.
[33] Ibid., p. 13.

behaviour of humans toward one another, but more frequently (ratio 3:1) describes the disposition and beneficent actions of God toward the faithful, Israel his people and humanity in general.'[34] The divine exercise of *ḥeseḏ* is closely linked to God's covenantal relationship with his people. '*Hesed* is the "essence" of the covenantal relationship', says one scholar.[35] The covenant is 'a prime exemplar of the *hesed* relationship', says another.[36] It is a relational term and one that calls for a corresponding obedience to God's prior grace. The loyalty of God calls for the loyalty of his people.

The other great word here is *ᵉmeṯ* ('faithfulness'). *ᵉmeṯ*, with its root in "truth", is the Lord's constancy, his ever being "true to himself", changeless in relation to his promises etc. but also true to his holiness and therefore to his law with its threats and judgements.'[37] 'What precisely', asks R. W. L. Moberly, 'does "faithfulness" mean in this context?' He answers:

> In general terms it must relate to Yahweh's willingness, in response to the intercession of Moses (Exod. 33:12–18), to show his true nature through renewing the covenant with Israel despite their sin with the Golden Calf, in which they had effectively forfeited their position as the chosen people of Yahweh. The general point is well expressed in the words of the NT, 'If we are faithless, he will remain faithful, for he cannot disown himself' (2 Tim. 2:13).[38]

Yahweh is 'abounding in love and faithfulness'. Abounding is the opposite of grudging. He is as quick to love as he is slow to anger; he is as eager in his love as he is reluctant in his judgments; his faithfulness to his people is a stickability no glue could adequately illustrate: he has welded together his life and ours, embracing us so close that there is an inter-penetration of his life with our lives and our lives with his life.

I heard it well expressed recently by a clergyman who said, 'God has been a part of my story for so long now that I cannot describe my story without speaking about God. And what is more, God has known me and loved me for so long that He cannot fully tell his story without speaking about me. He has loved me before I was born and will love me after I die; he will never allow his relationship with me to die. God's story is incomplete without me as my story is incomplete without God.' That is the God of grace, abounding in love and faithfulness.

[34] D. A. Baur and R. P. Gordon, '*ḥsḏ*', *NIDOTTE*, vol. 2, p. 211.
[35] N. Glueck, quoted in ibid.   [36] Sakenfield, op. cit.
[37] Alec Motyer in correspondence.   [38] R. Moberly, op. cit., vol. 1, p. 429.

d. 'Yet he does not leave the guilty unpunished'

If he did leave the guilty unpunished, where would his morality be? Where would we look for truth and justice? Walter Brueggemann writes:

> This second half of the sentence surprises us because it indicates that Yahweh takes affront (as in the case of Aaron in Exodus 32) very seriously, so seriously as to affect the relationship for as many as four generations . . . This second half of the sequence surprises, and at the same time it alerts Israel to the reality that Yahweh's full character is not subsumed under Yahweh's commitment to Israel in solidarity. There is something in Yahweh's sovereign rule – Yahweh's own self-seriousness – that is not compromised or conceded, even in the practice of solidarity.[39]

Israel can never say, in the spirit of Heinrich Heine's notorious death-bed witticism, 'God will forgive my sins, that's his job.' Israel knows too well that Yahweh's slowness to anger does not reduce by one degree his white-hot zeal for righteousness.

The meaning of 'faithfulness' in God is indicated by some of the words with which it is frequently combined. These include steadfast love, righteousness and justice, as well as other moral terms. The general significance of all this is that Yahweh's faithfulness towards Israel is combined with a strong sense of moral integrity and is in no sense morally lax or indifferent. In Exodus 34 the emphatic statement of God's graciousness and faithfulness to faithless Israel is combined with a set of clear stipulations as the covenant is renewed (34:11–26) and a statement that God's name, in other words, his character, is also 'jealous' (34:14), that is, tolerating no compromise in Israel's commitment to him. In Bonhoffer's famous phrase, there is no 'cheap grace'.[40]

Where there is no atonement for sin, where grace has been despised in its provisions, there can be only 'a fearful expectation of judgment'.[41] The wicked triumph only for a little while; a terrible reckoning is coming; sin unrepented of is morally continued in, and in the day of God's judgment it will receive its just recompense.

'But why punish the children?' it may be asked. Our modern (and largely Western) individualism finds it hard to recognize the essential and inevitable corporateness of human life. No doubt the 'children' in mind are the grown-up offspring who perpetuate their elders' wickedness. It is a grim fact of life that parents can breed and encourage many evils in their families: racism, aggressive behaviour,

---

[39] Brueggemann (1997), pp. 217–218.   [40] Ibid.   [41] Heb. 10:26–31.

dishonesty, pride, contempt and, the Bible would add (or rather put first), idolatry. The children who grow up following such ways are not guiltless and God says he will punish them – but how much more the 'fathers' who sow such seeds.

And so, at the personal revelation of God's moral being and majesty, *Moses bowed to the ground at once and worshipped.*

6. The renewal of the covenant (34:9–28)

Yet, even now Moses is not so taken up with God that he forgets the people of God; indeed, the revelation of God that has been given him prompts and encourages Moses' prayer for the full restoration of Israel: '*O Lord, if I have found favour in your eyes,*' he said, '*then let the Lord go with us. Although this is a stiff-necked people, forgive our wickedness and our sin, and take us as your inheritance*' (34:9). Notice how Moses identifies with his people: it is not 'their sin' but 'our sin' – though Moses was on the mountain with God when they engaged in worship around the golden calf.[42] His request 'take us as your inheritance' might seem to defy all reasonable expectations in view of the fact that within six weeks of God first meeting with the people on Sinai and while the wedding vows, as it were, were still being drawn up, many in the nation were already engaged in a debased and self-willed form of worship. Yet the very revelation God has made of himself gives a basis for Moses' plea, which recalls the original intent of Yahweh in Exodus 19:5 at the making of the Sinai covenant and it is not in vain.

Yahweh replies with an explicit and formal renewal of the covenant relationship in 34:10–28. The earlier promises of his presence as they go up to the Promised Land, the demand for loyalty, the references to the first two commandments, a series of requirements 'designed to present a broad summary of covenant obligation'[43] in prospect of their settlement in Canaan, all combine to form the terms of a fresh covenantal agreement. The prohibition of verse 26, *Do not cook a young goat in its mother's milk,* may seem an odd detail to be included in a summary of the covenant which has so many seemingly more important things in it; but it may refer to part of a Canaanite fertility rite and the purpose of its inclusion here at the end of the list would be to echo the prohibition of idolatry which began the list. To seal this renewal of the covenant, Moses, as the representative of the people, is to write it down (v. 27), and God (not Moses) writes again the Ten Commandments, the heart of the covenant, on the tablets of stone which Moses has prepared (v. 28).

---

[42] Cf. Dan. 9:5f.; Neh. 1:6–7.   [43] Durham, p. 461.

7. The radiant face of Moses (34:29–35)

For Moses and for the people, however, one requirement remains: the assertion or reassertion of Moses' mediatorial role between God and Israel and his authority as God's representative. This is established in the appearance of Moses as he comes down from Mount Sinai out of the presence of Yahweh: *he was not aware that his face was radiant because he had spoken with the Lord.* Literally the Hebrew text says that Moses' face 'sent out horns of light' or 'glowed'. Durham notes that because of the particular term used it is at least possible that the narrator 'intended to suggest a light or a shining that was separate from Moses' own person, an appendage-light, an exterior light, a light that was a gift to Moses from Yahweh, a sign precisely of an authority that was his by virtue of his special fellowship with Yahweh'.[44]

Aaron and Israel were afraid to come near him (v. 30) presumably because it recalled the frightening glories of the earlier theophany at Sinai, recorded in Exodus 19 – 20 and 24. Verses 31–32 suggest that when Moses had calmed their fears he repeated for them the revelation he had received. Moses giving and Israel receiving these representative commands is tantamount to Israel's recommitment to the requirements of covenant fellowship. The breach has been healed, the covenant has not been finally renounced.

Obviously we are meant to make something of the fact that Moses, after speaking, *put a veil over his face.* This process continued regularly through the wilderness period: Moses entering God's presence with unveiled face, emerging with face aglow with a supernatural glory, and replacing the veil over his face after speaking to the Israelites. 'The intent of the veil', says William Dumbrell, 'was that the Israelites might not continue to look upon the high point of the Old Covenant revelation.' In the New Testament, the apostle Paul gives as the reason that 'their hearts were hardened' and thus 'contact with the divine glory would have been dangerous'.[45]

Applying the lesson to his own time, Paul says that only in Christ is the veil taken away, enabling us to behold (or perhaps 'reflect') the glory of God and to be transformed by the Holy Spirit into the likeness of the God of glory.[46] For Israel to recover her initial and intended privilege a twofold operation is required: 'The veil must first be removed from the national heart (vs. 14) but also from the Mosaic narratives when read (vs. 15).'[47]

---

[44] Ibid., p. 467.   [45] Dumbrell, p. 108.   [46] 2 Cor. 3:18.   [47] Dumbrell, p. 108.

8. The lost privileges of Israel

William Dumbrell points out that the apostasy with the golden calf had decisive and long-term results:

> The position of the openness of Israel to the divine word which she had assumed in Ex. 19, has now disappeared, and indeed there is a hardness of national heart against which Israel is, from this time, constantly warned, which displays itself nationally ... Never again would Israel return to its original Sinai position or realise its Sinai potential. As a summary of lost opportunities and as an indication of the unfortunate state into which the Sinai covenant had lapsed, Ex. 34:29–35 appositely concludes the Sinai covenant.[48]

Sin weakens us; like a virus in the blood stream it can stimulate recurring bouts of sickness and disability. Even a nation can fall prey to typical sins: to national pride or violent prejudice or material greed or complacent indifference. The attitudes and decisions of earlier generations can precipitate a chain-reaction which affects future generations. Israel would never be quite what it could have been because of this apostasy.

Here is a warning to us all of the long-term results of great sin, even after the sin itself has been forgiven. I once heard of an evangelist who had lived a dissolute life as a young man. He had abused his body for years with drunkenness and violent gang fights. However, he had been wonderfully converted and eventually had become an effective preacher. But his body bore the scars and marks of those earlier years and he himself testified that every morning of his life, when his scarred face looked out at him from the mirror as he shaved, he was reminded of his past life. Grace had wiped the record clean but the scars would remain to the end of his life. Israel is scarred in her history by the golden calf incident and by the rebellions in the wilderness. They may have been forgiven but they will never be forgotten.[49]

[48] Ibid., p. 110.   [49] Heb. 3:7–19.

Leviticus
12. The God who reconciles sinners

It has been said that the book of Leviticus is the most evangelical book in the Old Testament. It may seem alien and impenetrable to the new reader of Scripture, but in fact it is a book which deals with the profoundest of human problems and the greatest of human needs. No part of the Old Testament had more relevance for or held out more hope to the people of God. They knew his law and loved it, yet so often failed to keep it in its fullness and perfection. Leviticus responds to the age-old question, how can a person be right with God:

> O how shall I, whose native sphere
> Is dark, whose mind is dim,
> Before the Ineffable appear,
> And on my naked spirit bear
> The uncreated beam?[1]

1. The God who is holy

The two focal points of Leviticus are holiness and sin. The book takes us from the alienation and danger which sin has produced to the reconciliation and safety which God has achieved through atoning sacrifice. The starting point of the book's thought is the holiness of God.

God's holiness is his total, unchanging and dynamic being and character out of which he expresses himself consistently and zealously. The two great corollaries of God's holiness are his love and his wrath. When confronted with purity, righteousness and obedience, God's love goes out in embrace and blessing; when confronted with impurity, rebellion or sin in any of its forms, it expresses itself in wrath. God's wrath is a necessary as well as a personal response to

---

[1] Hymn, 'Eternal Light! Eternal Light!', by Thomas Binney (1798–1874).

sin. It is the reaction of his truth and righteousness to what would invalidate them.[2] It is the revulsion of his holy being to what challenges its very existence and threatens to disintegrate his creation at every level. God's holiness includes what one scholar calls 'the death-dealing element'.[3]

John Stott puts it thus:

> The problem of forgiveness is constituted by the inevitable collision between the divine perfection and human rebellion, between God as he is and us as we are. The obstacle to forgiveness is neither our sin alone, nor our guilt alone, but also the divine reaction in love and wrath towards guilty sinners. For, although indeed 'God is love', yet we have to remember that his love is 'holy love'.

He quotes P. Carnegie Simpson, 'Forgiveness is to man the plainest of duties; to God it is the profoundest of problems.'[4]

The book of Leviticus shows that God in love has planned a way of reconciliation by sacrifice in which what was unclean can be made holy, in which those who were far off can be brought near, in which sinful men and women can be 'ransomed, healed, restored, forgiven' and brought into fellowship with God their Maker and Redeemer.

2. The God who is dangerous[5]

It is a basic principle in the Old Testament levitical laws that, as Gordon Wenham puts it, 'The unclean and the holy are two states which must never come into contact with each other.'[6] Contact between these ultimate opposites in God's universe is 'disastrous' and 'results in death'.[7] However, 'sacrifice, by cleansing the unclean, makes such contact possible. The holy God can meet with sinful man.'[8] Sacrifice enables God without compromise to elevate man to the level of the 'holy', consecrated to him in reconciliation and peace. 'Peace with God is the goal of sacrifice.'[9] We need to learn some important Old Testament words here, especially the idea of 'atonement'.

Repeatedly in the Old Testament we are told that sacrifice 'atones' for sin and uncleanness. What 'to atone' (Heb. *kipper*) actually means is the subject of much scholarly debate. Wenham argues that *kipper* is closely related to the Hebrew word *kōper*, which means 'ransom price'.[10] In Exodus 21:30, for instance, a man whose ox has killed a man or woman is allowed to escape execution by the

---

[2] Is. 5:16. [3] Otto Procksch, '*hagios*', *TDNT*, vol. 1, p. 93.
[4] Stott (1986), p. 88. [5] Much of what follows is taken from Lewis, ch. 18.
[6] Wenham (1979), pp. 19–20. [7] Ibid., pp. 22, 26. [8] Ibid., p. 26.
[9] Ibid., p. 55. [10] Ibid., p. 28.

payment of a *kōper*, or ransom price.[11] The idea of atonement being a *payment* for sin certainly seems more consistent with the general Old Testament attitude than the idea, now widely questioned, that it was a 'covering' for sin (*kipper* as related to *kāphar*, 'to cover'). The other main possibility is that the Hebrew word *kipper* comes from the Akkadian verb *kuppuru*, to cleanse or to wipe, a concept which Derek Kidner thinks 'lies close to the heart of what atonement signified'.[12]

The system of offerings under the Mosaic covenant was quite complex. For instance, there were whole burnt offerings, peace offerings of several types, sin offerings and guilt offerings. In these and their rituals, elements of penitence, consecration and joy are variously emphasized but in them all the element of atonement for sin and reconciliation is primary and essential.

3. The God who gives a substitute (1:1–4)

The LORD called to Moses and spoke to him from the Tent of Meeting. He said [2]*'Speak to the Israelites and say to them: "When any of you brings an offering to the LORD, bring as your offering an animal from either the herd or the flock.* [3]*If the offering is a burnt offering from the herd, he is to offer a male without defect. He must present it at the entrance to the Tent of Meeting so that it will be acceptable to the LORD."'*

The first reference to an offering, 'an offering to the LORD', uses the most general word for gifts and offerings and covers them all. The second is more specific. Of the 'burnt offering', Gordon Wenham writes: 'The burnt offering was the principle atoning sacrifice in ancient Israel. It was the sacrifice that reconciled the sinner with his creator. It was the most frequent sacrifice and also the most costly. Only unblemished animals could be offered and they had to be burned whole; there was no meat left for the priests to eat.'[13]

The worshipper himself had to slaughter, skin and cut up the carcass of the animal as well as collecting its blood for the priest to present before the altar. It is too easy for us to over lookthe value of the offering, unless, perhaps, we contemplate the burning of a car! Wenham remarks, 'In the overfed West we can easily fail to realise what was involved in offering an unblemished animal in sacrifice. Meat was a rare luxury in Old Testament times for all but the very rich (cf. Nathan's parable, 2 Sam. 12:1–6). Yet even we might blanch

[11] Cf. Exod. 30:15; Num. 31:50; Prov. 6:35.
[12] Derek Kidner, 'Sacrifice – Metaphors and Meaning', *TynB* 33 (1982), p. 128. For a useful survey and examination of *kipper*, its etymology and uses see R. E. Averbeck, '*kpr*', *NIDOTTE*, vol. 2, pp. 689–710.
[13] Wenham (1979), p. 95.

if we saw a whole lamb or bull go up in smoke as a burnt offering. How much greater pangs must a poor Israelite have felt.'[14] We can appreciate how serious and meaningful the offering was to such a person.

The 'burnt offering' was also a means by which the worshipper could give special thanks for some outstanding deliverance or blessing which had been received and by which he expressed the giving up of his whole being to Yahweh in adoration and consecration. The symbolism of sacrifice contained devotional as well as penal elements.

However, it is very important to note that the crucial features of substitution, atonement and reconciliation were present in all of the animal sacrifices. Even the thankful Israelite needed these. Even their gifts were unacceptable without the shedding of blood. Even their praises were polluted with their sin.

It is also crucial to note that in the first place it is *God himself* who provides the means of propitiation, of turning away his wrath, by instituting the system of sacrifice as a central part of the relationship between himself and Israel. Here begins the 'good news' of a remedy for sin, a way back to favour with God, atonement and reconciliation, joy and peace in believing. The worshipper was to present his offering in the appointed way: at the door of the tabernacle and with the laying on of hands by the offerer: *he shall lay* [lit. 'lean'] *his hand upon the head of the burnt offering* (1:4). That this symbolized both the worshipper's identification with the animal and the substitution of the animal in his place to become, by sacrifice, an atonement for his sin, is implied in the immediate context, for we go on to read, *and it shall be accepted for* (i.e. instead of) *him to make atonement for* (instead of) *him*. However, later, in instructions for the Day of Atonement, what was implied in 1:4 is made explicit in Leviticus 16:21–22 in connection with the 'scapegoat': *He* (Aaron) *is to lay both hands on the head of the live goat and confess over it all the wickednesses and rebellion of the Israelites – all their sins – and put them on the goat's head . . . The goat will carry on itself all their sins to a solitary place; and the man shall release it in the desert.* It may be too, that if the offering was for a particular blessing (such as a child) or deliverance (from a serious sickness, for example) this declaration was made with the dedication of the animal.

The crucial point in substitutionary sacrifice is that it is God who makes this provision. It is God, not the worshipper, who ordains that the animal shall go proxy for the man as a sacrificial substitute. It is God who accepts it as such from the hands of the priests. It is God who pronounces it to be an atonement for sin in Leviticus

[14] Ibid., p. 51.

191

17:11: '*I have given it* to you to make atonement for yourselves on the altar.' *He* is foremost in reconciliation, *he* provides the means of reparation, *he* is ready to be merciful, he longs to be gracious.

R. K. Harrison writes:

> Leviticus teaches that atonement for sin must be by substitution. The sinner must bring an offering which he has acquired at some cost as a substitute for his own life. The formal identification with it is followed by the presentation of the offering to God and a declaration by the priest that atonement has been made. The book thus makes it evident that no person can be his own saviour or mediator.[15]

4. The God who punishes sin

The blood-shedding does not simply represent the release of life to God: it represents that life given up *in death*. The central and primary purpose of the burnt offering was atonement by substitutionary sacrifice. Leon Morris points out that over two hundred times in the Old Testament 'blood' is connected with death, not just life, and with violent death at that.[16]

The death of the sacrifice symbolizes the judgment due to sin and due to every worshipper on account of sin. The devotion of the worshipper is clear in the act and its consequences, but its acceptability is grounded on a penal substitution in which payment is made for his sin in order that the sacrifice of a willing heart might be acceptable to a holy God. Probably the killing of the substitute represented the death-dealing aspect of the divine wrath, while the burning of the sacrifice represented the consecration of the offerer as well as the giving of a costly gift to Yahweh in thanksgiving or penitence.

Leviticus 17:11 is a very important verse since it offers a precise rationale of sacrifice. God has prohibited the eating of blood with the meat of a burnt offering or sacrifice and then he explains why: *For the life of a creature is in the blood, and I have given it to you to make atonement for yourselves on the altar; it is the blood that makes atonement for one's life.*

> In view of the consistent Old Testament tradition that sin was a most serious matter in God's sight, and merited the most drastic punishment, it is difficult to see how the slain sacrifices could be interpreted in any other than penal terms, with the animal acting

[15] Harrison, pp. 31–32.
[16] Morris (1965), pp. 112–128; see also, Leon Morris, *The Cross in the New Testament* (Paternoster, 1976), pp. 219–220.

192

as a substitute for the sinner ... Shed blood constituted visible evidence that life had indeed been offered up in sacrifice ... Only as atonement is linked with death, represented by shed blood, and not life set free, would it appear to become efficacious in the covering of human sin.[17]

5. The God who turns away his wrath

Both Leon Morris and Gordon Wenham assert that in the process of atonement the essential element of *propitiation* is the most revealing factor. In the ancient world, to propitiate meant to 'placate', to 'appease' and thus to turn away the wrath of the gods by persuading them to be merciful. The word had all sorts of connotations, most of them utterly unworthy of Israel's God. It is a dangerous and misleading word if wrongly used, but it is a vital and helpful word if properly understood. Among the heathen, to propitiate the gods meant to persuade them to change their minds and attitude by bribing them and appeasing their capricious anger: this was usually done by means of sacrifices, animal or even human. In ancient Israel, however, the idea of propitiation was cleansed from these impurities. True, God was indeed wrathful toward sinful man, but his wrath was the outgoing of his holiness not the expression of bad temper or an arbitrary sense of dignity.

The Old Testament takes the wrath of God very seriously because it takes the holiness of God very seriously. In the Hebrew Old Testament there are 20 different words for wrath and no less than 580 references to it. Examining the Old Testament vocabulary around the concept of God's wrath, Carl Henry comes up with an impressive list. He writes:

> An extensive vocabulary of dread emerges: *arar*, 'to curse'; *etseb*, 'grief', cf. *itstabon*, 'grievous thing'; *ebah*, 'enmity'; *oyeb*, 'enemy'; *garash*, 'to drive out'; *panim*, 'to hide', cf. *sathar*, 'to be hidden'; *dun*, 'to strive'; *shapat*, 'to judge'. A satellite vocabulary of anger, indignation and wrath appears: *aph*, *anaph*, *ebrah*, *naqam*, *neqamah*, *qatseph*, *qetseph*, *rogez*, *zaam*.[18]

God's holiness has two natural and necessary consequences: his wrath toward everything that contradicts it, that brings corruption into his creation, and his love for everything that is good and true, that serves its divinely intended purpose. In setting his love upon us in our fallen state, therefore, God had to deal with both our sin and his own wrath – wiping away the one and turning away the other.

[17] Harrison, p. 182.   [18] Henry, vol. 6, p. 327.

This involved what the Old Testament called 'atonement' – a process of sin-bearing and reconciliation. It was by this process that God's wrath was 'turned away' and the way opened for his love to re-establish that eternal fellowship with him for which we were made.

The ancient Greek version of the Hebrew Old Testament, the Septuagint, widely used before and during New Testament times, translates the Hebrew *kipper* (atonement), by the Greek word *hilasmos* (propitiation), usually in the context of averting and turning aside God's wrath. The Septuagint uses the verb *hilaskomai*, to propitiate, over a hundred times and the noun *hilasmos*, 'propitiation', well over a hundred times more – never in a crude pagan sense, and always with God as the merciful and gracious propitiator who himself provides for the satisfaction of his holy wrath. In this way God is both the object of propitiation and its subject: the sacrifice is given *by* him before it is given *to* him; his love provides what his holiness demands. In Scripture to propitiate means, not 'to make gracious' but 'to enable to be gracious'. God is *already* gracious in intention, and is making a way for his mercy to operate giving full honour to his justice and truth.[19]

Some trends in modern theology have opposed propitiation as crude and unworthy; and some modern Bible translations, such as the Revised Standard Version and the New English Bible, outlaw 'propitiation' and replace it with 'expiation'. The word 'expiation' (which simply means 'removal') is in itself valid enough, but it is limited since it does not tell us *how* God removes sin, whereas the Old Testament and the New are perfectly clear that God removes sin and guilt not by passing it over, but by visiting his holy wrath upon a sin-bearing substitute and satisfying the demands of his justice.

It is not enough therefore to speak of 'expiation'. As F. F. Bruce observes, 'If sins require to be expiated, it is because they are sins committed against someone who ought to be propitiated.'[20]

6. The God who reconciles

God's intention in providing the way of sacrifice in the Old Testament was not only to demonstrate something but also to achieve something. The goal of the entire process of sacrifice was the achievement of a restored relationship between the sinner

[19] Lewis, p. 266.
[20] F. F. Bruce, *A Commentary on the Epistle to the Hebrews*, NICNT (Marshall, Morgan & Scott, 1965), p. 41, n. 57.

and his or her God. Propitiation is the means, reconciliation is the end.

There were three ways, among others, in which Yahweh's acceptance of the sacrificial substitute and his goodwill towards the worshipper were expressed. Each of them in a dramatic and personal way exhibited aspects of the reconciliation which had been achieved. The ascending smoke of the whole burnt offering, rising as *an aroma pleasing to the LORD* (1:9), showed not only his acceptance of the worshipper but the real pleasure God had in the act of reconciliation. The symbolism is neither crude nor unworthy. The God who 'delights in mercy'[21] *savours* the moment of triumphant love!

On the human side, the joyful feasting on the peace offering by the offerer and his family and friends (7:15) expresses in the clearest and most familiar manner possible that God and sinners were now reconciled: Yahweh and his people were table companions! We also see, in connection with the sin offering, the obverse of this: the eating of the sin offering by the priests (6:26), which most likely indicates, as Kidner suggests, that in the persons of their priestly representatives, the offerers were the guests of God, sharing with him the reconciliation accomplished by the sacrifice for sin.[22]

In this way the Old Testament foreshadows and celebrates the truth of the next verse of the hymn quoted earlier:

> There is a way for man to rise
> To that sublime abode;
> An offering and a sacrifice,
> A Holy Spirit's energies,
> An Advocate with God.[23]

However, the New Testament book of Hebrews will show that these sacrifices and offerings were fundamentally inadequate to accomplish what they so vividly represented:

> The law is only a shadow of the good things that are coming – not the realities themselves. For this reason it can never, by the same sacrifices repeated endlessly year after year, make perfect those who draw near to worship. If it could, would they not have stopped being offered? For the worshippers would have been cleansed once for all, and would no longer have felt guilty for their sins. But those sacrifices are an annual reminder of sins, because it is impossible for the blood of bulls and goats to take away sins.

---

[21] Mic. 7:18, AV.   [22] Kidner, op. cit., p. 135.
[23] Hymn, 'Eternal Light! Eternal Light!' by Thomas Binney.

Therefore, when Christ came into the world, he said: 'Here I am . . . I have come to do your will, O God' . . . And by that will, we have been made holy through the sacrifice of the body of Jesus Christ once for all.[24]

7. The God who ordains mediators

'Although the word is not used,' writes Albrecht Oepke, 'mediatorship is at the heart of Old Testament religion.'[25] R. S. Wallace writes: 'When God reveals himself to mankind, or brings his authority, power and love to bear on the life of his people, scripture describes him as acting through some intermediary figure . . . Such mediating figures also led and directed the approach of people to God in response to his power and praise.'[26]

The main mediating figures of the Old Testament were Moses himself, the mediator *par excellence* (the greatest of Israel's prophets and a priest before the high priest was ordained), the prophets, the priests and the kings and, most mysterious and profound of all, the Servant of the Lord in Isaiah 40 – 53. The priests were appointed to work within the cultic activity of Israel, Israel's system of worship: 'The cult was meant constantly to re-establish and purify the covenant relationship, which cannot be broken. The cult not only brought back the people into a true outward relationship to God but also gave them a new inward communion with him.'[27] Crucial to an understanding of Israel's system of worship is an understanding of the holiness of God and the distance it set up between him and his people.

The holiness of God is the most important lesson taught in the Old Testament. It is the great glory of God and, because of sin and uncleanness, it is the danger of man. It is the great danger to human beings of the divine holiness that lies behind both sacrifice and priesthood in the book of Leviticus. Gordon Wenham writes:

A constant reminder of God's presence and holiness was needed together with the means of regular atonement for sin. This was provided by the tabernacle and the priesthood. The tabernacle stood in the centre of the camp to bring to mind God's glory and holiness, and it served as a centre for worship where forgiveness was offered to the people. The inauguration of this priestly ministry in the tabernacle, therefore, constituted a most significant step in the history of the nation.[28]

[24] Heb. 10:1–10.   [25] Albrecht Oepke, quoted in Lewis, p. 216.
[26] R. S. Wallace, 'Mediation', *ISBE*, vol. 3, p. 300.   [27] Ibid.
[28] Wenham (1979), p. 130.

Yahweh cannot be approached safely without the sacrifices which he had given to make atonement (17:11), but neither can those sacrifices be effective unless offered in the right manner. The priests are there to make sure that they were so offered. Leviticus 1 – 7 has been called a handbook for priests. The priests, in fact, operate as mediators between the worshippers and God 'in which God is approached, reconciled and besought on man's behalf by an appointed representative'.[29] The priests are taken from the tribe of Levi, that small tribe which was loyal to Moses in the rebellion of the golden calf.[30] Aaron and his sons are to be the main priestly family and the high priests are to be Aaron and his descendants, in each case the eldest sons.

a. The dignity of priesthood

The most immediately striking thing about the high priest was his robe of office. This robe is emphasized from the start: ' "You are to make sacral vestements for Aaron your brother, for splendour and for beauty" (Ex. 28–1 ff.; cf. ch. 39).'[31] The linkage with the beauty and splendour of Yahweh is brought out in Psalm 29:2: 'worship the LORD in the splendour of his holiness'. This is often translated 'in holy array', but as Kidner points out, the use of the phrase in 2 Chronicles 20:21 'tips the balance towards the "literal" sense, understood as speaking of God's holiness rather than man's'.[32] In Leviticus 8:6–9, Moses washes and dresses Aaron in his appointed robes of office: his tunic, sash, robe and ephod, breastpiece and turban. They were gorgeous and dazzling with their colours, materials, gold inlays and precious stones and reminded all who saw them of the splendour of God and the importance of this office. Gordon Wenham comments on this:

> Essentially a uniform draws attention to the office or function of a person, as opposed to his individual personality. It emphasises his job rather than his name ... Aaron's priestly robes are fully described in Exod. 28 and 39. Here we are simply told that in obedience to God's command these dazzling garments were now put on Aaron. In putting on these clothes he took to himself all the honour and glory of the high priesthood. In a religion the principal doctrine of which was the holiness of God, the high priest, who mediated atonement between God and man, was an extremely important person. His glorious clothing symbolised the significance of his office.[33]

[29] C. D. Hancock, 'Mediation', NDT, p. 418.   [30] Exod. 32:25–29.
[31] Durham, p. 381.   [32] Kidner (1973), vol. 1, p. 125.
[33] Wenham (1979), pp. 138–139.

In his vision of the glorified Jesus, John, the writer of Revelation, pictures him as dressed in 'a robe reaching down to his feet' and the single word used there is used in connection with the robes of the high priest in six out of seven of its occurrences in the Septuagint. Similarly the 'golden sash round his chest' recalls the sash of Exodus 39:29 which, according to Josephus, was interwoven with gold.[34] The recognition is essentially that of Hebrews and Paul, that Jesus Christ is our great and glorious high priest who has gone into heaven, the one mediator between God and man.

b. The duty of priesthood

Philip Jensen writes on this:

> Perhaps the central concept of priesthood is mediation between the sphere of the divine and the ordinary world. A priest through his ritual actions and his words facilitates communication across the boundary separating the holy from the profane. The priests represented God to the people in the splendour of their clothing, in their behaviour, and in oracles and instruction, while in sacrifice and intercession they represented the people to God ... The high priest represents the whole nation, regularly bearing the name of the twelve tribes into the Holy Place (Ex. 28:29–30).[35]

As far as the wider selection of priests who appear to have operated in later centuries was concerned, 'The main priestly functions (cf. Deut. 33:8–10) was care of the sanctuary, the performance there of major rituals (purification of major impurities, sacrifice), and the instruction of the people when they attended at the great festivals. Divination was a more occasional task, but could be one of national importance.'[36] The teaching and counselling ministry attached to the priestly office and developed subsequently is often missed.[37]

The most striking piece of the high priest's attire was the breast-plate. Wenham writes:

> In it there was a pouch for the Urim and Thummim (v. 8). These are Hebrew words which literally mean 'lights and perfections'. They seem to be some sort of dice by which God's will was made known. They were capable of giving a positive, negative, or neutral reply to a question. The king or leader of the nation would ask the priest whether a proposed course of action was approved by God and would meet with success.[38]

---

[34] Mounce, p. 78. [35] P. Jensen, 'khn', NIDOTTE, vol. 2, p. 600. [36] Ibid.
[37] See e.g. Deut. 17:9; 33:10; 2 Chr. 17:7–9; Neh. 8:7–11; Mal. 2:7.
[38] Wenham (1979), p. 140.

God had commanded, 'Whenever Aaron enters the holy place, he will bear the names of the sons of Israel over his heart on the breastpiece.'[39] 'Thus,' says Philip Hughes finely, 'the people of God were carried by name into the divine presence, supported as it were, in their weakness on the strong shoulders of their high priest and bound closely to his loving and compassionate heart. Their high priest was their remembrancer.'[40] The writer to the Hebrews recalls this when he demonstrates that the high-priesthood of Christ is far superior to that of Aaron. Aaron and his successors could only enter an earthly sanctuary in a symbolic yearly act of atonement for the sins of the nation; Jesus Christ, having made a once-for-all sacrifice for sin by the offering of himself, has entered heaven itself where he perpetually represents us as our great high priest:

> Therefore, since we have a great high priest who has gone through the heavens, Jesus the Son of God, let us hold firmly to the faith we profess. For we do not have a high priest who is unable to sympathise with our weaknesses, but we have one who has been tempted in every way, just as we are – yet was without sin. Let us then approach the throne of grace with confidence, so that we may receive mercy and find grace to help us in our time of need.[41]

c. The limitations of priesthood

There was no ground for the priests of Israel to arrogate to themselves any personal power or significance. Theirs was a function rather than a vocation, and one to which they were born, not self-selected. There were very strict rules of procedure laid down for them and no less than 16 times in three chapters we read the phrase 'as the LORD commanded Moses'. As shown by the fate of Aaron's sons, Nadab and Abihu, recounted in Leviticus 10:1–2, there could be terrible judgments for any proud violation of the God-given procedure. The greatest enemy to the integrity of Israelite religion would be the modification of her worship in response to the influences and expectations of her neighbours.

One of the main themes of the New Testament book of Hebrews is the sinfulness of the priests and the ultimate ineffectiveness of their sacrifices to remove sin.[42] This is not to say that their office and work did not answer to the requirements of God at the time, since their functions were meaningful and their blessings were effective. But in different ways their own sinfulness and need of atonement was clearly brought out from the start. They are themselves part of the problem and the solution lies beyond them; they themselves pollute

[39] Exod. 28:29.   [40] Hughes, pp. 351–352.   [41] Heb. 4:14–16.   [42] Heb. 5 – 10.

the tabernacle and so they too need purification. According to Exodus 30:17ff. the priests had to wash themselves every time they went on duty in the tabernacle.[43] 'Washing in the Bible is an outward physical action representing the desire for an inner spiritual cleansing, as the coupling "clean hands and a pure heart" (Ps. 24:4; 73:13; Isa. 1:16) makes clear.'[44]

There were special sacrifices which the priesthood was to make for itself and its own sins and which were needed at different times to purify and consecrate the altar, the curtain of the sanctuary, and the atonement cover or 'mercy seat' on the ark (8:14, 18, 22, 30; cf. 16:11). Wenham comments: 'If God was to be present at the sacrifices offered by the priests, his sanctuary had to be purged from sin's pollution, specifically of those pollutions introduced by the priests themselves.'[45] He observes further, 'These sacrifices are not just offered once; they have to be repeated, because sin is deep-rooted in human nature and often recurs. There is no once-for-all cleansing known to the Old Testament. It is the incorrigibility of the human heart that these ordination ceremonies bring into focus.'[46]

8. The final sacrifice for all

These sacrifices and rituals had profound meaning and real effects within their old covenant contexts. This was how God revealed himself and dealt with his people. However, Derek Kidner pinpoints the residual problem with all the sacrifices:

> As soon as we ask what were the iniquities that a sin offering could take away, we are answered (at least with any certainty) only by a list of negligences, accidents and what Hebrews 9:7 sums up as 'ignorances'. The climax of atonement in this elaborate sacrificial system could barely touch the matters that lie most heavily upon the sinner. Here above all, the Old Covenant cried out for the New.[47]

It is from within the new-covenant dispensation that the writer of Hebrews, after a careful examination of the old covenant's lessons and its limits, shows the utter superiority and all-sufficiency of Jesus Christ in his divine person and his atoning work. 'The law is only a shadow of the good things that are coming – not the realities themselves. For this reason it can never, by the same sacrifices repeated endlessly year after year, make perfect those who draw near

---

[43] Cf. Lev. 8:6; 16:4, 24.   [44] Wenham (1979), p. 139.   [45] Ibid., p. 141.
[46] Ibid., pp. 144–145.   [47] Derek Kidner, quoted in Lewis, p. 270.

to worship.'[48] He writes of a new priesthood and a new covenant, but crucial to both is the new sacrifice which has been made in the blood of Jesus Christ.[49] The sacrifices of the old covenant have been superseded by the all-sufficient sacrifice of Jesus Christ.[50] The offering which *this* high priest brought is incomparable and unrepeatable because 'he offered up himself'[51] an 'appointed' sacrifice,[52] fully acceptable and wholly accepted.[53] A word which the writer repeatedly uses of the sacrificial death of Christ is the unusual Greek word *ephapax* (a strengthened form of *hapax*), meaning 'once for all'.[54] It underlines the finality and unrepeatability of the historic act of salvation in contrast with the oft-repeated and finally insufficient sacrifices of the old covenant and its priesthood.[55] Nothing can equal this, nothing can perfect it, nothing can supersede it. Only Jesus Christ can save sinners:

> Not all the blood of beasts,
> On Jewish altars slain,
> Could give the guilty conscience peace,
> Or wash away the stain.

> My faith would lay her hand
> On that dear head of Thine,
> While like a penitent I stand,
> And there confess my sin.

> My soul looks back to see
> The burden Thou didst bear
> When hanging on the cursèd tree,
> And knows her guilt was there.

> Believing, we rejoice
> To see the curse remove;
> We bless the Lamb with cheerful voice,
> And sing His wondrous love.[56]

From the law to the prophets

From the law to the prophets may be a great step in history, but it is not a great step in theology. There, in a very different situation from the wilderness days of Moses, Sinai and Deuteronomy, we have a situation envisaged and prepared for from the start: Israel in the

[48] Heb. 10:1–2.   [49] Heb. 9:11–18.   [50] Heb. 10:11–14.   [51] Heb. 7:28.
[52] Heb. 7:29.   [53] Heb. 7:26.   [54] Heb. 7:27; 9:12; 10:10; cf. Rom. 6:10.
[55] Heb. 7:11–28; 9:6–12; 10 – 12.
[56] Hymn, 'Not all the blood of beasts', by Isaac Watts (1674–1748).

land. There too, we have the abiding demands of the law for justice, righteousness and truth faith. And there we have the successors of Moses, the prophets of God, confronting the people with the uncompromising character of the God of Israel. The prophets do not give us any new doctrine of God, but they proclaim and apply the truth set forth in the 'Books of Moses', Genesis to Deuteronomy. R. K. Harrison writes:

> ... these prophets are not to be described, as has often been done, in terms of great spiritual pioneers who discovered ethical monotheism. On the contrary, it is now clear that they were heirs to a spiritual tradition that was already centuries old. Their attacks upon the social and religious abuses of the day were made in the light of the Covenant provisions that themselves were firmly rooted in the historical past of the nation. The eighth- and seventh-century BC prophets added nothing that was specifically new and distinctive to the traditional *Torah*, or 'teaching', but instead concentrated upon a re-examination or a fresh interpretation of Mosaic tenets.[57]

I have chosen to illustrate three main aspects of the biblical doctrine of God from just three of the prophets: the righteousness of God from Amos, the love of God from Hosea, and, from Isaiah, the incomparability of God and his utter incompatibility with idolatrous forms of worshipping or styles of living. To these we now turn.

---

[57] R. K. Harrison, *Introduction to the Old Testament* (Tyndale Press, 1970), p. 413.

Amos
13. God the righteous judge

'The words of Amos burst upon the landscape of the Northern Kingdom, Israel, with all the terror and surprise of a lions roar,' writes D. A. Hubbard. Explaining his use of the vivid metaphor (which is Amos' own),[1] he continues, 'The lion-like roar was a divine "No" shouted through the prophet at every basic component of Israel's political, social, economic and religious life.'[2]

Amos lived over 750 years before the coming of Christ. He lived in a time when the moral legacy of the past was meeting the spiritual bankruptcy of the present; when the bills were coming in and in spite of Israel's present affluence, there was nothing in the bank with which to pay them.

Israel had become two kingdoms after Solomon. It was divided into the northern kingdom, consisting of ten of the tribes and called 'Israel', and the southern kingdom, consisting of Judah and Benjamin and called simply 'Judah'. Israel's first king, Jeroboam the First (reigned 931–910 BC), leader of the revolt against Solomon's son Rehoboam, had set up centres of national religion in Dan in the north of his territory and in Bethel in the south in opposition to Judah's Jerusalem temple. From the start the worship in these centres had been syncretistic, combining elements of calf-worship with the traditional Yahweh-worship.[3] The symbolism of a sacred calf was familiar in the fertility religions of the ancient Near East.

Through the succeeding two centuries there had been rivalry, uneasy peace and at times open conflict between the northern and southern kingdoms, and the moral and spiritual state of 'Israel' had steadily declined. Amos lived in Judah at a time when the northern kingdom was experiencing great material prosperity under another Jeroboam, King Jeroboam II (reigned 786–746 BC).

The cost of that prosperity, however, had been high. It had been gained at the expense of religion, morality and justice throughout the

[1] See Amos 3:8.   [2] Hubbard (*Joel and Amos*), p. 87.   [3] 1 Kgs. 12:25–30.

land. Israel's 'alternative' religion flourished at its cultic centre, Bethel, in Samaria, but it was a cancerous growth, a poisoned weed, an insult and an outrage to God, divorced alike from spiritual truth and social justice. It mixed Yahwism and Baal worship, sanctity and sexual orgies, a romanticized religion with a gross and ruthless materialism. The spirit that corrupted Israel's religious life corrupted everything else: politics, justice and commerce. Israel had not been so prosperous since Solomon's reign but the true prophets of God knew that she was nearing the end, nearing the catastrophic judgment of God on her national life.

The roar of the lion in Amos' prophecy, as Alec Motyer notes, is not the roar of a prowling lion but of a pouncing lion – a lion committed to the attack.[4]

1. God the judge of the nations (1:3 – 2:3)

Amos begins with a series of dramatic prophecies concerning the nations around Israel – north and south. The nations, sometimes identified by their capital cities, are all summoned, like criminals under arrest, to stand before the Judge of the whole earth. Each of them is indicted for crimes against humanity as well as against God and we are reminded that the writ of Yahweh runs through the whole earth and that it is not only from his own people that he looks for justice and fair treatment.

a. Syria (1:3–5)

Syria, with its capital city Damascus, is indicted for war crimes. In particular it is indicted for an atrocity committed against the trans-Jordan tribes of Israel fifty years before, reminding us that a nation cannot easily walk away from its history. A past unrepented of is morally continued in when the underlying pride, cruelty and moral indifference are still present. Nations have an identity as well as individuals. History too has its laws of sowing and reaping, and the judgment of God is in those laws. What this and the following chapter will show eight times over is that God judges *societies*.[5] We prefer to ignore that and often repudiate the idea from within our own (Western and recent) culture of a cushioned and protected individualism. However, the realities of life, as well as history, challenge that. The truth is that we rise and fall together to a very considerable extent. That is one reason why Christians cannot retreat to form their own ghettos or disown their own society, its present or even its past. We are connected to both and have a duty which arises from both.

---

[4] Motyer (1974), p. 27.   [5] Cf. Dan. 9:4–14.

b. Philistia and Tyre (1:6b–10)

These countries grew rich by means of a pitiless slave trade (1:6, 9). They saw only profit, but God saw whole communities of individuals and families and understood their sufferings. Even today according to statistics gathered by the UN, some 200–400 million people in the world, including at least 100 million children, live in actual slavery or in conditions amounting to slavery. They include chattel slaves in North Africa and the Arabian peninsula; feudal serfs in India, Asia, Africa and South America; bonded children in carpet weaving in India, Nepal and Pakistan; forced marriages (bride-stealing) in West Africa; and child prostitutes in Asia, Africa and South America. We see statistics, but their creator enters into the sufferings of whole communities.

c. Edom, Ammon and Moab (1:11 – 2:3)

Edom, Ammon and Moab (1:11, 13; 2:1) were all shooting the heroin of hatred, mainlining on it until it filled their veins with its fire and led them into sickening atrocities. Their tribal feuds led to the depersonalization and degradation of their traditional enemies and, of course, themselves. This story has been repeated too often in modern times for anyone to believe such things belong only to the past. Tribalism is alive and well in Europe in former Yugoslavia and the old Soviet Union, and in many parts of Africa and Asia. A major demonstration of the power and grace of the gospel is given when the church of God in divided communities is seen to overcome racial, political and social divisions in the name of Christ. Only God's grace is powerful and influential enough to overcome the forces of estrangement, suspicion and fear which keep men and women apart.

Surveying the judgments pronounced on these nations, David Hubbard writes: 'The degree of innovation that Amos brought to biblical prophecy should not be missed. Judgment speeches prior to his time were usually addressed to individuals ... Amos directed them against whole nations, demonstrating Yahweh's righteous concern for international politics and human welfare.'[6]

2. The God who acts and reacts

Throughout the entire book of Amos it is made clear that God is not only interested in religion, or, to put it another way, that religion is not only about formal acts of worship. God is concerned about all of life: about truth, righteousness and the love of humanity that cares

[6] Hubbard (Joel and Amos), p. 140.

for justice and mercy in his world. If these things are denied nothing can make up for their omission or stave off the righteous judgments of God for ever. Alec Motyer observes that 'It is a constant aspect of the Bible's view of life that earthly relationships have a heavenly dimension: actions directed towards men provoke reactions from God . . . e.g. Gen. 4:10; Ps. 51:3, 4 (cf. 2 Sam. 12:9–14); Mt. 25: 40, 45; 1 Thess. 4:6–8).'[7]

In these chapters it is not their false religions which are denounced but their inhumanity. They are condemned not for what they did not know but for their sins against what they did know. They did not have the law of Moses but they did have a God-given conscience and they ignored its claims, they were without excuse. We are accountable to our Maker with or without a Bible. The seventeenth-century Puritan preachers used to say that conscience was God's petty sessions in the mind of man and the final judgment his Grand Assize. Before that Grand Assize, there are interim judgments in life and history; fewer than we deserve but often more than we recognize.

These early chapters of Amos tell us that God is neither absent nor passive and uninvolved in human history. His patience must not be mistaken. In the face of widespread and deep injustices God is holding back a great and ever-mounting wrath. He indicates our danger by unexpected (but also in this world, uneven!) judgments. The apostle Paul speaks of these when he writes: 'The wrath of God is being revealed from heaven against all the godlessness and wickedness of men who suppress the truth by their wickedness.'[8] The wrath of God is a natural consequence or result of his holiness with its love of what is good and its hatred of what is evil. Our world and its nations deserve wrath every day, but God's judgments are held back time after time. Yet there are times when his interim judgments fall, swift and fierce or slow but inexorable. There are in-built penalties attached to both national and personal sin: for instance, social division and the abuse of minority groups brings trouble in future generations; neglect of the poor breeds an underclass and an increase in crime and violence; sexual promiscuity brings much human misery and a range of diseases. Permissiveness brings disruption of various kinds because it is a pervasive malady and not confined to one aspect of life. So, in various ways we learn that 'every sin has a boomerang factor'.[9]

The character of all God's judgment upon sin and sinners in this phase of things, however, is that all his judgments are partial, provisional and interim. Sometimes we feel frustrated and unhappy with that. People commonly say to us, 'If there is a God, why doesn't he do something about the evil in the world?' The answer of

---

[7] Motyer (1974), p. 46.   [8] Rom. 1:18.   [9] Motyer (1974), p. 45.

history is that he does, the answer of the future is that he will, and the answer of the cross is that he himself has born the greatest evil, and the guilt of it, for us and that unless we repent we shall none of us escape on the day he 'does something' about it *all*.[10] Critics would be wise not to hurry the Judge out of heaven – his 'cleaning up' will be very scrupulous indeed. Paul warns against easy judgmentalism which ignores its own sin.[11]

3. God the judge of his people Israel (2:4–8)

Amos' preaching of judgment against Israel's traditional enemies might well have found acceptance and even popularity, even in the northern kingdom, if he had stopped there. But he had only just begun! They would not have noticed that in cursing the nations around them he has in fact drawn an entire circle of flame, which would hem them in and then advance upon the centre: Israel north and south, the fire of the divine holiness consuming sin. Beginning at 2:4 the prophecy does just that. Judah has depised the revelation of God for a compound of lies; therefore Judah and her capital city Jerusalem, centre of the old faith and promises though she is, will fall to the divine judgment. God says, '*I will send fire upon Judah that will consume the fortresses of Jerusalem*' (2:5).

If God's judgment is to fall on Judah, what hope can there be for Israel? None, says Amos. Israel has corrupted its soul and now its whole body politic is sick. The rich and powerful have pillaged the poor of God. Creditors recovering debts are willing to inflict the greatest suffering for the smallest gain: '*They sell the righteous for silver and the needy for a pair of shoes*' (2:6). In court the poor were denied justice and their rights trampled upon as if they were less than human, as if they were dirt (2:7). Heads of families took advantage of their position and sexually abused their daughters-in-law (2:7). The vulnerable poor who owed money had even their cloaks left as pledges withheld through the cold Middle Eastern nights while the creditor caroused and worshipped his gods (2:8).

Alec Motyer notes:

> The absolutely devastating thing about all this is that these are precisely the sins discovered and condemned in the heathen. It was for this that Damascus, Gaza, Tyre, Edom, Ammon and Moab fell before the wrath of God and the charge as we saw was their failure to be and to act as human beings. But now these very things are the sins of the Church! There are lessons here to ponder. When the grace of God reaches out to man its purpose is to make

[10] Matt. 25:41–45.   [11] Rom. 2:3–6.

him truly human: as we would say, the purpose of God's saving work is to make us like Jesus, the perfect Man. It is a perversion, indeed a denial of his grace when we become wrongly isolated from the world and its needs and when we (perhaps unwittingly) restrict our awareness of sin to those offences which we commit against the first and great commandment and dismiss as even immaterial the sins against the second.[12]

Finally, Israel is reminded of her past. Yahweh had brought the nation up from Egypt and slavery, defeated formidable enemies and given her a land of her own (2:9–10), yet at almost every point she had proved unworthy, opposing the prophets and subverting the Nazirites (2:11). David Hubbard remarks: 'This attempt to throttle the Nazirite and prophetic ministries is a reminder that salvation-history, the account of God's gracious interventions and provisions, is precisely paralleled by sin-history, the record of Israel's rebellion and thanklessness.'[13] Today also, there are people and churches who would rather silence biblical ministries than sit under them, and intellectual free-wheelers who subvert the gospel they were set aside to defend.

4. God of the poor

God's evident concern for the poor of Israel in Amos and elsewhere has raised many questions and challenges in the church in our own time. Today 60% of the world's wealth belongs to 6% of its popula-tion, more than 950 million people are permanently hungry and in Britain today we spend more on our cats than the average worker in many of the world's poorest countries earns in a year. Gordon Aeschliman writes:

> One of five human beings on earth lives in poverty. When these 1.2 billion people (five times the size of the U.S. population) go to sleep at night, their bed is a dirt floor – they might not have any roof overhead, they might not have eaten that day. Should they fall ill during the night, no doctor will serve them. When the sun rises they will repeat their daily search for firewood, potable water and employment. Forty million of them are children who will die during their next twelve months of hunger and disease.[14]

John Stott, in *Issues Facing Christians Today*, notes three types of 'poor' in the Old Testament: the *indigent poor*, who are deprived of

---

[12] Motyer (1974), p. 57.   [13] Hubbard (*Joel and Amos*), p. 145.
[14] Gordon Aeschliman, *Global Trends: Ten trends affecting Christians everywhere* (IVP, 1990), p. 36.

the basic necessities of life; the *oppressed poor*, who are powerless victims of human injustice; and the *humble poor*, who acknowledge their helplessness and look to God for salvation. Here economic, sociological and spiritual categories may overlap. The lessons of the Bible are that God sees, understands and reacts to these conditions. As Stott says, 'God succours the indigent poor, champions the powerless poor and exalts the humble poor.'[15] The challenge to us is that he seeks to do so through us; to become visible in us and to be effective by means of us. John Stott insists that in the light of biblical revelation and in the sight of world-wide poverty, Christians must modify their lifestyles: 'We cannot maintain a "good life" (of extravagance) and a "good conscience" simultaneously. One or the other has to be sacrificed. Either we keep our conscience and reduce our affluence, or we keep our affluence and smother our conscience. We have to choose between God and Mammon.'[16] He counsels simpler lifestyles and sacrificial giving.

5. God the impartial judge

In an article in *The Times*, a former editor, William Rees Mogg, expressed his concern that we have entered 'a culture of corruption' in world politics to a new degree. Surveying financial scandals in America, the European Commission, France, Belgium, Ireland and Britain, some involving huge sums, he concludes with this point: 'In late 18th century and early 19th century Britain, honourable people, many of them evangelical Christians, were outraged by sinecures and corruption and successfully rooted them out of British public life. For more than a century the British even ran their huge empire without bribes. Now there is a new and global wave of corruption. We need a new sense of outrage which is lacking.'[17] In Amos and his fellow prophets there is just that: a sense of outrage burning in the prophet's words and in the heart of God; a voice of protest piercing the sham and the complacency of the times: 'The prophet's word is a scream in the night. While the world is at ease and asleep, the prophet feels the blast from heaven.'[18]

The very clear message of Amos's inexorable progression from the judgment of the nations to the judgment of Judah and Israel is that God judges impartially. It is a lesson that runs through Old and New Testaments. Just as under the old covenant Israel had to learn it (3:2), so under the new covenant the Gentiles have to learn it,[19] church

[15] Stott (1984), p. 220.   [16] Ibid.

[17] W. Rees Mogg, *The Times*, 5 November 1999.

[18] A. J. Heschel, *The Prophets* (Harper & Row, 1962), quoted in Hubbard (*Joel and Amos*), p. 115.

[19] Rom. 11:18–21.

leaders have to learn it,[20] and church members have to learn it.[21] Great privilege brings great responsibility and may bring great judgment.[22] That was spelt out by Amos at the beginning of chapter 3:

[1]*Hear this word the LORD has spoken against you, O people of Israel – against the whole family I brought up out of Egypt:*

> [2]*'You only have I chosen*
> *of all the families of the earth;*
> *therefore I will punish you*
> *for all your sins.'*

6. God the righteous judge

In Scripture one of the most frequently emphasized attributes of God is his 'righteousness' or 'justice' (the words belong to the same word group in the biblical languages). Often found in connection with this are such words as 'jealousy' and 'wrath'. Wayne Grudem's definition is helpful here: 'God's righteousness means that God always acts in accordance with what is right and [he] is himself the final standard of what is right.'[23] This means we must not bring to Scripture our own partial and often fashionable views of what is right and what is wrong, but must get from God and his revelation of his character and will what is so. Absolutes exist because God exists. Absolutes are rooted in God. God always acts according to his own nature which is good.[24] Everything God wills is right and God has the right to do and to command anything he wills.[25] Whatever conforms to his character and will is right and by that standard all morally responsible beings will be judged.[26] The justice God requires reflects his own perfect and entire standards of justice. It is not simply legal punctiliousness or only a matter of the letter of the law. As C. S. Lewis notes, 'Justice means more than the sort of thing that goes on in law-courts. It is the old name for everything we should now call "fairness"; it includes honesty, give and take, truthfulness, keeping promises, and all that side of life.'[27]

Against all that defies or violates God's standards and requirements his wrath goes out. 'God's wrath means that he intensely hates all sin.'[28] This is inevitable precisely because God is holy and just. Sin is the most destructive and corrupt force in this universe. It is the attempted overthrow of God's moral kingship over creation. God's

---

[20] 1 Cor. 3:10–15.   [21] 1 Pet. 1:17.   [22] Luke 12:48.
[23] Wayne Grudem, *Systematic Theology: An Introduction to Biblical Doctrine* (IVP/Zondervan, 1994), p. 203.   [24] Deut. 32:4.   [25] Ps. 19:8; Is. 45:19; Rom. 9:19–21.
[26] Gen. 18:25.   [27] C. S. Lewis, *Christian Behaviour* (Geoffrey Bles, n.d.), p. 14.
[28] Grudem, op. cit., p. 206.

wrath toward sin is the revulsion of his holy justice against its moral opposite, his maintenance of his own rule which is, alone, the hope of the world. Certainly God's wrath is an action,[29] but it is an action grounded in his nature as unchangeably and uncompromisingly holy. As one theologian puts it, the phrase 'the wrath of God' 'not only says something about what God does but about what he is in doing it'.[30] The remarkable thing is not that God should be capable of wrath but that he should be 'slow to anger', that is, slow to express the wrath which he invariably feels toward all sin, and 'abounding in love' to the unworthy.[31] Sometimes we read that God is a jealous God.[32] Here the word has no bad sense but means earnestly protective or watchful. 'God's jealousy means that God continually seeks to protect his own honour.'[33] He does so because that is the most important and precious thing in the universe. Far from being an unworthy concept of God it underlines his holiness and love.

In the book of the eighth-century prophet Amos, we find these attributes of God operative in dramatic and decisive ways in the history of Israel. The setting and the prophecy remind us that these attributes are not static in God but active in his government of human history, especially in the history of his people. In his *Theology of the Old Testament*, Walter Brueggemann reflects on the biblical image of God as judge as one of its most important metaphors, telling us of Yahweh's own moral seriousness and his uncompromising activity. He writes:

> It is evident that the metaphor *judge* presents Yahweh as committed to a rule of just law, as one who can be counted on to intervene on behalf of those who are treated unjustly or against what is regarded as inequitable treatment according to Israel's radical notions of justice, which stands against the exploitive 'realism' of much self-serving, self-aggrandising justice.[34]

God's law is a law of well-being for all, which Yahweh enforces and this has both positive and negative elements.

> This action of this judge will set the world right. This activity of the judge is given positive content in litigation against the other would-be gods who do not practise the justice of Yahweh ... In the end, the 'oracles against the nations' (Amos 1 – 2); Isaiah 13 – 23; Jeremiah 46 – 51; Ezekiel 25 – 32) are evidence that

[29] Rom. 1:18.
[30] H. Ridderbos, quoted in Lewis, p. 268; see also Lewis, pp. 262–263, 255–268, 425.
[31] Exod. 34:6; Ps. 103:8–9.   [32] Exod. 20:5; 34:14; Deut. 4:24; 5:9.
[33] Grudem, op. cit., p. 205.   [34] Brueggemann (1997), p. 234.

Yahweh exercises judicial control over the affairs of nations and metes out judgment according to Yahweh's own passionate justice.'[35]

Brueggemann recognizes that 'There is indeed a potential for severity and fierceness in Israel's rhetoric about Yahweh as judge', but he sees this as 'the foundation of Israel's affirmation that the world has moral coherence to it, on which even the weak can count. That moral coherence has credibility, moreover, because the judge is willing and able to effect sanctions against violators.'[36] Yahweh's 'vengeance' is not wild and capricious, but is in fact the exercise of a rule of order to which Yahweh is committed from the outset.[37]

7. Judgment past and future

One of the most significant additions to the Old Testament teaching that God is 'the Judge of all the earth'[38] is the New Testament revelation that 'the Father judges no-one, but has entrusted all judgment to the Son, that all may honour the Son just as they honour the Father'[39] and that 'we must all appear before the judgment seat of Christ'.[40] Such transfer of the prerogatives of God to Jesus are a main way in which the New Testament proclaims the deity of Christ. Jesus himself echoes the standards and concerns of God for justice and mercy in Amos when he warns that the standards by which he will judge will confront those who have not cared for the needy and the vulnerable as well as those who have committed outright crimes.[41]

The lines of God's justice in judgment are not softened in the New Testament and the words and warnings of Jesus are as terrifying as anything in Amos or the Old Testament.[42] To the end of biblical revelation, the uncompromising justice and judgment of God is made clear. The same perfect standard and the same divine concerns will mark the final judgment as characterize interim judgments. That is why we so desperately need the justification of God in Jesus Christ, the righteousness which is ours by faith in him.[43] The scene of the final judgment of the nations is graphically depicted in the last book of the Bible:

Then I saw a great white throne and him who was seated on it. Earth and sky fled from his presence, and there was no place for them. And I saw the dead, great and small, standing before the

---

[35] Ibid., p. 234.   [36] Ibid., pp. 234–237.   [37] Ibid., p. 236.   [38] Gen. 18:25.
[39] John 5:22–23; cf. 5:28–30.   [40] 2 Cor. 5:10.   [41] Matt. 25:31–46.
[42] E.g. Matt. 7:15–23; 25:44–46; Mark 9:42–49; Luke 16:19–31.
[43] Rom. 1:17; 1 Cor. 1:30.

throne, and the books were opened. Another book was opened, which is the book of life. The dead were judged according to what they had done as recorded in the books.[44]

The reference to the book of life follows from the entire biblical testimony that the people of God owe their salvation to God's grace and not to human merit.[45] Their salvation will be determined solely by their relation to Christ, 'For it is by grace you have been saved, through faith – and this not from yourselves, it is the gift of God – not by works, so that no-one can boast.'[46] Yet, in the New Testament, while salvation is always said to be by grace, judgment is always said to be according to works. Those who are 'in Christ' will be saved on the ground of his redemptive work, yet they will receive greater or less reward as they have lived in the use of that grace which they freely received.[47]

Meanwhile the people of God live to witness to Christ and the order of God. The enemies of that order are both human and non-human. They include the demonic agents which manipulate human institutions, human politics and the rush of events leaving people the helpless victims of, or even the unwitting participants in, economic oppression, political manipulation and social engineering which confuse our moral judgment and take things beyond our control. At both the personal and the corporate levels, Christians must recognize the truth and force of Paul's words to the Ephesians: 'For our struggle is not against flesh and blood, but against the rulers, against the authorities, against the powers of this dark world and against the spiritual forces of evil in the heavenly realms.'[48] These forces – demonic malice and human greed and self-interest – dishonour God and disfigure human existence. And they are the forces that shall finally be overthrown when God the righteous judge asserts to the uttermost his rule and reign in creation.

8. God's final victory

In the chapters that follow, the prophet Amos details his charges against Israel further: the defiance of God, the decadent luxury, the debased religion, the corruption of the legal system, and with scorching indignation and vivid imagery he shows both the justice and the inevitability of judgment. However, in the last verses of his uncompromising prophecy, Amos shows that the last word is with God and the final triumph is the triumph of his will. 'The days are coming' when Yahweh will reverse the sentence against Israel and

---

[44] Rev. 20:11–12.   [45] Rom. 11:5–6.   [46] Eph. 2:8–9.
[47] Matt. 5:11–12; 10:40–42; 19:28–30.   [48] Eph. 6:12.

restore the kingdom that had flourished in David's day. God has not finished with or abandoned his people.[49] While the more immediate fulfilment of these verses may lie in the return of a small remnant of 'Israel' with the larger remnant of 'Judah' to the land after the Babylonian captivity, the prophet's horizon lies in a final and universal restoration. His words signal not merely the triumph of good over evil. They are abstract concepts. It is the triumph of God, the reconciliation of a fallen world to God, the renewal of a broken natural order by the Creator who made it. It is the finality of his plan and the fullness of his joy. How will it come about?

Amos could hardly have known. But the key, the crucial event, would occur 750 years later with 'Great David's greater Son', a man who claimed to be the Son of God, sent by his Father to give his life a ransom for many, bearing their sins on a cross and removing the great barrier between them and eternal life with God.

We read the fierce judgments of God in Amos and elsewhere and we may be unsure how to present this or even defend it in an age of easy humanism where right and wrong are considered dubious concepts and where judgment is an alien word. But we must remember that the God of burning holiness who thundered his indignation through Amos and the prophets is the God who bore his own judgment at Calvary. It was love that cried 'No' to the society of Jeroboam and it was love that cried 'Yes' to the plan of salvation before the creation of the world.[50] And that uncompromising justice and unquenchable love met at the cross in one Man who cried, 'My God, my God, why have you forsaken me?' The Judge is judged and is at rest[51] in order that we might have a future as well as a past.

And Amos could not have known of the victory of the first Easter Sunday morning when death itself was overcome by a greater power and God raised up his Son, Jesus. He could not have known that at the right hand of God, gathering a people throughout history, and coming again to exercise the prerogative of God in a final apocalypse of salvation and judgment, the Christ of God would begin a new history in a new heavens and a new earth in which righteousness, truth and love would be for ever the character of men and women as it is for ever the character of God.

---

[49] Cf. Rom. 11:1.
[50] Eph. 1:3–4.
[51] Melito of Sardis, quoted in Lewis, p. 289.

Hosea
14. God the great lover

Imagine you are a young man about eighteen to twenty years old. The world is at your feet and God is at your side. The voice you know and love speaks one day as clearly as it has ever done: 'Son, I want you to marry now.'

You reply eagerly, 'Yes, Lord. Where is she? Who is she? An Elizabeth Elliott to go with my Jim Elliott! A Maria for my Hudson Taylor! I'm naming it and claiming it, Lord. Your best for my best: a cross between Miss World and the Virgin Mary!'

'No son, I want you to marry a prostitute – and she's not going to change because she married you!'

Something like that was the personal trial and tragedy of Hosea the prophet.

Now imagine you are in Britain in about 1936. For years one voice has spoken out with more and more urgency: 'A great evil is growing, a great danger is coming. The Nazi threat will engulf us all. We must rearm, we must be prepared for war, we must change course and alter our attitudes.' And imagine the nation and its leaders saying, 'No, we must have faith in peace, in progress, and in the honour of Herr Hitler.' So far history. But follow the course of what might have been. The clock ticks on unstoppably, inexorably to the midnight hour – and beyond. There is no last-minute awakening to reality; only a supine escapism with leaders and people waltzing on through 1939, 1940 and beyond, until an unstoppable invasion makes it the last waltz and the beginning of a thousand years of personal bondage and cultural oblivion.

Something like that was the national tragedy of Israel before the looming threat of the Assyrian Empire; but God and his prophets were calling on the nation not to rearm but to repent.

In Hosea's prophecy and in Hosea's pain we are going to discover the secret heart of God; his innermost feelings, his profound sorrow and his sovereign grace. Not until the Word becomes flesh will God appear so tender and so vulnerable as in the book of Hosea. He is

God of the cosmic drama and God of the domestic tragedy; he rides on the wings of the wind and he weeps with the heart of a rejected lover; he is catastrophic in judgment and tender in tears. 'I am God and not man' he cries (11:9) and yet we find he is more like us than we had dared to imagine.

Hosea, Israel, and God: three figures on a darkening stage. The high drama of redemption is moving through one of its saddest and most turbulent Old Testament periods.

1. Love's long trial

The story of the centuries after Moses is a story of contrasts: of good days under Joshua, chaotic days under the Judges, great days under King David, and days, years, centuries of decline after him. After Solomon a story unfolds in Israel of civil war, of two kingdoms and two rival centres of religion; of apostate as well as unworthy kings, and of national decline. During these times, again and again, the people followed their leaders into new forms of religion, mixing the prescribed worship of God with that of the Baals, the fertility cults of the surrounding tribes and the gods of other nations.

The prophets had a word for that. They called it adultery, spiritual adultery on a national scale which would lead to national disaster and judgment. Other nations might get away with it for a while but not Israel. What husband does not have a unique and exclusive relationship with his wife, including intimacies and loyalties that belong to them alone? Yahweh had been a husband to Israel but he had known more pain than pleasure in the relationship. His holy love had been violated and betrayed times without number. He would not tear up his marriage certificate, he would remain true to his purposes and promises, but he would bring judgment to these generations and express his holy wrath and husbandly outrage.

The result was the Assyrian invasion just a few years after Hosea's death in 722 or 721BC. Within a generation Israel, the northern kingdom, would be extinct.

Like that of his contemporary Amos, the book of Hosea is written in entreaty and warning, tender pathos and scalding indignation. For there is no pain like the pain of rejected love. Derek Kidner observes:

> It is the people you love who can hurt you most. One can almost trace the degree of potential pain along a scale – from the rebuff which you hardly notice from a stranger, to the rather upsetting clash you may have with a friend, right on to the stinging hurt of

a jilting, the ache of a parent-child estrangement or, most wounding of all, the betrayal of a marriage.[1]

In Hosea we discover God's capacity for pain and sorrow. For love makes us vulnerable and no body of people can grieve God like the Church, the people of God, whenever they are worldly, callous or hurtful to one another. Love is always vulnerable, including God's love. His Spirit can be grieved by us because he indwells us and we belong to him.[2] This prophecy challenges us to ask ourselves how we are treating God in our lives: with carelessness? with contempt? with a double life, a long backsliding? It will also warn us to beware the wrath of a betrayed and trampled love.

2. Love's human voice (1:2–3)

[2]*When the LORD began to speak through Hosea, the LORD said to him, 'Go, take to yourself an adulterous wife and the children of unfaithfulness, because the land is guilty of the vilest adultery in departing from the LORD.*[3] *So he married Gomer daughter of Diblaim, and she conceived and bore him a son.*

Hosea prophesied for forty years through the long reign of Jeroboam the Second, king over the ten northern tribes of Israel, and through the reigns of four kings in Judah. We might think it a fine thing to be a prophet but when we look at the lives of Jeremiah, Ezekiel or Hosea we begin to see the personal cost involved. Hosea had to *live* the history of Israel and the suffering of God. He had to endure while his own marriage became the parable of God's marriage to Israel. He had to make his heart the furnace of God's anguish. He had to make his children symbols of national apostasy and doom. He had no hope of another wife or a better one. It is a serious thing being a prophet! But then it is serious thing being God: God who bears the sin of the world and the sins of his own people; God whose love is taken for granted, abused and rejected by millions.

What follows in the prophecy gives us only by implication the serial adultery that marked Gomer's life in the early years of their marriage. She produced three children (could Hosea be sure that he was their father?) and God told his prophet to give them names that prefigured judgment to come upon Israel. The first was named 'Jezreel' (v. 4), the name of the place associated with the massacre-marked rise to power of an earlier king, Jehu, the founder of a long

---

[1] Kidner (1981), p. 17.　　[2] Eph. 4:30.

dynasty, which included the present king (Jeroboam II). Ironically Jezreel was not far from the scene of the assassination of the last king of Jehu's dynasty, Jeroboam's son Zechariah. The second child of the marriage, a daughter, was called 'Lo-Ruhamah' (v. 6), which means 'not loved', as a warning that God would no longer show love to 'the house of Israel' which had apostatised from him. The third, another son was called 'Lo-Ammi' (v. 9), which means 'not my people', for, God said, 'You are not my people, and I am not your God.'

3. Love's conflicting emotions (2:2–23)

Throughout Hosea's prophecy, often in contrasts of extreme emotion, we find three things repeatedly exhibited: the seriousness of sin; the reality of judgment; the certainty of love triumphing in the end. Superimposed upon the personal tragedy of Hosea urging his children to plead with the repeatedly unfaithful Gomer is the outrage and anguish of God toward unfaithful Israel: *'Rebuke your mother, rebuke her, for she is not my wife and I am not her husband'* (2:2), words which, says D. A. Hubbard, 'have an official ring to them, not unlike a divorce formula'.[3] While stopping short of immediate and irreversible judgment, Yahweh's wrath is explicit and real enough as the warnings that follow show. If Israel does not soon repent, says God: *'I will strip her naked and make her as bare as on the day she was born . . .'*

Yet, just as the reader (originally, the hearer!) is prepared for the worst with the 'therefore' of verse 14, the prophecy takes a completely unexpected turn into the 'impossibilities' of a transcendent love which does not allow human sin and failure to have the last word:

> [14]*Therefore I am now going to allure her;*
> *I will lead her into the desert*
> *and speak tenderly to her*
> [15]*There I will give her back her vineyards,*
> *and will make the Valley of Achor a door of hope.*
> *There she will sing as in the days of her youth,*
> *as in the day she came up out of Egypt.*
>
> [16]*'In that day,' declares the* LORD,
> *'you will call me "my husband";*
> *you will no longer call me "my master" . . .*
> [23]*I will plant her for myself in the land;*

[3] Hubbard (*Hosea*), p. 72.

I will show my love to the one I called "Not my loved one".
I will say to those called "Not my people", "You are my people";
and they will say, "You are my God."'

Just when we think the divorce is settled, a far different plan unfolds, reaching beyond the hopeless present to another generation and another future; a plan that is founded on what *God* will do above and beyond our poor devotion and our flawed obedience.

Sometimes, indeed often, the church of God has been a bad advertisement for her Lord. In her history, and even now, the church has often been corrupt or complacent or only half-alive. At such times you may be tempted to despair of it and withdraw in anger or disgust. But remember at such times that the church of God will always have a future with you or without you, and a glorious future at that. If you have been given the privilege of belonging to the people of God, bear with her inadequate present, work for a better day, and journey with God's sometimes tattered army to his final glory, when Christ shall present the church to God without spot or blemish – a bride prepared for her husband.[4]

4. Love's humiliation (3:1–5)

The LORD said to me, 'Go, show your love to your wife again, though she is loved by another and is an adulteress. Love her as the LORD loves the Israelites, though they turn to other gods and love the sacred raisin-cakes.'

[2]So I bought her for fifteen shekels of silver and about a homer and a lethek of barley. [3]Then I told her, 'You are to live with me for many days; you must not be a prostitute or be intimate with any man, and I will live with you.'

The lowest point of Hosea's experience is recorded in chapter 3. Whether viewed on a human level or a divine, this has to be one of the saddest scenes in the Old Testament. Gomer has left her home, her husband and her children and gone to live with one of her lovers. Then the word of the Lord came again to the prophet, 'Go, show your love to your wife again . . .'

Those words in verse 2, 'So I bought her', are filled with humiliation, pain and the priceless nobility of love. Gomer may have been a slave, a mistress, even a temple prostitute. The price and the method of payment are odd. Perhaps they reflect the prophet having to scrape together all he can for her 'redemption', as centuries later Another would give his all for our salvation. The sum paid 'seems to

---

[4] Eph. 5:27.

have amounted to about 30 shekels, which is the price set on a slave in Ex. 21:32'.[5] As Derek Kidner observes, 'This was no arm's-length settling of a legal battle or extracting of apologies.'[6]

From the start we are not allowed to forget that what Hosea is experiencing at a human level Yahweh is experiencing at a divine level as he contemplates the degeneration of the life of Israel and her spiritual apostasy (vv. 4–5).

'What is striking about this prophecy', writes Kidner, 'is first that it threatens the very pillars of life as Israel knew it, and then that it interprets the withdrawal of all these cherished things – good, bad and indifferent alike – as ultimate gain'.[7] At the end of exile, the nation will return, chastened and changed by God. 'Nothing less than such reverent awe is appropriate for Israel, who has learned in deprivation both who Yahweh is and who Baal is not, both the importance of covenant loyalty and the terror of its absence.'[8]

It is possible to deal with the first three chapters of the prophecy on their own since they form a close literary unit and give the essential message of the book. The second part of the book (chs. 4 – 14) deals with the corruption of the nation's moral, religious and political life, which also figure in the prophecy of Hosea's contemporary, Amos. These are covenant-breaking sins but God is a covenant-keeping God, the faithful Husband, the great Lover. Consequently the book ends with a moving call to the nation which has acted so shamefully: an invitation and a promise (14:1–5):

> Return, O Israel, to the LORD your God.
>> Your sins have been your downfall!
> [2]Take words with you
>> and return to the LORD.
> Say to him:
>> 'Forgive all our sins
> and receive us graciously,
>> that we may offer the fruit of our lips.
> [3]Assyria cannot save us;
>> we will not mount on war-horses.
> We will never again say "Our gods"
>> to what our own hands have made,
>> for in you the fatherless find compassion.'
>
> [4]'I will heal their waywardness
>> and love them freely,
>> for my anger has turned away from them.

[5] Kidner (1981), p. 42, citing H. W. Wolff, *Hosea* (Fortress Press, 1974), p. 61 for the calculation.
[6] Ibid., p. 40.　　[7] Ibid., p. 43.　　[8] Hubbard (*Hosea*), p. 95.

> [5]*I will be like the dew to Israel;*
> *he will blossom like a lily.'*

The call to return is an amazing act of grace at this late hour. It is astonishing that Hosea should want his Gomer again but even more that God should want this people, that he should still love Israel. Why not start again with a new Abraham, a new tribe, a new Moses? But it is the character of the divine love that it is neither a bland, universal benevolence nor a fickle, short-lived passion, but an altogether gracious and extraordinary love that chooses one out of a thousand and holds on to what it has chosen at all costs. And at Calvary, the divine love incarnate will pay *all* the costs. As with Amos so with Hosea, God has the last word, and the last word is grace.

5. God's serious love

As we can see from a reading of the prophecy of Hosea, anyone who imagines that the Old Testament presents a God of wrath and that it was left to the New Testament writers to discover God's love shows a pretty woeful ignorance of both Testaments![9]

The Hebrew Old Testament has a cluster of terms for love in general and for the divine love in particular, including *'āhēḇ* (well over 200 times, often stressing the free, spontaneous character of love), *ḥen* (68 times, in most cases with the sense of grace and favour), and *ḥeseḏ* (about 250 times, mainly with the sense of kindness or loving-kindness).

Throughout the Old Testament we meet the love of God in such close connection with his innermost being that we are prepared for the New Testament statement that 'God is love', a statement written by a Jew whose knowledge of God was rooted in the Old Testament, and who had seen its fullest expression in Jesus Christ. Carl Henry writes: 'Love is not accidental or incidental to God; it is an essential revelation of the divine nature, a fundamental and eternal perfection', it is 'the shaping principle of his creative and redeeming work'.[10] If holy is *what* God is, love is *how* he is. Yahweh's love, however, is not the bland benevolence of later Greek philosophy and religion.

It is interesting, notes Carl Henry, that 'the Old Testament uses the term "love" of God–man relationships much more cautiously than does Greek mythological literature where references to the *erōs* of the polytheistic gods abound'.[11] Ethelbert Stauffer very clearly

---

[9] Much of what follows is taken from Lewis, pp. 256–259.
[10] Carl Henry, quoted in Lewis, p. 256.   [11] Henry, vol. 6, pp. 344–345.

contrasts the heathen view of the divine love with the biblical view when he says that the distinctive characteristic of love in the Old Testament 'is of course its tendency to exclusivism'. He explains: 'Greek *erōs* is from the outset a universal love, generous, unbound and non-selective. The love extolled in the Old Testament is a jealous love which chooses one among thousands, holds him with all the force of passion and will, and will allow no breach of loyalty.'[12] Similarly, an older biblical theologian, Geerhardus Vos, points out that the Old Testament is consistently cautious about using the actual term 'love' outside of God's covenant relationship with his own people. 'The reason for this phenomenon', he suggests, 'lies in the absolute character the Old Testament ascribes to the divine love.' He continues, 'In his general goodness God bestows various gifts upon the creature; in His love He gives Himself and holds nothing back.'[13]

This is a problem for some, at first, but what mother loves the other children in the street in precisely the same way as she loves her own child? What husband loves all (or any) other women as much as he loves his wife? The higher a love becomes, the more distinguishing and specific it is. Time and again Israel is reminded that Yahweh has loved them in a special way. They are his chosen people.[14] His relationship with them is unique: Israel is his bride,[15] his child,[16] the apple of his eye.[17]

When Israel was tempted to forget the gracious nature of God's love to them, the prophets were at hand to remind them sharply that their history was a sorry reminder that apart from God they were no better than any other nation. There had been nothing in them to attract God at the start, and their repeated backslidings and treachery had forfeited his love a thousand times, yet he had remained true to his decision and oath to love the unworthy and to redeem his people in the end.[18] His love is free but not fickle, spontaneous in its rise but steadfast in its continuance. In a word it is *covenant* love. As such it is electing love,[19] suffering love[20] and enduring love;[21] which is to say, saving love.[22] We shall see its highest demonstration in the New Testament and in the life and death of Jesus Christ.

[12] E. Stauffer, 'agapaō', *TDNT*, vol. 1, p. 38, quoted in Lewis, p. 258.

[13] Geerhardus Vos, 'The Scriptural Doctrine of the Love of God', in R. B. Gaffin Jr (ed.), *Redemptive History and Biblical Interpretation: The shorter writings of Geerhardus Vos* (Presbyterian and Reformed, 1980), pp. 180–181, quoted in Lewis, pp. 257–258.

[14] Deut. 4:19–20, 34–35, 37–40; Amos 3:2; cf. Is. 43:3–4; Mal. 1:2–3.

[15] Hos. 1:2; Is. 54:5.   [16] Exod. 4:22–23; Deut. 32:18.

[17] Deut. 32:10; Zech. 2:8.   [18] Ezek. 16:1–6, 15–34, 59–63; cf. Ps. 89:19–37.

[19] Exod. 24; Deut. 7:6–9.   [20] Is. 53.   [21] Hos. 11; 14; Jer. 31:33.

[22] Is. 60 – 66.

6. Love's wide horizons

In the New Testament, however, we find both the breadth and the depth of God's love. The most famous of its statements, and one that summarizes the good news of the gospel is John 3:16: 'For God so loved the world that he gave his one and only Son, that whoever believes in him shall not perish but have eternal life.'

D. A. Carson notes: 'Jews were familiar with the truth that God loved the children of Israel; here God's love is not restricted by race. Even so, God's love is to be admired not because the world is so big and includes so many people, but because the world is so bad: that is the customary connotation of *kosmos* ("world").' He notes the dual stance of God which is found throughout biblical theology, that he hates sin and brings wrath and judgment upon those who violate his order and yet calls men and women away from sin and rebellion and to himself:

> The holy God finds wicked actions to be detestable things (Ezek. 18:10–13) but that does not prevent him from crying out, 'Do I take any pleasure in the death of the wicked?' declares the Sovereign Lord. 'Rather, am I not pleased when they turn from their ways and live?' (Ezek. 18:23). The same dual track is found in God's stance to other nations. Moab, for instance, is so wicked that God's decree has gone forth . . . 'Moab will be destroyed as a nation because she defied the Lord' (Jer. 48:42). At the same time, the God who takes no pleasure in the death of the wicked declares, 'Therefore I wail over Moab, for all Moab I cry out . . . So my heart laments for Moab like a flute; it laments like a flute for the men of Kir Hareseth' (Jer. 48:31, 36).[23]

The seriousness of the divine love is seen here in its uncompromising opposition to sin, in its correspondence with the divine righteousness, and in its undeserved mercy and costly grace. We ourselves, while we repeatedly find 'the world' in its fallenness to be the object of both God's wrath and his love, are told as his people not to love the world in its rebelliousness against God and yet to love all people in regard to their humanity and their need.

7. Love's final reconciliation

The prophet Hosea lived over seven hundred years before the coming of Christ. The full measure and dimensions of God's love would be made manifest only in the person and work of Jesus, his

---

[23] Carson (1991), p. 205–206.

incarnation and atoning death and exaltation to the right hand of God. We who live on the other side of that coming are best placed to recognize its cost and the extent of its victory. In the sacrificial death of Jesus Christ a work of reconciliation was achieved that makes possible the fulfilment and transcendence of every parable and promise, personal history and public prophecy, in the Old Testament. 'Inscribed upon the cross we see, / In shining letters, "God is love."'[24]

The New Testament message, its great 'good news', will be that God has opened up a way of reconciliation by which those who were his enemies: guilty, condemned and exiled, might again become his friends: ransomed, healed, restored, forgiven.[25] 'All this is from God, who reconciled us to himself through Christ and gave us the ministry of reconciliation: that God was reconciling the world to himself in Christ, not counting men's sins against them.'[26]

Jesus himself indicates the extent of that reconciliation in his prayer in the upper room recorded in John 17:24, 26: 'Father, I want those you have given me to be with me where I am, and to see my glory, the glory you have given me because you loved me before the creation of the world ... I have made you known to them, and will continue to make you known in order that the love you have for me may be in them and that I myself may be in them.' We can see the extent of God's love and our privilege only when we discover our destiny in the inter-Trinitarian life of God, our dearly bought place in the fellowship of love and joy which Father, Son and Holy Spirit have known from all eternity, which we were created to share and which we forfeited by our sin.

Miroslav Volf, in his book *Exclusion and Embrace*, gives us a sustained lesson in the 'ministry of reconciliation' which is committed to us by Christ. 'At the heart of the cross', he writes, 'is Christ's stance of not letting the other remain an enemy and of creating space in himself for the offender to come in ... The arms of the crucified are open – a sign of a space in God's self and an invitation for the enemy to come in.'[27] Later, he develops and applies this demonstration of the self-giving love of God:

> When the Trinity turns toward the world, the Son and the Spirit become, in Irenaeus's beautiful image, the two arms of God by which humanity was made and taken into God's embrace (see *Against Heresies* 5, 6, 1). That same love that sustains non self-enclosed identities in the Trinity, seeks to make space 'in God' for

[24] Hymn, 'We sing the praise of Him who died', by Thomas Kelly (1769–1855).
[25] Rom. 5:6–11; 2 Cor. 5:17–21. [26] 2 Cor. 5:18.
[27] Miroslav Volf, *Exclusion and Embrace: A theological exploration of identity, otherness and reconciliation* (Abingdon Press, 1996), p. 126.

humanity. Humanity is, however, not just the other of God but the beloved other who has become an enemy. When God sets out to embrace the enemy, the result is the cross. On the cross the dancing circle of self-giving and mutual indwelling persons opens up for the enemy; in the agony of the passion the movement stops for a brief moment and a fissure appears, so that sinful humanity can join in (see John 17:21). We, the others – we, the enemies – are embraced by the divine persons who love us with the same love with which they love each other and therefore make space for us within their own eternal embrace.[28]

His application of this is sustained, powerful and uncompromising: 'Inscribed on the heart of God's grace is the rule that we can be its recipients only if we do not resist being made into its agents; what happens to us must be done by us. Having been embraced by God, we must make space for others in ourselves and invite them in – even our enemies.'[29]

The apostle John shows that love which is the foundation of God's life must also be a principle of action in our own. He writes in 1 John 4:16–17: 'And so we know and rely on the love God has for us. God is love. Whoever lives in love lives in God, and God in him. Love is made complete among us so that we will have confidence on the day of judgment, because in this world we are like him.'

[28] Ibid., p. 129.   [29] Ibid.

Isaiah 40 – 48
15. The living God and dead idols

A shrewd observer of his own culture once wrote, 'Man is incurably religious ... The American who does not worship an authentic God is almost certain to have a substitute deity ... The Bible denotes remarkably little time to the menace of atheism. The biblical viewpoint seems to be that atheism is a rare and puny adversary compared to idolatry.'[1] Three hundred years before, the French philosopher Blaise Pascal, one of the great minds of Western intellectual history, reflected, 'It is natural for the mind to believe and for the will to love; so that for want of true objects they must attach themselves to false ones.'

More recently, David Wells, in his survey of Western society and the church in its midst, has written:

> The heart – no less the modern heart – is an idol factory. Idolatry, ancient and modern alike, consists in trusting some substitute for God to serve some uniquely divine function. These substitutes need not be supernatural: money, power, expertise, the location of the planets on the astrological charts, and a belief in progress are among the most popular idols of our time. We have used both our psychological and physical selves idolatrously – although, as the post-modern condition empties out the self, rendering it ever thinner and less substantial, we have increasingly begun to turn more to our bodies than to our psyches. One quite predictable turn in this regard is a revival of the worship of sexuality.[2]

Elsewhere, Wells warns that the modern Western church has to a large extent succumbed to the chief idolatry – the idolatry of the self, where a gospel of self-esteem has replaced a gospel of guilt and

[1] Chad Walsh, *From Utopia to Nightmare* (H. & R., 1962), pp. 143–144, quoted in Leland Ryken, *Work and Leisure* (IVP, 1989), p. 175.
[2] David F. Wells, *God in the Wasteland: The reality of truth in a world of fading dreams* (Eerdmans/IVP, 1994), p. 52.

forgiveness, and where God himself exists to promote the interests of the self. The self, he observes, is 'as powerful an organizing centre as any god or goddess on the market', but the gospel has power to free us from its grip: 'The emancipation that the gospel offers, after all, is not only from the judgement of God but from the tyranny of self as well. Its freedom is, in part, the freedom to be forgetful of the self and its imperious demands and its insatiable appetite for attention, the freedom to think that God is important in and of himself and not simply in relation to what he can do for us.'[3]

The greatest need of the church today is a true vision of God in his incomparable holiness, in his eternal majesty, his burning purity, and his utterly undeserved grace. It is this above all else which will dwarf our pretensions, sicken us of our God-substitutes and bring us back to where we belong in repentance and renewal.

That was also the greatest need of Israel in Isaiah's day and among the prophets no-one spoke more scathingly or more sublimely than Isaiah himself. In chapters 40 and 41 we have three main themes: the restoration of Israel; the incomparability of God; and the inadequacy of idols.

1. 'Comfort, comfort my people' (40:1–8)

> [1]*Comfort, comfort my people, says your God.*
> [2]*Speak tenderly to Jerusalem,*
> *and proclaim to her*
> *that her hard service has been completed,*
> *that her sin has been paid for,*
> *that she has received from the LORD's hand*
> *double for all her sins.*

Isaiah has been calling the people to repentance through many chapters and many years of prophecy. Here in the second half of his book he foresees both the greatest trouble and the greatest deliverance of his people, their exile to Babylon and their return to the land of Judah – and he sees this as the paradigm and promise of a wider and more ultimate salvation which would reach to the ends of the earth. The exile of Judah and the fall of Jerusalem do not mean that Yahweh has forsaken his people or that he is not Lord of history after all or that the gods of Babylon are stronger than him. God can reverse the expectations of men and revive the hopes of his people. Moreover, the nations at large will not be left in thrall for ever to superstition and spiritual darkness. The God who has such powers

[3] David F. Wells, *Losing our Virtue: Why the church must recover its moral vision* (IVP, 1998), p. 204.

of forgiveness and such purposes of grace for one nation is the God who has unfailing purposes and grace sufficient for all nations. As he himself will say to his Servant in Isaiah 49:6:

> *'It is too small a thing for you to be my servant*
> *to restore the tribes of Jacob*
> *and bring back those of Israel I have kept.*
> *I will also make you a light for the Gentiles,*
> *that you may bring my salvation to the ends of the earth.'*

In the second half of his great prophecy, Isaiah's prophetic vision scales height after height with increasing velocity as it soars upward, like a three-stage rocket, encompassing the future of the whole world in the purposes of God.

Isaiah 40 opens dramatically with three voices. The first cries out for comfort for the people of God, the end of their long punishment as a nation (40:1–2). It invites them to respond to the love that offers an ample forgiveness despite all their sins. The second voice calls for a highway to be prepared for our God, for all mankind will see his approaching glory:

> *³A voice of one calling:*
> *'In the desert prepare*
> *the way for the LORD;*
> *make straight in the wilderness*
> *a highway for our God.*
> *⁴Every valley shall be raised up,*
> *every mountain and hill made low;*
> *the rough ground shall become level,*
> *the rugged places a plain.*
> *⁵And the glory of the LORD will be revealed,*
> *and all mankind together will see it.*
> *For the mouth of the LORD has spoken.'*

And the third voice assures us that the salvation of God is for ever, his purposes cannot fail and his promises are sure:

> *⁶A voice says, 'Cry out.'*
> *And I said, 'What shall I cry?'*
>
> *'All men are like grass,*
> *and all their glory is like the flowers of the field . . .*
> *⁷The grass withers and the flowers fall,*
> *because the breath of the LORD blows on them.*
> *Surely the people are grass.*

> [8]*The grass withers and the flowers fall,*
> *but the word of our God stands for ever.'*

What stands in the way of God's purposes? Ultimately only men who are 'like grass' before the heat of Yahweh's unquenchable zeal (40:6–8). Nothing can match the power of God and nothing will deflect the grace of God. He wants to save and he will save. It may be that God is addressing other feelings too among the exiles: 'The glory of God does not look like much compared to the glory of the nations (cf. 30:1–17). Isaiah cries out, "Those great powers are as transient as the wild flowers! They are no more to be feared than a blade of grass!" '[4]

2. The God of power and tenderness (40:9–12)

Even the people of Judah, however, are grass when the fragility of their earthly lives is compared with the eternal immensity of God. Yet all that power, equalled by tenderness and love, is coming for his people's salvation not their destruction, for their vindication and recompense: *'Say to the towns of Judah, Here is your God!'* (v. 9).

> [12]*'Who has measured the waters in the hollow of his hand,*
> *or with the breadth of his hand marked off the heavens?*
> *Who has held the dust of the earth in a basket,*
> *or weighed the mountains on the scales*
> *and the hills in a balance?'*

The hand that cups the oceans in its palms, that marks off the galaxies between thumb and forefinger, that holds the dust of the earth and weighs the mountains, belongs to the arm that rules for Zion. He gathers the lambs of the flock like a shepherd who values and cares for each one of them. In him immense power and supreme tenderness meet:

> [11]*He tends his flock like a shepherd:*
> *He gathers the lambs in his arms*
> *and carries them close to his heart;*
> *he gently leads those that have young.*

3. The incomparable God (40:13–18)

> *Who has understood the mind of the LORD,*
> *or instructed him as his counsellor?*

[4] Oswalt (1986), p. 53.

> [14]*Whom did the LORD consult to enlighten him,*
> *and who taught him the right way?*
> *Who was it that taught him knowledge*
> *or showed him the path of understanding?*
>
> [15]*Surely the nations are like a drop in a bucket;*
> *they are regarded as dust on the scales;*
> *he weighs the islands as though they were fine dust.*

In an ancient world crowded with gods, the prophet asks this series of questions to expose the inadequacy of all rivals to Yahweh. He asks further, in mocking tones, Who advised Yahweh? How does he manage without counsellors? The nations have armies that outnumber Israel and counsellors that help kings to run their empires, even in the pantheons of the gods there was usually one who existed to give counsel to the others; but no-one can 'understand the mind' of God, or has 'instructed him as his counsellor' (v. 14).

'What are the nations – so impressive in their glory, and earthshaking in their power? They are the drop of water falling back into the cistern as the bucket is pulled up, the speck of dust on the pan of the balance scales that does not even cause the scales to flutter (v. 15).'[5]

John Oswalt shows us the relevance and importance of such a prophetic perspective in our own day:

With a series of rhetorical questions Isaiah asserts that the Lord is unique. This assertion implies several points that are at the heart of biblical religion: God is one, without any pantheon; he is the sole creator; he is beyond nature, not part of it. The daring, indeed, the near unintelligibility, of such ideas in the ancient world is lost on many modern Western readers because they take the propositions for granted. But they are by no means self-evident. Indeed, the history of world religions ought to suggest the very opposite: deity is the soul of cosmos, manifesting itself in many different ways to different cultures, but with no one manifestation being essentially different from any other. With the incursion of many Eastern religions and their mutations (such as the New Age movement) into Western culture, this idea is once more gaining currency. Nevertheless, the Bible insists from start to finish (Isaiah is clearly not trying to convince his hearers of some brand-new idea) on a set of ideas that flies directly into the face of the whole world's considered wisdom. Where did Isaiah get these ideas? Whence came this unique thought that there is one personal Being

---

[5] Ibid., p. 61.

who alone transcends the universe? Like the other biblical writers, Isaiah tells us he got this understanding by revelation (1:1; 2:1; 5:9, etc.). What better answer is there?[6]

4. Yahweh versus the rest (40:18–26)

The challenge to the idols and those who put their trust in them continues and will reappear again and again up to chapter 48 as the prophet refuses to let such people off the hook.[7] Idol worship is seen not only as a flight from reality but also as a flight from God. He is the 'Mover and Shaker', the 'Planner and Controller', but the idols, as Alec Motyer notes, are 'the product of the event, part of people's defensive arrangements against life'.[8]

The incomparability of God is utterly compromised when the radical discontinuity of the human and the divine is forgotten or denied and never is the denial made more foolish than in the use of idols and images as representations of the invisible God and ways of channelling and controlling his powers. With rising scorn Isaiah begins in chapter 40 to hold up to ridicule the idea that an idol which has to be prevented from toppling over can represent God or be a means of making him serve our purposes (vv. 18–20). Before him the gods of the nations are nothing, their idols are pathetic substitutes, man-made and helpless, needing help in standing upright, the crutch of man's wounded religiosity.

He asks in dramatic astonishment if they have not thought deeply about the origins of things (v. 21: *'Do you not know? Have you not heard?'*) and understood the difference between the Creator and the created. *'He sits enthroned above the circle of the earth'* (v. 22): so far above them that the entire creation project is to him as a tent which a man might put up overnight on his travels (*'He stretches out the heavens like a canopy'*), and the populations of earth, with their great armies and even greater egos are very small indeed, in comparison with him, *'like grasshoppers'*! Moreover, the God who stretches out the heavens in time-scales that exceed our imagination, reduces the proud rulers of this world and their empires to nothing in a few short years: *'he blows on them and they wither'* (vv. 22–25). The very stars that others worship as gods and powers ruling earthly affairs are no more to him than a flock of sheep to a shepherd who calls them all by name (v. 26). The stars that shine over Babylon were made by the God who dwells in Jerusalem!

Isaiah frequently uses hyperbole in this chapter in comparing human beings with God: 'All men are like grass'; 'Before him the

---

[6] Ibid., p. 59.   [7] See Is. 42:8; 43:10–13; 44:9–20; 45:16; 46:5–7; 47:12–15; 48:5.
[8] Motyer (1993), p. 311.

nations are as nothing; they are regarded by him as worthless and less than nothing'; earth's people 'are like grasshoppers'; its proudest, brightest and best are no sooner full-grown that 'he blows on them and they wither'. Yet he clearly does not mean that God does not value all human life since his plans for the nation's salvation have already been made clear. What is in view in such texts is humanity in its opposition to God, in its independence of God and its much-vaunted size and strength in comparison to that of God. All the glory of the nations does not compare to the glory of God.

The crucial message Isaiah has, however, is that it is not a matter merely of size and power. This God is both transcendent and personal. 'When all is said and done, the combination of these two may be Israel's greatest contribution to human thought.'[9] We too do well to remember this when the social, economic and political forces that hold God in easy contempt threaten to crush us and when we feel dwarfed in exile by alien values and impersonal pressures.

The gods are many; Yahweh is One. The creation is great; he is greater. He is greater not as a part of creation, not even as all of it, but he is 'Holy', 'different', he is greater not only in power but in being and nature. He is 'the Holy One of Israel' in control of the world and in covenant with his people.

5. A different timetable (40:27–31)

> [27]Why do you say, O Jacob,
>   and complain, O Israel,
> 'My way is hidden from the LORD;
>   my cause is disregarded by my God'?

In verse 27 we have 'the perennial question of all who suffer: "Why doesn't God take action to right this situation?" '[10] In this case it is the situation of exile and anguish for the oppressed people of God. Two major answers have already been given. It is not because God does not want to act (vv. 1–11) or because he cannot act (vv. 12–26). A third is now given: he will act but on his own terms, in his own way, and according to his own timetable (vv. 27–31). Meanwhile he calls on his people to wait in hope, to wait not as those killing time but as those confident in God, not as those finally defeated but as those assured of victory whose waiting is worship, whose expectation is faith:

> [29]He gives strength to the weary
>   and increases the power of the weak.

[9] Oswalt (1986), p. 70.   [10] Ibid.

> [30]*Even youths grow tired and weary,*
> *and young men stumble and fall;*
> [31]*but those who hope in the* LORD
> *will renew their strength.*
> *They will soar on wings like eagles;*
> *they will run and not grow weary,*
> *they will walk and not be faint.*

Times of distress are yet to come, but to the weary who seek him and to the weak who call on his name, to his people in all their distresses, to those who have come to the end of their tether and all their natural resources, he will bring relief and vindication and a future with him, strength from the unwearying God. What Isaiah has said in the earlier part of the chapter he says at its end. In the words of John Oswalt:

> The Spirit that breathes out destruction for all human pride is the same Spirit who speaks the eternal word of life over all withered and faded human hopes. Here is the paradox introduced at the beginning of the book: if I insist I am permanent, then I become nothing; if I admit that God alone is permanent, then he breathes his permanence on me.[11]

6. The God who holds the future

One of Isaiah's main points in the chapters that follow is that the only one who can predict the future is God because he is the one who shaped the future. Again and again Isaiah presses home the point that the idols of Babylon do not know the future because they do not command the future – or even the present. It is only Yahweh who knows what he will do and it is only Yahweh who can do a new thing, breaking the chain of cause and effect, entering in from outside the situation and the created order; and he will show this by bringing Israel back from exile in mighty Babylon and bringing them to their homeland – and even raising up a heathen king to do so! (41:2–4; cf. 45:1–7). There is no shared sovereignty, no dualism (45:7) and courage to face the future is not to be gained from man-made idols or occult forces (41:5–7, 21–24).

Yet recourse has been made to these in every period down to our own. Men and women's desperation to know the future that they might preserve themselves from its dangers or capitalize on its prospects for good has led them to seek predictions about the future in everything from stars to tea-leaves, from entrails to clairvoyants.

[11] Ibid., p. 54.

The great offence of such practices is that they bypass God, turning aside from his speech and honour to substitutes. In Isaiah, God says they are all 'but wind and confusion' (41:29) and insists, *'I am the LORD (Yahweh); that is my name! I will not give my glory to another or my praise to idols'* (42:8).

7. A choice that must be made

A feature of these chapters which is unwelcome to the modern or postmodern mind is the repeated use of exclusive claims and the choice which must be made between biblical religion and all other forms of religion. Here God says, in effect, 'If I am true, then these are false; you cannot choose God and idols, true religion and false, you cannot be loyal to the gods of the nations and to me.' So he forces a decision on Israel and on us all.[12]

To choose other gods over this God is to be fatally affected by one's decision. False religion cheats human hopes and exhausts human life; self-made religion is really a form of self-worship and finally a form of self-deceit, as Isaiah 44:9 shows:

> *All who make idols are nothing,*
> *and the things they treasure are worthless.*
> *Those who would speak up for them are blind;*
> *they are ignorant, to their own shame.*

The idols themselves are powerless to help the devotee, however hard or urgently he cries, for

> [18]*They know nothing, they understand nothing;*
> *their eyes are plastered over so that they cannot see,*
> *and their minds are closed so that they cannot understand.*

The result in the worshipper is that

> [20]*He feeds on ashes, a deluded heart misleads him;*
> *he cannot save himself, or say,*
> *'Is not this thing in my right hand a lie?*

In chapter 47 prophet says scornfully to the proud and impenitent followers of the Babylonian superstitions:

> [12]*'Keep on, then, with your magic spells*
> *and with your many sorceries . . .*

---

[12] Is. 42:8; 43:12; 45:6, 21–22; 46:9; 48:12.

> [13]*All the counsel you have received has only worn you out!*
>   *Let your astrologers come forward,*
> *those stargazers who make predictions month by month,*
>   *let them save you from what is coming upon you . . .*
> [14]*. . . They cannot even save themselves.'*

8. You are my witnesses (43:10–12)

The duty of those who know the true God is to speak of him in his unique and exclusive sovereignty and saving power: '*I have revealed and saved and proclaimed . . . You are my witnesses*', declares the LORD, '*that I am God . . .*' (43:12). In Babylon as well as in Jerusalem the people of God were to speak confidently and even boldly of the God they knew, whose witnesses they were chosen to be, and who would deliver them at the last. Their witness was not only to be of his existence but of his existence alone on the level of deity; he was not only God to them but, in his ultimate purpose, God to the world – for there were no other gods, not national gods or private gods, not gods in the heavens or gods on the earth.

Today, perhaps, we can scarcely grasp the outrage, even the incomprehensibility of such a claim to those of the ancient world whose religions were older than Abraham and whose cults far outshone that of Israel in splendour and prestige. Such considerations may well help us to face the challenge of a fashionable pluralism which stands aghast at exclusive and universal truth-claims in the field of religion and morality.

In this modern age all truth is perceived as relative and to the post-modern mind-set, looking back to times of religious wars and ideological persecutions, all exclusive claims to truth are seen as bids for power ('This is not only true for me, it must be true for you too'). No allowance is made for the possibility that any one claim is true to the contradiction of another. For some people, all religions are equal because all religions are wrong; for others all religions are matters of insight or of ethics or are fragments of a larger reality with no one religion having truth for all peoples and for all time. For the devotees of various New Age ideas and practices, all reality is part of what constitutes 'God' or religious-type experience and spirituality.

Isaiah's use of scorn and challenge sounds harsh to modern ears but for him what was at stake was all that mattered most: the glory of (the true) God, the comfort of his chosen people, and the salvation of the world in which the nations would worship together and be a blessing on the earth.[13] What stood in the way of God's glory

---

[13] See Is. 19:19–25.

and humanity's good was not the truth but substitutes for the truth. That is still the case.

The nations may be proud of their cultures and aware of their past, the ideals may be honourable and the ethics high, but what is of supreme importance is not whether a set of thoughts, convictions and rituals *help* but whether they are *true*, not whether they *satisfy* but whether they *save*, not whether they put us in a more positive mood but whether they put us *right with God* and please him and bring glory to him. Does he want everyone to know him personally or does he not? Is he equally happy with the spirituality that prays as he is with that which hugs trees; with the mind that dwells on his Word and that which empties itself of thought as it hums a mantra? Is he equally well-represented by a crucified Christ and a seated Buddha? These are questions of truth which can be answered only if the living God has finally spoken, breaking into our human consciousness and multiplicity of religious experiences. This involves the most foundational claims of Christianity as set out in Hebrews 1:1–4:

> In the past God spoke to our forefathers through the prophets at many times and in various ways, but in these last days he has spoken to us by his Son, whom he appointed heir of all things, and through whom he made the universe. The Son is the radiance of God's glory and the exact representation of his being, sustaining all things by his powerful word. After he had provided purification for sins, he sat down at the right hand of the Majesty in heaven. So he became as much superior to the angels as the name he has inherited is superior to theirs.

Here the self-revelation of God throughout the Old Testament period is affirmed, the ultimacy of Jesus Christ in that revelation is stated, and the universal relevance of Christ explained. He is the Creator of all people and the one who has made atonement for the sin which is, in all ages, cultures and individuals, the great human predicament. He is the one who now sits as God's equal, the victor over sin and death. There could not be, in one paragraph, a greater statement of ultimacy and universal relevance than this.

Moreover, this is the teaching of Jesus himself: that his representatives should 'go and make disciples of all nations, baptising them in the name of the Father and of the Son and of the Holy Spirit, and teaching them to obey everything I have commanded you.'[14] This is not a formula for religious pluralism: it insists that the God who is made known is the triune God, the God who is Father, Son and Spirit

---

[14] Matt. 28:20.

– Creator, Redeemer and Indweller; the God who saves and the God who sanctifies, the God who enters into personal relations with men and women and meets them at the point of their greatest need.

There are idolatrous systems as well as idolatrous objects, idols of the mind and of popular thinking as well as idols of the body and popular pleasure-seeking. As well as wealth, materialism, sexual immorality, drink and drugs, power, career and prestige there are idolatrous philosophies and systems of thought which leave out of the centre of human life and society the true God: secularism, relativism and pluralism have been three of the greatest forces in this regard in the past two hundred years or so.

9. The Holy One of Israel

'The concept of holiness is central to the whole theology of Isaiah', writes Otto Procksch,[15] and from it the prophet forged the expression 'the Holy One of Israel' to describe God in his relations with his chosen people. The expression, 'the Holy One of Israel' is 'obviously paradoxical' since God transcends everything creaturely and threatens everything sinful and corrupt. The holiness of God is often a danger to Israel, even a guarantee of judgment for her as well as for her enemies: 'The light of Israel will become a fire, their Holy One a flame.'[16] As Procksch puts it in another connection, 'In the holiness of God there is the death-dealing element which must destroy uncleaness (Hos. 5:3; 6:10; 9:4 cf. 2 Sam. 11:4).'

God is called 'The Holy One of Israel' twenty-five times in Isaiah. Alec Motyer writes:

> As a title it is full of majesty and mystery: the God who is transcendent in holiness has brought himself into close relationship with a specified people, whereby they may claim that he is theirs and he, that they are his. The whole Isaianic literature is an explication of this basic situation: the awesome threat which holiness constitutes to an unworthy, careless, rejecting and unresponsive people (chapters 1 – 37); the lengths to which the Holy One will go to deal with sin, reclaim the sinner and create a righteous people for himself (chapters 40 – 55); and the eternal state of holiness which he will prepare for them and wherein they will enjoy him for ever (chapters 56 – 66).[17]

Hence in the early part of Isaiah's prophecy, in the face of the unholiness of the people, it is supremely the divine Judge who is

---

[15] Otto Procksch, 'hagios', *TDNT*, vol. 1, p. 93. Cf. Is. 1:4; 5:19, 24; 10:20; 12:6, etc.
[16] Is. 10:17.   [17] Motyer (1993), p. 18.

introduced. However, in the later chapters it is in his very holiness that Yahweh shows himself to be the incomparable Saviour (40:25; cf. 57:15) who calls to forgiveness and reconciliation the fugitives from the nations and the foolish of Israel (40:1–2; 45:15–25). The ultimate mystery of God's being is disclosed in redemption. The holiness of God is also a tree of life for his people.

a. God the Holy One

It is difficult to give any one meaning to the term 'holy', as it is a description of what God is in himself in his infinite perfection. It is not one thing about God, it is everything about God. It is the most fundamental feature of the divine being and it is the total glory of all he is; it underlies and characterizes every attribute and it is the sum of all his attributes. Out of his holy being all his deeds and decisions proceed: his speech is the announcement of his holiness, his glory is the display of his holiness, his wrath is the revulsion of his holiness against sin, and his love is the embrace by his holiness of all that is good and true.

Hence God wants his people to know, as of first importance, that he is the holy God. God's holiness is the greatest jewel in his crown. No concept is more central to the biblical teaching about God. It is the very Godness of God. It is the way he subsists. It is the order of his being as infinite and eternal, just and good. He is holy in all that he is and does. He is holy in every aspect of his being, in his goodness, wisdom, power, righteousness, justice, love and wrath. He is holy in every aspect of his activity, as Creator, Sustainer, Redeemer and Judge.

The Hebrew word for holy (qāḏôš) probably comes from a root meaning 'cut off', 'separated', 'set apart'; and in the first place points not so much to his moral character as to his fundamental 'apartness' from everything else in his creation, his transcendence, his infinite 'otherness' as infinite and uncreated from everything finite and created. Hence the angels in Isaiah's vision who cover their faces in dread before Yahweh's holiness do so not because they are sinners but because they are creatures; they are awed by the infinite reaches and majesty of the the divine being.

God is holy, 'set apart', 'different' in his essential and mysterious being from everything else, from everything finite and created and also from everything sinful and corrupt. He is the infinite and eternal God, the uncreated Creator. He is a being of a different order and as such he has no equal and no fellow. He alone is God and there is no other.[18]

Moreover, the term 'holy' is also applied to whatever or whoever

---

[18] Deut. 4:39; 1 Sam. 2:2; Is. 43:10–11; 45:21–22.

God 'cuts off' from common use to serve him. The entire nation of Israel is made holy by an act of God at Sinai; they are 'set apart' from the other nations precisely in this respect[19] that they now exist to serve God and his purposes in the world. Furthermore, in Israel, where God has his earthly dwelling, the temple is holy, the priests are holy, even the vessels of the temple are holy because God has cut them off from common use and set them apart for himself. In different ways and in differing degrees, people, places and things in Israel are holy because they are set apart for God who is supremely holy.

b. Holy God, holy people

Closely allied with God's majestic holiness is his ethical holiness; for the God who is set apart from creatureliness is equally set apart from sin and corruption. This appears in the early chapters of Genesis in God's grief and anger at the corruption of the antedeluvian world and it continues throughout Scripture as the unceasing character of God's existence. The ethical implications of this for Israel's national life are made clear from the start.

In an act of sovereign grace God makes the nation a holy nation. Israel is made holy by an act of God in order that she might live out her holy standing as a nation. In Scripture sanctification is an act before it is a process; holiness is what God does to us before it is what we do for God. Hence God says repeatedly to the people: 'I am the LORD, who makes you holy.'[20]

This privilege, however, carries with it a corresponding duty: the nation that has God in her midst must be like him in character. Those who walk with God must live as God, in righteousness and true holiness. At the heart of Israel's life are the Ten Commandments,[21] and throughout the law moral and ethical commandments appear entwined with ceremonial and ritual laws. What makes Israel different among the peoples of the ancient near-East must include the standards of God lived out in her social and political life, as well as the claims inherent in her religious life. So the nation is to be consistently what God had made her definitively:

> For you are a people holy to the LORD your God. The LORD your God has chosen you out of all the peoples on the face of the earth to be his people, his treasured possession . . . Know therefore that the LORD your God is God; he is the faithful God, keeping his covenant of love to a thousand generations of those who love him and keep his commands. But

---

[19] Deut. 7:6.   [20] Exod. 31:13; Lev. 20:8; 21:8.   [21] Exod. 20:1–21.

those who hate him he will repay to their face by destruction;
he will not be slow to repay to their face those who hate him.

Therefore, take care to follow the commands, decrees and laws I give you today.[22]

'*Holy to the Lord*' defines both Israel's identity and her obligation. The story of her history is the story of what happens when a split is made between these two: when the holy nation forgets her calling and begins to live an unholy life. That split has become critical by the time of the eighth-century prophets and the consequences are spelt out by Amos, Hosea, Micah and Isaiah.

c. Holiness and the wrath of God

The holiness of God has two great corollaries in Scripture: they are, his *love* and his *wrath*. Both of these are essential to the integrity of God's being and character as holy. They are aspects of his holiness at work in relation to his creatures. His love goes out in embrace toward all that is good and true and upright in his creation and his wrath thrusts away from him all that is corrupt, rebellious and false.

Hence we have a very emphatic assertion of the wrath of God in the Hebrew Scriptures. Old Testament theologian Edmund Jacob points out that references to the divine wrath outnumber by five to one references to human anger[23] and Gerhard von Rad notes that the Hebrew prophets, especially Amos, Hosea, Isaiah and Micah, 'spoke of the divine wrath as a fact, and designated as its proper object their contemporaries' whole way of life, their social and economic attitudes, their political behaviour and, in particular, their cultic practice'.[24]

God is holy in himself and he is holy in his rule; holy in his love and in his wrath. The concept of wrath in God has long been dismissed as unworthy and untrue and is frequently caricatured. It is not, of course, to be confused with bad temper, outbursts of uncontrolled anger or the expression of a frustration suddenly detached from the other attributes of God. On the contrary, God's wrath proceeds from his whole character; it is the consequence of righteousness, the outgoing of justice, the reverse side of love. It is, in fact, an essential part of his moral seriousness in contrast to the fickleness of the heathen deities both in Mesopotamia and, later, in

[22] Deut. 7:6–11; cf. Deut. 26:16–19.
[23] Edmund Jacob, *Theology of the Old Testament* (Hodder & Stoughton, 1958), p. 114, quoted in Henry, vol. 6, p. 330.
[24] Gerhard von Rad, *Old Testament Theology* (Oliver & Boyd, 1965), p. 179, quoted in Henry, vol. 6, p. 330.

Greece.[25] In the context of Greek thought, which simply rejected anger as a disreputable emotion, 'the idea of the divine anger', notes Edwyn Bevan, 'was not something which penetrated into Christianity from its pagan environment; it was something which the Church maintained in the face of adverse pagan criticism'.[26] It is not the wrath of God which is an unworthy concept but the idea of a God who cannot be wrathful in the face of evil. A God void of wrath would be as heathen as a God void of love.

10. For God so loved . . .

The wonder of God's love can be appreciated only against the background of his holiness with its revelation of human sinfulness and corruption. It is this which makes for the costliness of his undeserved, and indeed, forfeited, love. God's holiness is the most essential and important thing about him. And God is determined to maintain his righteous rule as the Holy God: holy in creation, holy in salvation and holy in judgment. Hence we have, in the Old Testament, Sinai with its uncompromising demands and, in the New Testament, Calvary with its unsparing judgment. Nowhere is the indefectible holiness of God more fully revealed than at the cross. And there it is revealed in its love and wrath together. Sooner than compromise any part of his holiness, God himself would satisfy all its requirements and pay for our transgressions in our nature: 'God was reconciling the world to himself in Christ, not counting men's sins against them . . . God made him who had no sin to be sin for us, so that in him we might become the righteousness of God.'[27]

In profound explanation of the vicarious sufferings of Christ for us, the apostle Paul writes to the Galatians: 'Christ redeemed us from the curse of the law by becoming a curse for us, for it is written: "Cursed is everyone who is hung on a tree." '[28] The cost of the holy love of God is the bloody sweat of Gethsemane and the cry of desolation at Calvary where it was the will of the Lord to make his life a guilt offering, 'And by that will, we have been made holy through the sacrifice of the body of Jesus Christ once for all.'[29]

---

[25] See H. Kleinknecht, 'Theos: the Greek concept of God', TDNT, vol. 3, p. 70.
[26] E. Bevan, Symbolism and Belief (1938: reprinted by Folcroft Library Editions, 1975), p. 210, quoted in Henry, vol. 6, p. 329.
[27] 2 Cor. 5:19–21.   [28] Gal. 3:13; cf. Deut. 21:22–23.
[29] Heb. 10:10; cf. Is. 53:10.

PART 3: GOD IN THREE PERSONS

John 1
16. God incarnate

In the beginning was the Word . . . (1:1). *The Word became flesh and made his dwelling among us* (14). We all know something about the power of words. They are the vehicle of something bigger than themselves. Words can build us up and break us down. Words can be as sunshine on our souls and as whips across our backs. Many of our best and worst memories hang on words others said to us or we said to others.

Perhaps the most dramatic thing about words is that they can reveal in a moment what is otherwise entirely hidden. You may be in the same room as another person and yet you are a mystery to them until you speak. They cannot know what is in your mind until you choose to tell them. Your thoughts are invisible, inaudible, inscrutable until you speak out the secrets of your mind. Each worshipper in the congregation in church is sitting next to a mystery until that mystery is revealed in words. Now if you and I, as human beings, limited and familiar, are so far unknown until we speak, how much more is the infinite, eternal God a mystery until he speaks.

John at the start of his Gospel introduces us to Jesus Christ, not as the familiar baby of Bethlehem, not even as the easier to understand Son of the Father, but as the eternal *Word* (Gk. *logos*), the one who has always been with God and who alone can express God; the one who can make the unknown known; the one who is God's supreme self-revelation; the one who, by his Spirit, inspired the prophets and the one who, in his own person, enters our world: God speaking, God coming, God saving.

1. The Word of God in the Old Testament

Greek and Jewish philosophy also used the term *logos*, as we shall see later. However, Murray Harris, in his book *Jesus as God*, sees the resemblances between these and John's concept as 'only superficial' and writes:

Given John's demonstrable dependence on the O.T. for his formative ideas ... one should assume that his logos concept is informed principally by O.T. teaching concerning 'the word of the Lord' as God's agent in creation (Ps. 33:6), revelation (Jer. 1:4–5, 9), and salvation (Ezek. 37:4–6), especially since the Prologue proceeds to emphasise precisely these three spheres as the areas in which the Logos is mediator. He created the universe (1:3, 10), he personally and perfectly revealed the Father (1:4–5, 9, 14, 18), and he redeemed humankind (1:12, 16).[1]

a. The word that creates

In the theology of the Old Testament the 'word' of God is powerfully creative because it is God in action. It is no empty sound but a dynamic action which fulfils the intention of the Speaker: 'And God said, "Let there be light," and there was light . . . And God said, "Let the water under the sky be gathered into one place, and let dry ground appear." And it was so . . .'[2]

The word of God is the greatest creative and ordering force imaginable. As a psalmist puts it later, 'By the word of the LORD were the heavens made.'[3]

b. The word that destroys

On the other hand, the word of God can also be a terrible force for destruction because it is God in judgment: 'Nations are in uproar, kingdoms fall; he lifts his voice, the earth melts';[4] 'He will strike the earth with the rod of his mouth.'[5]

c. The word that saves

The word of God can also be a word spoken to one person to begin something new and far-reaching in human history, such as when God began a new phase of salvation-history: 'The LORD had said to Abraham ... "I will make you into a great nation and I will bless you ... and all peoples on earth will be blessed through you." '[6]

d. The word that heals

God's word can also be a healing word which forgives the offenders, which the lifts the downcast and heals the broken-hearted because it is God speaking in love and self-giving: 'He sent forth his word and healed them.'[7]

'So do not fear, for I am with you;
do not be dismayed, for I am your God.

[1] Harris (1992), p. 55. [2] Gen. 1:3, 9, etc. [3] Ps. 33:6. [4] Ps. 46:6.
[5] Is. 11:4; cf. Rev. 19:15, 21. [6] Gen. 12:1–3. [7] Ps. 107:20.

I will strengthen you and help you;
I will uphold you with my righteous right hand.'[8]

Such references as these are a way of describing God at work bringing into the visible world his unseen purposes. They are also a way of reminding us that there is no disjunction and no possibility of failure between what God determines to do and what he eventually does. There is no shortcoming between word and deed. He is the all-wise, all-powerful, Sovereign God. He is also the God who reveals himself as good and gracious and whose word is life-giving. God's word, even after the finished work of creation, can still initiate something new and powerful and gracious in world history.

e. The word that is reliable

Above all else, the word of the Lord that came to the prophets is a truthful and trustworthy revelation of the One God and his will and purposes for his people and for the world beyond Israel. F. R. Ames points out that the term 'the word of Yahweh' (the *dāḇār yahweh*) is repeated throughout the Old Testament no less than 242 times in the singular and 17 times in the plural ('the words of the Lord'), showing that 'Israel's God is a God who speaks'. Taking Psalm 33 as an example he says that it rehearses two theological themes that are prominent not only in Psalms but in the entire Old Testament, that 'Yahweh tells the truth so one can rely upon divine promises with confidence' and that 'Yahweh commands the universe so that no-one can thwart his will.'[9] Where the word of the Lord is personified or seems to have a life of its own, it in fact 'has power only because it is an expression and extension of Yahweh's knowledge, character and ability'.[10] This removes it far from the magic of ancient near-Eastern superstition. God's word is a power, not a magical but a moral power, and it is ultimately a saving power. God's speech is his activity.

f. God's word and God's wisdom

Closely connected with such concepts of the divine Word was the concept of the divine Wisdom. In the book of Proverbs, wisdom is personified as being with God in the beginning:

'Then I was the craftsman at his side.
I was filled with delight day after day,
 rejoicing always in his presence,
rejoicing in his whole world
 and delighting in mankind.'[11]

---

[8] Is. 41:10.   [9] F. R. Ames, '*dḇr*', *NIDOTTE*, vol. 1, p. 914.   [10] Ibid
[11] Prov. 8:30–31; cf. Prov. 8:1–36.

It is this same wisdom personified who stands at street corners and in noisy thoroughfares, offering men and women the saving truth of God as the most precious thing in life, but who is often ignored or rejected with tragic results.[12]

In the first-century world of John's day, in both Jewish and Greek philosophical traditions, the Word, considered as *logos*, had as much to do with mind, thought, reason and the rational principle which ran through the whole creation, as with the spoken word. I have given more detail in a section at the end of this chapter. However, for John, the Old Testament background is much more decisive with its emphasis on the word of the Lord in creation and in revelation, as later verses show (1:3, 4, 10, 18).

2. The Word in John's Gospel (1:1)

In the beginning was the Word, and the Word was with God, and the Word was God.

a. In the beginning was the Word

The words 'In the beginning' clearly recall the opening words of Genesis: 'In the beginning God created the heavens and the earth.' Here, John wants us to see that 'in the beginning the Word already was' – before heavens or earth, light or angels, beasts or human beings. Three times the word 'was' occurs, the imperfect tense of the verb 'to be', 'expressive in each case of continuous, timeless existence', as one scholar has put it.[13] This stands in contrast with later verbs: creation *came into* being (v. 3); John the Baptist *came on to* the scene (v. 6); even the incarnation of the Word *came about* at a point in time (v. 14); but the Word himself did not come into existence at any point, the Word was eternal, without beginning.

b. '... and the Word was with God ...'

The words of verse 1 contain a number of supremely important and foundational principles for what is truly Christian faith: that the Word was eternal, that the Word was a distinct person; that the Word was uniquely related to God; and that the Word was himself God. First of all, we learn that 'the Word' was not simply another name for the Deity. The Word is eternally all that God is in his divine nature, yet he is also a distinct person *within* the Godhead. Later in John's Gospel, we learn from Jesus himself the much easier concept of a Father-Son relationship within the Godhead.

Secondly, in the phrase 'the Word was *with* God', John uses the

---

[12] Prov. 1:20–33; 8:1–11, 32–36; 9:1–6.

[13] J. H. Bernard, quoted in Lewis, p. 104. Much of what follows is taken from Lewis, pp. 101–136.

Greek preposition *pros* with the accusative ('with', then, means literally 'towards', in the sense of 'in the company of', 'in communion
with', 'face to face') rather than *meta* or *para* with the dative. John is
telling us that the Word eternally existed in a person-to-person
relationship with God, no mere emanation from God but
maintaining communion and intercourse with God. The sense is,
says Murray Harris, that 'The Word was in active communion with
God', for, 'used of divine persons, this preposition points to eternal
intercommunion'.[14] John clearly means to proclaim the pre-
existence of Jesus Christ as the Word of God in eternity (vv. 14, 16,
18) but he begins by uncovering Jesus' eternal identity and life in a
very studied and special way. He is taking us into the inner life and
eternal existence of the Godhead in which more than one person
subsists in the one God.

c. '. . . and the Word was God'

The word 'God' in the Greek text is emphasized by placing it at the
beginning instead of at the end. The Greek reads literally: 'and *God*
was the Word'; it is as if John had written in English: 'and the Word
was nothing less and nothing other than – *God!*' There could be no
clearer statement of our Lord's deity than this.

In the Greek, the word 'God' does not have the definite article
'the', although the word *logos* does. It is not 'and the Word was *the*
God' (or, to follow the Greek word-order, 'and *the* God was the
Word') but it is simply 'and the Word was God' ('and God was the
Word'). Much is made of that fact by those who reject the orthodox
Christian understanding of the full deity of Christ. The Jehovah's
Witnesses' 'New World Translation' of the Bible, for instance,
translates our phrase as 'and the Word was a god'. However, this is a
completely unacceptable translation for several reasons.

First, in a pagan world which acknowledged many gods any such
statement would have been unthinkable to the New Testament
writers. It was a fundamental article of Jewish and Old Testament
faith that Yahweh alone was God:

> Before me no god was formed,
>   nor shall there be any after me.
> I, even I, am the LORD,
>   and apart from me there is no saviour.[15]

If in his pre-existent heavenly life Jesus had not been God in the
fullest sense, then John would not have dreamed of writing such a
statement as this.

---

[14] Harris (1992), p. 57.   [15] Is. 43:10–11.

Secondly, John deliberately avoids using the lesser word 'divine' (Gk. *theios*) in favour of the straightforward word 'God' (Gk. *theos*). He is making it clear that the Word, the Logos, is not divine in some lower sense than God himself.

Thirdly, there is also a reason in Greek grammar for the absence of the definite article before *theos* (God). In the Greek New Testament definite nouns which precede the verb in a construction like this commonly lose the article. A later example occurs in John 19:21, which literally reads in the Greek, 'King I am of the Jews', where it means, 'I am *the* king of the Jews.' The noun 'king' drops its definite article because it comes before the verb 'to be'. The *sense* of the article is there even if the article itself is not. No-one would imagine that it suddenly means, 'I am *a* king of the Jews'! Nor would a first-century Christian reader imagine that the Word was 'a' god.

There may also be a further theological reason why John used this particular sentence construction. He may have wanted to avoid giving the impression that the Word was all there was in God. As C. K. Barrett puts it: 'The absence of the article indicates that the Word is God, but is not the only being of whom this is true; if "*ho* theos" [*the* God] had been written it would have implied that no divine being existed outside the second Person of the Trinity.'[16]

It is true that such a direct statement as this concerning the deity of Jesus Christ is rare in the New Testament[17] and the New Testament writers usually avoid starkly saying 'Jesus is God'. But in the circumstances in which they wrote there were good reasons for this reticence. R. E. Brown writes:

> The reluctance to apply this designation to Jesus is understandable as part of the NT heritage from Judaism. For the Jews, 'God' meant the heavenly Father; and until a wider understanding of the term was reached, it could not be readily applied to Jesus . . . (The way that the NT approached the question of the divinity of Jesus was not through the title 'God' but by describing his activities in the same way as it described the Father's activities; see John 5:17, 21; 10:28–29).[18]

However, in these opening statements John makes his message about the ultimate identity of Jesus Christ as clear at the beginning of his Gospel as he will towards its end, when, in John 20:28, Thomas confesses the risen Christ as 'My Lord and my God!'

---

[16] Barrett, p. 156.

[17] Note, however, John 1:18; 20:28; Rom. 9:5; Col. 2:2; Titus 2:13; Heb. 1:8–9; 2 Pet. 1:1. See Harris (1992), passim.

[18] R. E. Brown, p. 367.

3. The Word in creation (1:3)

Through him all things were made; without him nothing was made that has been made (3). In the past two hundred years Western man, especially, has attempted to understand and explain his world in terms of an impersonal physics. Consequently he has left himself in a cold mechanistic universe in which humanity has no ultimate or objective meaning or purpose. John here gives us the key we threw away. He tells us that the ultimate explanation of the universe is not to be found in the formulas of physics but in the person of the Creator and in particular through the agency of this person who was with God in the beginning: 'Through him all things were made; without him nothing was made that has been made.'

In Genesis the word of God is not a distinct person; in John it is. 'The Logos is asserted to be the Mediator of creation.'[19] He is God's agent through whom it actually came into being. However, as Beasley-Murray stresses, it is important to note that the Word is not merely an intermediary between God and creation. There were many philosophical and religious notions of the relationship between God and creation which either viewed matter as evil, or God as far too elevated above the created universe to be in any sort of direct contact with it. They therefore positioned intermediary beings and powers, including the 'Logos' (however they conceived of it) between God and creation.

John is making the point here that *God* created the world, and that the creative activity of the true Logos is the activity of *God*, not of some deputy or intermediary. The Word is the fully divine and personal agent in creation. The apostle Paul makes the same point in Colossians 1:16. Jesus Christ is not another intermediary; he created every supposed being between God and humanity: 'For by him all things were created: things in heaven and on earth, visible and invisible, whether thrones or powers or rulers or authorities; all things were created by him and for him.'

Leon Morris makes a further point: 'He does not say that all was made "by" Him but "through" Him. This way of putting it safeguards the truth that the Father is the source of all that is.'[20] The apostle Paul similarly distinguishes the roles played by the Father and the Son when he writes: '. . . for us there is but one God, the Father, from whom all things came and for whom we live; and there is but one Lord, Jesus Christ, through whom all things came and through whom we live.'[21] Creation was not the solitary work of either. Both were at work, and still are.[22] In Paul's wording, however,

[19] Beasley-Murray, p. 11.   [20] Morris (1971), p. 80.   [21] 1 Cor. 8:6.
[22] Cf. John 5:17, 19.

'God and the *Word*' has become 'God and the *Lord* Jesus Christ'. The agency of Christ as the Son in creation is also taught in the opening statements of Hebrews where it is further said that the ongoing existence and life of the universe is upheld by the power of that same Son.[23]

Bruce Milne applies the words 'Through him all things ... without him nothing' to a fashionable pluralism in our own day:

> John is also addressing a first-century tendency to view Jesus as simply one of a series of intermediaries or emanations from God. A similar idea appears commonly in New Age writers, where Jesus is simply one of a series of spiritual masters who have been sent to bring enlightenment at different stages of human spiritual development. John's point is that it is through Jesus alone that all things exist, whether physical planets or spiritual hierarchies. He towers above all and cannot be reduced to one of a series, whether as a stage in the process of human evolution or in the history of human ideas.[24]

The entire statement tells us, furthermore, that nature is to be respected and our responsibilities with regard to it are to be fulfilled as honouring Jesus Christ's agency of creation. As Milne puts it:

> That species are being exterminated, forests denuded, soil eroded, rivers and seas polluted and the ozone layer depleted, contradicts the creative action of our Lord Jesus Christ who called all things into being. Although affected by fallenness, they remain his handiwork. A lack of concern for our natural environment is a sign of a limited view of Christ, or of a spirituality which is more spiritual than Jesus and in need of balance and healing.[25]

4. The Word became flesh (1:14)

The Word became flesh and lived for a while among us. We have seen his glory, the glory of the One and Only [Son], who came from the Father, full of grace and truth (14). To read verse 14 immediately after verses 1–3 is to get the full impact of John's great prologue, with its astonishing climax. What no Gentile philosopher would have believed, what no Jewish theologian had conceived, God had done. The *Word* became *flesh*: the highest being became a lowly creature; the source of life became a dying man; the ultimate Fact became a commonplace feature. While philosophers and mystics were seeking to escape the 'flesh' and be free in 'spirit', God who is Spirit became

---

[23] Heb. 1:1–3.   [24] Milne (1993), p. 39.   [25] Ibid., p. 40.

flesh! All power was his, yet he used his divine power to assume our human weakness, his perfect blessedness and freedom from all ill to share our vulnerability, our dying lives and painful deaths. In a vivid metaphor of Paul's, he who had everything 'made himself nothing'.[26]

The word 'lived' could be literally translated 'he pitched his tent' among us, and the impact of the phrase, at one level at least, is graphically captured by Eugene H. Petersen in *The Message*. He renders it 'The Word became flesh and blood and moved into the neighbourhood'!

a. 'We have seen his glory ...'

John's readers would recall here the wilderness period in Israel's journey to the Promised Land, and the tabernacle, the portable sanctuary which was constructed at God's command.[27] They would also recall the glory-cloud[28] which, in the words of W. A. VanGemeren, 'represented his presence and protection in the wilderness'. The cloud came to rest on Mount Sinai and 'formed a canopy for Moses as he communed with Yahweh and received the commandments'. When the tabernacle was completed it was crowned with the descent of the glory-cloud. 'The Pentateuch stresses that all Israel saw the cloud covering the tabernacle as evidence of the presence of the Lord's glory (Ex. 40:34–38; Lev. 9:23).'[29] Here John testifies that he and others have seen the glory of God in the flesh of Jesus, the 'tabernacling' of God in his presence, 'the glory of the One and Only, who came from the Father, full of grace and truth'. However, as D. A. Carson notes:

> As John proceeds with his gospel it becomes clearer and clearer that the glory Christ displayed was not perceived by everyone. When he performed a miracle, a 'sign', he 'revealed his glory' (2:11), but only his disciples put their faith in him. The miraculous sign was not itself unshielded glory; the eyes of faith were necessary to 'see' the glory that was revealed by the sign ... There is a hiddenness to the display of glory in the incarnate Word, a hiddenness penetrated by the Evangelist and the early witnesses who could say, *We have seen his glory.*[30]

b. '... the glory of the One and Only ...'

The term 'the One and Only' is translated 'the only begotten' in older versions. The Greek word is *monogenēs*. It literally means 'of a single kind' and its Old Testament equivalent is the Hebrew word *yāḥîd*, which is used of Isaac, the child of promise, who was the

[26] Phil. 2:7.   [27] Exod. 25 – 31; 35 – 40.   [28] Exod. 13:21–22.
[29] W. A. VanGemeren, '*Shekinah*', *ISBE*, vol. 4, pp. 466–467.
[30] Carson (1991), pp. 128, 130.

'only' in the sense of 'uniquely precious' son of Abraham.[31] We shall look at this word more closely in connection with verse 18.

This unique Son, however, 'came from the Father, full of grace and truth'. If, as Carson thinks, these terms are meant to modify the term 'glory' they will be an obvious reference to Exodus 33 – 34. In Exodus 33:18 Moses asks God, 'Now show me your glory', and God responds by passing by Moses, hiding him protectively from the dangers of his full glory and announcing as the very core of Yahweh's glory and goodness his incomparable 'love and faithfulness'.[32] These two words occur together again and again in the Old Testament and John here sums them up as 'grace and truth'. John is saying that the glory of God that Moses 'saw' is the very same glory that the disciples witnessed in Jesus, the incarnate Word.

5. God, unseen, but known (1:18)

a. No-one has ever seen God

No-one has ever seen God, but God the One and Only [Son], who is at the Father's side, has made him known (18). Some people love a mystery. They are fascinated by the unknown, particularly if it remains unknown. They love the elusive, the vague, the just out of reach. Now in all the universe there are no greater mysteries than God's infinite and eternal being. But God is not all mystery! Sin has made God the kind of mystery he was never meant to be; unbelief finds a God who stays distant and silent easier to live with than a God who speaks, challenges and comes near. The message of this chapter in John's Gospel is that the mysterious God is also the self-revealing God, and he is the God who has crossed the immeasurable gulf between his being and ours: he is the God who has come to our world in the only way it could survive his coming!

John writes 'No-one has ever seen God' out of a sense of the towering majesty and burning holiness of God. He is not writing as a disappointed investigator of the paranormal or a spectator whose curiosity has not been satisfied. He is writing as someone who knows the danger to sinners of the unmediated presence of God. He is again recalling Moses' request that he might see God, unveiled by darkness or the cloud that filled the tent of meeting. Moses had asked, 'Now show me your glory.'[33] That was love, not curiosity speaking. But even there, God replied to Moses, 'You cannot see my face, for no-one may see me and live.'[34] And Moses was sheltered in a rock on Sinai as God's glory passed by. Beyond this he was allowed to see the departing but not the approaching glory, the back but not the face of God.

---

[31] Gen. 22:2, 12, 16. [32] Exod. 34:6. [33] Exod. 33:18. [34] Exod. 33:20.

b. God the One and Only

The word translated 'One and Only' ('only begotten' in older versions) is the Greek word *monogenēs*, which means literally 'of a single kind.' When Jesus is called the *monogenēs* of God, John means that he is the same *kind* as God. Jesus as *monogenēs* is the one who can say, 'I and the Father are one.'[35] 'Applied to Jesus as the Son of God, it will mean that he is without spiritual siblings and without equals. He is "sole born" and "peerless". No-one else can lay claim to the title Son of God in the sense in which it applies to Christ.'[36]

G. R. Beasley-Murray sees this verse as recapitulating the essence of verse 1 and translates the lines: 'The only Son, by nature God, who is ever close to the Father's heart, has brought knowledge of him.'[37] Scholars are generally agreed that the best manuscripts actually read *monogenēs theos*, 'sole-born *God*', and not *ho monogenēs huios*, 'the sole-born *Son*', and this would form a suitable climax to the prologue. Murray Harris argues in great detail for this and concludes: 'It was not simply the only Son ... who knew and revealed the Father. It was an only Son ... who himself possessed deity ... and therefore both knew the Father and was qualified to make him known.'[38] Only God can reveal God.

Thus we can translate the term *monogonēs* 'God the One and Only', or 'the unique one [himself] God' or 'the only one who is the same as God'. Harris classifies a total of 41 versions and himself translates *monogenēs theos* as 'the only Son who is God'.[39] It is because he and he alone possesses the divine nature that the Son is qualified and able to reveal it. Only God can reveal God. 'Jesus Christ personally disclosed in item his own intimate, eternal knowledge of the Father.'[40]

c. ... who is at the Father's side, has made him known

'At the Father's side' is literally 'in the bosom of the Father', carrying ideas of depth and intimacy. His is no second-hand or partial knowledge of the Father. God has no secrets from him. He knows even as he is known. When he speaks of God he speaks out of the reality of an eternal communion. Even from within the constraints of a human mind and the limitations of a human experience, he reveals of God more than he knows at a human level and with an authority that comes from the mystery of his ultimate being. There is a profound compatibility between the speaker and that of which he speaks; his revelation of the Father is no intermittent thing nor is it confined to his words alone. It is in the entirety of his being, his divine–human being, that he reveals the life and character of God. In

[35] John 10:30.　[36] Harris (1992), p. 87.　[37] Beasley-Murray, p. 2.
[38] Harris (1992), p. 82.　[39] Harris (1992), p. 93.　[40] Ibid., p. 102.

the authenticity of his sinless humanity and in the fullness of his eternal and unchanging deity he is the consistent exegesis of God.

The word John uses for 'has made him known' (Gk. *exēgēsato*) is the word from which we get our word 'exegesis' – the critical explanation of a text. As a good exegesis unfolds the content and meaning of the text of Scripture, so the Word made flesh, the only, eternal and beloved Son of the Father, himself, in his own person, words and work, unfolds the character, will and purposes of God.

As the creating Word, the Son has revealed much of God's eternal power and deity in creation; as the inspiring and prophetic Word,[41] he has revealed more of God's love and saving purposes in the Old Testament revelation; but as Jesus, the incarnate Word, God with us, he has revealed the most of God in his saving work. He who has seen Jesus Christ and him crucified has seen the Father in the glory of his love and grace.[42]

After the prologue, the title 'Logos' is not used again in John's Gospel. There is a very good reason for this. He is to be known as Jesus of Nazareth now. The enfleshed Word becomes, in the words of C. F. D. Moule, 'the brilliant focal point' of God's activity,[43] and the eternal Logos is for ever identified with Jesus Christ the Lord. From now on the Word can never be understood and must never be described in abstraction from his identity as Jesus, the Son of God. Indeed, it is from the enfleshed Word that we know of the personal existence of the eternal Word.

6. One person, two natures

a. Fully God

When we read that the Word became flesh we are not to imagine that the Word ceased to be the Word, nor are we to think of the Son as leaving a sort of 'gap' in the Godhead, a vacancy in the Trinity, by coming into our world as a man. In his divine nature, as distinct from his human nature, the Word continued to uphold all things, filling the universe with his infinite and omnipotent presence as God. This did not change at the incarnation. What was new was that this same divine being became personally united with a complete human nature at its earliest stage. He took it as his own. In the language of classical theology, he 'assumed' (took to himself) a human nature; the second person of the Holy Trinity 'became' an embryo in the body of a young Hebrew woman. But though he became what he was not, he did not cease to be what he was and had been from all eternity. In the language of classical theology, he became one person with two natures, divine and human. Each of those natures retained

---

[41] 1 Pet. 1:11.   [42] John 14:9–11.   [43] Quoted in Lewis, p. 112.

its essential integrity; what was divine did not become less than divine and what was human was not less than fully human.

He who continued to fill all things and to sustain all things, also became contained in a virgin's womb, and was sustained by a human mother, living *simultaneously* the massive life of Godhead and the creaturely life of humanity. In the words of the great fourth-century theologian, Athanasius,

> The Word was not hedged in by His body, nor did His presence in the body prevent His being present elsewhere as well . . . at one and the same time – this is the wonder – as Man he was living a human life, and as Word he was sustaining the life of the Universe, and as Son He was in constant union with the Father.[44]

This early concern of the church not to misunderstand John when he says 'the Word became flesh', as if he had meant that the Word ceased to be the Word and became something else, is found in Calvin also, who writes:

> Even if the Word in his immeasurable essence united with the nature of man into one person, we do not imagine that he was confined therein. Here is something marvellous: the Son of God descended from heaven in such a way that, without leaving heaven, he willed to be borne in a virgin's womb, to go about the earth, and to hang upon the cross; yet he continuously filled the world even as he had done from the beginning![45]

This assertion of the Reformer has been called the *extra Calvinisticum*, the *extra* being that infinite 'more' which remained even when the Word became flesh. A twentieth-century theologian, Helmut Thielicke, comments that

> The point of the Calvinistic *extra* was that Calvin did not want to see the second person of the Trinity 'exhausted' in the historical man Jesus. The Logos is not completely absorbed by the flesh which he assumes. For he is the subject of this assuming. He thus transcends it. Consequently he is out of the flesh (*eksarkos*) as well as in it (*ensarkos*).[46]

It is all too common to hear explanations of the incarnation which say that God the Son set aside his incommunicable attributes such as

[44] St Athanasius, *The Incarnation of the Word of God* (Geoffrey Bles/The Century Press, 1944), 3.17.
[45] Calvin (*Institutes*), II.xiii.4.
[46] Helmut Thielicke, *The Evangelical Faith* (Eerdmans, 1974), vol. 1, pp. 292–293.

omnipotence, omnipresence and omniscience in order to become human. That is not true. If it were he would no longer be God, for the attributes of God are not optional extras which God can take up and put down and still be God. They are the very God-ness of God! When the historic creeds emphasize therefore that the Son was and remained God at and after his incarnation, they mean that he remained all that God was and is, in heaven and earth, in the depth and fullness of his divine being. There is no such thing as God minus some of his attributes. That is why Augustine, commenting on the phrase 'emptied himself' in Philippians 2:7 explained: 'He emptied Himself not by losing what he was but by taking to Him what he was not.'[47] 'Thus he emptied Himself, taking the form of a servant, not losing the form of God. The form of a servant was added; the form of God did not pass away.'[48]

b. Fully man

None of this means that the force of John's words are lessened when he writes 'The Word became flesh', for the incarnation involved a true entry into humanity and a real experience of creatureliness. Then the eternal and infinite Logos began to live in a new way and at a new level, possessing and experiencing a fully human life and consciousness; one divine person in two natures, a full and complete human nature and an undiminished divine nature. His humanity was not only an adding, an extension, a new horizon. It was also a boundary, an entrance into an authentic human experience of finitude. Therefore, although we must not think literally of 'our God contracted to a span', as Charles Wesley put it, we are nonetheless faced with a descent into creatureliness and into full humanity: 'For you know the grace of our Lord Jesus Christ, that though he was rich, yet for your sakes he became poor, so that you through his poverty might become rich'.[49] (2 Cor. 8:9). The Lord of glory became 'the Son in weakness'.

The eternal Logos assumed a full human psychology no less than a human physiology. He was – and is – not merely God in the form of man, but God in the nature of man; not God in disguise but God in the flesh. He did not only come among us; he became one of us, possessing as his very own, a true and full human nature from its conception. In that nature he, as the second person of the Trinity resided, and to him that nature properly belonged, so that God the Son consciously and experimentally lived his life through that humanity. In that humanity he felt pleasure and pain *as we* feel

---

[47] Augustine, quoted in Morris (1971), p. 114.
[48] Augustine, quoted in F. W. Beare, *The Epistle to the Philippians* (A. & C. Black, 1959), p. 164.
[49] 2 Cor. 8:9.

pleasure and pain. In that human nature he laughed and cried, hoped and feared, knew delight and disappointment. In that human nature he received and gave, blessed and suffered, was tempted as man and perfected as Mediator. The mystery and message of the incarnation is that, in Jesus, God acquired human nature, and deity became a member of the human race.

The real and true humanity of our Lord receives dramatic testimony from the Gospels' frequent references to his emotions. Repeatedly, for instance, we read of Jesus' *compassion*.[50] Surprisingly often we read of his *anger*.[51] We see him enjoying the *feasting and merriment* of life – so much so that his enemies slandered him as a drunkard and a glutton.[52] We also find him filled with *spiritual joy*[53] and we encounter him overwhelmed with *fearful sorrow*.[54]

The writer to the Hebrews is uncompromising in his statements relating to our Lord's deity[55] but is equally clear about his true and vulnerable humanity: 'Both the one who makes men holy and those who are made holy are of the same family ... Since the children have flesh and blood, he too shared in their humanity ... For we do not have a high priest who is unable to sympathise with our weaknesses, but we have one who has been tempted in every way, just as we are – yet was without sin.'[56] All that characterizes our humanity became his own – sin only excepted.

Of course the Gospels themselves do not give us an abstract account of the 'one person in two natures' mystery. They are concerned to show it in action. They show Jesus as being fully aware of himself in both respects. Hence, though he has only one area of self-consciousness, because he is but one person, yet he indicates two areas of consciousness. He both claims a knowledge of God that can only be divine,[57] and admits to an ignorance which is characteristic of human limitedness.[58] He can relate to God as an eternal equal[59] and also as a creature should relate to his Creator.[60] God is thus both his Father and his God.[61]

How all this could be the case without a division in the person must be for ever beyond us to understand or explain, but we should remember that it is a *divine* person of whom we speak. We cannot say that what would be impossible for us would be impossible for him. There is, of course, no adequate human analogy to this, or explanation of it, for in all the created world there is no greater

[50] Matt. 9:36; 14:14; Mark 1:41; Luke 7:13.
[51] Matt. 8:26; 17:18, cf. Matt. 23; Mark 1:43; 3:5; 11:15–17; Luke 4:39; John 2:13–17; 11:33, 38.
[52] Matt. 11:19.   [53] Luke 10:21.   [54] Matt. 26:37; Mark 14:33; Luke 22:44.
[55] Heb. 1:1–3.   [56] Heb. 2:11, 14, 17; 4:15; 5:7–8.   [57] Matt. 11:27.
[58] Mark 13:32.   [59] John 17:4–5.   [60] John 14:28.   [61] John 20:17.

mystery. Ranked only with the mystery of the Trinity, the Three in One, is the mystery of the incarnation – one person in two natures. Only the infinite intelligence of God can fully grasp it, as only the supreme wisdom of God could devise it and only the omnipotence of God could achieve it. Of it the apostle Paul speaks when he writes 'Great indeed, we confess, is the mystery of our religion: [God] was manifested in the flesh . . .'[62]

It has been said that 'a saviour not quite God is a bridge broken at the farther end'[63] and 'a saviour not quite man is a bridge broken at the near end'.[64] John takes us, as it were, from one end to the other and shows us the Son's uttermost deity and entire humanity. He has crossed the infinite gulf. The infinite and omnipotent God has built a bridge into finitude and creatureliness; indeed, God the eternal Word has become the bridge uniting heaven and earth, God and Man, the Saviour and the sinners who had forfeited heaven and lost their way home. And that bridge has borne the traffic of centuries and the weight of millions.

7. Jesus the only way

Christians are sometimes perplexed when they are told that the Christian doctrine of the incarnation of God is not unique and that Hinduism knows of many incarnations, emanations of the god Vishnu and others in the form of 'avatars', gurus and holy men through the ages. David Burnett, in his book *The Spirit of Hinduism*, shows in some detail the differences between the Hindu concepts and Christianity in this respect, and, after speaking of the uniqueness, death and resurrection of Christ, their different ways of salvation and concept of life after death, he concludes:

> The Hindu belief in the intervention of deity through avatars is inherently different from the Logos concept. Avatars entered the world to destroy evil, and this required repeated avatars. The mission of Jesus Christ was to deal with the problem of human sin . . . The Logos metaphor illustrates how the indescribable Creator, the ultimate meaning and logic, was manifest in human form. He may therefore be comprehended, appreciated, and adored. Devotion is given to him because he first loved us. This love was shown through his sacrificial death upon a cross . . . Christianity presents a picture of a God who takes the initiative in seeking those who have not yet turned to him. The divine Shepherd goes into the wilderness to seek the lost sheep. This contrasts with the Hindu image of a flock of sheep seeking guidance from the shepherd. As

[62] 1 Tim. 3:16, RSV.   [63] C. F. D. Moule.   [64] F. F. Bruce.

Daniel Bassuk concludes: 'Abba, the Christian God, loves to save; Baba, the Hindu Avatar, saves who love.'[65]

Islam affirms Jesus as a prophet but denies he is God incarnate; it agrees that he lived but it denies that he died, an atonement for sin. It does not have a doctrine of the universal fall of humanity or the spiritual bondage of the will; our weakness stems from our ignorance which must be corrected by understanding and submission to Allah and a *sunna* lifestyle. Islam does not normally use the word 'salvation' and the result of judgment to come is uncertain, but, after a life of submission to God guided by the Qur'an and the *hadith*, the Muslim hopes for a life of bliss in the world to come in the mercy of God.

Gautama Buddha himself made no claim to divinity and was considered to be divine only in a later form of Buddhism. He founded a moral philosophy rather than a religion and as he was dying told his disciples that what mattered was his teaching, not his person. Christianity, however, is the only religion in the world which rests on the person of its founder. Moreover the central message of the vicarious sufferings of Jesus in his sin-bearing death and personal resurrection are in utter contrast with the *arahant*, the Buddha saint who has reached fulfilment and who no longer feels suffering or joy and who has no desire, only a calm contentment as he waits for the entrance into *nirvana* at death and the extinction of personal, individual consciousness.

The religion of the Sikh includes belief that there is one God, the all-pervading creator and enlightener, who is the God of Hindu, Sikh, Muslim, Jew and Christian. The way of salvation is through meditation on God, truthful living and service to mankind, the study of the scriptures and reincarnation leading to the reabsorption of the individual soul into the eternal soul. However, the message of Jesus is that salvation lies beyond the Sikh's life of good works, patience, hospitality and care for others. Splendid as these are, they do not deal finally with our human sin and guilt before a holy God. The joyful news of Christianity is that God has not only sent prophets and teachers but has come in person to this planet and this race as one of us, the Word made flesh, Jesus Christ, the Saviour of the world, and has opened up a way of reconciliation to himself for each of us by the death and resurrection of the Lord Jesus.

Years ago, a Chinese Christian leader, C. K. Lee, spoke to an American audience and afterwards people were invited to ask questions. He gave this answer to a student who asked, 'Why should we

[65] David Burnett, *The Spirit of Hinduism: A Christian perspective on Hindu thought* (Monarch, 1992), pp. 254–256; cf. pp. 129–132, 138–141, 248–255.

send Christianity to China when it has Confucianism?' Mr Lee said: 'There are three reasons. First of all, Confucius was a teacher and Christ is a Saviour. China needs a Saviour more than she needs a teacher. In the second place, Confucius is dead and Christ is alive. China needs a living Saviour. In the third place, Confucius is one day going to stand before Christ and be judged by him. China needs to know Christ as Saviour before she meets him as Judge.'[66]

Against such backgrounds we can see the uniqueness of the New Testament faith and message. It is a uniqueness which needs to be made known today. John's Gospel, like those of Matthew, Mark and Luke, takes the reader on from the incarnation and teaching of Jesus to the essential work of his sin-bearing, sacrificial death and personal resurrection. As in all the gospels, so we learn from the New Testament teaching as a whole, Jesus of Nazareth was and is the one and only Son of God who came not only to enlighten but to save, who saves by his reconciling death, and who calls the world, not to his teaching, but to himself.

John's opening words speak to all faiths and philosophies and go beyond them all with their astounding message that God has come to do what we could never do: he has come to seek and to save the lost, to offer a righteousness infinitely beyond our own, and an eternity infinitely above our highest thoughts.

8. Jewish and Gentile backgrounds

John wrote his Gospel in Greek and in that language the word for 'word' is *logos*. However, the term was also used in a special way and loaded with special meaning throughout the ancient world. It had divine and philosophical connotations in both Jewish and Gentile philosophy quite apart from the Old Testament revelation. John would have been fully aware that his word *logos* was a term very widely used in Greek thinking and philosophy, and had been for centuries. Perhaps he has it in mind to attract the attention of enquiring Gentiles as well as fellow Jews in his opening sentences.

The Logos of God in the context of Greek philosophy could mean many things, but the most popular was the Stoic use of the term to describe the force that permeated the universe with order and growth and bestowed upon humankind the power of knowledge and moral behaviour. In this thinking the Logos was regarded as 'the rational principle of the universe'. Some Jewish philosophers, most famously Philo (c. 20 BC – c. AD 50), sought to bridge Jewish and Gentile philosophies with this term. Philo identifies 'wisdom' in Proverbs 8 with the Logos of Gentile philosophy and understands

---

[66] Norm Lewis, *Priority One* (William Carey Library, 1988), pp. 41–42.

the Logos as a divine mediating power between God and creation. He also 'combines OT statements of creation by the word, Stoic statements of the Logos as the world-soul and Platonic elements (the Logos as the archetype of the created world) with one another'.[67] The use of the wisdom concept abounds in Jewish intertestamental literature, but, like Wisdom in Proverbs 8, though often personified, it is not truly a person, and falls far short of John's Logos here.

John's use of the term 'the Word' is profoundly different from the Greek philosophers' or even the Jewish Philo's use of it. Philo's Logos is not really a person, but a force, a power, whereas John's Logos is clearly personal. It is true that Philo personifies his Logos and even poetically describes it as 'the captain and pilot of the universe', 'the Father's elder son' and the like.[68] But these are not meant to be taken as metaphysical statements. Philo's Logos, like the Greek philosophers' Logos, is a power that embraces the world: John's Logos is a divine person who became a baby in a manger, a boy in a carpenter's shop, a man among men, and the one who bears the sins of the world. It is the incarnation of the Logos of God which is the unique use of the term; there is nothing like it in Greek philosophy.

Many Jews and even Gentiles could have said, 'In the beginning was the Word', and would have affirmed that the Logos was 'with God' and was 'the true light', and perhaps John intended to capture their interest with his opening words. What would have startled them and taken them far beyond anything they had previously imagined or reasoned would have been his statement, *The Word became flesh and made his dwelling among us. We have seen his glory, the glory of the One and Only [Son], who came from the Father, full of grace and truth* (1:14). That is the great good news that John wants to bring to the Gentile and Jewish world.

---

[67] B. Klappert, 'Word', *NIDNTT*, vol. 3, pp. 1116–1117.
[68] Quoted in Milne (1993), p. 32.

Romans 3:21–26
17. God the redeemer

1. God the redeemer

But now a righteousness from God, apart from law, has been made known, to which the Law and the Prophets testify. [22]*This righteousness from God comes through faith in Jesus Christ to all who believe. There is no difference,* [23]*for all have sinned and fall short of the glory of God,* [24]*and are justified freely by his grace through the redemption that came by Christ Jesus.* [25]*God presented him as a sacrifice of atonement, through faith in his blood. He did this to demonstrate his justice, because in his forbearance he had left the sins committed beforehand unpunished* [26]*– he did it to demonstrate his justice at the present time, so as to be just and the one who justifies those who have faith in Jesus.*

Martin Luther used to distinguish between what he called, ironically, the *'theologia gloriae'* (theology of glory) of the philosophers and the *'theologia crucis'* (theology of the cross) of the New Testament. His point was that it is not in the lofty speculations and theories of the one but in the earthly suffering of the other that we see most clearly God's revelation of himself to the world. No philosophy that bypasses the cross will ever discover the wisdom of God or reach the true knowledge of him as God and Saviour.[1] A modern writer, David Wells, expresses it with similar insight and passion:

> Those who understand the Cross aright, grasp the meaning of Christ aright and can then see the entire purpose of revelation clearly. For Christ and his Cross stand at the centre of God's disclosure of his moral will and saving ways in Scripture. Indeed, without the Cross we are without the magnifying glass through which his love and holiness are most keenly seen. To stand beneath the Cross is to stand at the one place where the character

[1] 1 Cor. 1:18 – 2:5.

of God burns brightest and where his resolution of the problem of sin is sounded for all time.

It is hard to stand here, though. The cost of admission to this place is the humbling of our pride – intellectual, moral and religious. For to stand here is to repent of our proclivity to elevate our own standards of what is right and wrong to universal norms and to accept the judgement of God in their place. It is to repent of our trust in the innocence of self, which is the fount of our self-righteousness, and to acknowledge instead the corruption of the self. It is to displace ourselves from the centre of the universe we inhabit and to elevate Christ to that place of honour.[2]

This paragraph in Romans brings us to the very heart of the Christian message and Paul's letter. Martin Luther said it was 'the very central place ... of the whole Bible'.[3] If, as John Stott says, Romans is 'the fullest, plainest, and grandest statement of the gospel in the New Testament',[4] there is good reason for Dr Leon Morris's words that these verses constitute 'possibly the most important single paragraph ever written'.[5]

The paragraph opens with the dramatic 'But now' of verse 21. Paul has engaged in a sustained argument calculated to show the seriousness and the universality of sin. We cannot understand the gospel without that and we cannot understand that unless we have understood the holiness of God which shows sin to be what it is. Christianity, and the religion of the Bible as a whole, is distinguished by its understanding of the enormous seriousness of sin. One scholar writes, 'Nowhere do we see more clearly the difference between paganism and Christianity than in the conception of sin.'[6] In the ancient world generally, sin was not thought of as a serious matter. It is much the same with today's world, and it is always due to ignorance of the true God, who is above all else holy and whom we must one day face in judgment. J. I. Packer has remarked:

If you have not learned about sin, you cannot understand yourself or your fellow-men, or the world you live in or the Christian faith. And you will not be able to make head or tail of the Bible. For the Bible is an exposition of God's answer to the problem of human sin and unless you have that problem clearly before you, you will keep missing the point of what it says.[7]

---

[2] David Wells, *Losing our Virtue: Why the church must recover its moral vision* (IVP, 1998), p. 205.
[3] Quoted in Moo, p. 218.   [4] Stott (1994), p. 19.   [5] Morris (1988), p. 173.
[6] F. X. Steinleitner, *TDNT*, vol. 1, p. 295, n. 86, quoted in Morris (1988), p. 190.
[7] J. I. Packer, *God's Words* (IVP, 1981), p. 71.

Paul has argued that we all stand condemned before God on account of our sins, Jew and Gentile, the religious and the irreligious, the apparently moral and the openly immoral. In a devastating analysis of human sin he has concluded that in our own righteousness we can never hope to survive the judgment of God.

'But now', he says, with the coming of the Son of God and by his achievement at the cross, 'a righteousness from God', apart from our own failed morality, 'apart from law', has been made known to the world and is on offer to men and women everywhere. There has been a great turning point in human history and even in human destiny. God has come to save his people from their sins and to reconcile them to himself just as he promised in Old Testament times. He has found a way, not to crush us with his righteousness but to save us precisely by means of that righteousness; he has done something so momentous and decisive that his righteousness can justify us instead of condemning us. He has found a way of putting away our sins and of making his righteousness our righteousness for ever.[8] In this way the righteousness of God can be our confidence not our terror, our salvation not our damnation.

We all need this righteousness, concludes Paul, summing up his indictment carefully argued over the previous three chapters, 'for all have sinned and fall short of the glory of God' (v. 23). We were made to bear the image and glory of our Maker as unique beings, but we fell far and foully and that image was defaced, the glory sullied and dimmed. We have, as a race, lost the glory we had and forfeited the glory we could have had. Even the believer falls short of the glory which is yet to be given us in full. 'Attempts to soften this', says Charles Cranfield, 'or to explain it away have the disastrous effect of obscuring the transcendent majesty of the glory which is yet to be ours.'[9] By nature, and as a race, we stand under a great condemnation, our falling short is the sign, not of our incomplete evolution but of our initial and deep-seated rebellion. How far short we are from the standards of God! Bishop Handley Moule once put it this way: 'The harlot, the liar, the murderer are short of it but so are you. Perhaps they stand at the bottom of a mine, and you on the crest of an Alp; but you are as little able to touch the stars as they.'[10]

2. Justified in the law-court of God

What, then, has God done to make the gospel 'the power of God for the salvation of everyone who believes'?[11] In Romans 3:21–26 Paul

---

[8] Cf. Rom. 1:17.

[9] Charles Cranfield, *A Critical and Exegetical Commentary on the Epistle to the Romans* (T. & T. Clark, 1977), vol. 1, pp. 204–205.

[10] Quoted in Morris (1988), p. 177.   [11] Rom. 1:16.

introduces us to three pictures. The first is that of a law-court and it appears in the term 'justified' in verse 24 where believers are said to be 'justified by his grace'. The word 'justify' in the world of the New Testament was a legal word, a forensic term which literally meant 'to declare [someone to be] righteous'. It did not mean 'to make righteous' or even 'to treat as righteous' but to declare [someone to be] righteous. It was a judgment at law, a verdict, a pronouncement.[12] 'Justification' is not an ethical term but a legal one; it speaks not of a person's character, but of their status before the law, their legal standing. Among the Hebrews, as well as the Greeks, says Leon Morris, 'Righteousness was first and foremost a legal standing. The righteous were those who secured the verdict when they stood before God.'[13]

Of course, it was assumed that those who were pronounced righteous before the law were in fact personally righteous as well. It is here that Paul would have astonished both Jew and Greek, for his message is that God has found a way to justify, not the innocent but the guilty, not the righteous but the wicked,[14] not unfallen saints but helpless sinners. He has found a way of dealing with their sin, removing their guilt and investing them with his own righteousness. In John Stott's words, 'The "righteousness of God", then, might be defined as "God's righteous way of righteoussing the unrighteous". '[15]

That way is the way of the cross, the way of penal substitution, where 'the Judge was judged in our place'.[16] Behind the visible sufferings of Christ at the hands of cruel men, the apostolic teaching points us to his inner sufferings and a greater drama still, where 'God was reconciling the world to himself in Christ'[17] by meeting on our behalf his law's full claims.

From the start of his earthly life he had put himself under the obligations of the law of God on our behalf, acting as our representative: 'born of a woman, born under law, to redeem those under law'.[18] In his life he remained perfectly obedient, the sinless Son of God in our nature, achieving in our humanity the righteousness God required. On the cross the work was brought to a triumphant conclusion, but at unimaginable cost, when he stood in our place under the just judgments of God. There, 'Christ redeemed us from the curse of the law by becoming a curse for us',[19] standing

[12] See Morris (1965), pp. 224–274, for a more detailed treatment. See also Lewis, pp. 303–317.

[13] Morris (1988), p. 101. An important critique of some recent challenges to the traditional understanding of justification and, in particular, the views of N. T. Wright, James Dunn and Alister McGrath on the subject, can be found in Philip Eveson, *The Great Exchange* (Day One Publications, 1996), chs. 8 – 10.

[14] Cf. Rom. 4:5.   [15] Stott (1986), p. 210.

[16] Melito of Sardis, quoted in Lewis, p. 289.   [17] 2 Cor. 5:19.   [18] Gal. 4:4–5.
[19] Gal. 3:13.

in that relationship to the law which we should have occupied and bearing in our place its penalty for sin. So he becomes a sin-offering and more, for us,[20] bearing the curse of the law of God against sin and corruption in his world.[21] This is the basis of our justification before God and the basis of all our peace. Because of this we can be pardoned, and more: we can now have a righteous standing before God by faith in this Jesus, the righteousness that comes through faith in Jesus Christ to all who believe. In a word, we can be justified, not as a legal fiction but as an eternal reality by union with Christ the Righteous One, who has represented us in his sinless life and atoning death. This becomes effective in each believer's life when Christ is personally trusted as Saviour and Lord. Then the believer is 'justified by his blood' and being 'justified by faith' has 'peace with God' which is the fruit of justification.

Paul constantly makes it clear that God is in no way reluctant with regard to all this. We have been 'justified freely by his grace'. We have been justified by God as well as before God. It has been his plan, his initiative from the start (v. 25). It was not a unilateral action of Christ or a fearful attempt to wrest salvation from an unwilling God. This is as much the work of the Father as the Son; as Paul's repeated emphasis makes clear: this righteousness is 'from God'; 'God presented him as a sacrifice of atonement'; 'He did it.' It is all of God and all of grace; not only that God's justice might be satisfied but also that God's love might find a way of reconciliation, a restoration to fullest favour and final glory of the race that fell.

Justification itself is more than forgiveness and it goes beyond pardon. As Marcus Loane puts it: 'The voice that spells forgiveness will say: "You may go; you have been let off the penalty which your sin deserves." But the verdict which means acceptance [justification] will say: "You may come; you are welcome to all my love and my presence." '[22] Pardon says, 'You may go'; justification says, 'You may come.' This is the ground of the believer's assurance, this is the basis of all our peace.[23] John Calvin writes movingly: 'This is our acquittal: the guilt that held us liable for punishment has been transferred to the head of the Son of God (Is. 53:12). We must, above all, remember this substitution, lest we tremble and remain anxious throughout life.'[24]

Martin Luther used to tell of a dream he once had in which Satan, the Accuser, presented Luther with a long scroll on which his sins were written. There they were accurately and undeniably recorded: thoughts, words, deeds – of omission and commission – with dates, times and circumstances. Nothing was left out and they almost

[20] 2 Cor. 5:21.   [21] For more on both these verses see Lewis, pp. 283–289.
[22] Quoted in Stott (1994), p. 110.   [23] Rom. 5:1.
[24] Calvin (*Institutes*), II.xvi.5.

completely filled up the scroll from top to bottom. But at the bottom a space remained. And Luther, after Satan had recited them all, calmly and solemnly replied: 'Now write in the space at the bottom: "The blood of Jesus Christ, God's Son, cleanses us from all sin."' And the Accuser fled.

It is in knowing our free justification in Christ Jesus that we have peace with God,[25] a confidence without arrogance or anxiety as we face the judgment day of God. For us *the verdict has gone out already:* 'Not guilty!' because of Jesus.

> Bold shall I stand in Thy great day,
> For who ought to my charge shall lay?
> Fully absolved through these I am,
> From sin and fear, from guilt and shame.[26]

3. Redeemed from the law of sin and death

Paul then goes on to show further the basis of our justification by God; the ground on which God freely justifies guilty sinners. First of all, it is made possible 'through the redemption that came by Christ Jesus'. The word 'redemption' contains a new picture which Paul's Gentile readers in Rome would have recognized immediately. Justification was a legal term; redemption was a commercial term and one used in a familiar context. The Roman economy was a slave-based economy. It has been computed that in the Roman empire there were ten to twelve million slaves out of a total population of 50–60 million.[27] At the end of the first century BC there were some two million slaves in Italy. At its peak ancient Rome absorbed some half a million slaves in a year.[28] The sight of slaves being sold in the market-place was common enough. Furthermore, slaves were a valuable commercial property and a good slave did not come cheap.

A slave in such a context could be released only by the payment of a 'ransom', a sum of money large enough to cover the loss of years of work. That process was known as 'redemption'. In an earlier period the term 'redemption' was used for the release of prisoners of war on the payment of a price. 'To redeem' (Gk. *lytroō*) was a process of deliverance by payment, and the price paid was called a 'ransom' (Gk. *lytron*).

For Paul, and for Jews in Rome and elsewhere, however, there were also Old Testament associations with this idea. In Exodus 21:30, a man who had forfeited his life under the law by committing

---

[25] Rom. 5:1.

[26] Hymn, 'Jesu, Thy blood and righteousness', by Nicolaus Ludwig von Zinzendorf (1700–60), tr. by John Wesley (1703–91).

[27] Harris (1999), p. 34.   [28] Hugh Thomas, *The Slave Trade* (Picador, 1997).

an accidental homicide was allowed to 'redeem' it by the payment of a 'ransom' (Heb. *kōp̄er*). In Exodus 30:11–16, the population as a whole is ritually redeemed in the census, 'each one must pay the LORD a ransom for his life . . . making atonement for your lives'. In Numbers 18:15–17, every first-born Israelite male was to be redeemed by the payment of a 'redemption price' (Heb. *pāḏâ*) so that his life might be spared. For before the holy judgments of Yahweh the first-born of the Israelites were no more safe than the first-born of the Egyptians.[29] The idea of a ransom is also associated at a more intimate level with the 'kinsman-redeemer' (Heb. *gō'ēl*) whose duty it was to buy back land alienated from the family or a relation sold into slavery.[30] Again, in such cases it was necessary to pay a ransom price (*gā'al*).

Notice that in all these situations a price is paid for freedom. Leon Morris concludes from his own examination of these and corresponding terms in the Greek version of the Old Testament that 'the basic price-paying conception' remains 'as a stubborn substratum in every case'. He concludes his detailed survey: 'We see, then, that in Greek writings generally, in the Old Testament, and in Rabbinical writers, the basic idea in redemption is the paying of a ransom price to secure a liberation.'[31]

That is the difference between redeeming and merely releasing. Paul makes significant use of this term 'redemption' to help us understand what Christ has done as our Redeemer.[32] We too were prisoners. In our case the captivity was to 'the law of sin and death',[33] under which we were the helpless slaves of our own rebellious passions and the objects of divine retribution.[34] Moreover we were slaves to sin itself; its drives and its addictions, its mastery and its weakening power.[35] Christ's act of redemption at Calvary freed us from sin's guilt and grip, its condemnation and its power to keep us from God and godliness.

But this freedom, and the right to live as people free from the powers of 'the present evil age',[36] was dearly bought. It was not a work of power only but of purchase also. He did not simply release us, he *redeemed* us. Jesus used this imagery when he said, 'For even the Son of Man did not come to be served, but to serve, and to give his life as a ransom for many.'[37] Paul made the cruciality of the cross clear in this process when he wrote to the Galatians: 'Christ redeemed us from the curse of the law by becoming a curse for us, for it is written: "Cursed is everyone who is hung on a tree." '[38] He

[29] Cf. Exod. 12:13; 13:13–16.   [30] Lev. 25:25–28, 48; cf. Is. 49:7; 54:5–8.
[31] Morris (1965), pp. 26, 29.
[32] E.g. Rom. 3:24; 1 Cor. 1:30; Gal. 3:13; Eph. 1:7; Col. 1:14; Titus 2:14.
[33] Rom. 8:2.   [34] Rom. 6:17, 23.   [35] Gal. 1:4; Titus 2:14.   [36] Gal. 1:4.
[37] Mark 10:45.   [38] Gal. 3:13.

also made it clear to the Ephesians: 'In him we have redemption through his blood',[39] and to Titus, to whom he wrote of 'our great God and Saviour, Jesus Christ, who gave himself for us to redeem us from all wickedness'.[40]

Each of us needed that redemption and for each of us the price was high. How high, Paul makes clear in his third picture, that of a 'sacrifice of atonement'.

4. Saved from the wrath of God

God presented him, says the apostle in verse 25, *as a sacrifice of atonement, through faith in his blood.* Literally, Paul writes that God presented him as a 'propitiation' (Gk. *hilastērion*). Propitiation means the removal of wrath. Probably we should think of 'propitiatory sacrifice' here, as the book of Hebrews does when it looks back at the long line of Old Testament sacrifices and sees Jesus Christ, in his death for us, as the 'once for all' sacrifice for sin which 'makes perfect for ever' the people of God.[41]

The essential thing about the sacrifices for sin in the Old Testament is that in all of them the sacrificial animal was a substitute for the worshippers and died in their place. All of them 'atoned' for sin and cleansed the worshipper. Indeed, 'without the shedding of blood there is no forgiveness'.[42] Leon Morris approvingly quotes Sanday and Headlam's comment on this verse, 'It is impossible to get rid from this passage of the double idea (1) of a sacrifice (2) of a sacrifice which is propitiatory.'[43]

Paul often speaks of the death of Christ as the only atonement for sin, of faith in his blood (3:25), of being justified by his blood, of redemption through his blood and of peace with God by the blood of the cross.[44] Therefore there is abundant support for Marcus Barth's statement that the New Testament in general, and Paul's thought in particular, is 'saturated with the concept of sacrifice'.[45] Allied to the concept of sacrifice and integral to it was the concept of propitiation.

'Propitiation is one of the three main categories used in the New Testament to interpret the death of Christ.'[46] In the ancient world, 'to propitiate' meant to placate, to appease and thus to turn away wrath by persuading the gods to be merciful. It had all sorts of connotations, most of them utterly unworthy of Israel's God. Yet the term had a long history of biblical usage too.

Many people do not want to think of God as capable of wrath,

[39] Eph. 1:7.   [40] Titus 2:13–14.   [41] Heb. 10:8–14.   [42] Heb. 9:22.
[43] Quoted in Morris (1965), p. 120.   [44] Rom. 5:9; Eph. 1:7; Col. 1:20.
[45] Quoted in Lewis, p. 274; cf. 1 Cor. 5:7–8; 11:25; Heb. 9:18–20.
[46] S. R. Driver, quoted in Morris (1965), p. 182.

but Paul has built his argument and his presentation of the gospel on the fact of the divine wrath for sin and the liability of the entire human race to that holy wrath.[47] The wrath of God is not wild or immoral or capricious; it is precisely the wrath of *God* and so is holy as he is holy. It is, says Martyn Lloyd-Jones, 'his settled opposition to all that is evil arising from his nature as holy'.[48] That wrath might justly have gone out against our entire world, including you and me. But in his marvellous and costly love, God, in the words of Charles Cranfield, 'purposed to direct against his own very Self in the Person of his Son, the full weight of that righteous wrath which [we] deserved'.[49] In Christ, says John Stott, 'He bore the judgment we deserve in order to bring us the forgiveness we do not deserve.'[50] J. I. Packer gives us a comprehensive statement of this:

> The basic description of the saving death of Christ in the Bible is as a propitiation, that is as that which quenched God's wrath against us by obliterating our sins from his sight. God's wrath is his righteousness reacting against unrighteousness; it shows itself in retributive justice. But Jesus Christ has shielded us from the nightmare prospect of retributive justice by becoming our representative substitute in obedience to his Father's will and receiving the wages of sin in our place. By this means justice has been done, for the sins of all that will ever be pardoned were judged and punished in the person of God the Son, and it is on this basis that pardon is now offered to the offenders. Redeeming love and retributive justice joined hands, so to speak, at Calvary, for there God showed himself to be 'just and the one who justifies those who have faith in Jesus'.[51]

The story is told of a wagon train of early settlers who were faced by a distant but fast-approaching prairie fire. The leaders of the train immediately made a new fire downwind and as soon as the ground was cool enough, drove all the wagons, with their people, on to the charred ground. As the original wall of fire approached, hungrily eating up the vegetation and moving forward, one child looked up to its father and said, 'Father, are you sure we won't be burned up?' 'My child,' replied the father, 'the flames can never reach us here; we are standing where the fire has already been.' That is the safety of the children of God who stand on the finished work of Christ. We are standing where the fire has been. There is nothing to fear now.

This, as Paul adds in verse 26, was God's way of justifying his earlier dealings with his people and his forbearance of the nations.

[47] Rom. 1:18f.; 2:5f.; 3:5f.   [48] D. Martyn Lloyd-Jones, *Romans*, vol. 3, p. 75.
[49] Cranfield, op. cit., vol. 1, p. 217; cf. vol. 2, p. 828.   [50] Stott (1986), p. 89.
[51] J. I. Packer, *Knowing God* (Hodder & Stoughton, 1975), p. 211.

'Up to that time sins were neither punished as they deserve nor atoned for as they were going to be.'[52] In this way, too, God demonstrates his justice 'at the present time', in order, as Cranfield puts it 'that he might be righteous even in his very action of justifying'.[53]

5. The cross and the lifting of burdens

In a day when relativism rules, when tolerance is all and 'sin' is an obsolete word, it is strange that guilt remains a major problem for so many. The need for confession and absolution in order to 'move on' is still a deep-seated human experience. If this is true in psychology it is even more true in theology and before God. The message of the cross is that the burden of guilt can be lifted because the load of sin has been taken by Another for us, that the greatest drama in the history of the world was done for us, that the predicament involved us and the resolution is offered to us. 'Whether we like it or not,' says John Stott, 'our sins put him there.'[54] 'Only the man who is prepared to own his share in the guilt of the cross may claim a share in its grace.'[55]

A saintly African Christian once told a congregation that as he was climbing the hill to the meeting, he turned and saw a man carrying a very heavy load up the hill on his back. He was full of sympathy for him and spoke to him. He noticed that his hands were scarred and he realized that it was Jesus. He said to him, 'Lord, are you carrying the world's sin up the hill?' 'No,' said the Lord Jesus, 'not the world's sin, just yours!'[56]

---

[52] Cranfield, op. cit., vol. 1, p. 212.   [53] Ibid., vol. 2, p. 827.
[54] Stott (1986), p. 12.   [55] Canon Peter Green, quoted in ibid., p. 60.
[56] Roy Hession, *The Calvary Road* (CLC, 1988), p. 36.

Matthew 28:18–20
18. The Trinity: the biblical material

We know the true God only because he has revealed himself. He is not static or distant like some undiscovered planet waiting to be found. He is present and active in creation and history, reaching out in a personal love to men and women whom he has made for himself. God's self-revelation has been, in a number of ways, orientated to our humanness and to our history. His has been a historical self-revelation, given to patriarchs and prophets, culminating in his Son, Jesus Christ, the Word made flesh, and mediated by the Holy Spirit to Christ's apostles. He is the speaking God who has said at different times and in different ways, 'Stop! Listen! This is who I am and this is what I am like and this is my will for you and your world.' But God's 'This is what I am like' did not express everything at once; his was an unfolding, a progressive revelation and it led up to the most important and wonderful truth of all.

1. The God who is one, not many

The Old Testament believers lived in a world of many different and differing gods and philosophies. Yet they were taught that the true God was not 'many' but 'One'; a personal God, infinite and eternal, glorious and majestic, holy and wise, just and good. The Israelites were even given a name for this God, a name which was always intended to remind them that he was the God who had entered into a unique and personal relationship with them, who had chosen them as his people and who would always be committed to them. That name was Yahweh, rendered 'Jehovah' in older translations and hymns.

Our Bibles substitute 'the LORD' for 'Yahweh', but when we read in our Old Testament that 'the LORD' said this or 'the LORD' did that, we must be careful to remember that the original reads 'Yahweh' – this God and no other, Israel's God, our God – said this or did that. It is really a kind of personal name; it is very specific and very revealing in the way in which it is used. It is not enough to know that there is 'a god' of some sort, somewhere. It is of supreme importance that men and women know *this* God in his true character and from within a relationship based upon his love and grace and issuing in lives of devotion and obedience.

All this we find in one of the most famous Old Testament passages, Deuteronomy 6:4–5:

> Hear, O Israel: the LORD our God, the LORD is one [literally Yahweh is our God, Yahweh is one]. Love the LORD your God with all your heart and with all your soul and with all your strength.

The words of this passage have been called 'the fundamental monotheist dogma of the Old Testament'. They express 'not only the *uniqueness* but also the *unity* of God'.[1] The God of Israel is not merely the first among the gods. As Christopher Wright puts it, 'Yahweh is not the brand name of a cosmic corporation. He is one God, our God, and Yahweh is his personal name.'[2] This is said to distinguish the biblical God from all other powers, real or imagined, and from the religions of the peoples around Israel. 'He is the only member of a unique class.'[3] God is not 'everything', God is not nature, God is not the divine spark within us all and he is not the sum of all the other gods or the 'chief god' behind them.

This is very important for us today in a world where many religions live side by side. It is often said that 'God has many names', as if, behind them all, was one mysterious, unknowable reality of which they were more or less legitimate expressions. That might sound impressive or attractive but it leaves the ultimate God unnamed, unknown and characterless. Such a god may be 'the ground of all being' but he is not the God who helps the helpless, comforts the sorrowing and lifts the burden of guilt and death; the God who saves sinners.

All this underlines the personal character of Israel's God who, in his grace and mercy calls sinners into a personal relationship with him as their Saviour and their Lord: 'Love the LORD your God with all your heart and with all your soul and with all your strength.'

2. The God who does not live alone

There are, however, a number of Old Testament references which hint at something more than the oneness of God; which hint that the

---

[1] Craigie, p. 169. [2] Wright, p. 96.
[3] Millard Ericksen, *Christian Theology* (Baker, 1985), p. 323.

God who is One does not dwell alone within that oneness. From the start of the biblical revelation we hear of God and his Word or his Spirit or his Wisdom as in some way distinguishable. There were various Old Testament hints of some kind of plurality in the One God such as the plural of the divine name, *Elohim*, and its personal pronouns;[4] the extension of God in his Spirit,[5] his Word,[6] his Angel,[7] his Wisdom,[8] and mysterious references such as Psalm 2:7 and especially 110:1.[9]. There are even occasions when three subjectivities are referred to with the same divine connotation, as in Isaiah 63:7–10, where we read of 'the LORD', and of 'the angel of his presence', and of his 'Holy Spirit'. These references come short of compromising or confusing the necessary emphasis on the oneness of God in the Old Testament period but they do, along with other developments in Jewish thinking in the period between the Testaments, produce a 'hospitable atmosphere' for the New Testament revelation of distinct persons in the Godhead.[10]

Nevertheless, it is important that we do not claim that the trinitarian being of God is a revealed truth in Old Testament times. Gerald Bray writes on this:

> There is a very good theological reason for not accepting Old Testament texts as evidence for the existence of a trinity of persons in God. To admit belief in the Trinity without belief in Christ would be to confuse irretrievably the logic and purpose of revelation . . . the redeeming work of the Son of God is fundamental to the whole pattern of Trinitarian faith . . . To know the Trinity is to know the gospel, to have passed from the old dispensation to the new. It is therefore not surprising that we find no clear evidence for such a doctrine in the Old Testament.[11]

3. The God who is Father, Son and Holy Spirit

The Old Testament looks forward to a time when all the nations would know this God as their God. How would Israel teach the nations? Yahweh was Israel's own special name for God. How would he then be known? The answer to that, given by the church's highest authority, is found in Matthew 28:18–20:

Then Jesus came to them and said, 'All authority in heaven and on

---

[4] Gen. 1:1, 26; 3:22; 11:7; Is. 6:8.
[5] Gen. 1:2; 6:3; Is. 42:1.
[6] Gen. 1:3; Ps. 33:6.
[7] E.g. Gen. 18:13; 32:30; Exod. 3:2, 4; 23:20–21.　　[8] Prov. 8:22–23, 30–31.
[9] Cf. Matt. 22:41–46.　　[10] Cornelius Plantinga, 'Trinity', *ISBE*, vol. 4, p. 915.
[11] Bray, p. 141.

earth has been given to me. ¹⁹*Therefore go and make disciples of all nations, baptising them in the name of the Father and of the Son and of the Holy Spirit,* ²⁰*and teaching them to obey everything I have commanded you.'*

The nations would come to know the true and only God not as 'Yahweh' but as 'the Father, the Son and the Holy Spirit', a truth about God not revealed before, even to Israel. At first it had been necessary to stress the oneness of God against all other gods. But now a further revelation of God is made, and an astounding one: that the God who revealed himself in the Old Testament 'is not an undifferentiated, solitary, oneness. Instead God is a multiplicity – the three members of the Trinity.'[12] This one supreme being is 'not a solitary unity but a composite unity';[13] within the oneness of God is a threeness, within his essential and complete unity there is a personal trinity, God *is* the Father, the Son and the Holy Spirit, one God existing in three persons.

Notice too that believers are not baptised 'in the names' (plural) but 'in the *name*' (singular) of the Father and of the Son and of the Holy Spirit. The unity is as clearly affirmed as the Trinity. Notice too that it is not 'in the name of Father, Son and Holy Spirit' but 'in the name of *the* Father, *the* Son and *the* Holy Spirit'. The Trinity is as clearly stressed as the unity.

This is not one divine person acting in three different ways, assuming three modes of appearance in the external world (the heresy of 'modalism'); but a real distinction of persons within the unity of God. The unity is *essentially* (in respect of the essence of God) inviolable but it is *personally* complex: the true God is a tri-unity of persons.

4. The holy Son

It is, of course, in connection with Jesus that this tri-unity of persons becomes known.[14] We have it at his baptism for instance.[15] There we have the voice of the Father and the descent of the Spirit and the distinct person of the Son to whom they both relate. The Father acclaims his divine identity and the Spirit anoints and empowers his humble humanity and the Son himself stands with sinners in the water of John's baptism, a man among men, God with us, God for us.

[12] Stanley J. Grenz, *Created for Community: Connecting Christian Belief with Christian Living* (Victor Books/S P Publications, 1996), p. 45.
[13] D. Bloesch, *God the Almighty: Power, Wisdom, Love* (Paternoster, 1995), p. 184.
[14] For a sustained examination of the New Testament witness to the deity and humanity of Christ, see my *The Glory of Christ.*
[15] Matt. 3:13–17, etc.

We also see something of this pluralty of divine persons in the constant references of Jesus to the Father who sent him (forty times in John alone), the Father with whom he is one,[16] the Father whom he knows as no-one else knows or can know.[17] God is not his Father as he is our Father and from eternity they have lived in the glory of a unique communion.[18] In this connection too we may note that Jesus constantly refers to his Father as 'you', maintaining the personal distinction between himself as the Son and the Father with whom he is 'one' just as he will refer to the Holy Spirit as 'he'.[19] The distinction of persons within the Godhead is maintained.

The full Godhead of the Son from all eternity is taught by John at the beginning of his Gospel[20] and this is dealt with in some detail in chapter 16 of this book. For John it is of cardinal importance and at the very heart of his message.[21] Hence, at the end too, he makes a clear statement about our Lord's full deity as he records the words of Thomas to the risen Christ: 'My Lord and my God!'[22]

Paul, in Philippians 2:6,[23] speaks clearly of Christ being 'in very nature God', or 'in the form of God' – a phrase immediately explained as 'equality with God', which he did not exploit for his own advantage. Paul speaks of this confession as reflecting the faith of the early church. It may even have been part of an early Christian hymn giving expression to the great self-sacrifice of the one who 'being in very nature God' made himself 'nothing' and who has now been given the very place of God ('the highest place') and the name of God (Jesus Christ is 'Lord').

In Colossians 1:19,[24] Christ is called 'the image of the invisible God' by which is meant *not* (as in our day) a copy, like the original but inferior to it, but a counterpart of the original, sharing the substance of the thing it 'imaged'.[25] Verses 16–20 show that he 'images' God in the great works of God: creation, sustenance, salvation and judgment. Later, Paul makes it clear again that he posseses, not merely a fragment of the divine nature, but the fullness of it: 'For in Christ all the fulness of the Deity lives in bodily form.'[26]

In Hebrews 1:3,[27] the Son is called 'the radiance of God's glory and the exact representation of his being, sustaining all things by his powerful word'. The first reference in this verse recalls the Shekinah of Old Testament times and the bright glory of God that is so often recorded.[28] Only one who was in himself

[16] John 10:30, cf. 5:23. [17] Matt. 11:27. [18] John 17:5. [19] John 16:8.
[20] 1 John 1:1–3, 14, 18. [21] Cf. John 5:23; 6:51; 8:23, 42, 58; 17:5.
[22] John 20:28. [23] For a more detailed comment see Lewis, pp. 228–238.
[24] For a more detailed comment see Lewis, pp. 239–251.
[25] See Kittel, in Lewis, p. 241. [26] Col. 2:9; cf. 1:19.
[27] For a more detailed comment see Lewis, pp. 112–121.
[28] E.g. Exod. 24:15ff.; 33:9ff.; 40:34–38; Ezek. 43:1–5; cf. Mark 9:22ff.; Acts 9:3.

God, however differentiated or distinguished, could be described in this way.

The next words, '. . . and the exact representation of his being', mean that there is an exact correspondence between the Son and the Father, even to the very 'essence' (being) of God. The Son is able to reveal God perfectly because he is one with God essentially. When Jesus reveals God he does not reveal something other than himself. The persons are distinct, but the same divine nature is common to both. Once again, the divine prerogatives of creation and salvation are affirmed of the Son, who is also said to 'sit at the right hand of the majesty in heaven'. The right hand of God, says B. K. Donne, 'is metaphorical language for divine omnipotence and omnipresence',[29] and it affirms that he is reigning everywhere as King and Lord, wielding the power of divine authority.

It is very likely that the title 'God' is given to Jesus quite explicitly in a few places (Romans 9:5, Titus 2:13, Hebrews 1:8 and 2 Peter 1:1), as Murray Harris has shown with careful scholarship.[30] However, perhaps to counter the crude polytheisms of the day, the Godhead of Christ is often expressed in more subtle terms in Scripture.

One of the most astonishing and revealing things about Jesus in the New Testament is the way the exclusive rights of God are claimed by him, transferred to him or shared with him: the forgiveness of sins, the judgment of the world, the rule over the nations, the throne of God. This is another way of showing the true and full Godhead of Jesus in the New Testament. The same is true of the centrality of Jesus in his own teaching in the gospels and his place at the centre of the church's worship, as we see in Acts and Revelation as well as in the various prayers and hymns in the epistles. He is central to his own gospel and shares with the One who sent him the honour which is due to God alone. The Father is not sidelined when the Son is worshipped.[31]

The church must always remember that it has no gospel without this. If Jesus is not God, then God has not entered our race and experienced our human suffering. If Jesus is not God then he is not the perfect revelation of the Father, 'the exact representation of his being',[32] and then after all the *real* God remains shadowy and unknown to us, a God of uncertain grace and terrible possibilities. Moreover, if Jesus is not God then God has not borne our guilt and condemnation and we are still faced with the terrible prospect of

[29] Brian K. Donne, *Christ Ascended: A Study of the Significance of the Ascension of Jesus Christ in the New Testament* (Paternoster, 1984), p. 60.
[30] See Harris (1992), pp. 143–185, 205–227, 230–238.
[31] See R. T. France, 'The Worship of Jesus', in H. H. Rowdon (ed.), *Christ the Lord: Studies in Christology presented to Donald Guthrie* (IVP, 1982), pp. 17–37.
[32] Heb. 1:3.

bearing our own sins and their punishment. There is no gospel, no good news, unless 'he who has seen [the Son] has seen the Father', no gospel unless '*God* was reconciling the world to himself in Christ'.[33] But in fact the very name of the God of Israel is given to Jesus when he is acknowledged as 'Lord' in the New Testament writings. The Greek word *kyrios*, Lord, was the term used in the Greek version of the Hebrew Scriptures to translate 'Yahweh' over six thousand times. It was the name given to Yahweh in the synagogues of Greek-speaking Jews throughout the Roman world and in their common speech. In the New Testament writings it is used to distinguish the Lord Jesus from God the Father so that when we read of 'God our Father and the Lord Jesus Christ' we have the two sacred names of the two sacred persons. 'Lord' is now 'the inter-Trinitarian name of the risen Christ'.[34] That is why the apostle Paul can write repeatedly, 'Grace and peace to you from God the Father and the Lord Jesus Christ.'[35]

An outstanding example of the lordship of Jesus Christ being aligned with the lordship of God is in 1 Corinthians 8:6: 'yet for us there is but one God, the Father, from whom all things came and for whom we live; and there is but one Lord, Jesus Christ, through whom all things came and through whom we live'. Here, against the background of the many gods of the ancient world, Paul recalls the famous Jewish Shema of Deuteronomy 6:4 (which we examined earlier) and strikingly Christianizes it. Quoting N. T. Wright, D. R. de Lacey writes: 'It is hard to conceive of a clearer means by which Paul could indicate *both* that he was aligning Jesus with the *Kyrios* of the LXX [the Septuagint, the Greek Old Testament] and that he was doing so within a thoroughly Jewish framework of thought.'[36]

Paul is not inventing a new religion but unfolding an old revelation; this is the God of Abraham, Isaac and Jacob, the God of Moses and the prophets, but he is now to be known as the Father, the Son and the Holy Spirit. Gordon Fee states: 'Although Paul does not here call Christ God, the formula is so constructed that only the most obdurate would deny its Trinitarian implications.'[37]

5. The Holy Spirit

What then of the Holy Spirit? In some ways he is the hidden person of the three; he hides, as it were, behind the incarnate Son who is the focal point of salvation throughout the Gospels. That is why we have more about the Son in the New Testament as a whole. Yet, even in

[33] John 14:9; 2 Cor. 5:19.   [34] Warfield (1974), p. 231.
[35] E.g. Gal. 1:3; Eph. 1:2; Phil. 1:2; 2 Thess. 1:2; 1 Tim. 1:2.
[36] D. R. de Lacey, 'One Lord in Pauline Theology', in H. H. Rowdon (ed.), op. cit., p. 201.
[37] Fee, p. 375.

the three-year public ministry of our Lord, the Spirit of God is an emerging figure who is (clearly) different from Jesus himself and who empowers and guides him from the start and yet, further, becomes in some way distinguishable from the Father also. At first the Spirit appears, as in many Old Testament texts, simply as the activity of God,[38] but at the baptism of Jesus we have this third identity,[39] distinct from Father and Son. We see this same Spirit hurry the Son to his confrontation with the tempter in the wilderness[40] and empower him for an extraordinary ministry of healings, exorcism and miracles, demonstrating that the kingdom of God had come.[41]

John, however, goes far beyond the other Gospel writers in his explicit teaching about these things. 'Indeed,' writes Gerald Bray, 'the fourth gospel is in parts a trinitarian tract.' He continues, 'From the very first verse, we are introduced to the relationship between the Logos and God, and this theme is developed in the many references throughout the gospel to the intimacy of the relationship between the Father and Son.' The great trinitarian exposition of chapters 14 – 16 'provide a passage which for centuries has formed the cornerstone of orthodox doctrine'. Bray concludes: 'What is so striking about these texts is the way they so closely parallel the teaching of Paul.'[42]

In John's Gospel we have been confronted at many points by divine claims for Jesus, who is clearly a distinct person from the Father who sent him and yet shares with him an eternal oneness. With regard to the Holy Spirit, however, we are faced with different and opposite problems. With regard to the Son there is the need to establish his deity, not his personality; with the Spirit there is the need to establish his personality, not his deity. Jesus himself, however, shortly before his death, speaks of the Spirit more clearly than ever and indicates the distinct and divine personhood of the Holy Spirit, and indeed the whole Trinity of sacred persons, in John 14:17, 26. Here he speaks of 'the Spirit of truth . . . the Counsellor, the Holy Spirit, whom the Father will send in my name' in response to the request of the Son, and in the Son's name to continue Jesus' work: 'All this I have spoken while still with you. But the Counsellor, the Holy Spirit, whom the Father will send in my name, [he] will teach you all things and will remind you of everything I have said to you.'[43]

Only a person can take a person's place and represent him. Jesus distinctly uses a personal pronoun for the Spirit as he tells his disciples, '*He* will teach you.' The use of the masculine pronoun 'he' with the neuter noun 'Spirit', as Morris and Westcott note, 'brings

---

[38] Luke 1:35.
[39] Matt. 3:16–17. [40] Mark 1:12; Luke 4:1. [41] Luke 4:14; 11:20.
[42] Bray, p. 148. [43] John 14:25–26.

out the personability' of the Counsellor.[44] Similarly in John 16:7–8 Jesus tells his disciples: 'But I tell you the truth: It is for your good that I am going away. Unless I go away, the Counsellor will not come to you; but if I go, I will send him to you. When he comes, he will convict the world of guilt in regard to sin and righteousness and judgment.' Here, too, the personhood of the Holy Spirit is clearly indicated. He is not an influence or a force or a power but a Counsellor. The Greek term is *paraclētos*, which basically means 'an advocate who takes up one's case or an ally fighting on one's side: someone who strengthens and encourages',[45] someone called alongside to help. Jesus does not say, 'I will send you help', but 'I will send you a helper.' The Spirit, then, is a some*one*, not a some*thing*, and so Jesus says in John 16:8, 'When *he* comes', not 'When *it* comes'. He also speaks of the intensely personal work the Spirit will do: convicting the world, enlightening and inspiring the disciples in their mission, and always pointing to Jesus, glorifying him and bringing his grace and truth from the right hand of God to the apostles on earth: 'He will bring glory to me by taking from what is mine and making it known to you.'[46]

Jesus is clearly showing that he himself is not the Spirit. He must go that the Spirit might come to do his work. And that work will be the conviction of the world about the things of God. As Lesslie Newbigin says: 'It is he [the Holy Spirit] who is, properly speaking, the missionary', not the church through which he works.[47]

Earlier Jesus had said to his disciples, 'The Counsellor . . . whom the Father will send in my name, will teach you all things and will remind you of everything I have said to you.'[48] There the Spirit is distinguished from both the Father and the Son, though his work is done in perfect harmony with theirs. That perfect harmony is reflected too in that the sending of the Spirit in his new work on earth is attributed to the Father in John 14:16 and to the Son in John 16:7. Indeed, the risen, ascended Lord Jesus is so much one with the Spirit he sends to take his place, that he can say, 'And surely I will be with you always, to the very end of the age.'[49] But it is the Spirit's coming which is the means of his presence.

I have much more to say to you, more than you can now bear. But when he, the Spirit of truth, comes, he will guide you into all truth. He will not speak on his own; he will speak only what he hears, and he will tell you what is yet to come. He will bring glory to me by taking from what is mine and making it known to you.[50]

---

[44] See in Morris (1971), p. 656.   [45] Milne (1982), p. 176.   [46] John 16:14.
[47] Newbigin (1998), p. 40.   [48] John 14:26.   [49] Matt. 28:20; cf. 2 Cor. 3:18.
[50] John 16:12–14.

Here Jesus tells his disciples that the Spirit who will convict the world of sin will also enlighten the disciples. He will continue Jesus' ministry and teaching, bringing to their minds and hearts the meaning of the central truths of Jesus' death and resurrection, truths as yet unclear to them that could be explained only after the event.

Max Turner thinks that here, in verses 12–14, we have the most convincing statements suggesting that the Spirit is a divine person. This is no mere personification of the Spirit, intended to take the matter no further than the Old Testament revelation of the Spirit as the mode of Yahweh's presence. This is a clear recognition of his distinct personality.

As Turner points out, John's 'whole presentation of the Paraclete as a *parallel figure to Jesus* in the relationships sustained to the Father and the Son, to the disciples and to the world' arguably 'requires that John views the Spirit as a divine figure who relates to the Father and to the exalted Son after the analogy of Jesus' relation to the Father in the ministry'. Important too is the consideration that 'in the theology of the Fourth Gospel, the Son glorifies the Father, and the Father the Son: they do not glorify *themselves*. When it is said that the Spirit will *not* glorify himself, but the Son, the Spirit is being portrayed as a separate Person (16:13–14) ... The Spirit enables the Johannine community to confess Jesus, and worship the Father, but he is distinct from both – no mere extension of their personality.'[51] Turner notes the profound significance of Jesus 'sending' the Spirit both here and in Acts[52] for the developing trinitarian thought of the church. The Spirit, as in the Old Testament, is clearly divine and the Spirit of God. In the Old Testament the Spirit is God in action. Jesus' promise of the Spirit ties the sending closely with the Father.[53] Yet it is the exalted Christ who sends him[54] and in the event pours out the Spirit of God from the throne of God.[55] The exalted Christ becomes Lord of the Spirit.[56] This is very clear in Paul's theology of the Spirit too. Turner notes:

> Essentially he regards the post-resurrection gift of the Spirit as 'an ambassador acting on behalf of both God and Christ, and thus as the power of Christ exercising his lordship in the church'. In the light of this, such expressions as 'the Spirit of Christ' (Rom 8:9), 'the Spirit of his Son' (Phil. 1:19), and 'the Spirit of Jesus Christ' (Phil 1:19 cf. Acts 16:7) should be understood after the analogy of the expressions 'the Spirit of God' or 'the Spirit of the Lord'. That is 'they were used to express the belief that the Spirit acted on behalf of God and of Christ, and under the sovereignty of both'.[57]

[51] Turner, p. 179.   [52] See Acts 2:16–17, 32–33; cf. Luke 24:49.
[53] John 14:16, 26; cf. Acts 1:4.   [54] John 15:26; 16:7.
[55] Acts 2:33; cf. John 20:21–22.   [56] John 16:7, 12–15.
[57] Turner, pp. 174–175, quoting his earlier essay, 'The Spirit of Christ in Christology', in H. H. Rowdon (ed.), op. cit., p. 188.

First of all this has enormous significance for the deity of Christ since it is inconceivable that any creature could assume such a position of lordship over the Spirit of God.[58] Before the resurrection the Spirit acts upon Jesus. After his resurrection Jesus acts upon the Spirit. His lordship over and through the Spirit 'appears to accord Jesus a lordship within God himself, i.e. over the Spirit which is his [God's] own personal presence in action ... the outpouring of God's Spirit by Jesus entails that the Father and the Son are together one God'.[59] This, as he notes, is tantamount to calling Jesus 'God'.

But it also has implications for a developing doctrine of the Trinity, since it is not the Father Jesus sends but the Spirit, and the Spirit, while being in closest relation to him, is also distinct from him in his (the Spirit's) own personality. Turner writes:

> It would be natural enough for Jewish Christians to maintain their pre-Christian commitment to the full divine nature of the Spirit. In the light of Jesus' exaltation-Lordship, however, they would need to distance the Spirit from the Father in some way, in order to avoid speaking of the Son sending the Father ... In other words, it would be natural for the Spirit increasingly to become perceived as the locus of personhood within God, but one *other* than the Father and the Son. One can see strong hints of this in Paul at e.g., 1 Cor. 2:10, 11; 12:5–7; 2 Cor. 3:17–18; 13:13; Rom. 8:26–27 and in the whole trinitarian 'shape' of the rest of Paul's pneumatology.[60]

Elsewhere in the New Testament, the Holy Spirit 'searches, speaks, testifies, commands, reveals, strives, makes intercession, raises the dead',[61] can be grieved, resisted, lied to and provoked,[62] indwells us, works in us, and sanctifies and saves us.[63] He unites us to Christ at our conversions[64] and is the immediate Agent of every act of God upon us whether of conviction or joy.[65] He is the divine agent of the church's new covenant life and power,[66] its growth and multiplication[67] and its various ministries.[68] He is the Spirit of God and he is the Spirit of Christ, but he is also, in his own Person, the Holy Spirit.

---

[58] Acts 2:36.   [59] Turner, p. 175.   [60] Ibid., p. 178.
[61] Berkhof (*Systematic Theology*), p. 96.   [62] Acts 5:3–4, 9.
[63] 1 Cor. 6:11; Gal. 5:16–26.   [64] John 3:5–6; 1 Cor. 12:13.
[65] Acts 13:52; Rom. 15:13; Gal. 5:22.   [66] Acts 2:4, 17, 38; 10:44–48; 19:1–7.
[67] E.g. Acts 4:31; 8:5–7; 19:11–20.   [68] Rom. 12:4–8; 1 Cor. 12:4–11.

6. The church's privilege

This is how God makes himself known, this is the God who is made known, and this is how God wants us to know him. This, after all, is God's full being and identity. Moreover, this is how God is *best* known. The doctrine of the Trinity is not a piece of ancient dogmatic lumber; it is the fullness of God and the features of his love and the activity of his grace. We know him most fully in this truth because this is his fullest revelation of himself. We know him most fully because the Father sent the Son, because the Son is the image of the invisible God, and because the Son sent the Spirit to be the witness to Jesus in the world of men and women.

In Galatians we have what Gerald Bray calls 'one of the most strikingly trinitarian as well as one of the earliest Pauline texts': 'God has sent the Spirit of his Son into our hearts, the Spirit who calls out "Abba, Father."' Bray remarks, 'There can be little doubt that Paul's mind was fundamentally trinitarian in cast.'[69] And a reading of other texts such as 1 Peter 1:2 and Jude 20–21 shows that this thinking was not unique to Paul. Furthermore, while 'the fourth gospel is undoubtedly the main biblical source for trinitarian doctrine', it is 'probably true to say that it has one rival . . . the Book of Revelation'. It is here, more than anywhere else, that

> . . . the perfect unity of the Trinity is demonstrated, so that while the persons remain fully distinct, it becomes almost impossible to distinguish between them . . . Indeed we are barely aware that we are passing from one person to another. The sense of the presence of God is so overwhelming that we can move among the persons almost without noticing, yet we are always fully conscious of their presence . . . The doctrine, culled from the rest of Scripture and laboriously constructed, is here presented to us in all its profound complexity and splendid simplicity . . . The Book of Revelation is first and foremost a revelation of the Trinity.[70]

The baptismal formula of Jesus, which would be repeated down through the ages in countless baptisms, and the apostolic benediction in Paul, which would be repeated in countless acts of worship,[71] make it clear that this is a truth that God wants to preserve at the forefront of the church's consciousness at all times and in all places.

---

[69] Cf. Rom. 15:16, 30; 1 Cor. 1:21–22; 2 Cor. 3:3; Eph. 2:18.
[70] Bray, pp. 149–151. Cf. Rev. 1:8 with 17–18; 1:18–19 with 2:7, 11, 17, etc.
[71] 'May the grace of the Lord Jesus Christ, and the love of God, and the fellowship of the Holy Spirit be with you all' (2 Cor. 13:14).

Matthew 28:18–20
19. The triune God

1. The importance of this truth to God

Of all the truths about God that he has made known, of all his perfections, achievements and purposes, the truth about God in which God most delights is that he is the triune God. It is the infinite and endless joy of God that he is the Father, the Son and the Holy Spirit in self-giving love and eternal communion. Even before the universe was created, when there was nothing whatsoever but God in eternity, God was not lonely, nor was he alone.

In his earthly life Jesus could say, 'I am not alone for the Father is with me', and in his heavenly life he could say, 'I am not alone for the Father and the Spirit are with me.' The Father could say, 'I am not alone for the Son and the Spirit are with me', and the Spirit could say, 'I am not alone for the Father and the Son are with me.' In that eternity before time and space were created, God was alone but he was never solitary. In knowledge, joy and love each person within the one essence acted and interacted face to face,[1] giving their life to one another and receiving their life from one another. And for this reason we can say that God is 'community'. God is the community of the Father, Son and Holy Spirit, who enjoy perfect and eternal fellowship.[2]

This understanding of the trinitarian love of God prevents us from seeing the divine love as a static, or indeed, an impersonal quality. 'God is love' not in abstract definition or unfulfilled potential but in infinite and eternal activity within the relations of the persons of the Godhead. Each divine person loves and is loved by the other divine persons in a community of loving and being loved. These relations are relations within a shared being and of a unique kind. Colin Gunton writes:

[1] Cf. John 1:1.
[2] Stanley J. Grenz, *Created for Community: Connecting Christian Belief with Christian Living* (Victor Books/S P Publications, 1996), p. 51.

The persons do not simply enter into relations with one another, but are constituted by one another in the relations. Father, Son and Spirit are eternally what they are by virtue of what they are from and to one another. Being and relation can be distinguished in thought, but in no way separated ontologically; they are rather part of the one ontological dynamic. The general point, to use the words of John Zizoulas, is that the being of God is not a blank unity, but a being in communion. To adapt Gregory of Nazianzus, we may say that to think of divine being is to have one's mind necessarily drawn to the three persons, to think of the three to be led ineluctably to a concept of shared, relational, being.[3]

2. The importance of this truth for us

a. Our knowledge of God

Gerald Bray reminds us that 'the Reformers believed that the essence of God is of secondary importance in Christian theology. They did not deny that he has an essence ... They said only that God speaks sparingly of his essence, because he wants us to focus our attention and our worship elsewhere.'[4] Calvin did not systematize the being of God in terms of a list of 'attributes' as others had done in the medieval tradition, and were to do, in the Reformed tradition also. He was content to recognize the two main attributes of God's 'immensity' and 'spirituality' by the revelation of which God 'suppresses all gross imaginations and checks the audacity of the human mind'.[5] He warns: 'Those who propose to enquire what the essence of God is, only delude us with frigid speculations, it being much more our interest to know what kind of being God is, and what things are agreeable to his nature.'[6]

After making the point that God's nature is immeasurable and spiritual, Calvin writes:

> But God also designates himself by another special mark to distinguish himself more precisely from idols. For he so proclaims himself the sole God as to offer himself to be contemplated clearly in three persons. Unless we grasp these, only the bare and empty name of God flits about in our brains, to the exclusion of the true God.[7]

A great fourth-century theologian, Gregory of Nazianzus, used to say, 'When I say God, I mean Father, Son and Holy Spirit', and a

---

[3] Gunton (1993), p. 214.   [4] Bray, p. 199.
[5] Calvin (*Institutes*), I.xiii.1, quoted in ibid., p. 80.
[6] (*Institutes*), I.ii.3, quoted in ibid., p. 80–81.   [7] Calvin (*Institutes*), I.xiii.2.

great twentieth-century theologian, Karl Barth, used to say, 'Trinity is the Christian name for God.'[8] These statements remind us of the fundamental importance of this truth and its teaching for those who call themselves Christian. The trinitarian being of God is what distinguishes him from all other supposed gods and alternative mysticisms and philosophies. Our belief in God as being Father, Son and Holy Spirit distinguishes us as Christians who know and worship the true and living God. That it is foundational to the church's existence and her proclamation is the burden of the great early church creeds, including the 'Nicene' Creed and the Chalcedonian Creed (AD 451).

The subject leads us to consider the way God himself exists. There can be no higher or deeper mystery than that. The puritan theologian, John Owen, said it is a matter of *revelation* not of *explanation* and therefore we should be content to listen to Scripture. We may know that God *is* three-in-one rather than *how* he is so. It is not a matter of trying to understand the manner of it but of humbly listening to the truth of it and grasping those elements of it that clearly pertain to our salvation: 'Where reason fails and all her powers, / There faith prevails and love adores.'[9] The revelation of Father, Son and Holy Spirit in Scripture has led the church to confess that God is a personal Trinity within a numerical unity. Notice that the distinctions within the Godhead are personal not mathematical. It is sometimes scornfully said that 'in mathematics one plus one plus one equals three, but in theology one plus one plus one equals one!', with the implication that theology, especially trinitarian theology, is illogical, self-contradictory and absurd.

But the teaching is not that God is *mathematically* three in one but that he is *personally* three in one, that the one God exists eternally as three persons, who each possess the same 'essence' and who share it equally, eternally and completely. God is one essential being within which there are three personal distinctions: the Father, the Son and the Holy Spirit: co-existent, co-equal and co-eternal. God is not three in the same way that he is one, nor is he one in the same way that he is three – that would indeed involve an inherent contradiction. Here there is a perfect unity of essence and that unity is shared *alike* by each of the three divine persons. God is 'The undivided Three / And the mysterious One'.[10] This means that each divine person has the fullness of God's being or essence or substance in himself. God is a triune being but not a divided being. Their unity is perfect; each possesses the whole being of Godhead and each is completely open to, known by and enjoyed among the others in

---

[8] Quoted in Fee, p. 586.
[9] Hymn, 'We give immortal praise', by Isaac Watts (1674–1748).   [10] Ibid.

perfect and self-giving love. If we could point to a part of the divine essence (which, of course, we cannot do because God is not spatially defined), we could not say, 'This part belongs to the Father and that part belongs to the Son and that part belongs to the Spirit.' Each part would be the possession of all three persons simultaneously. They each and all subsist in every 'part' of the divine being. In the sonorous words of the Athanasian Creed:

> And the Catholic Faith is this: That we worship one God in Trinity, and Trinity in Unity; neither confounding the Persons; nor dividing the Substance. For there is one Person of the Father: another of the Son: and another of the Holy Spirit. But the Godhead of the Father, of the Son, and of the Holy Spirit, is all one: the Glory equal, the Majesty co-eternal.[11]

Calvin, going beyond the Nicene caution and talk of 'eternal generation', insisted that each person was *autotheos*, 'self-existent'.[12] The essence of both the Son and the Spirit is unbegotten. Each person is 'God in his own right'.[13] The Father is the fountain-head of the order, not the essence, of the Godhead. The Son of God is begotten according to his personal relationship with the Father but not according to his participation in the divine essence. 'Calvin held to the absolute equality of the persons in the Godhead.'[14]

b. Our confidence in God

It is to be expected then, that God would want to communicate to us what is the most treasured and glorious truth about himself. God has made it clear that he is the relational God – God is the social Trinity. Moreover, foundational to our knowledge of God is the knowledge that 'God is love'.[15] As we have seen, love has never been a static property in God, a potential benevolence, a mere capacity to love if the right objects to be loved should appear. This love has been the inter-trinitarian principle in the eternal life of God. Father, Son and Holy Spirit have loved one another with infinite self-giving and delight. Stanley Grenz writes: 'Through all eternity, therefore, God is the social Trinity, the community of love.' Applying this to our lives he continues:

> When we become believers, the Spirit makes his abode in our hearts. But this indwelling Holy Spirit is none other than the Spirit of the relationship between the Father and the Son. When

---

[11] Quoted in Wayne Grudem, *Systematic Theology: An introduction to biblical doctrine* (IVP/Zondervan, 1994), p. 253.
[12] See Warfield (1956), p. 275.   [13] Bray, p. 201.   [14] Berkhof (1978), p. 95.
[15] 1 John 4:8, 16.

he comes to live within us, therefore, the Spirit brings us to share in the love the Son enjoys with the Father. No wonder Paul exclaims, 'Because you are sons, God sent the Spirit of his Son into our hearts, the Spirit who calls out, "Abba, Father"' (Gal. 4:6).[16]

Where would we be without this truth? How much of God would we know personally if we had never heard of Jesus Christ or if he had never come into the world? For many God is a dark and distant deity precisely because they do not know the Father in the Son. How close would we personally be to God in love and obedience if the Holy Spirit had not been given to us in the work of rebirth?[17] It is because of the third person of the Holy Trinity that we know God as *our* God, that a person becomes a Christian and continues as one.[18] We know God is love because he is a community of persons who live in self-giving love. We know we shall be saved in the hour of death and at the last day because we have been taken up into the company of the holy Three from whose circle of fellowship none of us will be cast out.[19] As Michael Ovey observes:

> The Bible stresses God's faithfulness. But faithfulness is possible only within an existing personal relationship. The same arguments apply to faithfulness as do to love. A non-Trinitarian God means a God for whom faithfulness is either irrelevant since he is not personal, or else a God who is finding out about faithfulness as he experiences personal relationships with his creation for the first time. This is devastating since it means we do not actually know that God is permanently faithful – he might turn out not to be. That doubt eats away at the assurance of our destiny with Him.[20]

Without this truth of the trinitarian being of God our knowledge of God will be impoverished and our understanding of the way of salvation in Christ will be impossible. The truth about God as a tri-unity of divine persons is not obfuscation but revelation, clarification and celebration. It is not darkness but light.

c. Our praying

In Scripture it is normal to pray *to* the Father, *through* the Son and *by* the Holy Spirit. This is because of the way in which they work. The Father is the fountainhead of the *order* of the three persons and of the plan of salvation. He is the one who has 'chosen us from the foundation of the world' in Christ. The Father is the author of elec-

---

[16] Grenz, op. cit., p. 47. [17] John 3:5–6. [18] 2 Cor. 13:14; 1 Pet. 1:2.
[19] John 6:37–40; 14:23; 1 John 1:3; 3:1–3; 4:13; 5:11–12.
[20] Michael Ovey, 'The Human Identity Crisis: Can we do without the Trinity?', *Cambridge Papers*, vol. 4, no. 2 (June 1995).

tion.[21] The Son is the mediator who represents God to us and us to God, who mediates God's blessing and our prayers; and the redeemer who makes a full atonement for sin in the nature that sinned – our human nature.[22] The Holy Spirit is the perfector of what God has done, the sanctifier who brings us the grace of new birth and the gift of faith and who will bring us to heaven through many temptations, tests and trials.[23]

These divisions, of course, are not absolute since each member of the Trinity owns and cooperates in the work of the other, but each does so according to their eternal plan and external operations, so that for instance it was the Son and not the Father or the Spirit who became a baby at Bethlehem and who was crucified at Calvary. Yet it was the Father who sent him and the Spirit who prepared a human nature for him. It was the Father who gave him up for us all and never left him alone but upheld him with unknown grief and pain through the entire work of salvation.[24] Similarly it was 'through the eternal Spirit' that Christ offered himself up to God[25] and by the power of the Spirit that he was raised from the dead.[26] And so we could speak of each of the external acts of God in which each have their part and all have their place, including creation which is revealed as having been the work of the Father as the author of creation, the Son as the agent of creation and the Spirit as the instrument of creation.[27]

All this means that when we pray we can also turn to each of the divine persons and express our love and thankfulness for the part that they have played and still play and always will play in our creation, preservation and salvation unto eternal life. Stanley Grenz speaks of this as 'trinitarian praying' and writes, 'Our knowledge of the Triune God ought to motivate us to address our prayers to the Father, Son and Spirit.'

It is clear from the Lord's Prayer that we are to pray to the first person of the Trinity as 'Our Father'. And we ought not to forget how startling such a term of intimacy applied to a mere individual would have been to the Jewish mind, with its profound reverence for God. But we should recognize, too, the worship of Jesus which we find in the New Testament. Believers are even characterized as those who 'call on his name'.[28] We find it there from Thomas's confession,[29] Stephen's prayer and those of others in Acts,[30] right through to the worship and praise which are offered to Jesus equally with the Father in the book of Revelation.[31] We also find it underlying the

[21] Eph. 1:3–6.   [22] 1 Tim. 2:5–6.   [23] Rom. 8:9–17.   [24] Rom. 3:25; 8:32.
[25] Heb. 9:14.   [26] Rom. 1:4.   [27] Gen. 1:1–2; Col. 1:16; Heb. 1:1–3.
[28] 1 Cor. 1:2.   [29] John 20:28.
[30] E.g. Acts 7:59; 9:10–17, 21; 22:16, cf. 1 Cor. 1:2.
[31] Rev. 1:5f.; 5:8–14; 7:9–12; 22:3.

great Christological passages, some of which may have been sung as hymns by the early congregations.[32]

In the New Testament, the Holy Spirit's connection with prayer is usually seen as his prompting the believer's prayers or his own intercession in the heart of the believer,[33] and we rarely hear of someone praying to the Spirit, though he too is explicitly invoked in the threefold benediction of 2 Corinthians 13:14. And the church has not forgotten to praise and to invoke the third person also in her prayers and hymnody: from the *Veni Creator Spiritus* of the seventh century, splendidly rendered by John Dryden in his hymn 'Creator Spirit by Whose aid / The world's foundations first were laid', to the beautiful 'Come down, O love divine' of the fifteenth-century Bianco Da Siena, and the great revival hymns of Charles Wesley, such as 'Come, Holy Ghost, all-quickening fire', 'Come, Holy Ghost, our hearts inspire' and 'Spirit of faith, come down'.

The public worship of the church has always been decidedly trinitarian and the same may be, and should be, true of our more private prayers. The great Puritan theologian, John Owen, wrote a classic devotional work on this, the title of which advertises its contents: *Of Communion with God the Father, Son, and Holy Ghost, Each Person Distinctly, in Love, Grace and Consolation; or The Saint's Fellowship with the Father, Son and Holy Ghost Unfolded.*[34] In this great work Owen taught that the believer, while normally praying to the Father, through the Son and by the Holy Spirit, may also distinctly and directly praise and thank and love each person in the Godhead for the part they have played in our lives: the Father in election, the Son in redemption and the Holy Spirit in conversion and sanctification. He is careful to say that all three get the glory directed to each since they all cooperate at every point in creation and salvation and we are reminded of the famous words of Gregory of Nazianzus, a passage which, said John Calvin, 'vastly delights me': 'I cannot think on the One without quickly being encircled by the splendour of the Three; nor can I discern the Three without being straightaway carried back to the One.'[35]

3. The importance of this truth for the church

a. In mission

It has been said that mission is not primarily an activity of the church but an attribute of God. God is a missionary God: 'It is not the Church that has a mission of salvation to fulfil in the world; it is the

---

[32] Phil. 2:6–11; Col. 1:15–20; Heb. 1:1–4; John 1:1–18.
[33] Rom. 8:14–16, 26–27; 1 Cor. 14:15–16; Eph. 6:18; Jude 20.
[34] See *Works of John Owen* (Banner of Truth, 1966), vol. 2.
[35] Quoted in Calvin (*Institutes*), I.xiii.17.

mission of the Son and the Spirit through the Father that includes the Church.'[36] Mission is thereby seen as a movement from God to the world; the church is viewed as an instrument for that mission. 'There is church because there is mission, not vice versa. To participate in mission is to participate in the movement of God's love toward people, since God is a fountain of sending love.'[37]

The trinitarian being of God is a truth which is, from the beginning in the New Testament, related to the church's world-wide mission. Jesus began the missionary movement of the New Testament with this truth in verses 18–20: *Then Jesus came to them and said, 'All authority in heaven and on earth has been given to me. Therefore go and make disciples of all nations, baptising them in the name of the Father and of the Son and of the Holy Spirit, and teaching them to obey everything I have commanded you. And surely I will be with you always, to the very end of the age.'*

As Lesslie Newbigin observes,

> When one goes outside the 'Christendom' situation to bring the Gospel to non-Christians, one soon discovers that the doctrine of the Trinity is not something that can be kept out of sight; on the contrary, it is the necessary starting-point of preaching as the name of Jesus is related to the one true God and as the Spirit's past and present work is acknowledged in the hearers ... Even in the simplest form of missionary preaching, one finds that one cannot escape dealing with this doctrine. When an evangelist goes into an Indian village where the name of Jesus is unknown and preaches the Gospel for the first time, how is he to introduce the Name? How does one say who Jesus is in a pagan situation? ... I have always found, in talking to such village groups, that they had already in their minds the consciousness, however vague, of the one God behind all the gods, One who was their creator and judge. If this consciousness is present, how does one relate the name of Jesus to it?[38]

The reality of God as the Father, the Son and the Holy Spirit is the first truth of all mission and the gospel cannot be preached adequately without it. The message of the good news is that 'God so loved the world that he gave his one and only Son, that whoever believes in him shall not perish but have eternal life',[39] and it is in the

---

[36] Jurgen Moltmann, *The Church in the Power of the Spirit: A Contribution to Messianic Ecclesiology* (1975; SCM Press, 1977), quoted in David Bosch, *Transforming Mission: Paradigm Shifts in Theology of Mission* (Orbis, 1991), p. 390.

[37] Johannes Aagard and Anne Maria Aagard, quoted in Bosch, op. cit., p. 390.

[38] Newbigin (1998), pp. 35–36. [39] John 3:16.

power of the Holy Spirit that the light of that truth enters the minds and the joy of that truth grasps the heart. Trinitarian truth lies at the core of the gospel and is implicit in its first proclamation.

b. In fellowship

This truth about God also teaches us a profound truth about ourselves: that as persons created in the image and likeness of the tri-personal God we are made to live in fellowship with others. In God there is both unity and diversity and he has so ordered human life that in marriage, the church, and even the wider society and its creation-context there is also unity and diversity at various levels. As Stanley Grenz puts it, 'Because God is a plurality-in-unity, the ideal for human kind does not focus on solitary persons, but on persons-in-community. God intends that we reflect the divine nature in our lives. This is only possible as we move out of our isolation and into godly relationships with others. Consequently, true Christian living is life-in-relationship or life-in-community.'[40]

This truth, therefore, models how the community of believers are to relate to one another. Jesus prayed for all believers shortly before his passion: 'I pray also for those who will believe in me ... that all of them may be one, Father, just as you are in me and I in you. May they also be in us so that the world may believe that you have sent me ... I in them and you in me.'[41] Here Jesus himself is the link between the inter-trinitarian relations in the Godhead which we cannot enter (the 'ontological' trinity) and the trinitarian activity (the 'economical' trinity) that in various ways we can reflect in our church life together and in the oneness we discover when we encounter Christians in general.

Not only in our unity but in our diversity too we reflect the Trinity of God. One of Paul's favourite metaphors for the local church is that of a body, where the different members combine to achieve the life-in-community that God wants for us and which he himself has always lived. Paul writes:

> The body is a unit, though it is made up of many parts; and though all its parts are many, they form one body ... If one part suffers, every part suffers with it; if one part is honoured, every part rejoices with it. Now you are the body of Christ, and each one of you is a part of it.[42]

---

[40] Grenz, op. cit., p. 51.   [41] John 17:20–23.   [42] 1 Cor. 12:12, 26–27.

4. The importance of this truth for all human society

a. *Our understanding of ourselves*

Today, Western individualism is in a crisis of loneliness and confusion. We have lost the co-ordinates of family, community and craft so necessary to knowing our place and even our worth in the world. We need others in order to know who we are. We endlessly affirm our worth as individuals, but answering voices confirm an ideology rather than an appreciation. We are encouraged to express and promote our own self-image, but as everyone else is doing the same it is somehow losing its force, its relevance and even its point. We are losing our uniqueness in the very age that affirms our individuality. Apparently the centre of the universe is getting rather crowded.

The doctrine of the Trinity tells us that relations are essential to personhood; that persons are people-in-relation, that we do not flourish or even know ourselves in isolation. God himself lives in relationship. The Trinity is being-in-relation. The Father, Son and Spirit know themselves in relation to each other and in the reflection of themselves in each others' knowledge of them. They have their identity in relation to one another. Their perfect unity precludes an independent (in the sense of 'cut off' or 'set apart') knowledge. So we, who have been made persons, made in the image of our Maker, are taught the lesson of human unity: the unities of family, group and society. We need each other at the deepest levels of our existence and our call is to serve each other in love and faithfulness.

b. *Our understanding of marriage*

Wayne Grudem writes:

> Because God himself has both unity and diversity, it is not surprising that unity and diversity are also reflected in the human relationships he has established. We see this first in marriage. When God created man in his own image, he did not create merely isolated individuals but Scripture tells us, 'male and female he created them' (Gen. 1:27). And in the unity of marriage (see Gen. 2:24) we see, not a tri-unity as with God, but at least a remarkable unity of two persons, persons who remain distinct individuals yet also become one in body, mind and spirit (cf. 1 Cor. 6:16–20; Eph. 5:31).[43]

c. *Our understanding of human society*

Even outside of the unique forms of diversity in unity in marriage and the churches, we neither live to ourselves, nor love to ourselves,

---

[43] Grudem, op. cit., pp. 256–257.

nor sin to ourselves; our interconnectedness is a necessary part of human life and society. Humanity in its widest relationships and its common interdependence and in its mutual obligations mirrors faintly the nature of its creator who is Three in One.

There is a message for human society at large in this truth about God. We need others in order to know who we are and it is from others that we receive our value. When we become a law unto ourselves, when we boast our self-sufficiency and give ourselves up to a gross and swollen individualism, when we become self-determining, making up our own ethic and standards, careless of what others think of us or expect from us, then it is that we begin to lose ourselves. We do not grow, we shrink; we do not become stronger, only more fragile, and we weaken the society of which we form a part. Colin Gunton observes: 'The logically irreducible concept of the person as one whose uniqueness and particularity derive from relations to others ... continues to be desperately needed in our fragmented and alienated society.'[44]

It is by others we know ourselves and by us that others know themselves. From our mothers' arms to the nurses' care in our dying hours we recognize our specialness and worth as human beings; from our central place in marriage and family we learn more of our uniqueness and our duty; from our place in work and society at large we learn our significance in the wider world which needs our skills and shows our calling.

When society fails to do this, by bad work practices or loss of community, when marriages and parenthood are deficient in love and its generous self-expression and self-giving, and when our old, sick, handicapped, poor or disadvantaged are ignored and unhelped, then the life of the triune God is not reflected in our humanity as it should be; then personhood itself is wounded and reduced. Where recognition of others, where kindness, gratitude and care are lacking, the person who has left these behind, however successful in other respects, has shrunk not grown in terms of their true personhood. They are diminished, not greatened, in their self-sufficiency; for in neglecting others they fail to receive from others – and what they refuse to receive from others only those others can give.

[44] Gunton (1997), pp. 95–96.

Romans 11:33–36
20. The sovereignty of God

In chapter 5 we considered the providence of God as his sustaining power, keeping our world in being, making human history possible, guaranteeing a future in spite of our past. Here we consider the providence of God as his rule, his government, his ordering of events toward a final victory of good over evil, grace over sin, salvation over our universal fall and condemnation. God's providence involves his wisdom, power and love, sovereignly at work in the world at large, in all its events, good and bad, and in all its people, saved and lost.

But what can we say of the providence of God in a world of global catastrophes? Who dares speak of the sovereignty of God after a century that has seen two world wars, scores of millions killed in their youth and their prime, the Jewish Holocaust and the genocides of more recent years? Haven't these things blown to bits both the traditional Christian teaching and, for that matter, the naïve optimism of the nineteenth century with its Enlightenment view of human progress and 'paradise around the corner'?

The harsh realities of life, especially when they are on the scale of events we see today, do indeed make mincemeat of selective, sentimental and ideological philosophies of life, whether they are religious, political or social. Neither a naïve humanism nor an unbiblical 'faith' can stand before the rigorous inquisition of blasted hopes, failed civilizations, and deeply flawed humanity. On what basis then can we speak of God's presence in human affairs and his government in human history, what has traditionally been called his providence and sovereignty? My own reply would be: on a biblical basis and with biblical realism, and, at the end of the day, with the humble confession that trusts where it cannot track the ways of God in the world of the fall.

1. The suffering and triumph of God

The biblical doctrine of providence is not the doctrine of a genial benevolence but the doctrine of a tenacious commitment. It is the doctrine of a God who bears as well as blesses, who groans as well as gives, who grits his teeth as he 'sends rain on the righteous and the unrighteous'[1] and who does so precisely because it is his provision which is being abused, his power which is being warped to manipulate and disfigure lives, his laws which are being used to spread death and destruction in the world he made and still sustains in all its parts. There is a cost to God, greater than we can ever imagine, in his providential government of the world he sustains. It is about suffering as well as sovereignty.

We do indeed have to be careful here and to make necessary distinctions. If God is to understand us and identify with us he must enter into our pain and sufferings. But if God is to help us, he has to be more than the God who suffers, he has to be the God who saves; and to be the Saviour God amid so many contradictory forces, he has also to be the Sovereign God. In classical theology God was said to be 'without body, parts or passions'.[2] The doctrine of the 'impassibility' [beyond suffering] of God was not meant to leave him cold and unfeeling toward us, though it could easily be confused with ancient Greek ideas which are far from biblical (as a reading of Hosea shows in the Old Testament and all the Gospels show in the New). The concern of the old Christian theologians was to show that God is not the temperamental god of old paganism and that there is an immovable stability and a depth of blessedness which is essential to God's being and necessary to our well-being.

There has been much stress on 'the suffering God' in modern theology since the horrors of the Holocaust, some of it going beyond the boundaries of classical theology. Gerald Bray attempts to correct a modern reaction to this and insists that 'The essential point which has to be remembered in this argument is the familiar one, that this attribute [God's impassibility] ... belongs to God's essence.' He goes on to write helpfully:

> The *persons* of the Trinity are indeed moved by our suffering, but ... God's essence is untouched by it. If this appears to be heartless and cruel, we need only look to the analogy of the doctor and his patients ... a hospital patient would not be greatly comforted by a doctor who got into the next bed and assured him that he understood the patient's sufferings because he had the same

---

[1] Matt. 5:45.
[2] The Westminster Confession of Faith (1647), ch. 2, and Bray, p. 98.

disease himself; the patient wants someone who understands but who can also heal. Over-identification does not help in this; it only destroys the healer's credibility.[3]

We need to hold together both the suffering and the sovereignty of God if we are to be true to Scripture and helpful to a world in desperate need of hope.

Yet providence is about something more than either a fruitless suffering or a bare sovereignty. It is supremely about salvation. The chief testimony of Scripture is that God's providence is fundamentally soteriological: that is, relating to salvation. His sovereign plan and government is 'motored' by his desire for the salvation of men and women and the redemption of the world. As D. M. Lloyd-Jones writes of *The Providence of God* by G. C. Berkouwer: 'The principle which is emphasised throughout is that there is an indissoluble link between Providence and soteriology, and that Providence must never be considered apart from this grand purpose and object of salvation.'[4] God's sovereignty in providence and grace is an absolute prerequisite to the triumph of his purposes and the certainties of salvation.

If ever sin is to be conquered, Satan defeated and the world brought into what Paul calls the 'freedom of the children of God',[5] then it will be by the involvement, not the abdication of God. He is *involved*, and in that inevitable proximity to human sin he suffers. For it is the very seamlessness and universality of God's providential sustaining, directing and overruling of all human life in all its activity which is the stabilty of our existence and the agony of his commitment to that existence. God suffers with the oppressed and suffers the more because it is his ongoing power which holds the tyrant in being. God could reduce the dictator to nonexistence in a moment, but one life touches others in a million unseen connections and God is committed to the creation as an interconnected whole where easy instant reversals are not an option. In such matters God is both sovereign and victim. Yet it is always God as Sovereign Lord who is victim: the one who chooses to suffer, the one who knows 'the end of a thing from the beginning', the one who is himself Alpha and Omega and who is the ever-blessed God, rejoicing at the very centre of his being as he contemplates an endless time when 'there will be no more death or mourning or crying or pain, for the old order of things has passed away', a time when he will dwell with men having made everything new.

[3] Bray, p. 250.
[4] From D. M. Lloyd-Jones' review of *The Providence of God* in *Evangelical Quarterly*, April 1953, vol. 25, no. 2.
[5] Rom. 8:21.

In the meantime, God's providence is not a 'pretty' doctrine nor is it genial and effortless. It is light and darkness, sunshine and storm, desolation and hope. It is God, the best of beings in the worst of situations: sustaining and suffering, directing and redeeming, staying in and pressing on, taking our fallen, corrupt and wicked history on to the day of his coming when every tear will be dried and every bad memory dissolved in a present of unending joy. We cannot know as much about the middle of human history as we do about its beginning and its end, but we can plot our course in faith and hope with these two reference points.

Perhaps the most famous biblical and comprehensive definition of the doctrine of God's providence is given in the Confession of Faith of the Westminster divines:

> God, the great Creator of all things, doth uphold, direct, dispose, and govern all creatures, actions, and things, from the greatest even to the least, by his most wise and holy providence, according to his infallible foreknowledge, and the free and immutable counsel of his own will, to the praise of the glory of his wisdom, power, justice, goodness, and mercy.[6]

From where did these seventeenth-century divines get the material for such a confident and comprehensive statement of the doctrine? There is only one answer to that: they were consciously summarizing a biblical truth, a truth taught in narrative and proposition, a truth taught in explicit statement and implied in personal history, a truth that strengthened Israel's faith and made her confident about the future, a truth that lies at the heart of the New Testament too.

2. The universal government of God

We see this celebrated as the faith of Israel throughout the book of Psalms where the kingship and providence of God are everywhere rehearsed as Israel's glory and the sinner's comfort. The tribal and national gods of the ancient world were thought by their devotees to have their specific territories and their spheres of operation, their areas of strength and their limits of authority and power. Yahweh, in entire contradistinction, is King over all the earth,[7] in judgment,[8] and in mercy.[9] He is the King of infinite wisdom and unbounded power[10] whose rule enfolds the entirety of creation from its begin-

---

[6] The Westminster Confession of Faith (1647), ch. 5.   [7] Pss. 50; 113; 135.
[8] Pss. 9; 46; 68; 79.   [9] Pss. 47; 66; 86; 96.   [10] Pss. 104; 147; 148.

ning[11] and for ever.[12] There is nowhere his writ does not run. The nations are called to rejoice in his bounty, his own people most of all.[13] His care for his people and his rule over their lives is personal[14] as well as national.[15] In the world as it is, that rule is often hidden, his presence often elusive and his wisdom mysterious and this leads to crises of faith in his people.[16] Yet his love is trustworthy and sure and again and again psalms which begin in desperation and crisis end in comfort and trust.[17] Such trust is not a mere whistling in the dark but is based on Yahweh's self-revelation in the history of Israel,[18] and the status of the psalmist as one of his own people.

We see God's providential government of the world, even in its fallenness, in the history of Joseph. Here we have God working for good even as the brothers work for evil. Joseph could say to his frightened and guilty brothers: 'And now, do not be distressed and do not be angry with yourselves for selling me here, because it was to save lives that God sent me ahead of you ... to preserve for you a remnant on earth and to save your lives by a great deliverance. So then, it was not you who sent me here, but God.'[19]

God was at work in all the twisting fortunes of Joseph: the envy of the brothers, the malice of Potiphar's wife, the dreams of Pharaoh's chief baker and chief cup-bearer, the forgetfulness of the cup-bearer, the dream of Pharaoh and the famines in Egypt and Canaan. Here we see God's hand in history as well as over it, an interweaving of the divine with the human: God working sinlessly even as men and women work sinfully; God working sovereignly even as men and women work responsibly and as those who are accountable for their decisions; God working for good even while others are working for evil and, most mysteriously, God's working *before* as well as behind their working.

We also see God's providential government at work in the later narratives of the Old Testament. He says of Pharaoh in Moses' time, 'I have raised you up for this very purpose, that I might show you my power and that my name might be proclaimed in all the earth.'[20] He speaks of the world-power of Assyria as being both used and judged by himself: 'Woe to the Assyrian, the rod of my anger, in whose hand is the club of my wrath.'[21] A hundred years later he will speak of the leader of another world power in even more striking terms: 'This is what the LORD says to his anointed, to Cyrus, whose right hand I take hold of to subdue nations before him and to strip kings of their armour.'[22]

[11] Ps. 90.
[12] Ps. 102.　　[13] Pss. 66; 67; 145; 146.　　[14] Pss. 1; 18; 23; 34; 139.
[15] Pss. 77; 78; 105; 106; 107.　　[16] Pss. 31; 73; 74.　　[17] Pss. 42; 43; 56; 69.
[18] Pss. 77; 78; 105; 106; 107.　　[19] Gen. 45:5–8.　　[20] Exod. 9:16; cf. Rom. 9:17.
[21] Is. 10:5.　　[22] Is. 45:1.

The book of Esther, whose setting is Susa, the diplomatic and administrative capital of the Persian kings, is striking in that the name of God is not mentioned once. Yet the hidden activity of God is everywhere indicated. Under the threat of an Old Testament holocaust, Mordecai the Jew says to his niece Esther, who has become the wife of the king, 'For if you remain silent at this time, relief and deliverance for the Jews will arise from another place ... And who knows but that you have come to royal position for such a time as this?'[23] The absence of the name of God is surely deliberate. The anonymity of Israel's God may be the writer's way of comforting and encouraging his readers. We live in a world where God often seems to be absent and where unworthy people or downright evil forces seem to have the upper hand. But the Esther story tells us that God is at work in that same world: furthering his plan and fulfilling his purposes despite all contempt and contradiction.

The opening of the book of Job, too, is uncompromising in its statement that Satan himself can act only by permission, that God's sovereign providence is not redundant in our times of suffering and that when nothing else makes sense, unfailing trust in an unfailing God has its own sense and is justified in the end.[24]

3. Sovereignty and Jesus

The greatest, clearest and also most mysterious instance of God's sovereign providence at work is given in the New Testament perspective on the crucifixion of Jesus Christ. The apostle Peter brings together the sovereign foreordination of God and the culpable responsibility of man when he preaches his sermon on the day of Pentecost: 'This man was handed over to you by God's set purpose and foreknowledge; and you, with the help of wicked men, put him to death by nailing him to the cross.'[25]

Similarly, the believers praying together in Acts 4 and giving thanks for God's sovereignty over their danger and Peter's deliverance from the Jerusalem authorities say: 'Indeed Herod and Pontius Pilate met together with the Gentiles and the people of Israel in this city to conspire against your holy servant Jesus, whom you anointed. They did what your power and will had decided beforehand should happen.'[26]

Jesus' own devotional life is shot through with an awareness of his destiny in the plan of God and the certainty of its fulfilment in accordance with the Old Testament prophecies.[27] He lived his life under the 'must' of prophecy. The apostle Paul shows the same

---

[23] Est. 4:14.   [24] Job 1:12, 20–21; 42:8–10.   [25] Acts 2:23.   [26] Acts 4:27–28.
[27] Mark 8:31; 9:12; Luke 22:37; 24:25–26; John 9:4; 12:27–28.

awareness when he writes of the death of Christ, 'God presented him as a sacrifice of atonement ... He did this ... He did it.'[28] When he speaks of God as the one who 'did not spare his own Son, but *gave him up* for us all',[29] he uses the same Greek verb *paradidōmi* that is used in a number of places in the Gospels: when Judas 'delivered up' Jesus;[30] when the chief priests and elders 'handed him over' to Pilate;[31] when the people of Israel in their corporate identity 'handed him over' to be killed;[32] and when Pilate 'handed him over' to be crucified.[33] In each case the same verb is used. A nineteenth-century writer, Octavius Winslow, summed up the force of this: 'Who delivered up Jesus to die? Not Judas for money; not Pilate for fear; not the Jews for envy; – but the Father for love!'[34]

Here, pre-eminently, we have what G. C. Berkouwer describes as 'the interlacing of divine and human activity'. He continues: 'God acts *in* men's acts: in Pilate's sentence, in Judas' betrayal, yes, in everything that men do with Christ. God's activity embraces all these and leads them along His mysterious way.' Yet, 'The New Testament sees human actions as being nonetheless fully responsible. Christ was nailed to the cross by unrighteous, responsible men.'[35] Here are two agencies involved in the same event, but they are not comparable; each acts according to their own being and nature and character; God acts in his Godness and human beings act in humanness. God is at work for good,[36] even in a situation where men are at work for evil. Where man acts sinfully, God acts sinlessly. Where man acts in huge abuse of his powers; God acts in undiminished exercise of his own.

We cannot resolve the problem but we can state both parts of the truth; and we can do so as those to whom God is not a dark and unknown mystery, a Fate, but 'our Father in heaven'. It is in the recognition that he who acts is the just and good God, our holy Father, that we find our comfort and safety in contemplating these things. Berkouwer writes:

In all this we can observe the overruling power of God. He is the Holy One, the Incomparable who fulfills His purposes in the actions of the sinners of all generations. To place God and man in one line as comparable powers is to fail to understand this activity of God. He who listens to the preaching of Scripture knows that God works thus for good. God is no blind force or foreign 'will' who plays His incomprehensible game to confound us. He who

[28] Rom. 3:25–26.   [29] Rom. 8:32.   [30] John 18:5.   [31] Matt. 27:2.
[32] Acts 3:13.   [33] Mark 15:15.
[34] Octavius Winslow, *No Condemnation in Christ Jesus* (London, 1857), p. 358, quoted in J. Murray, p. 324.
[35] Berkouwer, pp. 95, 96.   [36] Cf. Rom. 8:28.

does these things is the God of salvation, the God of Abraham, Isaac, and Jacob. And who has withstood His will? God does not give the initiative for His work over to the Devil, though He allows sinners to serve Him. In the light of revelation, God's own initiative is disclosed in its invincibility, mysteriously disclosed even in the acts of His enemies.[37]

4. Sovereignty and history

a. Israel and the Gentiles

The apostle Paul recognizes the sovereignty of God at work throughout Israel's history. He writes in Romans 9–11 of God's choice of Israel as the favoured people of God and within that the choice of Jacob over against Esau. He recalls from the biblical narrative God's determination to harden Pharaoh's heart and deduces a broader principle: 'Therefore God has mercy on whom he wants to have mercy, and he hardens whom he wants to harden.'[38] This principle he brings to bear on Israel's rejection, as a nation, of Jesus Christ, but always with the background of God's wider purposes of mercy for the Gentiles[39] and his ultimate plan to re-include Israel into the household of faith.[40] It is the sight of this ultimate goal and, even more, of the character of God who has ordained it, which is decisive for Paul over any tendency to mute the revelation of God's sovereign providence:

Again I ask, Did they [Israel] stumble so as to fall beyond recovery? Not at all! Rather, because of their transgression, salvation has come to the Gentiles to make Israel envious. But if their transgression means riches for the world, and their loss means riches for the Gentiles, how much greater riches will their fulness bring ... I do not want you to be ignorant of this mystery, brothers, so that you may not be conceited: Israel has experienced a hardening in part until the full number of the Gentiles has come in. And so all Israel will be saved ... As far as the gospel is concerned, they are enemies on your account; but as far as election is concerned, they are loved on account of the patriarchs, for God's gifts and his call are irrevocable ...

> Oh, the depth of the riches of the wisdom
> and knowledge of God!
> How unsearchable his judgments,
> and his paths beyond tracing out![41]

[37] Berkouwer, p. 97.   [38] Rom. 9:18; cf. 9:14–24.
[39] Rom. 9:25–33; cf. 10:6–21.   [40] Rom. 11:7–32.
[41] Rom. 11:11–12, 25–26, 28–29, 33.

G. C. Berkouwer comments:

And when Paul ends his discussion with: 'O the depth of the riches . . .' he is not moved by an inscrutable, arbitrary force that puts the finger over one's lips. It is the fulness of God's love and wisdom that inspires Paul to exultation. It is said that there are accents in Paul which the Church has hesitated to assume. Where the Church has thus hesitated she has impoverished herself and blurred her outlook on God's activity. Hesitation where Paul was bold has caused the Church often to make only a problem of God's rule and man's responsibility. She thus undermines either the providence of God or human responsibility. They do not exist together in the scriptures as something problematic. They both reveal the greatness of Divine activity, in that it does not exclude human activity and responsibility but embraces them and in them manifests God on the way to the accomplishment of His purposes.[42]

b. All human history

It is one thing to affirm that God is working in all human history, but it is another thing to tell how and where God is working. The intrinsic danger in such attempts is that they can give the impression that God is at work only in some events or in one kind of event and not in others. The testimony of the Scriptures is that there is nowhere in the world where God's writ does not run, there is no event where he is locked out, no process of thought and act where he is helpless. God is not at work in some things in history but in all of history: in all its events, processes, agents and actors. He is at work sinlessly but nonetheless sovereignly: in advance and setback, war and peace, in the rise and fall of empires, in the powerful and in the powerless, in all things both good and bad.[43] The decisive thing, however, is that it is God acting always in his own character: the one who is holy and just, wise and good but whose justice can be terrible and whose goodness has long been abused in our world and whose wisdom is beyond our partial assessments.

It is true that there are salutary laws of cause and effect, decisions and their consequences at work in the history of individuals, families and nations. Here too we reap what we sow, as a race, as a society and as individuals. However, Scripture does not give countenance to an amoral and atheistic view of history as impersonal, inevitable, historical processes, and as Christian believers we confess God's providence to be at work in history. Nevertheless, it is *fallen* history and God's work is in various ways hidden, provisional and

---

[42] Berkouwer, p. 98.   [43] See Is. 45:5–7; Amos 3:6–8; Rev. 8 – 11; 15 – 16.

related to that fallenness. We live between the 'already' and the 'not yet' of his kingdom. That kingdom is both present and future: present in the world but not yet filling up the world, present in principle and activity but not yet reigning undisputed in the world. Hence the church which celebrates the coming of the King also prays: 'Your kingdom come.'

c. Interpreting history

Still the question recurs: Can we see God's ways in history, especially his hand in certain events, in such a way that we can deduce his favour or his anger? The Old Testament prophets did so of course. However, they were not offering an opinion but giving voice to an inspiration.[44] But we ourselves must be very cautious here. Jesus warned against what seemed to be the obvious interpretation of events when recalling Pilate's massacre of the Galileans and the deaths of others when the tower of Siloam fell on them.[45] Such rash interpretations of history can be as cruel as they can be crass, as with the attitude of the disciples to the man born blind.[46] The difficulty of 'reading' events in terms of God's providential judgment or blessing is that the same event can be differently 'read' by different people – including Christians!

For instance, when Rome, the great centre of Western civilization, was sacked by the Visigoths certain pagan Romans attributed the event to the wrath of the ancient gods and the adoption of Christianity as the official religion of the empire. Augustine, Bishop of Hippo in North Africa, saw it as the inevitable outcome of paganism's moral impotence. Silvianus the monk interpreted it shortly afterwards as God's judgment, not on the pagans, but on the low standards of contemporary Christians. One event – three readings of it!

There is not only difficulty but also real danger when events in history are isolated from revelation in Scripture and used, as they have been, to draw self-serving and ambitious conclusions about God's favour. A particular event can be given revelatory status quite independent of Scripture:

> The so-called 'German Christians' saw the special finger of God in Hitler's rise to power in 1933. The Church, it was said, could not without fault fail to recognise this providential sign. A fragment of history was in effect canonised as a new revelation. God's Providence, they claimed, was here setting Germany, after years of sorrow and misunderstanding, again on the way of blessing and greatness. In the background was Hitler's continual call upon

---

[44] 2 Pet. 1:20–21.   [45] Luke 13:1–5.   [46] John 9:2.

'Providence', leading to the all too popular conviction that his was a 'word of redemption'.[47]

Karl Barth, like others, openly protested against such an interpretation of history. He wrote: 'The freedom of the gospel is dependent on this, that there is no other source for the church's proclamation: no book of fate, of history, of nature, of experience, of reason, nor the currently so zealously quoted book of "the hour of destiny".'[48] A few years later, in Soviet Russia, Patriarch Sergius of the Russian Orthodox Church spoke of Stalin as 'the divinely appointed leader of our armed and cultural forces, leading us to victory'.[49] Such use of providence can be used to justify and strengthen any politics, religion or ideology, as we see in the resurgent nationalism and tribalism and civilizational identities of our own day where true Christianity falls victim to both 'Christian' and non-Christian patriotisms and other loyalties. We may even beware of the danger, nearer home, of placing the flag on a level with the cross.

This does not mean that there can be no gratitude for providential safety and deliverances of which our lives are often fuller than we realize.[50] Nor does it mean there can be no such gratitude on the part of nations. But it does mean that an event cannot be construed as indicating the favour of God apart from ongoing faith and obedience. God's mercy is not the same as his favour. Berkouwer writes wisely:

> If the faith of a people is real, and the Church more than a fallen power, the thankfulness for prosperity is more than a selfish interpretation of Providence. There *can* be a meaningful 'Thou hast set us free'. There can also be a jubilation that construes God's favour from a neutral fact, apart from faith and apart from 'the service of the Lord'. The success of the Normandy invasion in 1944, in and by itself, does not prove a special favourable disposition in God toward the West European people any more than the liberation of Stalingrad, in and by itself, proves a special favourable disposition in God toward the Russian people. The Providence of God included West and East, but everything depends, for both, on how the facts are understood. In the absence of true faith, liberation can be turned against a people, as Israel's resting its case for unexpected blessings on the mere fact of the Exodus was turned against her. God's way with the world cannot be summarised with charts or statistics. Each of his acts and each

[47] Berkouwer, p. 162.   [48] Quoted in ibid., p. 163.   [49] Quoted in ibid., p. 164.
[50] E.g. Ps. 91.

of his gifts is charged with a new summons to obedience and new reminders of responsibility.[51]

5. The problem of evil

The problem of evil is undoubtedly recognized in Scripture at many levels. Historians and prophets struggle with it, psalmists agonize over it and the New Testament writers confront it in unique ways in the light of the cross. Always, however, the problem is set against the background of God's unalloyed goodness and his final self-assertion over against evil in the last judgment and the renewal of the earth.

This is why evil is a problem but not a pre-occupation in the Bible. There is no dualism in Scripture which makes evil an eternal fact or sees God as having a dark side as well as a light. The problem of evil is not peripheral but neither is it central; it is regarded with intense seriousness but always approached as from the presence of the Sovereign Lord who is holy, just and good. Always it is God who is central. Evil is not ultimate, inevitable or final. The first and last word is with God.

When this is not the case, then there arise all the unhealthy and despairing forms of preoccupation with 'the problem of evil'. Some of these are found in the context of a high ethic and a profound, if ultimately hopeless, concern; as in early Buddhism, which begins with the problem of suffering in the world and ends in the 'freedom' of unconsciousness. In others, however, the 'problem of evil' eclipses the even greater problem of sin and the concern with it masks the more immediate challenge to repent and obey the gospel of salvation from sin and death in Jesus Christ. It can even be made the justification of sin, as if evil were as natural as good and the survival of the strongest and the most ruthless were a part of the inevitability of things.

The Bible never allows us to consider the problem of evil apart from the problem of sin – and our own status as sinners. The first chapters of Genesis explain why, as a race created for better things, we fell prey to the forces of sin and death, change and decay, natural and man-made disasters in a damaged and unfulfilled world.

The book of Ecclesiastes faces the facts of futility and frustration, unfairness and even meaninglessness which now run through human life like ripples in marble.[52] Ecclesiastes exposes the fallenness of the world with unsparing honesty and frequent irony and prescribes accordingly. But it also tells its readers not to be so preoccupied with the problems of life that it misses life's real good: its joy and laughter, its sweetness and gifts.[53] Above all, and at the end of life, it sets

---

[51] Berkouwer, p. 179.   [52] Eccles. 1:1–2; 2:12–16.   [53] Eccles. 3:12–13; 9:7–10.

before us *God* who is to be feared (honoured) and obeyed whatever the gains and losses of life; God who stands at the limits of life with the promise of something more and something better.[54]

The prophets too, like Habakkuk, have their unanswered questions: 'Why then do you tolerate the treacherous? Why are you silent while the wicked swallow up those more righteous than themselves?'[55] Yet Habakkuk's starting point in all his anguish is not the fact of evil but the fact of God, his existence and his character.[56] It is because of this primary truth of God that Habakkuk can wait for an answer to his questions.[57] It is because of this that he can journey on to God's future for humankind,[58] meeting the distresses of the present with the joy of the future.[59]

The mystery remains, for Habakkuk and for us, as to *how* God can use evil to achieve his purposes without himself doing evil or approving evil or excusing the evil that sinful human beings and demons do.[60] Yet Scripture is clear in its testimony that nothing comes to pass apart from the plan of God, from the best act in the world[61] to the worst;[62] all falls within his plan and under his sovereign control.[63] This is because God is God and in order that the triumph of good over evil might be guaranteed. Wayne Gruden writes:

> There are literally dozens of Scripture passages that say God (indirectly) brought about some kind of evil . . . Christians are often unaware of the extent of this forthright teaching in Scripture. Yet it must be remembered that in all of these examples, the evil is actually done not by God but by people or demons who choose to do it.[64]

Many examples follow. We read repeatedly, 'the LORD hardened Pharaoh's heart',[65] as he does many others[66] as a punishment for sin. We read that in Saul's later life an evil spirit 'from the LORD' tormented him[67] and in David's later life that the anger of Yahweh incited him to count the people, the writer short-circuiting Satan's part in it.[68] Job looked beyond secondary causes and said, 'The LORD gave and the LORD has taken away; may the name of the LORD be praised.'[69] Yet in all that happened, Job did not charge God with

---

[54] Eccles. 12:1, 13–14.   [55] Hab. 1:13.   [56] Hab. 1:12–13.   [57] Hab. 2:1.
[58] Hab. 2:14.   [59] Hab. 3:17–18.   [60] Jas. 1:13–15.   [61] John 15:13.
[62] Luke 23:33.   [63] Eph. 1:11.
[64] Wayne Grudem, *Systematic Theology: An introduction to biblical doctrine* (IVP/ Zondervan, 1994), p. 323.
[65] E.g. Exod. 4:21; 7:3; 10:20.   [66] Rom. 9:17–18.
[67] 1 Sam. 16:14; cf. 16:15–16, 23.   [68] 2 Sam. 24:1.   [69] Job 1:21.

wrong.[70] It was Yahweh who 'put a lying spirit in the mouths' of Ahab's false prophets[71] as a judgment on court and people. Then in the New Testament the apostle Paul warns that those who 'refuse to love the truth' will have no excuse or defence when God 'sends them a powerful delusion so that they will believe the lie'.[72] God's greatest judgment on earth is to punish sin with sin, to 'give them over' to greater and greater corruption with its corollary of greater and greater judgment to come.[73]

Always God is in ultimate control, always God is sovereign; evil cannot keep him off the ground that it has scorched. The cost to God of the triumph of his sovereignty in grace is the exercise of his sovereignty even where grace is refused and opposed. It involves too the pain of interim decisions: the burning of his heart and the staying of his hand when people suffer, including his own people. It is through much tribulation that we must enter the kingdom of God[74] and to this day the church which he bought with the blood of his Son sheds its own blood for the testimony of that same Jesus.[75] God is our deliverer but he is not a good-luck charm; he gives us protection,[76] but not immunity; hope in trouble, but not freedom from trouble.[77]

Every thoughtful Christian must feel the difficulties associated with this area of revealed truth, and the temptation is to 'soft pedal' the doctrine of the divine sovereignty over all human affairs and over all the details of life. But what if it were otherwise? Would we feel better, safer, more in control if God had withdrawn from the chaos of evil, leaving history to blind forces? Then indeed we should despair, falling victims daily in areas where God was not in any control. More than that, a universe where God was not in moment-by-moment control would cease to exist. There would be no human story, no history, no grand redemption, for God's sustenance of all things and his government of all things go together. The sovereignty of God is the condition of all created existence, present and future.

6. Sovereignty and free will

Do we then have free will? Much depends on how we define our freedom. Too often our theoretical definitions are not true to life. If by free will we mean a position of complete neutrality then we are being untrue to reality. Other facts have to be recognized. Many things combine to affect our choices and limit our options, to shape us psychologically and to limit us circumstantially and even to weaken us morally and spiritually. We 'choose', but it is usually in

[70] Job 1:22.   [71] 1 Kgs. 22:23.   [72] 2 Thess. 2:10–11.   [73] Rom. 1:24, 26, 28.
[74] Acts 14:22, AV.   [75] Acts 20:28; Rev. 1:9; 6:9; 12:11.   [76] Ps. 91.   [77] Ps. 42.

accordance with our mood or cast of thought or perceived goals and in accordance with the prevailing bent or inclination of our nature. Martin Luther wrote a famous book entitled *The Bondage of the Will*, to promote not a philosophical determinism but a biblical understanding of the seriousness of sin and the need of a God-centred understanding of salvation. We are not neutral and God is not idle.

a. The bias away from God

We may choose abstractly in our thoughts and intentions, but the way our choice works out (and what we really choose to do or not do) tends to be brought down to earth by these things. Think of New Year resolutions as an example, or giving up smoking, or alcohol, or deciding to be, in everything, others-centred instead of self-centred! The serious matters of sin and our fallen nature are involved here and they affect not only how we treat each other but most important of all how we treat God. The old theologians wrote about the bias of the rebellious human will away from God (rather like the bias of the 'wood' in the game of bowls). We might speak of an allergy against God deep in our fallen nature (as long as we do not think of sin as merely a disease!), as well as a powerful bent to selfishness and other sins. It is this anti-God[78] and pro-sin[79] inclination that drastically reduces and even redefines our 'freedom'. We are free to be ourselves – but so often our cry is to be delivered from our selves.[80] Our will is not a sovereign faculty, existing apart and above the rest of our nature; it is affected by that nature and so weakened and misdirected by the force of our own sinfulness. Walter Chantry illustrates the predicament vividly:

> In modern times we observe rockets fired so that they escape from earth's gravity. To accomplish this there is a great complex of electrical wires, all woven into one control centre, called in the U.S., 'Mission Control'. According to the Bible, the heart is the Mission Control of a man's life. The heart is the motivational complex of a man, the basic disposition, the entire bent of character, the moral inclination. The mind, emotions, desires and will are all wires which we observe; none is independent, but all are welded into a common circuit. If mission control is wired for evil, the will cannot make the rockets of life travel on the path of righteousness ... 'Will' may be the button which launches the spacecraft. But the launching button does not determine the direction ... Your will cannot choose without consulting your intel-

[78] Rom. 8:7.
[79] Jer. 17:9. [80] Rom. 7:24.

ligence, reflecting your feelings and taking account of your desires. You are free to be yourself. The will cannot transform you into someone else ... Here is the tragic truth about man's will. While free from outward coercion, it is in a state of bondage.[81]

The predestination of God is not the contradiction of our freedom but the true context of it. We are not more free as we depart from God, but less. We find our freedom in obedience to his revealed will.

b. First and second causes

In speaking of the way our world works we usually attribute action directly to second causes. Biblical teaching does not deny the place or integrity of second causes in the working of the world but it does look beyond them to the supreme cause which is God. We say the clouds brought rain, the ancient Israelite said God sent rain. Both perspectives are right. Second causes do not have an existence *independent* of God, for he holds them in being and the laws by which they operate. They do not fall outside of his power or beyond his concern. Yet they have their own integrity within the created order so that they operate according to their own nature and laws. At the summit of the created order in our world are human beings uniquely made in the image of God, uniquely gifted, and uniquely endowed with the power to make rational and free moral decisions. To say 'human being' is to say this. Wayne Grudem writes:

> God's providential direction as an unseen, behind-the-scenes, 'primary cause' should not lead us to deny the reality of our choices and actions. Again and again Scripture affirms that we really do *cause* events to happen. We are significant and we are responsible. We *do have choices* and these are real choices that bring real results. Scripture repeatedly affirms these truths as well. Just as a rock is *really hard* because God has made it with the property of hardness, just as water is *really wet* because God has made it with the property of wetness, just as plants are *really alive* because God has made them with the property of life, so our choices are *real choices* and do have significant effects, because God has made us in such a wonderful way that he has endowed us with the property of willing choice.[82]

c. Human responsibility

The knowledge of God's sovereignty was never meant to cut the nerve of our responsibility. God acts in our acts but they remain our

[81] Walter Chantry, 'Man's will: free yet bound', *Banner of Truth Magazine*, May 1975, no. 140, pp. 3–10.
[82] Grudem, op. cit., p. 321.

acts still. We make real choices and have real responsibilities. As we read the Bible we must get used to thinking along two lines simultaneously – the line of divine sovereignty, predestination and government and the line of human freedom, decision and responsibility. What is more we must learn to see these in the same event and at the same moment so that we do not think of God as the divine juggler making the best with what we give him, always accommodating himself to our acts with an infinite number of variations, adjustments and achievements, simply coming in to clean up our mess. That would leave everyone with free will except God. He alone would not have the freedom to do as he chooses. Then indeed the roles would be reversed with a vengeance. No, but God acts and we act; he with his properties and we with ours; he with the freedom proper to God and we with the freedom proper to human beings. The eternal mystery of course is how his freedom operates, how he achieves his will without violating ours. But the testimony of God in Scripture is that he does. 'Continue to work out your salvation with fear and trembling, for it is God who works in you to will and to act according to his good purpose,' writes the apostle Paul.[83]

We are bound to see this as contrary in logic, something akin to denying that two physical objects cannot occupy the same space at the same time, if we insist on putting the divine will on a level with our human will or defining it in the same way. But it is God's will we are talking about and that, like his essence, is unfathomable in its full purpose and beyond our comprehension in its way of working.

Calvin laid great stress on the irrefragable sovereignty of God and spoke of the divine will from two aspects: God's revealed will and his hidden will. His revealed will was the ground of all obedience and the supposition of all human responsibility and choice. His hidden will was grounded in his utter sovereignty and was the guarantee of the final victory of God and his plan over all contrary forces.

Not only theologians of the Calvinistic tradition but others too have wanted to do justice to the teaching of Scripture on this point. Howard Marshall writes: 'The basic difficulty is that of attempting to explain the nature of the relationship between an infinite God and finite creatures. Our temptation is to think of divine causation in much the same way as human causation, and this produces difficulties as soon as we try to relate divine causation and human freedom. It is beyond our ability to explain how God can cause us to do certain things.'[84]

[83] Phil. 2:12–13.   [84] Quoted in Grudem, op. cit., p. 322.

d. Revelation and mystery

At the end of all our thinking, we have to recognize two things: revelation and mystery, or, to put in another way, revelation and the limits of revelation – and the limits of our logic too! What is revealed is the fullness of the divine sovereignty and the reality of human responsibility; what is not revealed is how they cohere and the point at which they come together. It may be that this is not explained to us because it is inexplicable in our terms. Or it may be so because we need to know the two truths but not the resolution of our difficulty in reconciling them. Scripture is not so much concerned to satisfy our curiosity as to glorify God and draw us to himself in adoration, trust and grateful obedience. I have always liked the words and shared the attitude of the great nineteenth-century preacher Charles Haddon Spurgeon:

> It is a difficult task to show the meeting-place of the purpose of God and the free agency of man. One thing is quite clear, we ought not to deny either of them, for they are both facts. It is a fact that God has purpose for all things both great and little; neither will anything happen but according to his eternal purpose and decree. It is also a sure and certain fact that oftentimes events hang upon the choice of men. Now how these two things can both be true I cannot tell you ... They are two facts that run side by side, like parallel lines ... Can you not believe them both? And is not the space between them a convenient place to kneel in, adoring and worshipping him whom you cannot understand?[85]

7. Prayer and providence

The biblical doctrine of prayer is not in contradiction of its doctrine of providence but in correspondence with it. Prayer is among God's ordained means to God's ordained ends: he who has purposed to accomplish his will has also purposed to do so through and with the prayers of his people. Even the second coming of Christ will come as heaven's final response to the prayer of millions over the centuries: 'Your kingdom come, your will be done on earth as it is in heaven'; 'Come, Lord Jesus.'[86]

Prayer often seems to us the weakest of all our works and sometimes the most irrelevant. But the power of prayer is, quite simply, the power of the divine response to prayer; it finds its power in the strength of his love, as the power of the baby's cry lies in the devotion of the baby's parent. Its relevance is asserted by God who

[85] C. H. Spurgeon, *The Metropolitan Tabernacle Pulpit*, vol. 39, p. 169.
[86] Matt. 6:10; Rev. 22:17, 20.

tells us to pray.[87] It is part of our partnership with him to persist in prayer as he persists in a world which continually resists his grace. That his grace may conquer in the end in a world of apathy and injustice,[88] our God has chosen to take us into his purposes, to make us integral to his rule and blessing, to call us into partnership with what he is doing in the world. The God who has ordained what he will do has also ordained what prayer will do. There is no contradiction and there should be no apathy; only a searching for the divine wisdom and a submission to the divine will.

Here in a quite special way we bring together theory and practice, and here we are turned from problems to solutions. For in prayer we practise the sovereignty of God and address ourselves to him as responsible moral agents praying to a sovereign God about other responsible moral agents! Indeed, by his command to us that we pray, both for things we know are in his decrees[89] and for things we do not know,[90] God teaches us that the doctrine of his sovereignty in providence and grace is not a paralyzing knowledge but an encouraging one. It stirs us up to pray and fires our prayers, making us confident that if we ask according to his will nothing will prevent the victory of our prayers.[91] Even if our prayers are not valued by those we pray for, our prayers will never be lost, but the answering blessing of God will be redirected upon us[92] or upon others, even in future generations.

---

[87] Matt. 6:5–13.   [88] Luke 11:5–13; 18:1–8.
[89] E.g. Dan. 9:2ff.; cf. Jer. 25:11–12.   [90] Hab. 2:1.   [91] 1 John 5:14–15.
[92] Luke 10:5–6.

Revelation
21. Alpha and Omega:
the worship of the living God

It is generally thought that the book of Revelation was one of the last books of the New Testament to have been written. However, it is not a book of retrospects, for at its centre is the ongoing Christ, Lord of heaven and history, risen, reigning and coming again. It is not a book shot through with nostalgia. It does not look wistfully back at Peter's life or Paul's journeys or John's youth or even Jesus' ministry. It faces the present and the future with the confidence that Jesus Christ has already won the decisive victory at the cross and at the empty tomb, a victory that is good for all time. George Beasley-Murray writes:

> The whole book of Revelation is rooted in its portrayal of God almighty as the Lord of history and his redemptive activity in Christ. So surely as Jesus has accomplished the first and most important stage in the redemption of humanity, so will he complete his appointed task of bringing to victory the kingdom of God and thereby the total emancipation of humanity from the powers of evil.[1]

In the meantime his church must share his suffering, *faithful unto death* (2:10) in the knowledge of her eventual vindication and share in his victory.

1. The big story (1:1–3)

The revelation of Jesus Christ, which God gave him to show his servants what must soon take place. He made it known by sending his angel to his servant John, ²who testifies to everything he saw – that is, the word of God and the testimony of Jesus Christ. ³Blessed is the one who reads the words of this prophecy, and blessed are those who hear it and take to heart what is written in it, because the time is near.

[1] George R. Beasley-Murray, 'Revelation, Book of', *DLNT*, p. 1035.

The word 'revelation' (Gk. *apocalypsis*) means 'unveiling', the revealing of what could not otherwise be known and must remain hidden. The revelation given to John concerns history and eternity. It takes him behind the scenes of human history with its turmoil, wars and changing fortunes and shows him other powers at work, both evil and good, manipulating and restraining, exploiting and protecting. Above all it shows that history is an ordered chaos, that God is still sovereign, even over the world of the fall, and that he has appointed Jesus Christ to take history on to an appointed goal, a timed and final end.

From the beginning, John wants his hearers to know that this is no private dream, no merely personal philosophy. This is not just 'his truth' but God's truth, truth for everyone and for all time. It is indeed the 'big story', the metanarrative behind and alongside all other narratives and no-one can hide from it or opt out of it by hiding in their own self-made 'little story'. This is a drama in which we are all actors; we are born into it and are part of something bigger than ourselves.

This book, says John, is 'the word of God and the testimony of Jesus Christ'. It is to be read in the churches, as the words of a prophecy on a par with the prophecies of the Old Testament. That is why he says, 'Blessed is the one who reads the words of this prophecy, and blessed are those who hear it.' Books (scrolls, really) were not the commonplace things they are today. They were hand-written and precious. As a result, Scriptures were 'heard' more than read, and here the 'one who reads' is the public reader of Scripture in the Christian meetings and 'those who hear' are the congregation.

But they are not merely to be listeners. They are to 'take to heart' a prophecy which encourages, warns and urges them on, even in times of great persecution, pain and loss. This is truth for tough times. It is to affect their lives as well as their opinions. It may make them martyrs but it will also make them 'more than conquerors'[2] in tribulation and final victory.

After the early greetings and doxology of verses 4–6, John proclaims the coming of the once-crucified Christ and the despair of those who have rejected him (v. 7). He hears the voice of God and sees the exalted Christ in divine glory (vv. 8–16). He is given his commission to write what he has seen (and, by implication, what he is about to see) and heard (vv. 17–20). At first this takes the form of a series of letters to the seven churches of Roman Asia, shortly to face fresh persecution for the sake of Christ. Then, in chapter 4, the first vision of heaven is given to him and expressed by him in the highly symbolical, apocalyptic language which characterizes the

[2] Rom. 8:37.

book. If John is to understand earth he must see it from heaven: 'A true insight into history is gained only when we view all things from the vantage point of the heavenly throne.'[3]

2. Worship: the priority of heaven (4:1–8)

After this I looked, and there before me was a door standing open in heaven. And the voice I had first heard speaking to me like a trumpet said, 'Come up here, and I will show you what must take place after this:' [2]*At once I was in the Spirit, and there before me was a throne in heaven with someone sitting on it.* [3]*And the one who sat there had the appearance of jasper and carnelian. A rainbow, resembling an emerald, encircled the throne.* [4]*Surrounding the throne were twenty-four other thrones, and seated on them were twenty-four elders. They were dressed in white and had crowns of gold on their heads.* [5]*From the throne came flashes of lightning, rumblings and peals of thunder. Before the throne, seven lamps were blazing. These are the seven spirits of God.* [6]*Also before the throne there was what looked like a sea of glass, clear as crystal.*

The first thing John sees in heaven is the glory and the worship of God. God sits in majesty on a throne (the symbol of sovereignty). He is surrounded by an angelic order of beings who may be, as R. H. Charles put it, 'the heavenly representatives of the whole body of the faithful',[4] that is, representing the people of God in both Old and New Testament times,[5] or their number may echo the twenty-four courses of priests and Levites who were responsible for the music at the temple service.[6] Their only calling is to worship God unceasingly (the most common use of the number is for the twenty-four hours in a day). Their white robes suggest holiness and their crowns suggest royalty.

The figure on the throne cannot be described directly but only by a series of interweaving references. He has the appearance of light flashing from semi-precious stones, he is surrounded by a rainbow resembling an emerald. The flashes of lightning, rumblings and peals of thunder proceed not from the throne as such but from God, as in the great Sinai appearance.[7] They symbolize his awesome power and majesty. Even the throne is, as Morris notes, 'a reverent way of referring to Him who sat on it'.[8]

Similarly, the 'seven lamps' blazing before the throne are part of the total description of God; they are 'the seven spirits of God' or,

[3] Mounce, p. 133.   [4] Quoted in Morris (1973), p. 88.
[5] Twenty-four is twelve plus twelve, indicating the twelve tribes of Israel and the twelve apostles.
[6] 1 Chr. 24:4; 25:9–31.   [7] Exod. 19:16.   [8] Morris (1973), p. 88.

as we might read it 'the sevenfold Spirit of God'. Seven is the number of completeness or totality, and often recurs in the book. I agree with those writers who think that this is a reference to the Holy Spirit,[9] over against those who see here a reference to angels.[10] In Revelation 1:4–5, 'grace and peace' are said to come from *him who is, and who was, and who is to come, and from the seven spirits before his throne, and from Jesus Christ, who is the faithful witness, the firstborn from the dead, and the ruler of the kings of the earth.* Nowhere are grace and peace said to come from the angels and it is, to my mind, unlikely that they are here sandwiched between references to God and the Son of God.

The symbolic element of the book is soaked in Old Testament allusions and in this section the writer has probably drawn on the vision in Ezekiel 1 in which the throne appears like a sapphire surrounded by a rainbow.[11] Leon Morris, however, sees here a reference to Genesis 9:18 and the covenant God made with Noah: 'The rainbow round the very throne of God then is a way of saying that the covenant is eternal. It will never be repudiated.'[12]

Throughout the Bible light is used in various ways to describe the glory of God. The psalmist speaks of God who 'wraps himself in light as with a garment',[13] and Paul writes of him as 'God, the blessed and only Ruler, the King of kings and Lord of lords, who alone is immortal and who lives in unapproachable light, whom no-one has seen or can see.'[14] The 'sea of glass' before the throne is part of the larger scene and heightens the sense of God's separateness from his creatures.

> [6]*In the centre, around the throne, were four living creatures, and they were covered with eyes, in front and behind.* [7]*The first living creature was like a lion, the second was like an ox, the third had a face like a man, the fourth was like a flying eagle.* [8]*Each of the four living creatures had six wings and was covered with eyes all around, even under his wings.*

The four living creatures around the throne, who are so strangely described in verses 6–8, again echo Ezekiel's vision of God and the cherubim attendant upon him.[15] Mounce writes of them as an exalted order of angelic beings 'who, as the immediate guardians of the throne, lead the heavenly hosts in worship and adoration of God'. He adds, 'It is possible that they also represent the entire animate creation. That they are full of eyes before and behind (cf. v. 8: "round about and within") speaks of alertness and knowledge.

[9] E.g. Morris, Caird and Hendriksen.   [10] E.g. Mounce and Aune.
[11] Ezek. 1:26–28.   [12] Morris (1973), p. 87.   [13] Ps. 104:2.
[14] 1 Tim. 6:15–16.   [15] Ezek. 1:5–14; cf. 10:2, 20.

Nothing escapes their notice.'[16] Morris agrees that they stand in some way for the whole creation and remarks, 'Nature, including Man, is represented before the Throne, taking its part in the fulfilment of the Divine Will, and the worship of the Divine Majesty.'[17] The symbols, 'like a lion . . . like on ox . . . like a man . . . like a flying eagle' may stand for 'everything that is noblest, strongest, wisest, and swiftest in nature'.[18]

a. Holy, holy, holy (4:8)
Day and night they never stop saying:

> *'Holy, holy, holy*
> *is the Lord God Almighty,*
> *who was, and who is, and is to come.*

The living creatures worship God in his holiness, power and eternity. His holiness is his 'difference', which sets him infinitely apart from all created things including the most superior of the angelic orders. His holiness is also his 'separateness' in uttermost purity from everything corrupt and sinful. As in Isaiah 6:3 his holiness is given threefold expression as the central truth of his entire being. His power is honoured in the title Lord God Almighty. Caesar may be mighty but only God is *almighty*. John's readers are to remember that fact in the dark times to come. Evil can be mighty, but it will never be almighty. The final outcome is not in doubt: their God reigns.[19]

God's eternity is proclaimed here in the words 'who was, and is, and is to come'. This phrase has already occurred twice in the book. First in 1:4, where Mounce refers to it as a 'paraphrase of the divine name' which stems from Exodus 3:14–15 'and calls attention to the fact that all time is embraced in God's eternal presence'.[20] The second appearance of this phrase is in 1:8: 'I am the Alpha and the Omega,' says the Lord God, 'who is, and who was, and who is to come, the Almighty.' Mounce notes: 'Alpha and Omega represent the Hebrew *Aleph Tau*, which was regarded not simply as the first and last letters of the alphabet, but as including all the letters in between. Hence, God is the sovereign Lord of all that takes place in the entire course of human history. He is the beginning and he is the end.'[21] The final power is not with evil but with the Holy One, God Almighty and eternal. Here we have the three great truths about God which engaged our attention in our earlier study of Genesis 1.

---

[16] Mounce, p. 138.   [17] Morris (1973), p. 91.
[18] Barclay, vol. 1, p. 200, citing H. B. Swete, *The Apocalypse of John* (Macmillan, 1907), in loc.
[19] Cf. John 16:33.   [20] Mounce, p. 68.   [21] Ibid., p. 73.

In verse 11 God as the Creator God is the object of the worship of these heavenly beings, called the twenty-four elders. 'Here', says Mounce, 'is direct refutation of the dualistic idea that God as spirit would not himself be involved in a material creation.'[22]

[10]*They lay their crowns before the throne and say:*

> [11]*'You are worthy, our Lord and God,*
>   *to receive glory and honour and power,*
> *for you created all things,*
>   *and by your will they were created*
>   *and have their being.'*

They lay their crowns or wreaths at the foot of the throne and in doing so 'acknowledge that their authority is a delegated authority'.[23] In verse 11 we see God's origination and ownership of the creation which is not abandoned or given over to the powers of evil and corruption. Morris writes: 'In view of the troubled state of the little church this is a noteworthy affirmation in the first heavenly vision. God has not abandoned the world, and it is indeed his world. He made all things and made them for his own purpose. John's readers must not think that evil is in control. Evil is real. But the divine purpose still stands.'[24] Creation exists to bring him glory and it does so not only by its existence[25] but by the understanding and admiration of sentient and personal beings – heavenly and earthly.[26]

From this first vision of the heavenly court, we learn the central awareness in true worship.

b. The central awareness in worship

The central awareness in true worship is the centrality of God. In worship we practise most fully the centrality of God. For once it is not the priority of our needs but the priority of God's glory that gets precedence and attention. For once it is not our domestic concerns or our professional problems or the world news which predominate but God. Here we have time and space to think about him, to touch eternal matters for which we were made, to read and hear the word of God which is so often drowned out by everyone else's words. To get God in central and undivided focus is the first concern of worship. It is only as we get God in perspective that we get other things in our life and world into focus and perspective, including our own concerns and self-understanding.

In worship we respond most immediately to the centrality of

---

[22] Ibid., p. 140. [23] Ibid., p. 139. [24] Morris (1973), p. 92.
[25] Pss. 19:1–2; 103:22; 148. [26] Ps. 104.

God: his presence not only everywhere but in our midst; his presence with the awesome priorities of holiness, power and eternal being. In heaven, the beings nearest to God cover their eyes (v. 8)[27] and the twenty-four elders fall down before him (v. 10). These are expressions of reverence and awe among beings which are themselves awesome. They remind us that awe is an essential and proper part of true worship. It is also in danger of becoming the forgotten emotion whenever insufficient thought or teaching is given to the essential character and being of God. We have seen in our study of Leviticus the awesome antipathy of holiness to sin and the consequent need of an atonement if men and women are to survive the presence of God. We see too, in the inauguration of Isaiah, that we never leave behind the need of cleansing, and that God's holiness is, in itself, a threatening power to the best as well as the worst.

The ancient Hebrews may have something to teach the modern Westerner here. They knew the danger of a close encounter with God. Tradition has it that at one period in their history, when the High Priest went into the Most Holy Place on the Day of Atonement, they tied a rope to his ankle. If he was struck dead in the presence of God, his body could be dragged out under the curtain without anyone else going in to the dangerous territory of the Most Holy Place. One writer has remarked, 'If an ancient Hebrew rode the time machine to the front door of a church one Sunday morning, and understood what we were doing, he would not expect us to come out alive!'[28]

This, of course, is only a part of the truth, and we would fall far short of our privileges in the gospel if we stopped here. New-covenant worship is not only awe before the eternal holiness and power of God, but it certainly includes that and if these things are forgotten or devalued, his love will become unsurprising and even commonplace. In his book *The Trivialisation of God*, Donald W. McCullough writes:

> Unaccustomed as we are to mystery, we expect nothing even similar to Abraham's falling on his face, Moses' hiding in terror, Isaiah's crying out 'Woe is me!' or Saul's being knocked flat... The NT warns us 'to offer to God an acceptable worship with reverence and awe, for indeed our God is a consuming fire' (Heb. 12:28–29). But reverence and awe have often been replaced by a yawn of familiarity. The consuming fire has been domesticated into a candle flame, adding a bit of religious atmosphere, perhaps, but no heat, no blinding light, no power for purification ... We

---

[27] Cf. Is. 6:2.
[28] Jamie Wallace, quoted in Paul Beasley-Murray, *Faith and Festivity* (Monarch/ MARC, 1991), p. 23.

prefer the illusion of a safer deity, and so we have pared God down to manageable proportions.[29]

3. Worship: worthy is the Lamb! (5:1–14)

Leon Morris writes:

> Chapter 4 recorded a vision of God, the Creator. Now [in chapter 5] comes a vision of God the Redeemer, the Lamb who conquered through his death. The last chapter ended with a scene of worship of the Creator, this will end with the worship of the Redeemer. These two chapters are very important for an understanding of the message of the book. There are mysteries in life. Men feel themselves caught up in the world's evil and its misery, and they cannot break free. Some become rigid determinists, and we must all, at times, feel a sense of hopelessness and helplessness in the grip of forces stronger than we. The world's agony is real. And the world's inability to break free from the consequences of its guilt is real. This chapter with its seals which no man can break stresses man's inability. But it does not stop there. More important is the fact that through the Lamb the victory is won. The seals are opened and God's purpose is worked out.[30]

Many suggestions have been made as to the contents and meaning of the scroll in verse 1, but it seems best to take the views of Mounce, Caird and Morris as pointing in the right direction: 'Filled to overflowing and sealed with seven seals to ensure the secrecy of its decrees, it contains the full account of what God in his sovereign will has determined as the destiny of the world';[31] 'The scroll is God's redemptive plan [and] contains the world's destiny, foreordained by the gracious purpose of God';[32] 'The book surely is that which contains the world's destiny, and its contents are revealed to us pictorially as the seals are broken.'[33]

> *[2]And I saw a mighty angel proclaiming in a loud voice, 'Who is worthy to break the seals and open the scroll?' [3]But no-one in heaven or on earth or under the earth could open the scroll or even look inside it.*

The call of the angel is for someone who is worthy, not merely to look at the contents of the scroll, but to put them into action, to

---

[29] Donald W. McCullough, *The Trivialisation of God: The dangerous illusion of a manageable deity* (NavPress, 1995), pp. 14, 18.
[30] Morris (1973), pp. 92–93. [31] Mounce, p. 142. [32] Caird, p. 72.
[33] Morris (1973), p. 94.

mediate the work of God and achieve his purposes of judgment and mercy, defeating evil and establishing for ever his kingdom. Swete sees the angel's call travelling through the angels of heaven and the populations of earth and the world of departed spirits and, when each declines the challenge, hope vanishes away.[34] The world, with all its resources, does not have within itself the solution to its problems or the ability to fulfil its true potential; there is not in all our secular humanism anything that can substitute for God.

The call of the angel pointed up a critical moment. 'Unless the seals are broken and the scroll of destiny unrolled, God's plan for the universe will be frustrated. Hence the Seer breaks out in unrestrained weeping.'[35] He has grown up with the Messianic hope of the Old Testament, the promise that one day God will reign over this runaway world bringing peace and truth, justice and blessing to the nations, overthrowing evil and vindicating the faith of his people. But now 'John weeps with disappointment because the hope of God's action appears to be indefinitely postponed for lack of an agent through whom God may act.'[36] But it is to those very hopes, so long cherished, that the elder refers when he comforts John in verse 5, with the news that *the Lion of the tribe of Judah, the Root of David, has triumphed.* 'Both of the titles ascribed to Jesus are taken from the common stock of Jewish messianism.'[37]

John turned to see a lion, but he saw a lamb! This lamb, however, is a combination of the Passover or temple lamb of sacrifice and safety and the apocalyptic lamb of leadership and conquest. Again John uses traditional apocalyptic imagery, which would have been familiar to his hearers, and we are to *understand* the imagery rather than to try to envisage it. The seven horns stand for perfect strength and the seven eyes for perfect vision and complete knowledge. He is the decisive figure of human history and the defining figure of human destiny. Yet John sees him as a *Lamb, looking as if it had been slain,* and 'in one brilliant stroke John portrays the central theme of NT revelation – victory through sacrifice'.[38] What qualifies this figure, what gives him the perfect right to fulfil the decrees of God for judgment and salvation, is not only his possession of power but his accomplishment of redemption as set out in the song of 5:8–10.

[8]*And when he had taken it, the four living creatures and the twenty-four elders fell down before the Lamb. Each one had a harp and they were holding golden bowls full of incense, which are the prayers of the saints.* [9] *And they sang a new song:*

---

[34] H. B. Swete, op. cit., p. 76, quoted in Mounce, p. 143.   [35] Mounce, p. 144.
[36] Caird, p. 73.   [37] Mounce, p. 144. See Gen. 49:9–19; Is. 11:1.
[38] Mounce, p. 144.

> *'You are worthy to take the scroll*
> *and to open its seals,*
> *because you were slain,*
> *and with your blood you purchased men for God*
> *from every tribe and language and people and nation.*
> [10]*You have made them to be a kingdom and priests to serve*
> *our God,*
> *and they will reign on the earth.'*

'With the handing of the scroll to the Lamb we enter into one of the greatest scenes of universal adoration anywhere recorded.'[39] At its centre is the once-crucified, now risen and glorified Christ. He is not leading the praise but receiving the praise with God, as one who is himself the incarnate God: God is 'worthy' (4:11) and he is 'worthy' (5:9). The heavenly beings fall down before him in worship themselves and as representing the worship of believers. The song they sing is called a new song 'because the covenant established through his death is a new covenant'.[40] The Lamb is worthy to head up salvation-history in its widest and final phase, not simply because of his power or glory as God but because of his atoning and reconciling death which qualifies him to be the Saviour of the world. It was with his blood (as an atoning sacrifice) that he purchased (redemption regularly carries with it the element of a price paid for the freedom achieved) people, not only from Israel, but from all nations and people-groups through the centuries, people who have been redeemed 'for God' as his possession, his people, his glory. 'What was promised to the Israelites at Sinai ("You shall be to me a kingdom of priests, and a holy nation," Ex.19:6) is fulfilled in the establishment of the church through the death of Christ. Corporately believers are a kingdom, and individually they are priests to God.'[41] These will share in the eschatological reign of Christ and all that it involves (2:26–27; 20:4; 22:5).

[11]*Then I looked and heard the voice of many angels, numbering thousands upon thousands, and ten thousand times ten thousand. They encircled the throne and the living creatures and the elders.* [12]*In a loud voice they sang:*

> *'Worthy is the Lamb, who was slain,*
> *to receive power and wealth and wisdom and strength*
> *and honour and glory and praise!'*

---

[39] Ibid., p. 146.   [40] Ibid., p. 149.   [41] Ibid., pp. 148–149.

[13]*Then I heard every creature in heaven and on earth and under the earth and on the sea, and all that is in them, singing:*

> *'To him who sits on the throne and to the Lamb*
> *be praise and honour and glory and power,*
> *for ever and ever!'*

[14]*The four living creatures said, 'Amen', and the elders fell down and worshipped.*

In verse 11 expression is piled on expression to bring out the innumerable number of the heavenly host. They sing again of the worthiness of the Lamb and we should note Mounce's observation: 'Power, riches, wisdom, and might are not benefits which the Lamb is about to receive but qualities he possesses and for which he is worthy to be praised.'[42] These qualities are ascribed to him elsewhere in the New Testament. However, 'honour and glory and praise' are responses in which we can share. As William Barclay says of the last, it is 'the one gift that we who have nothing can give to Him who possesses all'.[43]

Of verses 13–14 Barclay says, 'Now the chorus of praise goes so far that it cannot go farther, for it reaches throughout the whole of the universe and the whole of creation.'[44] John hears 'the roar of the great acclamation as it rises to heaven'[45] and at its centre, receiving the homage of the redeemed creation, are 'him who sits on the throne' and 'the Lamb'. The two, observes Morris, 'are joined in a way which is characteristic of this book (6:16; 7:9, 10, 17; 14:1, 4; 21:22–23; 22:1, 3). There cannot be the slightest doubt that the Lamb is to be reckoned with God and as God.'[46]

4. The dominant theme in worship

We learn here, in Revelation, as everywhere in the New Testament, that central to the worship of God is the Son of God, that the person and work of Jesus Christ are to be the dominant theme in the worship of the church. Indeed there can be no worship, or aspect of worship, outside of his person or divorced from his work.

Firstly, we address God through Jesus Christ as the mediator between man and God, the one who in his own person and by his incarnation, is for ever both man and God, and whose atoning work makes even our best works and prayers acceptable to God.[47] It is only because Jesus Christ is 'our righteousness, holiness and

[42] Ibid., p. 150.   [43] Barclay, vol. 1, p. 227.   [44] Ibid., p. 228.
[45] H. B. Swete, quoted in Mounce, p. 150.   [46] Morris (1973), p. 102.
[47] Heb. 9:15; 1 Tim. 2:5.

redemption'[48] that we can please God in our best works and worship. It is 'in Christ' that our prayer, praise and our very persons are acceptable to God and it is as Christ dwells in our hearts that God dwells in each of us.[49] The very act of worship takes place in Christ, the Son of God, our 'great high priest who has gone through the heavens'.[50] The knowledge of that makes us humble but also confident: 'Let us then approach the throne of grace with confidence, so that we may receive mercy and find grace to help us in our time of need.'[51]

Secondly, we thank God, among all his gifts to us, chiefly for Jesus Christ as the once-for-all sacrifice for sin.[52] We find all the goodness and mercy and love of God focused and revealed at the cross and the giving up of Christ his Son.[53] As in heaven the focus of worship is the Lamb slain, so on earth the church in bread and wine, in prayer and praise, in preaching and witness calls men and women to this central truth: 'that God was reconciling the world to himself in Christ, not counting men's sins against them'.[54] It is as we contemplate this and Christ's self-giving, that we say: 'Love so amazing, so divine, / Demands my life, my soul, my all.'[55]

Worship that sidelines the cross has lost its way and will soon degenerate into a vague mysticism or religion as 'morality touched with emotion', in Matthew Arnold's words. It is only at Calvary that we see what sin deserved, what holiness demanded and what love was prepared to do for our salvation. It means more to God than we shall ever know and it must mean more to us than we can ever tell; yet tell it we must: to God in our worship and to people around us in our witness.

Thirdly, we must learn the lesson the New Testament everywhere emphasizes: that worship is not to be divorced from the way we live and serve other people. The writer of Hebrews urges his addressees: 'Through Jesus, therefore, let us continually offer to God a sacrifice of praise – the fruit of lips that confess his name.'[56] Yet it is not only in vocal praise that we worship but in serving others in Christ's name and spirit. As the same writer immediately goes on to say, 'And do not forget to do good and to share with others, for with such sacrifices God is pleased.' It is in such lives that we are fulfilling our priesthood under the new covenant: 'As you come to him, the living Stone – rejected by men but chosen by God and precious to him – you also, like living stones, are being built into a spiritual house to be a holy priesthood, offering spiritual sacrifices acceptable to God through Jesus Christ.'[57]

[48] 1 Cor. 1:30.   [49] Eph. 3:14–21.   [50] Heb. 4:14.   [51] Heb. 4:16.
[52] Heb. 10:10.   [53] Rom. 3:25; 1 John 4:10.   [54] 2 Cor. 5:19.
[55] Hymn, 'When I survey the wondrous cross', by Isaac Watts (1674–1748).
[56] Heb. 13:15.   [57] 1 Pet. 2:4–5.

Paul makes the point very clearly when he writes to the Christians in Rome in application of all the great doctrine he has taught them: 'Therefore, I urge you, brothers, in view of God's mercy, to offer your bodies as living sacrifices, holy and pleasing to God – this is your spiritual [Gk. *logikē*, "reasonable", even "logical"] act of worship.'[58] The assertion that worship must take place in the 'embodied' life, not just the thought life, of the worshipper, in their outward relationships and not just their inward thoughts, was a main message of the prophets as well as of the Lord himself. Worship divorced from life is, by implication, 'unspiritual' and even 'unreasonable' or 'illogical'. God had made the same point vividly through Isaiah and Micah[59] and Jesus consistently shows up the failure of the Pharisees and others in this regard.[60] Miroslav Volf defines worship as adoration and action:

> There is no space in which worship should not take place, no time when it should not occur, and no activity through which it should not happen . . . Because the God Christians adore is engaged in the world, adoration of God leads to action in the world and action in the world leads to adoration of God . . . Without adoration action is blind; without action adoration is empty.[61]

5. The essential Spirit in worship

The presence in us of the Holy Spirit is the necessary pre-condition of all true worship. The seven-fold Spirit who blazes before the throne of God must burn in us and conduct us in worship if we are to glorify the great God who is Father, Son and Holy Spirit. We must always remember that worship is as much God's approach to us as our approach to God. Throughout the Bible it is assumed that the initiative in true worship is God's. God's grace is always the ground of our goodness. A thing is good if it serves the purpose for which it was made. We were made to worship God. But in our fallenness we would have expended all our energy and passed all our lives running from him, if his grace had not brought us to our first purpose. That grace comes from the Father through the Son and by the immediate operations of the Holy Spirit who works in us all manner of conformity to Christ and who draws us to the feet of God in love and gratitude.

The Holy Spirit does not do his work disconnected from all other

---

[58] Rom. 12:1.   [59] Is. 1:10–17; Mic. 6:6–8.   [60] Matt. 6:1–14; 23:1–32.

[61] Miroslav Volf, 'Worship as Adoration and Action: Reflections on a Christian Way of Being-in-the-World', in D. A. Carson (ed.), *Worship: Adoration and Action* (Paternoster, 1993), pp. 204–209.

human beings. That is not the way of God's working. Rather, he meets us in one another in public worship and ministers to us by one another in church life. As Heribert Muhlen rightly says: 'Every Christian is for everybody else a place of God's presence and it is just because of that that this becomes manifest in a special way when people are gathered for prayer "altogether in one place"', and 'When we hear how other people surrender themselves to God in praise, thanksgiving and faith, then we see and hear something of the Spirit of Jesus himself (Acts 2:33).'[62]

In a sustained correction of local abuses in worship, the apostle Paul shows the Corinthians how the Holy Spirit is the author of gifts and the orderer of worship, building up the congregation by means of one another's ministries and orchestrating their worship for the strengthening of the church and the glory of God.[63] Yet that orchestration is not the ordering of lifeless instruments but the educating and encouraging of personal agents. Therefore they are to act responsibly as they give utterance to the praises of God and the revelations of his will and ways.

The Holy Spirit is the immediacy of God in our lives. Every time we are stirred and enlightened in worship, lifted in adoration, humbled in confession, drawn out in intercession, integrated in all levels of our being for the service and praise of God, it is the Holy Spirit at work in us. Siegfried Grossmann offers a corrective to merely cerebral action in worship when he writes: 'Every genuine religious experience is in essence an experience of the *presence* of God . . . of contact in the here and now with the overwhelming, joy bringing, terrifying, saving and judging power of the transcendent.'[64] The experience of meeting God, he says, 'will so affect a person that it is not just his intellect but every level of his personality that is involved'.[65] That is the work of the Spirit of God on the human person who becomes more and more what he or she was always meant to be as they grow nearer to God in worship.

6. Worship yesterday, today and for ever

It is in worship that the Bible closes, but it is a worship that opens to us the future of God and his world. It does not leave us disengaged from the creation of which we form so significant and unique a part, made in his image, made to rule, and made to serve him for ever. Worship turns us out as well as in, and orientates us to the future as well as the past and the present. As Miroslav Volf notes:

---

[62] H. Muhlen, *A Charismatic Theology*, pp. 290, 348.   [63] 1 Cor. 12 – 14.
[64] S. Grossmann, *Stewards of God's Varied Grace*, p. 64.   [65] Ibid., p. 67.

As Christians worship God in adoration and action they anticipate the conditions of this world as God's new creation. Through action they seek to anticipate a world in which Satan will no longer 'deceive the nations', a world in which God will 'wipe away every tear' from the eyes of God's people, a world in which peace will reign between human beings and nature. Through their adoration they anticipate the enjoyment of God in the new creation where they will communally dwell in the triune God and the triune God will dwell among them (see Rev. 21 – 22).[66]

If the supreme purpose of human life is 'to glorify God and to enjoy him for ever,'[67] then the patient reader of this book should know that 'the first purpose of theology is to lead us to his feet'.[68] The biblical revelation calls to us as a human race in mid-flight from the Creator – Father, Son and Spirit – who is the reason for our very existence. It arrests us as the grace of God, proceeding from the love of God, accompanies the message of the living God and draws us back to our knees and to his arms. For this we were made and to this we have been redeemed. This is our duty here and this is our destiny hereafter. The glory of the future, wherever it may take us and whatever we may do, lies in this: that we shall never cease to worship, serve and love the living God.

[66] Volf, op. cit., p. 208.   [67] The Westminster Shorter Catechism, Q.1, A. 1.
[68] Thomas Howard and J. I. Packer, *Christianity: The true humanism* (Word, 1985), p. 98.

Study guide

The aim of this study guide is to help you to get to the heart of what Peter has written and to challenge you to apply what you learn to your own life. The questions have been designed for use by individuals or by small groups of Christians meeting, perhaps for an hour or two each week, to study, discuss and pray together.

The guide provides material for each of the sections in the book. When used by a group with limited time, the leader should decide beforehand which questions are most appropriate for the group to discuss during the meeting and which should perhaps be left for group members to work through by themselves or in smaller groups during the week.

In order to be able to contribute fully and learn from the group meetings, each member of the group needs to read through the section or sections under discussion, together with the passages in the Bible to which they refer.

It is important not to let these studies become merely academic exercises. Guard against this by making time to think through and discuss how what you discover *works out in practice* for you. Make sure you begin and end each study by focusing on God in praise and prayer. Ask the Holy Spirit to speak to you through your discussion together.

Introduction: How can we know God? (pp. 15–25)

1 Why is the 'Woody Allen' way of seeking God flawed?

> 'We have a deep dissatisfaction with life without God, and yet are runaways from him. As Augustine famously said, "You have made us for yourself, and our hearts are restless until they rest in you" ' (p. 16).

1. Points of contact

2 How can it be possible for us simultaneously to long for God and to reject him?

3 What it is that enables us to overcome the problem?

2. Knowing God

4 According to the author, seeking God from a simply intellectual perspective is pointless. Why?

5 How do we begin to 'see him by his own light and not just by our own' (p. 17)?

3. The need for special revelation

6 Why are the Scriptures vital in arriving at the knowledge of God?

4. The historic Christ

7 The historicity of Jesus is largely undoubted. Why is this?

5. The risen Lord

8 How is it possible to know that Jesus actually rose from the dead?

6. The claims of Jesus

9 If Jesus was only pretending to be God's Son, how do you think he would have acted?

10 What does the character of Jesus say about the character of God?

> 'No-one meets the deepest needs of our flawed and dying humanity like the Christ who said, "Come to me, all you who are weary and burdened, and I will give you rest . . ." ' (p. 22).

7. *The inspired Scriptures*

11 What part does the Old Testament play in proving the authenticity of the Christian faith?

8. *The need of God's Spirit*

12 What are your experiences of God's Spirit working to show 'that this is the word of the Lord' (p. 24)?

9. *The people who listen*

13 'God is a speaking God – and a speaking God calls for a listening people.' How can we listen to God better (p. 25)?

Part 1. God and his world

Genesis 1:1 – 2:3
1. God the Creator (pp. 27–45)

1. *God! (1:1)*

1 What aspects of life make you marvel at God's creation?

2. *The eternal God*

2 Why doesn't the Bible try to prove the existence of God?

3. *The creator God*

3 What does the author of Genesis say in verse 1? Why?

4. *The present God (1:2)*

4 To what extent is the character of God revealed through the picture of his Spirit hovering?

'He is the God who is "in touch" with his creation at every level: subatomic, macrocosmic, and every level between' (pp. 31–32).

---

5. The God of order

5 What do 'formless and empty' really mean?

6. The purposeful God (1:3–25)

6 'And God said' or 'Then God said' appear eight times in Genesis 1 (p. 33). Why?

7. A good creation (1:31)

7 'If God rejoices in what is material as well as in what is spiritual, then so may we' (p. 36). What is your attitude towards this statement? How does it challenge you?

8. Good – but not God! (1:14–16)

8 Why is seeking God through astrology misguided?

9. Human beings: the masterpiece of God (1:26–28)

9 In what ways do we see the image of God in ourselves?

'In the last analysis the image of God probably does not lie in any one thing but in a uniquely human complex of qualities and relationships. It is our humanity in its fullness, not some detached part of it, which makes us "like God"' (pp. 39–40).

---

10 God speaks directly to humans in Genesis 1:28. Why didn't he speak to animals in the same way?
11 Why did God choose to create two genders?

11. The rest of God (2:2–3)

12 What is the purpose of God's rest?
13 'God's act of creation was no experiment; it was an act of commitment' (p. 42). In what ways was it an act of commitment?

12. A tract for the times?

14 Why were the early chapters of Genesis written as they were?

Genesis 1
2. Genesis for today (pp. 46–65)

1. The God who continues to reveal himself

1 How does God reveal his character in Genesis?
2 Why do you think Martin Luther described Genesis as 'the foundation of the whole of Scripture' (p. 46)?

2. The infinite-personal God

3 In what ways is God both infinite and personal? Why is it so important that he is both?

'I can hug the yew tree but the yew tree cannot hug me back. The entire Milky Way cannot love and comfort me and dry my tears as can a person, or the God who is a person' (p. 50).

---

3. The God who creates out of nothing

4 What is the doctrine of creation out of nothing? Identify some of the implications of this doctrine for human behaviour.

4. The God who is not nature

5 What are the problems in proving the existence of God scientifically?

5. God and the recovery of purpose

6 How are belief in God and having purpose in life linked?
7 What does Psalm 8:3–5 say about our status in creation?
8 What separates humans from the rest of creation?

6. The God who entrusts us with his world

9 How has the command to 'subdue' the earth been abused? What is the command's true meaning and what are our responsibilities as a result?
10 Why is claiming equal rights for animals not the right outcome of subduing the earth?

7. God's Sabbath rest

11 What does 'the Christian weekly commemoration of the resurrection of Jesus Christ' (p. 63) point towards?

12 Given that Christians are destined for heavenly rest, what should our attitude be while we wait for it?

'In a restless world and an uncertain life, where many are looking for meaning and for security, we need to point men and women to the Creator God who is the meaning of life' (p. 64).

---

8. The creation call to worship

13 What is the relationship between creation and the cross?

Genesis 2
3. God the betrayed (pp. 66–82)

1 Why was it costly for God to create as he did?

1. God the final authority (2:16–17)

2 List the results of humans choosing their own morality. What is the irony in this approach to life?
3 What figure does the Genesis serpent represent?

2. The slandered God (3:1)

4 Read Genesis 2:16. How does this misrepresented view of God affect people's lives today? What is your personal experience of this?

3. The distanced God (3:2–5)

5 How does the woman misquote God?
6 What does this show about her relationship with God?
7 In what ways do we misquote God to justify our own means?

4. The first lie (3:4–5)

8 What was the serpent's purpose in lying?

5. The fatal results (3:7–15)

9 'The rebels failed; for our Utopia was the home we fought to leave' (p. 72). Does this statement have any significance for you?
10 In what ways does the reality of sin oppose its promise?

11   What is the first thing sin does in a person?

6. God seeking (3:9–13)

12   How does God go about his search for Adam? How do Adam and Eve respond? How would the scenario play out if the pair had not sinned?

7. God promising (3:15)

13   What does God promise (3:15)?
14   How are these struggles won?

8. God judging (3:16–19)

15   Though Jesus has come, the curse is still part of reality. How is the curse seen at work today?

9. God staying (3:20–24)

16   What is so remarkable about God's going out from the garden with Adam and Eve?

10. God's second Adam

17   Who is the second or last Adam?
18   Why is it significant that God's grace came through one man (Romans 5:15–17)?

Genesis 6 – 9
4. God the committed (pp. 83–94)

1. The God who shelters

1   Why did God send the flood?
2   Who was saved?

2. The God who grieves over sin (6:1–8)

3   If Noah was equally fallen, why was he chosen to build the ark?

'It is of first importance that we see the flood as God's judgment upon sin, as the expression of his holy wrath on account of sin, and as the demonstration of his grief and indignation in the face of universal human sin' (p. 84).

---

3. The gods who are helpless

4 List the biblical and mythical attitudes towards the divine. What are the differences?

4. The moral seriousness of God (6:9–17)

5 What do we learn about God from the story of the flood?
6 How does knowing that God isn't 'safe' impact you?

5. The covenant of God (6:18)

7 What is a covenant relationship?
8 What was God's covenant in this case?

6. The covenant-keeping God (8:1, 20–22; 9:1–17)

9 How does God confirm his covenant?
10 Why is the rainbow an appropriate sign of commitment? What do you feel when you see one today?
11 What does God's covenant with Noah show?
12 According to Peter Lewis, how should the term 'establish my covenant' be understood (p. 89)?
13 What does this say about God's commitment to creation?

7. The God who enters into relationships

14 Why is a covenant necessary for God to enter into relationship with us?

Genesis 8 – 9
5. Providence: God who sustains (pp. 95–104)

1. The reliability of God (8:22; 9:12–16)

1 What is God's providence?

2. Providence as sustenance (8:22)

2 In what ways does God sustain his creation?

3. The everywhere-active God

3 How do you define 'dynamic stability' (p. 98)?

> *'The "rest" of God in Genesis 1 does not mark the end of God's involvement with creation, only a transition of his working into a new phase of activity'* (p. 97–98).

4. God's two books

4 Why is there no conflict between 'God's two books'?

5. God and the scientist (9:12–16)

5 How does modern science challenge unbelief?
6 What do the 'laws of nature' (p. 101) show about the God of the covenant?

6. The question of miracles

7 How does natural order work?
8 What are miracles? How are they related to laws of nature?
9 Why are there fewer miracles recorded in the New Testament than in the Old?
10 Why are miracles rare?

Part 2. God and his people

Genesis 11 – 18
6. God of the promise (pp. 105–125)

1. From the city of mankind to the city of God (11:31–32)

1 Why does God need to intervene?

2. God's elective call (12:1)

2 Why would it have been difficult for Abram to follow the call?
3 What is the doctrine of election?
4 Why do we have to go through an elected group or person to be saved?

> *'God invests the knowledge of himself in one man, one family, one nation, that it may be communicated to all men and women, families and nations through the meeting of mind with mind, heart with heart, and life with life'* (p. 110).

3. God's disruptive call

5 Give some reasons for not supporting mission. Why are these reasons invalid?

6 What similarities are there between the call of Abraham and Jesus' call on our lives? How has following Jesus been difficult for you?

7 What is the significance of the detailed records in Joshua 15 – 22?

8 Of what place is the Promised Land symbolic?

4. Great nation . . . great name . . . great blessing (12:2–3)

9 Contrast Genesis 11:1–9 and 12:2–3. Why will Abraham's project succeed?

10 What is God's plan and strategy for salvation?

5. Human pain and God's promise (15:1–5)

11 Why was childlessness such an issue in the ancient world?

12 Imagine yourself as Abraham. How would you have dealt with his test of faith? What benefit do we have today in trusting God?

6. The righteousness of faith (15:6)

13 On what basis was Abraham credited with righteousness?

14 Whose righteousness was Abraham credited with?

7. The God who covenants (15:7–18)

15 Why did God appear to Abraham in this way?

8. The demands of the covenant (17:1–9)

16 Why isn't God's covenant to Abraham in any danger of breaking?

9. The sign of the covenant (17:10–14)

17 What are circumcision's religious and symbolic meanings?

10. El Shaddai

18 How is the nature of El Shaddai illustrated (Gen. 18:14)?

11. Trusting the promise-maker

19 On what basis can we trust God's promises? How are we to keep our faith when waiting is hard?

> *'It is a lesson that has to be learned in the life of faith, that many of God's cheques are post-dated. The promise is given but we cannot read the time of their fulfilment'* (p. 123).

20 What is our relationship with Abraham?
21 How do promise and faith work together?
22 Imagine you are the man crossing the Mississippi on foot (pp. 124–125). How do you feel when you see the other man whizz by on the sled?

Exodus 3; 7 – 12; 15
7. The God who rescues a people (pp. 126–140)

1. Our decisions and God's delays (3:1–3)

1 What is your experience of being most useful when you have felt useless?

> *'Our greatest work and our greatest victory in life is to place our hearts and lives into the hands of God with each aspiration and achievement, and with each failure and disappointment also'* (p. 127).

2. When God meets a man (3: 4–6)

2 What is holiness?
3 How should we approach God?

3. The God who answers prayer (3:7–10)

4 What is significant about God answering the Israelites' prayer?

4. The God who names himself (3:11–15)

5 What is behind the question 'What is his name?'
6 How might 'I AM WHO I AM' be translated?
7 What does this statement reveal to the Israelites about God?
8 What is reassuring about God saying, 'I will be to you all that I am' (p. 131)?
9 What does the name 'Yahweh' mean?

5. God's 'strong hand' and 'outstretched arm' (7 – 12)

10 What is the danger of separating the natural and supernatural?

11 What should our response be to signs and miracles?

12 According to Peter Lewis, what is the purpose in sending the plagues?

13 How are the Israelites' firstborn saved?

14 What are the implications of being redeemed people?

15 'Perfect love casts out one type of fear' (p. 000). What do you think this type of fear is?

6. God, sovereign in judgment and salvation

16 What role did God play in the hardening of Pharaoh's heart?

17 Why does God give some people over to their sin?

'When God is kept out of a life he can allow sin and forces beyond a man or women's power to take them further than they ever meant to go . . .' (p. 137).

---

7. God as kinsman-redeemer

18 Who was the kinsman-redeemer in ancient Israel? Who is the divine kinsman-redeemer?

8. God as cosmic ruler (15:1–21)

19 How is the redemption from Egypt symbolic of the ultimate redemption of the cross?

Exodus 19:1–25
8. The unapproachable God (pp. 141–147)

1. Israel at the mountain of God (19:1–6)

1 What is God's special relation to Israel?

2 What is meant by Israel being God's *treasured possession* (Deut. 19:5)?

3 How did/does Israel act as a 'priestly' nation?

4 Why did God make Israel holy?

5 What does God's special relation to Israel mean for us? How can our churches be a 'kingdom of priests'?

2. *Unapproachable holiness (19:7–25)*

6 What makes God unapproachable without special access?

'... *God is dangerous because he is holy and the people are unclean, and when the holy comes into contact with the unclean there is a reaction which spells death for the sinner*' (*p. 146*).

Exodus 20:1–21
9. God in ten words (pp. 148–162)

1. *The God who speaks (20:1–2)*

1 What are the Ten Commandments and who are they for?
2 Why should they be obeyed?

2. *The Ten Commandments*

3 How are the commandments expressions of God's nature?

3. *New Lord, new lifestyle (20:3–11)*

4 Why have we been saved?
5 How is the first commandment often abused?
6 How is this abuse justified?
7 Why does God forbid worship of other gods?
8 What is the only image of God that is permitted? Why?
9 How does Jesus' command in Matthew 5:34–37 (p. 153) challenge you?
10 With the increase in seven-day working practice, how can we obey the fourth commandment?

4. *God's laws and our lives (20:12–17)*

11 Contrast the first four commandments and the last six. Why was it necessary to have this division?

'*Surely the first foundation of righteousness is the worship of God. When this is overthrown, all the remaining parts of righteousness, like the pieces of a shattered and fallen building, are mangled and scattered*' (*p. 155, quoting John Calvin*).

---

12 What is foolish about the search for eternal youth?

13 How should God's view of us influence our views on issues like capital punishment, abortion and euthanasia?

14 What are the wider social implications of adultery? How can we 'show a better and wiser way' (p. 157)?

15 What is a thief?

16 *You shall not give false testimony* (Exod. 20:16). What did this commandment first relate to? How should we apply it to our lives now?

17 How does the tenth commandment relate to the other nine?

5. Wanted – a mediator (20:18–21)

18 Why do we need and want a mediator? What do you think would happen if we didn't?

Deuteronomy
10. God the lawgiver (pp. 163–173)

1 Define the covenant at Sinai (p. 163). What did it achieve?

2 What does Exodus 21 – 23 contain?

3 Why did God need to give the law twice?

1. Guidance and gratitude

4 What is the significance of law following salvation?

5 Why is the word 'law' an unfortunate translation of *tôrâ*?

6 How can we learn from the psalmists' attitude towards the law?

2. Law and grace, then and now

7 What means does God use to write his law on our hearts (Jer. 31:33)?

8 What happens when the law is kept, but the originator of it isn't acknowledged?

3. God's law and likeness

9 How did Jesus see this book (Matt. 5:17–20)?

10 What does Deuteronomy mean? What is the purpose of the book?

4. God, the foundation of life (6:4–7; 7:6–11)

11 What is the correct motivation for a life of obedience?
12 Why will we never fulfil our potential and destiny without God?

'Israel's law is rooted in a relationship with God, a unique, undeserved and challenging relationship' (p. 167).

---

5. God's model community

13 How is God's character shown in Deuteronomy?

6. Church and state

14 What is the role of the church in politics?

Exodus 32 – 34
11. God of glory and grace (pp. 174–187)

1. A great apostasy (32:1–8)

1 Why did the people disobey God?
2 What is the warning about worship without the living God?

2. The God who rages (32:9–14, 27–35)

3 How is God's divine wrath expressed?

3. The God who withdraws his presence (33: 1–6)

4 Why does God send an angel instead of himself?
5 What similarities does the end of the chapter have with the expulsion from Eden?
6 When have you been tempted to 'chuck' (p. 177) Christianity? What happened?

4. The God who relents (33:7–23)

7 What is life like without the presence of God?
8 What is Moses asking by his request, *'Now show me your glory'* (p. 178)?
9 What makes it impossible for Moses to see God?
10 How does God reveal himself? Why?

5. What is God like? (34:5–8)

11 How does God want us to know him?
12 What is God's compassion and grace like?
13 'God is never closer to us than when we feel he is far from us' (p. 223). What is your experience of this?
14 What would happen if God was short-tempered?

'... *while we can never persuade him to compromise his righteousness, we can count on him to help us in our struggle with our sins and failures*' (p. 182).

---

15 How may *abounding in love and faithfulness* (34:6; p. 182) be described?
16 How does this picture of God fit with his 'abounding in love and faithfulness'?

6. The renewal of the covenant (34: 9–28)

17 What is the significance of the renewal?
18 Why does God write down the Ten Commandments?

7. The radiant face of Moses (34: 29–35)

19 What is the purpose of the veil?
20 What effect does Christ have on the use of the veil?

8. The lost privileges of Israel

21 How does the golden-calf incident end? What can we learn from this?

Leviticus
12. The God who reconciles sinners
(pp. 188–202)

1. The God who is holy

1 Why is the starting point of Leviticus God's holiness?

'When confronted with purity, righteousness and obedience, God's love goes out in embrace and blessing; when confronted with impurity, rebellion or sin in any of its forms, it expresses itself in wrath' (p. 188).

2. The God who is dangerous

2 Gordon Wenham says that the unclean and the holy are two states that must never come into contact with each other (p. 189). How is contact between the two made possible, and why this particular means?

3 What does atonement mean and why is the meaning important?

3. The God who gives a substitute (1:1–4)

4 Describe the features of a 'burnt offering' (p. 190). Why was it important to give something that 'cost' the person?

5 What might be today's equivalent and how do you think you would feel making that sacrifice?

6 'I have given it for you to make atonement for yourselves on the altar' (Lev. 17:11). Why is there an emphasis here on 'I have given it . . .'?

4. The God who punishes sin

7 Why is atonement's link with death so vital?

5. The God who turns away his wrath

8 How did people in the ancient world 'propitiate' the gods?

9 Why can't the wrath of Israel's God be appeased in this way?

10 How would you explain propitiation to someone unused to theological terms?

6. The God who reconciles

11 Name the three ways in which God's goodwill was expressed to worshippers. How are these expressions linked to reconciliation?

'The ascending smoke of the whole burnt offering, rising as an aroma pleasing to the LORD (1:9), showed not only his acceptance of the worshipper but the real pleasure God had in the act of reconciliation' (p. 195).

7. The God who ordains mediators

12 What role do the priests fulfil?

13 Why is so much importance placed on Aaron's robes of office?

14 Contrast the priesthood of Aaron to the high priesthood of Jesus. What are the similarities and differences?

8. The final sacrifice for all

15 What was the main problem in having human mediators?

16 How does the sacrifice of Jesus solve the problem?

Amos
13. God the righteous judge (pp. 203–214)

1 Describe some characteristics of the two kingdoms of Israel.

1. God the judge of the nations (1:3 – 2:3)

2 'Nations have an identity as well as individuals' (p. 204). Why does God judge societies? What is difficult to accept about the idea of a collective responsibility?

3 What is the overall theme of Amos' prophecies?

2. The God who acts and reacts

4 'We are accountable to our Maker with or without a Bible' (p. 206). How will God judge us?

5 Think about the statement, often made by unbelievers, 'If there is a God, why doesn't he do something about the evil in the world?' (p. 206). Is there any validity in it?

'Our world and its nations deserve wrath every day, but God's judgments are held back time after time. Yet there are times when his interim judgments fall, swift and fierce or slow but inexorable' (p. 206).

---

3. God the judge of his people Israel (2:4–8)

6 What is the lesson here for today's church?

4. God of the poor

7 'Either we keep our conscience and reduce our affluence, or we keep our affluence and smother our conscience' (p. 209, quoting John Stott). How are you challenged by this observation?

5. God the impartial judge

8 How would you describe the 'new and global wave of corruption' (p. 209) that William Rees Mogg refers to? Why are we so complacent in protesting against it?

6. God the righteous judge

9 Why must our views of right and wrong come from God?

7. Judgment past and future

10 '... salvation is always said to be by grace, judgment is always said to be according to works' (p. 213). If you died tomorrow, how do you think you would be judged?

8. God's final victory

11 '... uncompromising justice and unquenchable love met at the cross in one Man who cried, "My God, my God, why have you forsaken me?"' (p. 214) Give thanks to God for what he has done.

Hosea
14. God the great lover (pp. 215–225)

1 Why does God choose this devastating way of life for Hosea?

1. Love's long trial

2 Why does Israel, and not other nations, come under judgment?

2. Love's human voice (1:2–3)

3 'He had to endure while his own marriage became the parable of God's marriage to Israel' (p. 217). In what ways does Hosea's marriage mirror God's?

4 Gomer's three children were given names referring to the judgment on Israel. What is the particular significance of each name?

3. Love's conflicting emotions (2:22–23)

5 Think of a time when you have been disillusioned with the church – perhaps even wanting 'divorce'. How does Hosea's prophecy speak to you?

'Just when we think the divorce is settled, a far different plan unfolds, reaching beyond the hopeless present to another generation and another future; a plan that is founded on what God will do above and beyond our poor devotion and our flawed obedience' (p. 219).

---

4. Love's humiliation (3:1–5)

6 How does the 'character of the divine love' (p. 221) contrast with our human notion of love?

5. God's serious love

7 Why is God's love so unfailing?
8 What is the name for this love?

6. Love's wide horizons

9 How does God's love differ in the Old and New Testaments?

7. Love's final reconciliation

10 'Having been embraced by God, we must make space for others in ourselves and invite them in – even our enemies' (p. 225). How do these words of Miroslav Volf challenge you?

Isaiah 40 – 48
15. The living God and dead idols
(pp. 226–241)

1 'Atheism is a rare and puny adversary compared to idolatry' (p. 226, quoting Chad Walsh). Why do you think this should be so?

> '... the modern Western church has to a large extent succumbed to the chief idolatry – the idolatry of the self, where a gospel of self-esteem has replaced a gospel of guilt and forgiveness, and where God himself exists to promote the interests of the self' (pp. 226–227).

1. 'Comfort, comfort my people' (40:1–8)

2 What does Isaiah foresee in the second half of his book?

3 Why would these things be comforting to the people?

2. The God of power and tenderness (40:9–12)

4 How do power and tenderness meet in God?

3. The incomparable God (40:13–18)

5 How does this set of rhetorical questions reveal that God is unique?

4. Yahweh versus the rest (40:18–26)

6 Read Isaiah 40:21–24. How do these verses help when the world seems out of control?

7 What is Isaiah's crucial message?

5. A different timetable (40:27–31)

8 How would you counsel somebody who says, 'Why doesn't God take action to right this situation?'

6. The God who holds the future

9 How do practices like tea leaf-reading amount to idolatry?

7. A choice that must be made

10 'You cannot be loyal to the gods of the nations and to me' (p. 234). Why isn't it possible to serve both God and idols?

8. You are my witnesses (43:10–12)

11 Why are Hebrews 1:1–4 and Matthew 28:20 key in answering questions about the existence of absolute truth?

9. The Holy One of Israel

12 How does the expression 'Holy One of Israel' describe God's relations with his chosen people?

13 Why is holiness such a central concept to the biblical teaching about God?

14 'Those who walk with God must live as God, in righteousness and true holiness' (p. 239). Why is living as God a condition of walking with God?

15 Why has the concept of wrath in God often been dismissed?

10. For God so loved ...

16 How is the holiness of God revealed at the cross?

Part 3. God in three persons

John 1
16. God incarnate (pp. 243–261)

1 What is your experience of the power of words?

1. The Word of God in the Old Testament

2 What 'functions' does God's Word serve?

3 Why is the 'Word' of God so powerful?

4 How is God's Word linked to God's wisdom?

2. The Word in John's Gospel (1:1)

5 Who was Jesus before he became known as Jesus?

6 '... and the Word was God'. Why does John use this sentence construction, instead of '... and the Word was *a* god' or '*the* God'?

7 Why do New Testament writers avoid saying bluntly, 'Jesus is God'?

3. The Word in creation (1:3)

8 If God created the world, why did he need an agent to work through?

4. The Word became flesh (1:14)

9 Reflect on John 1:14. Why is the fact of this verse so incredible?

5. God, unseen, but known (1:18)

10 What is John saying in verse 18?
11 What is the message of John's Gospel?

'Sin has made God the kind of mystery he was never meant to be; unbelief finds a God who stays distant and silent easier to live with than a God who speaks, challenges and comes near' (p. 252).

---

12 How does the term *monogenēs* translate into 'God the One and Only' (p. 253)?
13 What does Jesus the Son reveal of God the Father?

6. One Person, two natures

14 How can God the Son be both fully God and fully man?
15 Read the statements in Hebrews about the Lord's deity and his humanity. Why is it important that God keeps his divinity and humanness?

7. Jesus the only way

16 Why is Christianity unique?

8. Jewish and Gentile backgrounds

17 Why would *the Word became flesh* be so shocking for Jews and some Gentiles?

Romans 3:21–26
17. God the redeemer (pp. 262–271)

1. God the redeemer

1 How do these verses bring us to the heart of the Christian message?
2 Why is the Christian view of sin unique?

'No philosophy that by-passes the cross will ever discover the wisdom of God or reach the true knowledge of him as God and Saviour' (p. 262)

---

2. Justified in the law-court of God

3 Peter Lewis asks, 'What ... has Good done to make the gospel "the power of God for the salvation of everyone who believes"? ' (p. 265). Put his answers into your own words.

3. Redeemed from the law of sin and death

4 How does Paul go on to show further basis of our justification by God?

5 What does the word 'redemption' add to our understanding of 'justification'?

4. Saved from the wrath of God

6 Why is the word 'propitiation' so important in Paul's explanation of what God has done through Christ's death?

5. The cross and the lifting of burdens

7 How does the message of the cross answer the major problem of guilt that afflicts so many of us?

Matthew 28:18–20
18. The Trinity: the biblical material
(pp. 272–283)

1. The God who is one, not many

1 Why is the use of 'Yahweh' significant?

2. The God who does not live alone

2 How is a 'hospitable atmosphere' produced for the New Testament revelation of three people in the Godhead?

3. The God who is Father, Son and Holy Spirit

3 Why are believers baptised in the *name*, not names, of the Father, the Son and the Holy Spirit?

'The nations would come to know the true and only God not as "Yahweh" but as "the Father, the Son and the Holy Spirit", a truth about God not revealed before, even to Israel' (p. 275).

---

4. The holy Son

4 Give three examples from the Bible of where Jesus is shown to be a distinct person within the Godhead. How does Jesus reveal God perfectly?

5. The Holy Spirit

5 'With the Spirit there is the need to establish his personality, not his deity' (p. 278). Why should this be so?

6 How does Jesus show that he is not the Spirit?

6. The church's privilege

7 Why is the doctrine of the Trinity vital to the church today?

Matthew 28:18–20
19. The triune God (pp. 284–294)

1. The importance of this truth to God

1 'God was not lonely, nor was he alone' (p. 284). It is sometimes said that God created us because he was lonely. If God wasn't lonely, why did he create us?

2 What is divine love?

2. The importance of this truth for us

3 Why do we need to stress the Trinity when speaking about God?

'God is a triune being but not a divided being. Their unity is perfect; each possesses the whole being of Godhead and each is completely open to, known by and enjoyed among the others in perfect and self-giving love' (pp. 286–287).

---

4 How do we know that God is faithful?

5 Think about or discuss your experience of 'trinitarian praying'. How do you feel about the concept? What action could you take in your prayer life?

3. The importance of this truth for the church

6 In what way does the Trinity lie at the core of the gospel?

353

7 How should the church be modelling relationships? Why do you think this doesn't happen?

4. *The importance of this truth for all human society*

8 'We need others in order to know who we are' (p. 293). Why is Western individualism in crisis?
9 How is it possible to change the way we live as a society?

Romans 11:33–36
20. The sovereignty of God (pp. 295–313)

1 How can we reconcile our faith in a sovereign God with world events as they are?

1. *The suffering and triumph of God*

'The biblical doctrine of providence is not the doctrine of a genial benevolence but the doctrine of a tenacious commitment' (p. 296).

---

2 In what way does God suffer with us?
3 How would you define the doctrine of God's providence?

2. *The universal government of God*

4 Look at one of the listed psalms in detail. How does it celebrate the universal government of God?
5 'If you remain silent at this time . . .' (Est. 4:14). What would have happened to the Jews had Esther stayed quiet?

3. *Sovereignty and Jesus*

6 What does the crucifixion of Jesus tell us about God's overruling power?

4. *Sovereignty and history*

7 In what ways does Paul recognize God working throughout Israel's history?
8 What are the dangers in reading God's hand in events through history?

5. *The problem of evil*

9 Why are the problems of evil and sin intrinsically linked? How does this view differ from that of other religions?

6. *Sovereignty and free will*

10 'Do we ... have free will' (p. 308)?
11 'God acts in our acts but they remain our acts still' (p. 310). How should we make our decisions, knowing that God is sovereign, but that we still have choices and responsibilities?

7. *Prayer and providence*

12 Why do we need to pray?

'Prayer is among God's ordained means to God's ordained ends: he who has purposed to accomplish his will has also purposed to do so through and with the prayers of his people' (p. 312).

Revelation
21. Alpha and Omega:
the worship of the living God (pp. 314–328)

1. *The big story (1:1–3)*

1 What is the overall message of Revelation?

2. *Worship: the priority of heaven (4:1–8)*

2 Read Revelation 4:1–8. Who do you think the twenty-four elders and the four living creatures represent? What is their purpose in surrounding the throne?
3 How is God's eternity proclaimed?
4 What do we learn from the vision in Revelation 4?

3. *Worship: worthy is the Lamb! (5:1–14)*

5 Read Revelation 5. What is the significance of the Lamb's taking the scroll?

4. The dominant theme in worship

6 How should our worship on earth reflect the worship of the Lamb in heaven?

'... we must learn the lesson the New Testament everywhere emphasizes: that worship is not to be divorced from the way we live and serve other people' (p. 325).

---

5. The essential Spirit in worship

7 Why is the presence of the Holy Spirit in us essential for true worship?

6. Worship yesterday, today and for ever

8 'The glory of the future, wherever it may take us and whatever we may do, lies in this: that we shall never cease to worship, serve and love the living God' (p. 328). How does this final statement challenge the way you live your life?